Trading Systems

Second edition

Trading Systems

A new approach to system development
and portfolio optimisation

Second Edition

Urban Jaekle and Emilio Tomasini

Hh

Hh Harriman House

HARRIMAN HOUSE LTD
18 College Street
Petersfield
Hampshire
GU31 4AD
GREAT BRITAIN
Tel: +44 (0)1730 233870
Email: enquiries@harriman-house.com
Website: www.harriman-house.com

First published in Great Britain in 2009
This second edition published in 2019

Paperback ISBN: 978-0-85719-755-9
eBook ISBN: 978-0-85719-756-6

British Library Cataloguing in Publication Data
A CIP catalogue record for this book can be obtained from the British Library.

Urban Jaekle:

To my family Inna, Till, Hannah and Thomas who support me day and night.

"If you want a guarantee, buy a toaster."

Clint Eastwood

Emilio Tomasini:

To the loving memory of my mother Carla Ferrarini and of my father Ercole Tomasini.

When days are dark and friends are few how I long for you

Disclaimer

This book, including all free code examples, is an educational document. Nothing in this book is intended, nor should be taken, as investment advice.

The views expressed herein are the personal views of Urban Jaekle and Emilio Tomasini. Investing and trading is risky and can result in loss of principal. Neither this book in its entirety, nor any portion thereof, nor any follow-on discussion or correspondence related to this book, is intended to be a recommendation to invest or trade currencies, stocks, commodities, futures, options, or any other financial instrument. Neither the authors nor the publisher will accept any responsibility for losses which might result from applications of the ideas expressed in the book or from techniques or trading systems described in the book.

The programs used as examples have been tested and are believed to be correct. Even so, this book may contain typographical errors and other inaccuracies. Past performance, whether hypothetical, simulated, back-tested, or actual, is no guarantee of future results. Results will depend on the specific data series used. Please verify the accuracy and correctness of all programs before using them to trade.

Contents

Appendices: Systems and Ideas 289

Acknowledgements

Special thanks to all people and companies who helped us to write this book.

Thanks to Otmar Licht, Victor Burwitz, Joachim Lenz, Jens Castner, Thomas Wirth, Daniel Tydecks, Andrea Angiolini and Francesco Placci for the precious contribution and support during recent years: they deserve credit for having helped us survive so far in the markets.

And we can assure you that this is not an easy task. A major part of this book derived from conversations and mutual help with them.

Further thanks go especially to Cesar Alvarez, a professional trading consultant and successful quantitative trader, who helped us verifying the AmiBroker codes (alvarezquanttrading.com/services).

Special thanks to MultiCharts (www.multicharts.com) and TradeStation (www. tradestation.com) for providing such powerful platforms which allow full back-testing and trade execution all in one. A big part of this book on how to develop a basic trading system relies on EasyLanguage which is used by these two platforms. Because of their importance we updated this second edition with more free code examples.

An indispensable software if you want to perform tests on huge portfolios of stocks is certainly AmiBroker (amibroker.com). This software package provides high speed and comes at a reasonable price, including all you need from back-testing and optimisation, from Monte Carlo up to walk-forward analysis. Thanks for this to Tomasz Janeczko, the founder of this platform.

The most important thing to perform professional back-tests like those shown in this book is reliable and clean market data. Therefore we want to thank Norgate Data (norgatedata.com). They are one of the few providers in the world who offer price data for US stocks going back as far as 1950, including delisted stocks.

Last but not least we want to thank you, our readers, for all the valuable feedback within the last ten years on our first edition. We took it seriously, added a complete chapter about back-tests on portfolios and also more practical examples with open codes as you desired.

We hope that these free EasyLanguage and AmiBroker codes, provided for educational use, can be a starting point for you to create your own trading strategies and to become a better systematic trader!

Preface

Our lives are deeply interlinked with trading systems. We have both been systematic traders since the 1990s and we can say we were only lucky to start this job when systematic trading and technical analysis were still considered by the academic world as being within the boundaries of fraudulent activity. You need to consider that we were born in an era where the tenet of the financial world was, at best, you cannot make money or at least not more money from the financial markets than from a properly optimised portfolio of assets.

Since then it has been shown in many research papers that this old academic assumption is wrong. Every day the sun rises on the horizon, there are many traders that die and some of them that make a fortune. It happens seldom, but it happens, as the names of William Eckhardt, Ed Seykota, Jim Simons, and many others remind us. And you can be one of them. We do not know if we are to be counted among those lucky quantitative traders, but we know that we have done it for so many years and we have met so many dead bodies of systematic traders that we can proudly state that luck cannot be the only driver of our survival.

Sometimes your experience will help you to understand what you are and where you are heading to. The story of this book started with this premise and it was developed to explain and demonstrate what a system developer should know and do in order to achieve success in the markets with trading systems. That is, in short, to make money with a return higher than the majority of his fellow traders. We do not think that in order to build a winning trading system you need to be a rocket scientist; we are not rocket scientists ourselves. We are systematic traders that trade institutional money.

We think that part of our survival is due to the meeting of other fellow traders and to the huge amount of research we have done over the years. If your research is a lonely trip, then your way to success must be a long one. We owe so much to other fellow traders, both from the retail market and from the institutional side of the market, that we felt it our duty to share our experience with all the traders that will buy this book. Thanks to the frequent speeches we make in Frankfurt, London, Paris, Budapest and Milan we got in touch with quantitative traders from all around Europe, Asia and the US. These meetings were the driver of our success as traders. We hope this book will help you in finding your way through the uncharted waters of systematic trading, as other books and other fortunate relationships with fellow traders helped us in achieving our trading success.

Preface to the Second Edition

What has happened since 2008?

When we wrote the first edition of this book in 2008 it was in the middle of a financial crisis which only became clear afterwards. Such events can change the market structure by affecting the direction of trends and especially volatility.

But it's not only the financial crisis that changed the markets. There were many changes in the industry that had a huge impact and changed the playing field. Some of these changes were the growth of passive index funds and exchange traded funds (ETFs). Others were the increasing volume of trades executed by fully automated high frequency trading systems (HFT).

All these developments have an impact on the markets and therefore on the outcome of your trading systems. As a consequence, markets today tend to be more *choppy* than they were ten years ago or in the last century. Of course trends and consolidation phases still occur and will always be there. But they have become more difficult to exploit since they are often accompanied with huge volatility. Tremendous moves often manifest more suddenly.

On the one hand, this increases the risks. But if you are able to catch a part of the big moves, then today's markets, on the other hand, give you the opportunity to grab huge profits.

How this book is presented

The book is divided into three parts. Part one is a short practical guide to trading system development and evaluation. This section tries to condense our experience into a few practical tips and forms the basis for part two – a step-by-step instruction of how to develop a trading system, illustrated with a concrete example. The trading system development process is demonstrated from the initial code writing up, through optimisation to walk-forward and Monte Carlo analysis, up to risk and money management.

To rely only on one trading system and only one market is risky. Therefore, in the main part of the book – part three – we cover portfolio construction and provide you with solutions on how to lower your risks and at the same time make your profits more stable. We show two completely different ways in order to achieve this same goal.

The first possibility deals with the topic of how to combine trading systems with each other (chapter 8). In the second case, we deal with one trading system applied to different portfolios of stocks (in the brand new chapter 9).

The LUXOR system – when performance decays

The trading system development process in part two is shown using the example of a simple strategy consisting of two moving averages. It is called LUXOR, of which you see the result in fig. i.

Figure i: Equity Curve of trading system LUXOR. White, left part: Development area, Part II of this book, which had its first publication in the year 2009. Green, right part: Out-of-sample area. Performance of the system afterwards. Test on GBPUSD, (cable), 30-minute data.

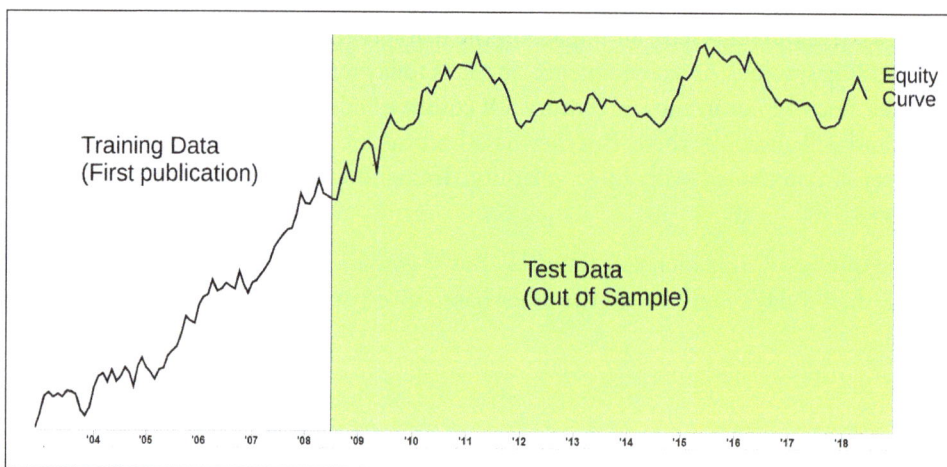

Chart created with TradeStation 9.

The equity curve shows the behaviour of this example trading system during its lifetime. The white, left-hand area is the phase in which the system is developed and tested. You see a steady equity curve with only little drawdowns. In the first two to three years after the training period, the good performance continued.

The performance decay after 2010 can always happen in a trading system (e.g. see 'Out-of-sample deterioration', chapter 5.2). All systems have to be switched off sooner or later. But when exactly to do this is a difficult question. We will discuss this topic within the context of dynamic portfolio construction in chapter 8.

If you have done your homework, such situations will not affect you since they are not the exception but rather the normal, every day, behaviour. When markets change, which they do more or less all the time, you have to listen to them and notice what they do. Don't try to predict the future, since none of us can do this. Just react based on what the market tells you!

The importance of controlling losses

To make your money in any market conditions you need two things:

1. A trading plan which consists of a portfolio of trading systems.

2. The discipline to follow this trading plan, which includes risk and money management to avoid big losses.

Most traders only take care of point 1 and lose their shirt when events such as those in 2000 or 2008 happen. Keep in mind that the amount of losses is the **only** parameter which you can control in your trading. Therefore, in our opinion, chapter 3.5 and chapter 7 about risk and money management are the most important one of this book. This is the place where the money is essentially made.

Examples of working trading systems

Besides such indispensable methods, another goal of this book update is to present example systems and ideas which still work. One fascinating simple approach of this kind of system is the 'Beginning of the month' (BOM) strategy (fig. ii).

This system produces steady results with only small drawdowns for over 80 years up to today! It is discussed in detail within the newly added chapter 5.6, right after the topic of 'rule complexity'. The simpler a system, the more robust it should turn out to be.

We also provide a completely different approach to avoid the over-optimisation trap, in the newly written chapter 9 on systematic portfolio trading.

Here you do not look for a trading system which works on a certain market. Instead you take a huge number of stocks and buy only the ones for which a special situation occurs, e.g. a volatility breakout. In this chapter we discuss in depth an example of a Bollinger Band system that is applied to huge portfolios of stocks on the main US indices and the Australian stock market.

If you, for example, apply such a system to all stocks of the S&P 500 index in the correct way, you get a trading result like in fig. iii.

Figure ii: BOM System on S&P 500. A system that buys every last day of the month on close and stays in the market four days. Back-test result on the S&P 500, daily, including $40 slippage and commissions per trade. Back-test performed with AmiBroker.

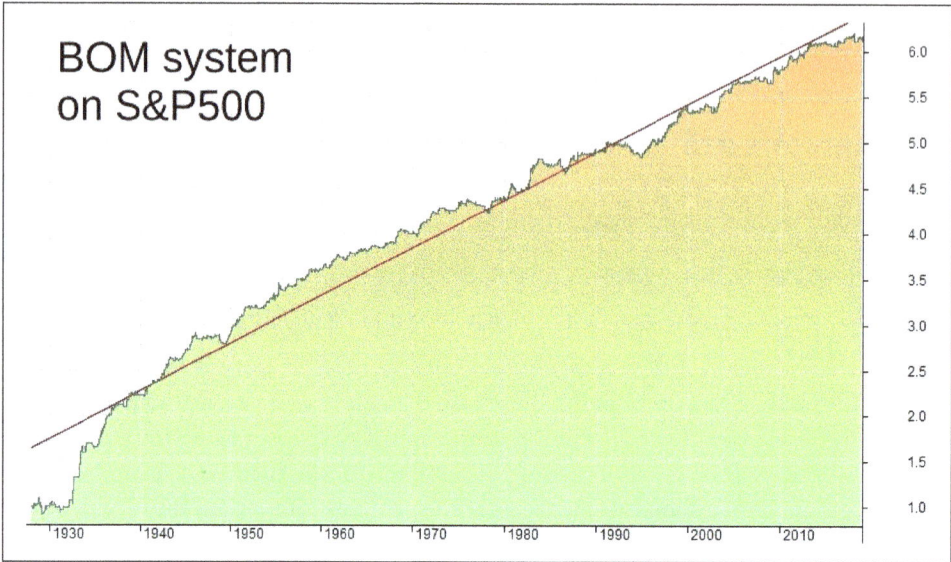

Data supplier: Norgate Data.

Figure iii: LOG equity S&P 500. A Bollinger Band breakout system applied to a portfolio of the S&P 500 stocks 1/9/1962–31/12/2018. Back-test performed with AmiBroker.

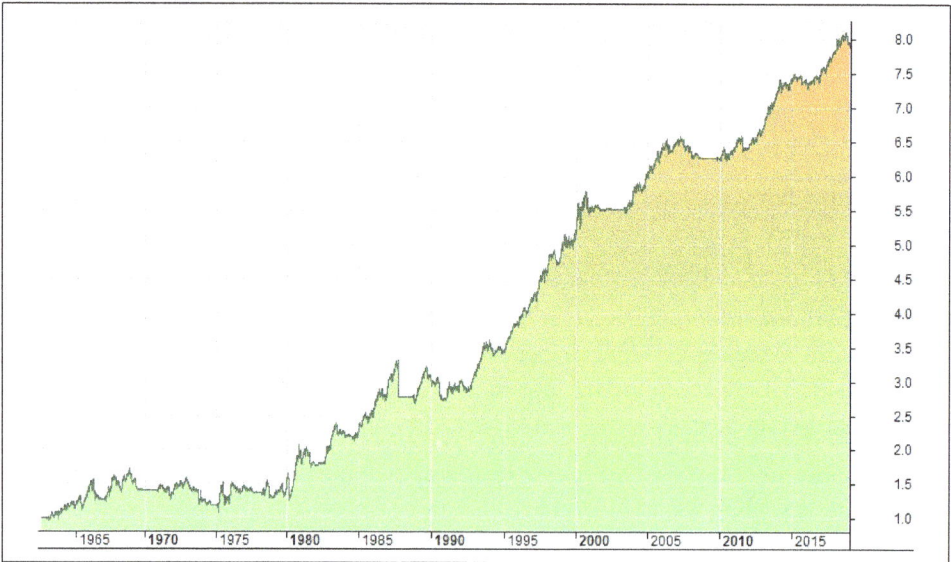

Data supplier: Norgate Data.

Software and data

For testing trading systems that span multiple markets, you need two imperative components: a suitable portfolio testing software and clean market data.

For back-testing and development on this topic we use AmiBroker – in our opinion the most powerful tool on the market for this task (amibroker.com).

To supply AmiBroker with data, we use Norgate Data (norgatedata.com). Norgate Data has a plug-in for AmiBroker, which allows the data to be integrated neatly and provides access to rich data features such as historical index constituent information for US stocks. Norgate Data can also supply data for US delisted stocks, making it the ideal data source for survivorship-bias-free system tests in AmiBroker.

In order to develop single trading systems for single markets we use TradeStation (www. tradestation.com) – a powerful platform which combines a real-time intraday datafeed with back-testing possibilities and automated trade execution, all under the same roof. All intraday tests in this book were therefore performed with TradeStation. Of course, you could also use AmiBroker, MultiCharts (www.multicharts.com) or another backtest software here as well – choose what you think fits best to your needs.

In order to give you the maximum value you can find all AmiBroker codes together with the EasyLanguage codes (for TradeStation and MultiCharts) for free in the appendix of this book. Take them as a short basis to start building your own trading system portfolio with the help of the tools given to you within this book. Be advised, however, that most of our back-tests in this book are for demonstration purpose only.

Urban Jaekle: www.urban-stocks.com; info@urban-stocks.com

Emilio Tomasini: www.sharetips.ch; tomasini@emiliotomasini.com

Part I

A Short Practical Guide to Trading System Development and Evaluation

What is a Trading System?

N OWADAYS THE TERM *trading system* conveys many meanings that can sometimes be misleading. A trading system is a precise set of rules that automatically defines, without any human discretionary intervention, the entry and the exit on the markets. Since rules are precise there is no doubt over when and where to apply them and this makes the trading system statistically testable. This means that we can figure out how the system performed in the past and how it could perform in the future with a certain degree of confidence. If you add a money management rule and a portfolio rule to the set of rules that define entry and exit on the market then you have a *trading strategy* or, in other words, a completely automatic approach to the markets, given a starting capital.

When we talk about money management we are not talking about what is commonly believed to be risk management; that is, where to place an initial stop loss or a target price and so on. We are talking instead about how much to invest on a particular trade; that is, the position sizing or how many shares and how many futures contracts to buy and sell. And if we move to the construction of a portfolio of systems on uncorrelated price series, then money management plays an important role in maximising the portfolio returns relative to the risk. Thus this process is also called *portfolio management*.

In more practical terms we can conclude that in order to develop and implement a trading system you need to have a software that easily performs all the programming and testing facilities and above all that goes directly to the market without any interference by the user. So we need to distinguish from a purely linguistic standpoint what a *trading system* is (or algorithmic trading) and what *automated trading* is. Indeed the latter could not exist without the first, but not vice versa. You could have algorithmic trading signals provided by a computer but not automatically place them on the markets. The main hindrance for the trading systems user is to produce trading signals that he is not mentally fit to place in the marketplace. To have a trading platform which automatically trades the mechanical signals produced by the trading system is thus a major advance.

1.1 An easy example of a trading system

So what does a trading system's pseudo code look like? It could be the following:

```
Buy 2 contracts at the highest high in the last 20 days;

Sell short 2 contracts at the lowest low in the last 20 days;

If marketposition = 1 then sell at last close - avgtruerange(14) stop;

If marketposition = -1 then buy to cover at last close + avgtruerange(14)
stop.
```

We have an entry rule and we have a stop loss rule. This is a trading system. Its risk management is quite poor since we just wrote an initial stop loss which works also as a trailing stop, but the example is easy and quickly shows what a trading system is.

When the investor or the trader has a predefined set of rules that she or he applies discretionally in order to enter or exit the market, without any testing process and without any automation of the orders, and resting on a final judgement if and when to enter or exit the markets that could not be eventually classified ex ante, we could more appropriately talk of a *trading methodology*. If the investor or the trader conducted detailed research on the past behaviour of the trading methodology, supporting it with statistical tests, and he has a disciplined character so that all the signals are equally placed on the market, we have something that is much closer to a trading system, without actually being one. Since the *trading system* is much more precisely defined and it conveys an idea of a scientific work that underwent a strict statistical test, many investors or traders are tending to profess the use of a trading system instead of a trading methodology. A trading methodology always involves a bit of judgement and discretion.

Recently the financial industry has been swamped by the 'quants', that is by money managers and traders that apply quantitative methods in order to produce buy and sell signals. What the difference is between a trading system and a quantitative forecasting method nobody knows, but since the term *quantitative finance* conveys an idea of something which is rigorously scientific and surely beyond the retail-oriented trumpery wares of common technical analysis, expect to meet many system traders that resell themselves as *quantitative traders*. If the term quantitative finance serves to divide the system traders that base their decisions on statistics from those analysts that just grasp the artistic and esoteric side of technical analysis, we all agree on calling ourselves quantitative traders.

Since a scientific appeal is the best way to sell something, there is nowadays a wide rush in the markets to give a deep scientific status to the trading systems industry. This approach seems to take for granted that a trading system must be a long series of rules, programmed in a complicated way, and full of breathtaking algorithms. Salesmen know that complexity raises prices. But it also raises the probability that a trading system will fail in the real world, and there is no approach more false than this.

Many commercially available formulas that you will find in any technical analysis software, when properly tested and applied to price series, show a real market bias; that is they have a realiable predictive power. Trading systems may be simple in their logical implementation – like a channel breakout, an indicator, a moving average – and to base your trading decisions on something that is *easy* will not reduce your success probability; on the contrary it will increase it. On the way to success, a lot will be done by money management and portfolio construction, risk management and timeframe, so do not be worried when you examine a trading formula that is simple and produces an equity line that appears unexciting, because you need to always reason under the portfolio constraint. It must be clear from the outset that a mediocre trading system – if applied to a portfolio of markets – will easily produce a good looking equity line.

1.2 Why you need a trading system

Evidence from economic literature shows without any doubt that just a few percent of traders are able to beat the market year after year. Most of both the retail and institutional traders sooner or later will go bust. If you do not belong to the lucky category of winning discretionary traders, then the only option for you in order to survive is the use of trading systems. If you have purchased this book you are most likely not a successful discretionary trader: in my experience successful discretionary traders are intuitively blessed and are unconsciously able to predict the market moves with their gut feeling. On the contrary there are many successful money managers, institutional and retail traders that profit from predetermined trading strategies and investing methodologies. But it would be misleading to think that a trading system could easily overcome all the hindrances trading creates. A trading system from one side could help the trader to beat the market but from the other side will create a new set of problems that a discretionary trader does not know.

First of all, if the trader has problems in terms of physical courage and some difficulties in pulling the trigger, trading systems will not be the ultimate solution. Like Larry Williams says, "trading systems work, system traders do not". There is no bigger infamy for a systematic trader than not to take a signal, as Bill Eckhardt wrote:

> *"If you make a bad trade, you have money management, you have a whole bunch of things that will come to your aid, and you're really not in so much trouble if you make a bad trade. But if you miss a good trade there's really nowhere to turn. If you miss good trades with any regularity you're finished, you're doomed in this game."*

Second, in order to trust a trading system, especially during gloom periods when drawdown will erase the trader's confidence in the trading system's capabilities, you really need to do a huge amount of research and statistical work that not everybody is able to do. To develop, implement, test and evaluate a trading system is not an everyday job.

Finally, many of the drawbacks that affect discretionary trading still affect systematic trading, e.g. lack of sufficient starting capital, possibility to diversify the portfolio, full-time, 24-hour, dedication.

More importantly we can say that trading is not a rational enterprise, it is not an activity where you can, given some premises, arrive at a unique conclusion or where everything could be explained in a logical way. Fear and greed manipulate prices in a way that the human mind is unable to grasp. There are of course some fortunate discretionary traders that can beat the market with gut feeling but in these instances they do not often manage to fully explain why they buy or sell. If all this is true the consequence would be that you need a tool that is not rational and not logical to enter and exit the market, something that you could not fully understand, something that is counterintuitive. Usually the signals that you believe to be illogical or simply prone to failure will be the big winners.

To use a mechanical trading system means that you need to discard widely held beliefs about finance and, above all, discard the feel-good approach to trading: everybody usually feels comfortable buying dips and uncomfortable buying the highest high, but it may be the case that just the latter methodology is the good one. Testing a trading system could mean being forced by the brutal power of numbers to a trading attitude where you do not feel at ease. To be a fully mechanical trader means, in conclusion, to use violence against yourself. This is the only way to profits, unless you are one of the fortunate gun slingers that make money day after day and do not even know how.

1.3 The science of trading systems

It would be inappropriate to mix all the kinds and breeds of technical analysis available nowadays. There is a broad distinction between subjective and objective technical analysis.

> Objective technical analysis methods are well-defined repeatable procedures that issue unambiguous signals. This allows them to be implemented as computerised algorithms and back tested on historical data. Results produced by a back-test can be evaluated in a rigorous quantitative manner. Subjective technical analysis methods are not well-defined analysis procedures. Because of their vagueness, an analyst's private interpretations are required. This thwarts computerisation, back testing, and objective performance evaluation. In other words, it is impossible to either confirm or deny a subjective method's efficacy. For this reason they are insulated from evidentiary challenge.[2]

Subjective technical analysis did not gain a good reputation among the academic community or among serious market practitioners because of its vagueness and lack of scientific method. To be a chartist or a technical analyst, instead of a portfolio manager, using hidden technical analysis could be the least promising career launching pad in the financial industry. There is a wide sociological and psychological literature about why people believe weird things such as dogma, faith, myth and anecdotes so that it is much easier to isolate good scientific technical analysis using the approach of the scientific method. Without the intention to lecture here about philosophy of science we need to briefly remind readers what scientific knowledge is. Scientific knowledge is empirical or it is based on observations of reality:

> *"The essence of technical analysis is statistical inference. It attempts to discover generalisations from historical data in the form of patterns, rules and so forth and then extrapolate them to the future."* [2]

So technical analysis, utilising the tools of statistical inference, starts from a sample of observations in order to gauge some statistical properties of the whole population. In this way technical analysis, like statistics, is quantitative. Further, technical analysis, like science, tries to predict the future through functional relationships among variables. If this variable does this then the dependent variable will do that. What in technical analysis is a rule in statistics is a functional relationship, which a certain probability is attached to. There is no barrier between scientific technical analysis and statistics so that all the doubts raised by those that dislike subjective technical analysis suddenly disappear. Quantitative technical analysis uses the typical method of analysis in applied sciences: the hypothetic-deductive method initiated by Newton and made famous by Popper. The hypothetic-deductive method has five stages [2]:

1. *Observation.* The system developer, through the continuous observation of the daily and intraday activity of the financial markets, devises a relationship among variables, i.e., among the daily volume activity and the closing price, or among the value of an indicator and the next day opening.

2. *Hypothesis.* This comes from the innovative mind of the system developer – an intellectual spark, the origins of which nobody knows. The system developer understands that the relationship he hypothesises is not due by chance to the particular nature of the sample he analysed, but it is common to the majority of the samples he can deduct from the whole population of data.

3. *Prediction.* If the relationship is true then a conditional proposition or a prediction can be constructed and "the prediction tells us what should be observed in a new set of observations if the hypothesis is indeed true".[1]

4. *Verification.* The system developer verifies if the prediction holds true in a new set of observations.

5. *Conclusion.* The system developer, through the use of statistical inference tools such as confidence intervals and hypothesis tests, will decide if the hypothesis is true or false weighing whether new observations will confirm the predictions.

This process is in no way different from the scientific appraisal method used in applied sciences like chemistry or biology.

---

[1] Aronson, David, *Evidence-Based Technical Analysis*, Wiley, 2006, see [2].

2

Design, Test, Optimisation and Evaluation of a Trading System

2.1 Design

A TRADING SYSTEM starts from an idea like an entrepreneurial vision. Innovation is something that lies between creativity and fancy, and it can come independently from how much time you are dedicating to it. There are system traders that say a good trading system idea comes when you are least expecting it, but conversations with good traders could help and it is highly recommended you attend seminars, congresses and friendly meetings among professional traders. Even watching discretionary traders at work can be useful. Unfortunately there is no sure path for innovation, but the following tips can prompt you to walk beyond the boundaries of imagination.

Getting started

A good place to begin is to look to the internet. Just search for "trading systems", "AmiBroker", etc., and you will find plenty of videos and explanation of existing codes and ideas.

Further, have a look at existing literature on algorithmic trading: you can take the bibliography of this book as a starting point.

Finally the forums of the software platforms MultiCharts, TradeStation and AmiBroker deserve a particular mention. They are full of free trading codes and ideas.

The programming task

Usually beginners are scared when they are faced with the necessity of learning to program in a language like EasyLanguage (for MultiCharts and TradeStation) or the AmiBroker formula language.

The jitters are apparently greater for programming than for learning a foreign language, even though nobody could explain how a foreign language differs from a programming language. This is perhaps due to the fact that programming sounds mathematical and logical, while to speak a foreign language is something most people are more accustomed to, and it is an endeavour where in any case you can help yourself with gestures and mimics.

As far as we are concerned, the contrary is true and it is much more difficult to learn Russian as a foreign language, for example, than to learn to program in EasyLanguage.

A system is comprised of an entry formula, an exit formula and a money management formula. The exit formula is concerned with *risk management*, that is initial stop loss, trailing stop, target exit and generally how much money we risk and how we risk it in every trade. *Money management* is concerned with how much we invest on every trade, that is how many stocks or futures contracts we buy or sell.

What beginner system traders tend not to trust is that returns will be astonishing only through an extensive and aggressive use of leverage and money management techniques or, put in another way, not even breathtaking trading systems can become viable investment tools if appropriate money and risk management tools are not applied.

Which timeframe to trade?

Usually retail traders are inclined to trade intraday because they think risks are lower, while institutional traders could not usually endure the effort to watch the markets for 24 hours per day. Nowadays traders are unlikely to consider using daytime trading sessions alone, since most futures contracts are traded on the Globex market 24 hours a day. Even though major price moves still often happen during the US daylight trading sessions, if you project into the future what has happened so far and how fast globalisation has shaped financial markets, we anticipate that in the future there will be increasingly no difference between trading in the morning or during the night, since shocks and counter shocks will affect the markets 24 hours per day.

Liquidity is really changing the markets' behaviour, moving from one part of the world to another without any difficulty, and it is not rare today to meet US traders that trade German DAX futures. This is something that was absolutely impossible even to think about just five years ago, and if you think ahead in this direction you will recognise that it is impossible now to even mull over what the markets will be like in the next ten years.

There is no difference between intraday and daily approaches since there are so many liquid contracts around.

Risks can be controlled choosing those markets and contracts where systems are efficient and stop losses will not destroy the initial capital even in the most unfortunate of starts. Trading intraday, even with a platform that automatically places trades and stop losses like TradeStation, is a demanding task and it is not compatible with any other work. Those thinking of the intraday business will be better off if they combine with a team of at least three fellow traders with whom to share the burden of following markets 24 hours per day. Life is full of unexpected woes and to approach intraday systematic trading without a range of strategies applied by a team of at least three traders is pure suicide.

Trading a daily timeframe is a more relaxing enterprise than intraday trading and can be approached even by those traders that have another daylight occupation. The discipline of placing orders every day, either in the morning or at midday, and of checking positions as many times as possible during the day, is very important.

The biggest side effects of this approach – drawdown and risk – can be levelled out with the choice of the most suitable futures contracts in terms of margin, volatility and liquidity. Trading intraday exposes the traders to huge unexpected price movements, energy blackout and platform inefficiencies. Conversely, trading a daily price series will raise the drawdown by a monetary absolute amount and it will also enlarge the flat equity line period. But nowadays traders have so many possibilities around the world that every account will find its appropriate futures margins and price volatility.

2.2 Test

The importance of the market data

The testing process is particularly difficult since the first problem a trader encounters is the market data. Today the access to market data is cheap and easy, but notwithstanding this a trader must apply great care in deciding the trustworthiness of the data. If 20 years ago data accuracy was a sheer nightmare for the serious trader, today the facility with which data can be retrieved often overlooks drawbacks almost every data vendor has.

For example, there are data vendors that for unknown reasons consider the closing price to be something different from the last traded price and, if your trading algorithm uses the closing price as a filter, test results will consequently be different from what you expect.

Other data vendors provide open prices systematically different from the real ones, usually when the opening price is the result of an auction that takes place before continuous trading begins, and some data vendors have different daily highest high or daily lowest lows. They can also get confused when the trading session is different from the ordinary one, as is the case with CME futures on Sundays, when the trading session starts one hour earlier than usual during the week.

So, even if everything looks simple, a systematic trader should always pay great attention to the accuracy of the price data, and it is a worthwhile exercise to compare the price series of one data vendor with the price series of a different one in order to understand what will happen when applying the system with real money.

For commodities and futures the daily data sources most commonly used by traders nowadays are CSI data (csidata.com), Pinnacle data (pinnacledata.com), TradeStation (tradestation.com) and Norgate Data (norgatedata.com)

When you are considering stock prices there is nothing more destructive than if you go on the long run with a bad data supplier. In the long run stock prices will inevitably be fallacious because a company may sooner or later merge with another one, it may change its core business, undergo a corporate split, or the company may simply go bust and be delisted. For example, the acquisition of Mannesmann by British Vodafone in 1999, where the takeover doubled Vodafone's value and changed its company structure. A more current example is the merger between Dow Chemical and DuPont to the new company DowDuPont, which took place in 2017.

When you apply a system to a 40-year stock price series you really need to wonder what you are trading. This is the major drawback in relation to which other difficulties – such as the dividend policy – can be easily dealt with. Obviously the gap due to dividend payment must be taken into consideration and price series accordingly rectified, a task that is performed, more or less promptly, by every serious data vendor. To be on the safe side as a serious trader it is advisable to use a high quality data supplier like Norgate Data.

Futures price series do not have any lesser problems: futures last from one month (like, for example, futures on energy products like NYMEX Crude Oil) up to 14 months (like, for example, on cereal futures markets), so if you want to apply a system to a 50-year grain price series you will have the problem of connecting one expiration date to the following one. Usually literature about futures relies on three major methods:

1. Same expiration contracts

The individual contracts are connected according to the expiration months. That is, for example, you connect September Corn 2001 with September Corn 2002 and September Corn 2003 and so on. This approach is possible where every single expiration month goes close to its peer forthcoming expiration month, the closer the better, and it is best when it overlaps the forthcoming contract by some months as in the case with cereal markets. Surely this approach is not possible on a stock index that usually lasts three months, or on an energy futures index that usually lasts one month.

On commodities that have a seasonal stocking industry that brings the unconsumed production on a given year to the following one, prices tend to assume a similar pattern according to the expiration months. With US corn, for example, which is harvested from September to October, the same players are involved (farmers, stocking industry entrepreneurs, cattle breeders, etc.) on the September expiration contract each year and so they tend to assume the same behavioural pattern. In other words, it makes more sense to create a price series with all the September expiration months connected together than a continuous or perpetual price series that mixes up different delivery months that have nothing in common.

2. Continuous contracts

The continuous contract is an artificial collage of the different forthcoming delivery months. The rationale of the continuous contract is that the forthcoming contract is the most liquid and the most traded so that if you add up all the forthcoming contracts you will have a significant price series. The problem is that on the delivery day you will have a gap between the old expiration month and the new one. This gap is what happens in reality when you are trading real money. If you are in a trade and you need to switch to the successive contract before the delivery day of the expiration contract, you will add up or subtract the difference in prices on the expiration day from the eventual result of the trade.

3. Perpetual contracts

In order to avoid the above mentioned hurdle from the price gap on the expiration day, the perpetual contract was created. This is a mathematical representation of the past data series where the old prices are updated according to the gap in the last expiration day. On the *point-based* update the difference in absolute terms is subtracted or added from the whole price series. On the *ratio-adjusted* price series it is usually subtracted from or added to a percentage equal to the price gap. In this way the relative difference in historical price swings is kept constant. More complex methods for perpetual contracts exist but they go beyond the scope of this paragraph [1]. The ultimate result of a perpetual price series is that it is not a real one and the more extrapolated, the more you are applying a system to something that is far from reality.

The length of your back-testing period

Literature points to the fact that a trading system, in order to be robust and consistent, must be more or less successful on a multi-period multi-market test. This is an important point that, with the newest generation of computers, has been put under scrutiny thanks to the fast speed of making calculations and cheap availability of historical price series. According to some mechanical traders the multi-market rule should be limited since systems have their own personality that suits only a certain batch of markets but not all. Rare are the systems that can withstand the multi-market test in the sense that they work equally well on many different markets (bonds, equity, commodities, currencies, stocks, etc.). We share the same opinion with these traders – after 20 years experience we can today count the real multi-market systems on the fingers of just one hand.

Conversely, as far as multi-period tests are concerned, other mechanical traders point to the fact that past is past: markets change continuously because economy, institutional structure and society change. So why expect markets to behave in the same way year after year? There are many system traders that for intraday trading systems will never test back more than 12 months and others will test back just three months. We will see shortly how optimisation and reoptimisation will fit into this whole picture. So far we can just express our point of view, which is neither permissive nor strictly rigid.

We think that the length of the back-testing period should be decided with some ordinary acumen based on experience. For example, let's consider a banking stock that traditionally had a choppy price series. Suddenly this bank merges with an online bank during the 2000 bubble. In 2001 it would be inappropriate to test a system on the price series before the merger because it is something that has changed so abruptly. Another example is with euro/dollar. Many data providers offer customers a euro/dollar price series derived, or worse extrapolated, in some way before 2003. Other data vendors simply extrapolate the euro/dollar price series before 2003, making a proportion with the Deutsche mark/dollar pair. It is obvious that it would be fatal to test a system on a euro/dollar price series starting from 1960 (yes, there are data vendors that sell this dubious data) expecting it to perform in the same way in 2008. Or it would be inappropriate to test a system on a Bund data series when it was still traded on open outcry in London in the 1980s. It is also clear that a serious trader should cut away abnormal circumstances like the stock bubble in 1999–2000 or the crude oil spike in 2008. Every system works when volatility is huge and market movements are the widest. But only a robust and consistent system will always work in normal conditions. Abnormal conditions will happen and we know that we will face them. But markets will be normal 80% of the time and a good system knows when a market is really out of control and risks are too high.

Rule complexity and degrees of freedom

The first aim of a multi-market test is to check if a system performs in the way it is supposed to (that is signals, if checked manually, are in the same position the programmer wants) and if it is profitable on the average of the markets on which it was applied. We should not expect a system to be profitable on every market we test it with but the more markets the system tests positively with the better.

Testing serves the need to check the system's statistical validity at a first glance, while optimisation serves the need to fine-tune the system to the particular behavioural feature of a market. Although this is only a partial definition it helps to clarify that optimisation comes after testing – that is after we have decided the system is sound.

The usual result will be that a system performs profitably on similar contracts; that is, for example it will perform the same way on all the energy futures but worse on all the different bond contracts and moderately well on currencies.

The most important choice while testing a system is to decide the size of the test window; that is how much of the price series we need to apply the system to. This decision does not follow a clear-cut schedule or rule of thumb but it needs to respect two statistical requirements: the price series must be long enough to cover different market situations and to produce a significant number of trades.

The number of variables and the data they consume are also considered in relation to the whole data sample under an approach known as *degrees of freedom* – that is, the number of variables and conditions and the data they use should not be more than a 10% fraction of the whole data sample considered. It is of critical importance to avoid a situation where we have 500 trading days and a trading system with 500 different conditions. It could be that each condition is different from the remaining 499 and it only fits to that particular trading day, so that every day will have its own proper condition that will make the most money from the market in sample, but it will have no forecasting power (see chapter 5).

Rule complexity and degrees of freedom are a hard topic for those not mathematically oriented. But even among mathematicians there are many that would not be at ease in explaining what degrees of freedom are. When explaining degrees of freedom (usually indicated as df) maybe the most appropriate and easy to grasp explanation is the joke of the married man that comments, "There is only one subject, my wife, and my degree of freedom is zero. I should increase my 'sample size' by looking at other women."

Coming to a more serious approach we should say that there are many definitions of the concept degrees of freedom varying from statistics to mathematics, geometry, physics and mechanics. An interesting paper available free on the internet performs the difficult task of making the concept simple[3]. A first definition (Larry Toothaker, 1986) could be "the number of independent components minus the number of estimated parameters." This definition is based upon the Walker (1940) definition: "The number of observations minus the number of necessary relations among these observations." But the best practical way to explain the concept is an illustration introduced by Dr. Robert Schulle (University of Oklahoma):

> In a scatter plot when there is only one data point, you cannot make any estimation of the regression line. The line can go in any direction … Here you have no degrees of freedom (n-1 = 0 where n = 1) for estimation (this may remind you of the joke about the married man). In order to plot a regression line you must have at least two data points (a wife and a mistress). In this case you have one degree of freedom for estimation (n-1 = 1 where n = 2). In other words, the degree of freedom tells you the number of useful data for estimation. However, when you have two data points only, you can always join them to be a straight regression line and get a perfect correlation (determination index = 1.00). Thus the lower the degree of freedom is, the poorer the estimation is.

So even in an intuitive way we arrive at the conclusion that the wider the sample size and the lower the number of variables, the better the estimation. Robert Pardo is the only author in the current literature that is able to keep the topic manageable and he gives the following short-cut guidelines in his book [4]:

```
Calculation of the degrees of freedom = whole data sample - rules and
conditions - data consumed by rules and conditions
```

Generally, less than 90% remaining degrees of freedom is considered too few. Beyond the Pardo's formulas that can help from a practical standpoint it is important to remember that a system with 20 variables cannot be tested on just 6 months of daily data in order to decide, if going ahead with a proper optimisation. The number of variables and conditions of the trading system are intimately connected to the length of the testing period. Put in another way, some estimates are based on more information than others. The number of degrees of freedom of an estimate is the number of independent pieces of information on which the estimate is based. The more information, the more accurate the estimate. The more information the higher the number of the degrees of freedom.

The same concept of the at least 90% degrees of freedom left could be applied in reverse as a rule of thumb with a multiple of 10 to the relationship between data used by the system's calculations and the testing window length. If you apply a 30-day moving average of the closing price you need to test it over at least 300 days (30 × 10).

Let's make one example: we consider a data sample of three years of highs, lows, opens and closing prices for a total 260 day per year × 3 × 4 = 3120 data points. We consider then a trading strategy uses a 20-day average of highs and a 60-day average of lows. The first average uses 21 degrees of freedom: 20 highs plus 1 more as a rule, and the second average uses 61 degrees of freedom: 60 lows plus 1 as a rule. The total is 82 degrees of freedom used in the example. The result in percentage terms is 82/3120 = 2.6% so that 97.4% degrees of freedom are left.

Data points used twice in calculations are counted once so that if you are using a five-day moving average of the closes and a five-day moving average of the closes you will have for the latter condition 10 data + 1 rule while for the first condition you will have just 1 rule. The total is 12 data consumed. It is obvious that since the five-day moving average is included into the longer one only the latter will be relevant for the degrees of freedom calculations.

The number of trades required in order to trust a system is also connected to the length of the testing windows. A test is significant if it produces a number of trades that will allow the risk of being wrong to be kept at the lowest level. The test window's length should take care of this. Let's say that the obvious standard error should be added to or subtracted from all the trading system's report parameters according to the trade sample. Standard error is:

```
Standard Error = square root of n + 1
```

```
Where n = number of the trades
```

The higher the number of trades, the lower the possible error in the trading system's metrics. In other words if we have few trades, the risk that these trades are profitable by accident is high. If you shoot once and you hit the bull's-eye it is possible either that you are a good marksman or simply that you are lucky. Conversely if you shoot 100 times and you hit the mark every time the probabilities that you are a good marksman are higher.

To be considered trustworthy, a system needs at least 100 trades, so that its standard error will be the square root of 100 + 1 = + – 10.04%.

All the trading system metrics will vary between the boundaries of +10% and –10%. That is, if the net profit is $100 the possible real net profit will vary more or less as a rule of thumb from a high at $110 to a low at $90.

2.3 The forecasting power of a trading system

Optimisation

Optimisation has earned a bad reputation among many traders. It can even be an offence for a systematic trader. Optimising a system means to find those inputs in the system's variables that maximise profits or that fulfill whichever constraints a trader decides to be the leading criteria for optimisation (for instance instead of maximising profits a system could tend to minimise drawdown). Let us give an example: you have a moving average crossover system; that is, the system buys when the short-term moving average crosses the long-term moving average. The question optimisation replies to is how many days will be the input of the short-term moving average and how many days will be the input of the long-term moving average. Optimisation means to make fit a system; that is, to adapt a system to the market we intend to trade [4].

But optimisation is a two-edged sword: it is one thing to adapt a system to a market in terms of volatility, initial risk, return, etc. But it is another thing to look for those inputs that by chance made the most money in the past but have no forecasting power. Let's assume that we have a system that every day will buy at the lowest price and sell at the highest price with two inputs that will have the precise entry and exit price by which the maximum profit is reaped. This is a wrong kind of optimisation since we looked for a value that changes every day and only with hindsight is the best value for that particular day able to be defined. This system has no forecasting power.

It is absolutely impossible to avoid optimisation in trading systems' development. Just think of what every trader is currently doing and you will understand that optimisation is something we need to face. There are traders that refuse the inputs optimisation process since, according to their view, a system should work forever with the same inputs. But then they decide to trade a system among a batch of other systems simply because in the past it made more money than other systems. Isn't this a kind of optimisation? Again they change the original system code adding constraints and conditions in order to adjust the system to market price behaviour and then they chose the variation of the system that worked the best in the past: isn't this also a kind of optimisation? If you are currently not so much inclined towards optimisation please review your standpoint and consider how many times you have used optimisation involuntarily.

Optimisation is something useful in system trading and we need to distinguish between the normal optimisation process and its aberration, namely curve fitting or over-optimisation. For example: we trade a daily system on bond futures that will be consequently affected by monetary policy. Monetary policy is not something that changes every day but it suits the economic cycle of expansion-recession so that we are talking about something that lasts years. It will be clear in this case that we need to have an optimisation window that is 6, 12 or 18 months long – something of a reasonable length in order to fine-tune the system with the market and the monetary policy.

Provided the system produces a significant number of trades, we will test the system on the preceding two years at the beginning and then we will fine-tune the system, re-optimising it every 6, 12 or 18 months. This approach is directed toward real trading and not a theoretical appraisal of the system. Surely the system must be tested on the longest price series we have at our disposal and optimised accordingly in order to check at a first glance if the system is viable. But this process is not something that will help us in finding the appropriate parameters to place the next trades. It is simply an evaluation process that will help us in deciding if the system is suitable for that particular market; that is, if the equity line is growing (the equity line may not be growing in a smooth way as we would wish, but it should at least be decisively on the upside).

In other words during testing over the longest price series available we check if the system is adapted to catch the moves of a particular market, while during optimisation we see if there is room for improvement with a change of inputs. Then through periodic reoptimisation within a six- to 12-month window we fine-tune the system, in terms of inputs, to the characteristics of that particular market and keep the system abreast of the market changes.

For an intraday system all the testing, optimising and re-optimising periods will be shorter than for daily or weekly systems.

Walk-forward analysis

In conclusion we can state that optimisation is something variable in terms of data window since systems need to be kept in synchronisation with the market. Before computer power became so cheap and easy to employ for the majority of market players, an out-of-sample period was always recommended after optimisation by all trading systems' developers. The out-of-sample period is a data window (usually 10–20% of the whole optimisation data window) we keep outside the optimisation process and which we apply to the optimised trading system in order to verify its forecasting power over unseen data. If the system performs in the same manner over the unseen data of the out-of-sample data it means that the system is a robust one and it can be traded with confidence.

So far we have only discussed ideas that you can read in any of the books in circulation about trading systems. But this is an obsolete view of optimisation, maybe dating back to those times where computer power was neither cheap nor widely available. Today optimisation has evolved into a more efficient and proper method of testing and making a system fit over a long price series. This method goes under the name of walk-forward analysis or walk-forward testing.

Walk-forward testing is a kind of multiple and successive out-of-sample test over the same data series. Let us give an example: a system is optimised over the first two years of the data history and then applied over the subsequent six months of unseen data. Then the optimisation window moves ahead by a six-month period and a new optimisation takes place in order to find the new inputs that will be applied over the forthcoming six months of data. And so on. This kind of optimisation is a *rolling* walk-forward analysis since the starting period of the optimisation window is always moving ahead by a six-month period each time we re-optimise the inputs. If the starting period is always the same and the optimisation period gets longer and longer as the time goes by we have an *anchored* walk-forward analysis. For intraday systems the *rolling* walk-forward analysis is more appropriate since intraday trading systems are more suited to the changing market conditions.

Figure 2.1: A graphical description of a rolling and anchored walk-forward analysis

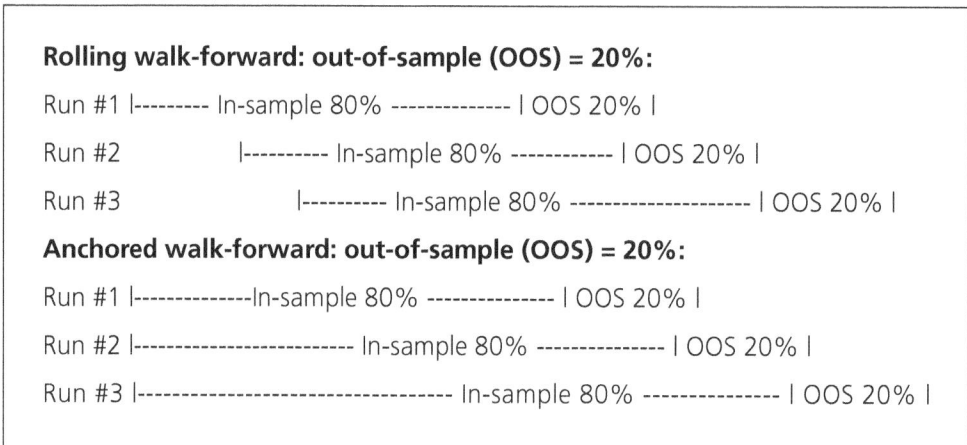

```
Rolling walk-forward: out-of-sample (OOS) = 20%:

Run #1 |--------- In-sample 80% -------------- | OOS 20% |

Run #2          |---------- In-sample 80% ------------ | OOS 20% |

Run #3              |---------- In-sample 80% -------------------- | OOS 20% |

Anchored walk-forward: out-of-sample (OOS) = 20%:

Run #1 |--------------In-sample 80% --------------- | OOS 20% |

Run #2 |------------------------- In-sample 80% --------------- | OOS 20% |

Run #3 |----------------------------------- In-sample 80% --------------- | OOS 20% |
```

The equity line resulting from a walk-forward run is where we are closest to reality in trading systems development since it is what real trading will produce in our pockets. And with no surprise this walk-forward analysis equity line will be deeply different from the equity line we can produce with testing and optimising a trading system on the whole price series. So often traders fool themselves deciding whether a trading system is to be discarded or not based on a whole price series equity line that in reality reveals nothing about the real trading situation after periodic reoptimisation.

A widely accepted way to gauge the forecasting power of a system and its consistency is to calculate the ratio between the annualised net profit relating to the walk-forward tests and the annualised net profit reaped during the optimisation periods. This is the walk-forward efficiency ratio. If the ratio is above the 100% threshold then the system is efficient and the probability that it will keep its forecasting power during real trading is high. If a trader decides to trade a system with a walk-forward efficiency ratio of just 50% (and many traders accept this level as the lowest possible) they should expect a system that performs at least at half the level of the performances indicated into the optimisation test. Statistical evidence also pinpoints that a poorly optimised system could make good performances on some lucky one or two walk-forward tests. To avoid this trap the highest possible number of tests should be performed or at least ten walk-forward analysis tests with a test window (that is the data window where we apply the optimised trading systems) of at least 10–20% of the whole optimisation price series.

Every comment on the old type of static out-of-sample testing on the last part of the price series or on how to optimise a trading system is nowadays obsolete since most professional trading system development software has a walk-forward analysis feature (like for example most of the RINA Systems products and in particular Portfolio Maestro). This does not mean that traders should not become accustomed to the ordinary testing and optimisation process. We recommend before using WFA you should do the ordinary homework about optimisation in order to acquire a full view of the system and its performances. To run a full walk-forward analysis takes much time, so it is quicker to check the robustness of the system with a shift test and then another shift optimisation. In any case, for the sake of simplicity we will summarise some good tips about optimisation.

If we have many inputs to be optimised the best methodology is to test one or two inputs per turn while all other inputs are kept static. In this way the risk of over-optimisation is kept at the lowest level since it is impossible to find the batch of inputs that will maximise the constraint we gave to the equation simply because the inputs will not be optimised together in the same run.

Robustness

But can we deduce from the post-optimisation window if the system is robust or whether it is the product of over-optimisation? We do not need to trust the area of the best performing inputs as a sure way to victory. If enough darts are thrown at the board, a high-scoring grouping will occur or, put in another manner, if a monkey is put in front of a piano and enough time is allotted, it will eventually compose a sonata. This joke suggests that, at least, the average of the results should be profitable if we want to trust the most performing inputs. If just 1% to 5% of the results are profitable this could have happened by accident: if the system's variables are given wide enough input ranges eventually the system will make a fortune over the past data. A robust system will show post-optimisation positive performances not only in 5% of all the tests but on the average of the tests. In other words, if the average results are positive then we can assume that the trading system is a robust one. If you are more statistically inclined you can also subtract the standard deviation (or a multiple of it) from the average net profit and check if the average net profit remains positive in this case.

So the number of inputs, conditions and variables must be kept under control and reduced to its minimum term. But how many inputs, conditions and variables are too many? This is a controversial area where the unique hallmark is the number of degrees of freedom that must always respect the numerical condition we depicted in the previous paragraph. Before taking an input into consideration it is obviously important to check with a rapid and cursory optimisation if the input varies or if it does not have any change under optimisation. If not, keep it constant in order to increase the degrees of freedom.

Another point to be considered is what scan range to choose for each input. An example will give a clearer picture of this problem: if you want to test a moving average crossover system with a short-term moving average and a long-term moving average on daily data, you cannot test the short moving average from 1 to 20 (this is what is considered the short term with daily data) and the long moving average from 20 to 200 (the latter is the interval that is usually considered long term with daily data). Indeed a step from 1 to 2 is a 100% change and a step from 19 to 20 is a 5% change. But a step change from 199 to 200 is just a 0.5 % change. You need to put the step scan range in an almost parallel relationship so that the scan from 1 to 20 will be performed with a step of 2 and the scan from 20 to 200 will be performed with a step of 20.

After optimisation is done a critical decision should be taken: which inputs' batch should we choose? First of all what we need to do is create a function chart that puts the variable's inputs scan range in relation to the net profits (or whichever other criteria was chosen for optimisation).

Figure 2.2: In the middle of the chart as the variable varies the net profit stays almost at the same level.

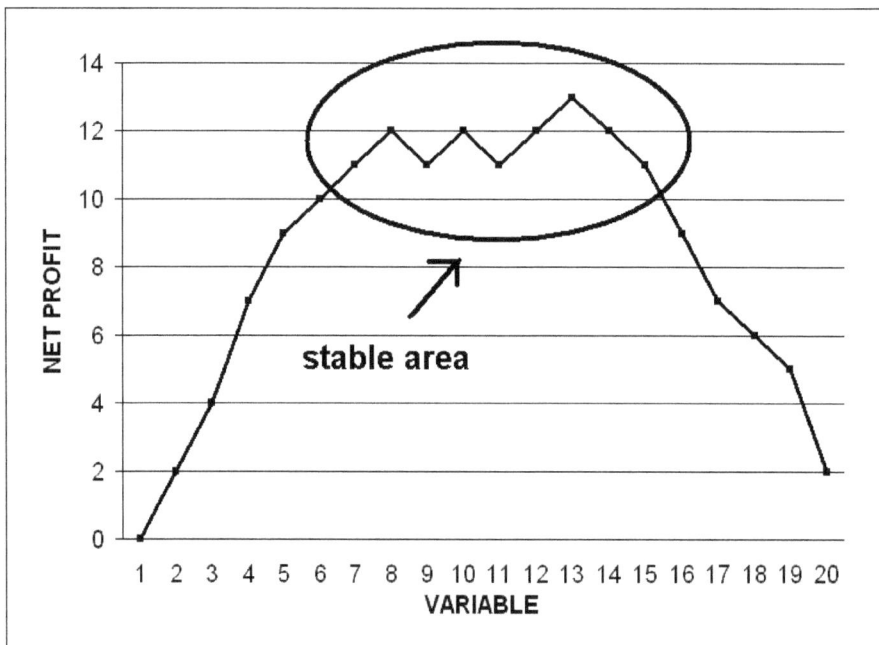

What we are looking for is a line that ideally would be as close as possible to a horizontal line, so that the net profit is not dependent on the input values. Reality is much different from theory so that we should be content with a line that grows lightly, then tops for a while and then decreases. The topping level is what we are looking for, that is an area where, even when changing the inputs, the net profits stay almost constant. This is the area where the robust input values are. This is diametrically opposite to a profit spike, that is a point in the line where net profit is high but it decreases deeply in the surrounding values. In other words we need to find an area where even after changing the input values net profit stays stable.

Figure 2.3: As much as the variable changes the net profit shows deep and wide swings: there is no area where at the variable's changing net profit stays more or less stable.

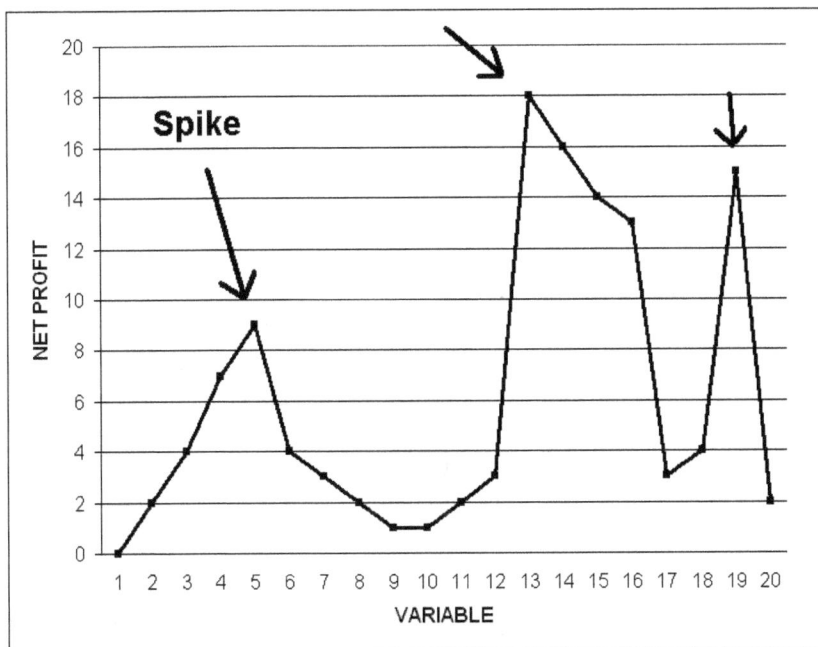

In summary we can state that there should be a logical path into the inputs' results so that something coherent in terms of inputs' batch should arise. When there is not a linear relationship with inputs and net profits, or drawdown, or whichever constraint you are putting as a primary rule of the optimisation, the whole set of results must be regarded as suspicious.

2.4 Evaluation of a trading system

Evaluating a trading system can look easier than it is in reality. In the end what a prudent trader must do is something which is counterintuitive: at first glance we indeed would say that the higher the net profit the better the system. Unfortunately nothing is further from reality than this impression. We will put forward some general methodological criteria not based on net profit and absolute numbers in order to weed out this deceptive approach. Then we will introduce the indicator RINA index, which was elaborated by TradeStation. RINA index is more and more common among system traders and we believe that it comes closer to a good analysis than any other tool.

What to look for in an indicator

Net profit is how much money the system brought home during the testing period. Even if the absolute number can lure the reader, it fundamentally says nothing about real performances of the system and moreover it says nothing about risk. Talking about profit without quantifying risk is a fatal error in system analysis. Furthermore, if you add proper commissions and slippage the equity line shape could change up to the point it becomes downward sloping or indeed negative.

So the two starting general considerations are the following:

1. A versatile return indicator should be normalised so that it can be easily comparable among multiple asset classes or multiple trading systems.

2. A prudent indicator always compares return to risk.

Net profit has neither of these features.

Moreover an indicator should always convey the idea of how much the measure he is trying to catch is *consistent*. What is consistency? A synonym of consistency could be *stability*: consistency measures how stable an indicator is. Let's take the example of the net profit: net profit in itself says nothing about when the profit was reaped. It could be that profit varied a lot from year to year or even that it was made just in a single year and all the other years the system lost money. Would you place more trust in a system that makes money year after year or simply a system that made money ten years ago and then lost money every year since? In the end this later system made money because the profit was so huge ten years ago and the following losses were acceptable; but who would be able to follow this system in the future? Nobody will trade such a system because it is apparent that the windfall ten years ago could likely be an outlier, an abnormal occurrence that will never be repeated.

So we can conclude that a consistent trading system has an even distribution not only of profits and losses but also of the series of consecutive winning and losing trades. If you cut the statistics of a consistent trading system year by year you will find all the indicators will be almost the same. If substantial differences arise from year to year or from month to month the trading system is not consistent. An intraday system could also be gauged by weekly performances.

Average trade

An important indicator of the quality of a trading system is the *average trade*, that is the net profit divided by the number of trades. Average trade tells us how much money we make or lose per trade. In absolute terms the average trade should be capable of covering slippage and commissions and then still leave some profit for the trader. In percentage terms the average trade should be consistent throughout the whole testing period. Usually traders compare the absolute average trade with the entry price of that particular trade so that it is expressed in percentage terms. Other traders compare the nominal average trade value with the nominal value of the contract in a given period. What we can recommend is to plot the historical average percentage value of the trades in order to have a clear picture of the profitability trend of the system over the years.

Percentage of profitable trades

The *percent profitable trades* number expresses the number of winning trades out of the number of the total trades. It is important not by itself (a trend-following system can have a low percent profitable trades number such as 35% and still be a viable system) but because it can be used to gauge how the system is balanced in relation to the average winning trade/average losing trade ratio. Usually the logic is that if you win a lot of times the average winning trade/average losing trade ratio will be low, while if conversely your percentage of profitable trades is low then the ratio will be high (inverse relationship). A 50% percent profitable trades number is a healthy one. If it grows significantly over 50% (for example to 60% or 70%) be watchful because something could be wrong: to counterbalance such a high percentage the average winning trade/average losing trade ratio should be particularly low, often even under the alarm level of 1. If you are using target exit (let's assume you exit 50% of the position at a price limit over the entry) it is normal for the percentage of profitable trades to go over 60% and the average winning trade/average losing trade to go under 2.

The percentage of profitable trades number is also important for calculating the mathematical expectancy of a trading system. The percentage of profitable trades multiplied by the average winning trade should be higher than the percentage of losing trades multiplied by the average losing trade. Mathematical expectancy, in other words, should be positive and the higher the better. You can use this measure of mathematical expectancy to rank systems and pick up the best.

As far as the percentage of profitable trades is concerned there is a caveat that must be regarded with careful attention: a 50% profitable trades ratio does not mean that a loss is followed by a win or vice versa. It is a controversial area if a trade sequence suggests it is possible to claim that a win follows a win or vice versa in some order. Even if the topic is fascinating, a prudent trade should always fight against the worst and hope for the best so that in our experience to trust on trade dependency is particularly risky since the assumption is quite strong. Indeed you are assuming that there is a recurring order in the trade sequence; that is, probabilities in the past show that after three wins in a row it was more likely to have two losses instead of a fourth win.

There are roulette players who really believe that the chance of getting a red number in the next run increases if you just had a black one. And even worse, they believe that the chance of getting a red number becomes bigger and bigger if a row of subsequent black numbers occurs, for example seven or ten times in a row. From logical thinking and statistical theory, however, you know that each run of the roulette in the casino is completely independent from another. So it has no meaning, neither good nor bad, if in the run just before there was a red number, a black one or the green one. Each occurrence of a number is completely independent from the other ones. So betting on a colour in the next run your chance is always the same: 18/37 = 48.6% (since there are 18 black and 18 red numbers plus one green 0).

Although the financial markets, especially for beginners, sometimes look like a casino, they are very different and more complex. In many cases they behave accidentally, with many movements happening up and down and nobody knows why. There are however some special situations which are created by human psychology of greed and fear when the market behaves differently to accident. It is these movements where, in special trading systems in special situations, trade dependencies can occur [5]. But this is a sophisticated topic that goes beyond of the scope of this book. In any case we recommend readers approach this topic with extreme prudence.

Profit factor

Profit factor is a perfect indicator for comparing different systems or the same system plotted over different markets. Of course this indicator is a ratio so it does not suffer from the usual drawback of the other absolute number ratios. Profit factor is gross profit divided by gross loss and basically reveals the size of gross profit in relation to gross loss. The higher the better. Usually a healthy trading system has a profit factor of 2, an average winning trade/average losing trade ratio of 2 and a percentage of profitable trades number equal to 50%. But there are also good systems with a profit factor of between 1.5 and 3. Think again about what you did during optmisation and your system's design and development when your profit factor goes over 3.

Drawdown

A broad definition of *drawdown* could be the largest loss or the largest losing streak of a trading system, whichever is the biggest [4]. In a more graphical way we can depict drawdown as the dip in the equity line between a highest high point and the successive lower point before a new high is made. In other words total equity drawdown is the open trade profits and losses plus the already closed out equity on your account. But drawdown has more subtle meanings according to whether we consider only open positions or closed out positions. In fact it is important to distinguish between three different types of drawdown:

1. An *end trade drawdown* tells us how much of the open profit we had to give back before we were allowed to exit a specific trade

2. A *close trade drawdown* is the difference between the entry and the exit price without taking into consideration what is going on within the trade

3. A *start trade drawdown* measures how much the trade went against us after the entry and before it started to go our way [6].

For sake of simplicity we will use the close trade drawdown definition since it is the most significant. But it is important to remember that while trading real money we can endure an open trade drawdown much bigger than the theoretically calculated closed trade drawdown.

It is undeniable that the absolute value of a drawdown has a deep psychological impact on the trader because he will be forced to deal with it and this could be painful. But with drawdown, as with profit indicators, we need to be careful to use this measure in a comparative way. For this purpose the concept of underwater equity line is useful; that is, the absolute drawdown value divided by the equity line's previous highest high value. This expresses the drawdown relative to the equity line in percentage terms. So even if we are testing a system on a 40-year long price series in which the value of the contract changed dramatically, we still have a percentage point reference value in order to spot what is the real expected drawdown at current values: just plot the highest underwater equity line percentage at the current market value.

Many analysts try to fight against drawdown by optimising the exits and the initial stops while it would be more appropriate to further understand the reason why drawdown is taking place. If there was a freak occurrence in historical terms on the markets then it is obvious that an abnormal drawdown occurred. If nothing special occurred then there is something wrong in the logic of the system.

In order to evaluate which kind of drawdown we have to worry about, and which kind of drawdown is normal, it is paramount to calculate the average drawdown and its standard deviation. If the largest drawdown lies between one and two standard deviations from the average than we should expect a future drawdown quite close to what we had in the past. If the average drawdown is beyond two standard deviations from the mean then we need to rethink the logic of the system, provided that nothing special happened in the past that could justify the freak drawdown.

The average tolerance of a drawdown for most professional traders and money managers ranges from 20% up to 30%. Let's say that a drawdown of 10% is a wonderful accomplishment while a drawdown of 30% is much more painful and worrisome. A drawdown of 40–50% would be unbearable for most market players.

Time averages

Other important indicators include the *time averages*. Average time in trades displays the average time (years, days, minutes) spent in all completed trades, during the specified period for the strategy. Other trading platforms have similar indicators. Average time in trades is vital for portfolio construction since to exploit negative correlation among equity lines your systems need to be in the market at the same time or at least to have the same average time in trades. If you make up a portfolio with a system that trades seldom and stays in the market for long periods of time, and another that trades often but with short individual trades, you will never level off the cumulative equity line.

A trading system should be balanced between the profit and risk it produces on the long side and on the short side. AmiBroker and TradeStation split the system report between long and short trades and except in particular cases, when you can find a logical reason for it, longs should always keep pace with short in profit generation. A trading system which is not balanced in between long and short must always be regarded with suspicion.

In this section, we have tried to figure out some practical guidelines for a system developer without delving into much theory or philosophical considerations. Without fretting about being considered sloppy system traders, we dare to openly recognise that even after 25 years' experience we cannot understand at the first glance whether a trading system deserves to be considered with attention or not.

The first aspect we check is the *equity line*, which needs to be growing smoothly and without many deep drawdowns. Personally we also appreciate many flat times, that is parts of the equity line that are horizontal: it means that no trading was done in that period since a filter took the system out of the market. We believe that there is no need to trade continuously and a good system should know when there is some edge to be exploited over the markets and conversely when it is more appropriate to sit on the sidelines. Then, after the equity line, we immediately check average trade, profit factor, percent profitable, average win/average loss and how the monthly returns were distributed throughout the years. Just from these indicators a proper judgement about the trading system can be drawn without much worry about being on the wrong side.

2.5 Conclusion

So far we have covered the most important theoretical aspects of the trading systems' optimisation and performance evaluation. It was a quick overview of the universe of notions that this topic embraces, but we hope that this brevity will lead to a much more powerful understanding.

We can assert in conclusion that trading systems are a scientific approach to trading where nothing is left to discretion. It is not a certain business, obviously, but it is a business that deals with probability and that allows the trader to trade the markets exploiting a statistical edge.

You will be able to expand this knowledge, delving into the nuances of trading systems evaluation and optimisation, by reading the texts we included in the bibliography at the end of the book.

Unfortunately it is impossible to have a full grasp of the subject without dealing with the practical application of trading systems. Trading systems' development is not a theoretical intellectual challenge, but a practical experimental approach to markets. Writing codes, testing them and then optimising them is a process that allows the trader to acquire a practical view of the markets that is sometimes much more important than theory. Knowing how to follow this process will save much demanding work and it will help to solve situations that otherwise will be out of reach for the average trader.

In the following chapters you will have a practical view of what a systematic trader does when they develop, evaluate and optimise a trading system. We believe that this is the most important part of our work.

Part II

Trading System Development and
Evaluation of a Real Case

3

How to Develop a Trading System Step-By-Step – Using the Example of the British Pound/US Dollar Pair

Introduction

THE CURRENCY MARKETS are attractive to all types of traders including individual day traders, trading companies, financial and non-financial companies, banks and governments. They trade 24 hours a day from Monday morning in New Zealand until Friday night in America. Markets with strong movements like the British pound offer you all the possibilities to develop any type of trading system from any different idea on any time scale.

In this chapter we will not present the absolute best trading system, which promises the highest profits. Instead our goal is to show you a trading system which is based on a sound idea and improved for a high robustness. As an aid to understanding our concept of trading system development you will find in the following pages a step-by-step explanation of how a new trading system is developed and tested for stability.

As an example we choose a trend-following system with a breakout component. We take this system and show how you can improve it up to become a profitable trading system in the following steps.

3.1 The entry logic and code. How to improve a normal moving average crossover system with a breakout filter.

3.2 Evaluation of the trading system without parameter optimisation and exits – the importance of commissions and slippage.

3.3 Variation of the input parameters: optimisation and stability graphs.

3.4 Inserting an intraday time filter: the importance of time for short-term trading.

3.5 Determination of appropriate exits for your system by checking the development of all the system's trades. How John Sweeney's Maximum Adverse and Maximum Favourable Excursion can support you.

Let's start with the description of the logic of the system.

3.1 The birth of a trading system

As mentioned in the introduction there are lots of sources for developing your own pool of trading systems. One of them is certainly the Strategy Trading and Development Club (STAD) of Omega Research (TradeStation). As a starting point we take the following entry logic, as explained in STAD, volume 13:

> The Luxor system identifies set-ups for new trades by the crossing of two moving averages – a fast one and a slow one. Of course, there are many types of moving averages; Luxor is the first strategy in STAD Club to use triangular moving averages. The purpose of the triangular moving average (TMA) is to increase the smoothing of the price data without also increasing the lag time between prices and the indicator. TMAs begin with the calculation of a simple arithmetic average of prices (the close is the price field most commonly averaged). Then, the TMA indicator calculates a simple arithmetic average of the first average.

So the key point in the description is the special type of moving average. When we tested the trading system we found, however, that the type of moving average did not matter and the best results were produced with a simple moving average instead of the more complex triangular moving average! So you can forget how this triangular, complex moving average works and stay with the normal ones. This confirms our observation when developing trading systems that often the simplest things work best.

The main steps in system development are the following: to get ideas which fit the personality of the traded market, to test them and to adapt them to your own needs. We do this here for the LUXOR system. We only take the main idea of how to use the moving averages and make some minor changes.

The free LUXOR system code

The programmers who want to implement this logic can find the code of the trading system in TradeStation's EasyLanguage below. (Other readers can skip this paragraph and continue on to the description of the trading system.) We added some comments into the code so that you know what is done and so that you can change the code easily according to your needs.

Text 3.1: EasyLanguage Code of the LUXOR trading system. Bold letters: Code for the entries. Normal letters: added time filter. In comment brackets: possible simple exits.

```
{Copyright 2000. OMEGA RESEARCH, INC. MIAMI, FLORIDA.
Strategy Trading and Development Club STAD, Volume 13,

Modified 18 June 2006 and 15 July 2008 by Urban Jaekle
Modified 1 January 2007 by Russell Stagg}

{1. Definition of necessary inputs and variables}

Inputs:

FastLength( 3 ),    {The input parameters of the two moving
averages... }

    SlowLength( 30 ),

tset(1600),      {...start time for the intraday time window
filter...}

WindowDist(100);  {...window distance for the intraday time window
filter...}

               {...can be changed - this makes optimisation
possible}

Variables:       {Definition of needed variables}

    MP(0), Fast(0), Slow(0), GoLong(False), GoShort(False),
BuyStop(0), SellStop(0), BuyLimit(0), SellLimit(0), tEnd(1700);

MP = MarketPosition;

{2. Time window filter; see below: 3.4, "Inserting an intraday time
filter"}

tend=tset+WindowDist; {time window of 1 hour}
if time > tset - 5 and time < tend then begin

{3. Definition of moving averages and entry conditions}

Fast = Average(Close, FastLength);
Slow = Average(Close, SlowLength);

GoLong = Fast > Slow;
GoShort = Fast < Slow;

{4. Entry Setup}

If Fast crosses above Slow then begin
    BuyStop = High + 1 point;
    BuyLimit = High + 5 points;
end;

If Fast crosses below Slow then begin
    SellStop = Low - 1 point;
```

```
        SellLimit= Low - 5 points;
  end;

  If GoLong and C < BuyLimit then
        Buy ("Long") next bar at BuyStop Stop;
  If GoShort and C > SellLimit then
        Sell Short ("Short") next bar at SellStop Stop;

  {5. Exits: Derived from the slow moving average. These exits
  are not used here since we take different standard exits! Feel
  free to change the exits according to your needs}

  {If MP = 1 then Begin
        Sell next bar at Slow - 1 point Stop;
  End;
  If MP = -1 then Begin
        Buy to Cover next bar at Slow + 1 point Stop;
  End; }
  end;
```

The EasyLanguage Code can be divided into different parts:

1. Definition of inputs and variables

2. Time filter (discussed below in 3.4)

3. Entry and exit setup

Since this first section of this chapter focuses on the entry logic we have put the exit part of the trading system in the EasyLanguage Code in brackets. This means that first we leave the exits out and only take the entries from this system. Later in this chapter we use these entries and apply our own exits to them.

The entry logic

Now let's explain what this code means for the construction of the entries (fig. 3.1). The entry is based on a usual moving average system and works as following: you enter the market long on the bar where a fast moving average crosses above a slow moving average and in the same way you go short if the fast moving average crosses below the slower moving average.

Trend-following methods like these are well known to be able to capture huge profits during long steady trends. The LUXOR entry logic takes this basic idea of such trend-following methods by just using two simple moving averages as an entry signal generator. However it is modified in the following way: an entry after the average crossover is only allowed after a confirmation of the price itself occurs. The crossing of the moving average alone is not enough to initiate a market position. In case of a long entry you want the current price to exceed a recent high to enter a trade (fig. 3.1). Analogously the price must go below a recent low to trigger a short entry. Please note that we only explain here the long side in the system code since the short entries are built symmetrically.

Figure 3.1: Entry Logic. The entry is not triggered by the crossing of the two moving averages. Instead, at the crossover bar the high is kept and used as a long entry level. Short entries are taken symmetrically. Chart example was taken from British pound/US dollar, 30 min, FOREX from 26 Dec 2007. Chart and datafeed from TradeStation 8.

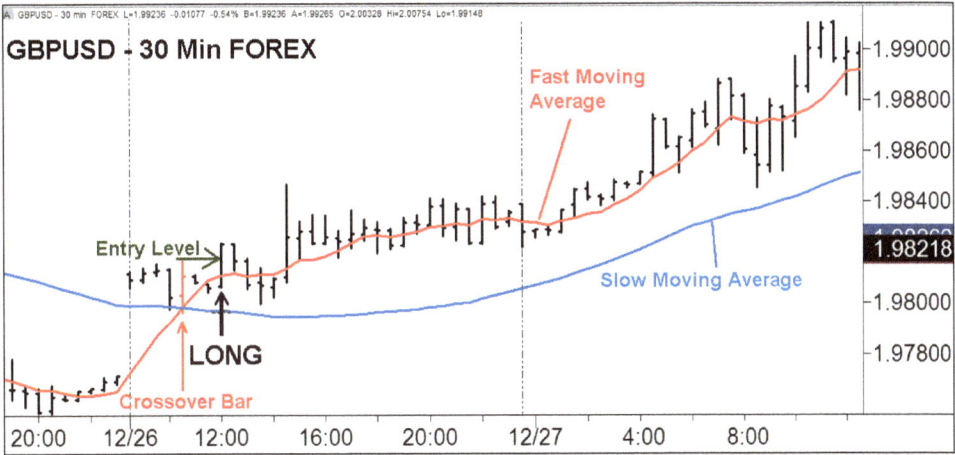

The system has the following two input parameters which can be varied and optimised:

```
Inputs: FastLength (3), SlowLength (30);
```

These two input parameters "FastLength" and "SlowLength" are used for the fast and slow moving average:

```
Fast = Moving Average (Close, FastLength);
Slow = Moving Average (Close, SlowLength);
```

Now the important breakout filter is added. At the bar when the fast moving average crosses above the slow moving average the trade is not directly initiated. We take the high of this bar (crossover bar, marked in red colour in fig. 3.1) and keep it as the entry stop point as long as the fast moving average stays above the slow moving average:

```
If Fast crosses above Slow Then EntryLevel = High;
If Fast > Slow then Buy ("Long") next bar at BuyStop Stop;
```

This simple but effective condition improves the probability of the simple trend-following system capturing the most profitable breakouts and not just any moving average crossover which occurs. It is different to common moving average crossover systems where every trade is taken, since the additional filter has to confirm the moving averages and in this way prevents trading some false breakouts.

3.2 First evaluation of the trading system

Calculation without slippage and commissions

The strategy is now applied to 30-minute FOREX data from 21/10/2002 to 4/7/2008. All the following calculations in this chapter are based on a one contract basis. Keeping the beginning simple we calculate the trading system's results without any slippage and commissions. These will be added in the next section where we will examine their impact on system performance. Furthermore please note that at first we check the system just with entries and trade reversals, leaving out exits.

As first input parameters for the trading system's entries we choose 10 bars for the fast and 30 bars for the slow moving average. With 30-minute bars this means the fast moving average is calculated from the last five trading hours whereas the slow moving average relies on the last 15 hours. Fig. 3.2 shows the resulting equity curve in a detailed form. By *detailed form* we mean that this curve shows all run-ups and drawdowns of the trades which happen during their lifetime. Like this the equity line is more informative compared to a form where just end-of-day or even end-of-month results are shown.

Figure 3.2: Detailed Equity Curve of the trading system LUXOR on British pound/US dollar (FOREX), 30-minute bars, 21/10/2002–4/7/2008. Input parameters: SLOW=30, FAST=10. System without exits, always in the market. Back-test without any slippage and commissions. Chart from TradeStation 8.

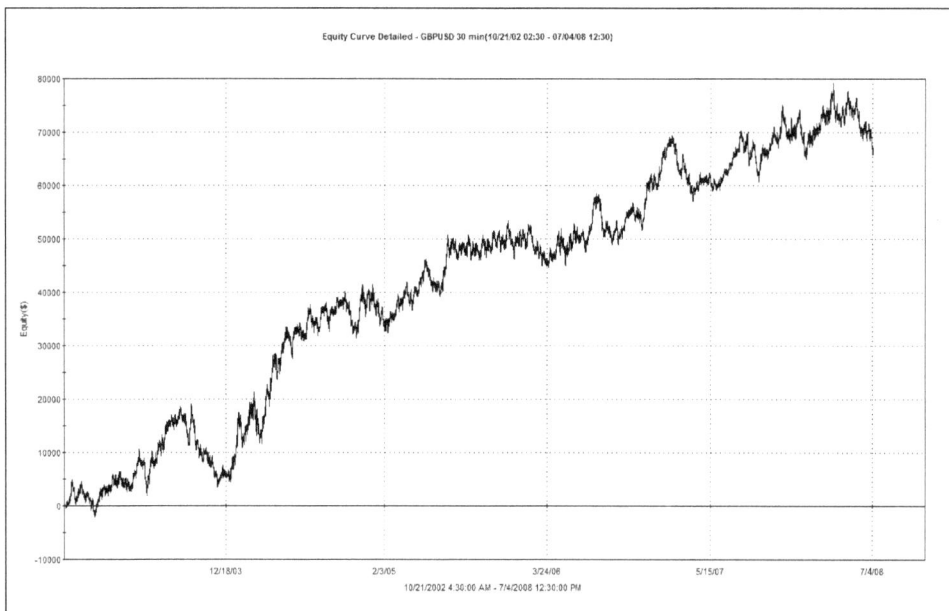

The equity line looks like a good starting point for a viable trading system. Although some drawdowns occur the system always recovers quickly and achieves new highs, so that you get a relatively steady growth of the initial capital. The profitability of the trading system is also revealed by the trading figures (table 3.1). Here you see that LUXOR gains a total net profit of $66,000 with only one traded contract within the testing period from October 2002 until July 2008. The biggest drawdown within this period was $16,000. If you assume a starting capital of $30,000 then this would mean that your total profit is more than 200% in the last six years, with a maximum drawdown of about 50%.

Table 3.1: Main system figures of the LUXOR system. British pound/US dollar (FOREX), 30-minute bars, 21/10/2002–4/7/2008. Input parameters: SLOW=30, FAST=10. System without exits, always in the market. Back-test calculation without any slippage and commission.

	All Trades	Long Trades	Short Trades
Total Net Profit	$66,318	$56,918	$9,400
Gross Profit	$590,530	$310,301	$280,230
Gross Loss	($524,213)	($253,383)	($270,830)
Profit Factor	1.13	1.22	1.03
Total Number of Trades	1913	957	956
Percent Profitable	36.49%	39.81%	33.16%
Winning Trades	698	381	317
Losing Trades	1215	576	639
Avg. Trade Net Profit	$35	$59	$10
Avg. Winning Trade	$846	$814	$884
Avg. Losing Trade	($431)	($440)	($424)
Ratio Avg. Win:Avg. Loss	1.96	1.85	2.09
Largest Winning Trade	$5,628	$5,628	$4,338
Largest Losing Trade	($2,522)	($1,652)	($2,522)
Max. Consecutive Winning Trades	6	6	6
Max. Consecutive Losing Trades	16	10	11
Avg. Bars in Total Trades	37.77	39.18	36.36
Avg. Bars in Winning Trades	61.84	62.96	60.5
Avg. Bars in Losing Trades	23.94	23.45	24.38
Max. Drawdown (Intraday Peak to Valley)	($15,644)	($11,133)	($19,746)
Date of Max. Drawdown	27-Nov-03		

The considered system shows the main properties of trend-following trading strategies:

- The percentage of profitable trades is low (36.5%). From the 1913 performed trades, only 698 are profitable whereas the majority (1,215) end with a loss.

- The overall gains of the system result from the high ratio of average win/average losing trade. The average winning trade is with $846, which is bigger than the average losing trade ($435) by a factor of two.

- The average time in winning trades is about three times longer than the average time which the system stays in losing trades (62 bars versus 24 bars).

This shows that the system logic follows perhaps the most important rule in trading which everybody knows but which is yet difficult to follow: cut the losses short and let the profits run. This trading rule is psychologically hard to adhere to since you often suffer directly from your losses and on the other hand you have to wait a long time until you can earn your rare but hefty gains.

It is worth mentioning that the long side of the trading system is much more profitable than its short side ($56,900 vs. $9,400 net profit). This observation will be examined in chapter 5.3 again when we discuss the *market bias*. The market bias means the tendency of a market to favour special features or parts of a trading system, like in this case the better profitability of the trend-following system's long side in an overall upward trend of the tested market. The good point for our trading system here is that although there is such a market bias with an up-trend, the short side of our trading system is still in the profitable range. This underlines the stability of this symmetrically built system.

Furthermore, you of course get nearly the same number of short trades (956) as long trades (957) because the trading system only reverses positions. Since we have not added any exits the system stays in the market 100% of the time, holding either a long or a short position.

Finally we want to underline a fact which should never be underestimated when developing trading systems: the statistical significance of your performed tests. If you develop a new system and in testing you have only 100 signals, or even less, the probability of achieving profitable results just by accident is high. With nearly 2,000 trades in our back-test the statistical probability is high that this strategy will perform in a similar way in the (near) future.

So what have you gained so far? Statistics show that the entry logic is sound and has a certain probability of maintaining its behaviour in the future. If you however take a closer look at the trading figures you will see that the system produces only an average profit of $35; this level of average profit per trade without any trading costs is very low! So what you have so far is just a trading rule which detects a tiny profitable bias in prices.

Therefore we are now at a point when the trading system development work has just started. There are lots of steps to perform until you can work out a complete trading system. The profitability of this system must be increased and exits must be added. Before we do this we take trading costs into consideration to make the whole approach more realistic.

Calculation after adding slippage and commissions

When subtracting $5 of commission and $25 of slippage (which is three pips in total) per round turn from the above mentioned average per trade profit of $35 only a $5 average profit per trade is left. The detailed equity curve and the drawdown graph show the result of this more realistic calculation (fig. 3.3). Whereas the equity curve is now moving sideways with lots of oscillations, the underwater equity curve reveals big drawdowns (up to 15%) and long phases which the trading system needs to recover from these drawdowns.

The situation for the LUXOR-trading system seems to be hopeless. With this system you are far away from gaining any profits on the pound/dollar FOREX pair. Keep in mind however that we have just chosen two arbitrary input parameters. They could be suitable or not. The key question which has to be answered now is: is this trading system useless overall, or is it a trading system that has its strengths but is suffering from the inappropriate choice of input parameters?

To answer this question more system tests like the one shown above will be necessary for multiple different input parameters. In order to prepare these tests we first want to explain what we are looking for when we perform such optimisations since there are some pitfalls to avoid.

Figure 3.3: Result of the trading system LUXOR with added $30 slippage and commissions per round turn. A: detailed equity curve; B: underwater equity curve. British pound/ US dollar (FOREX), 30-minute bars, 21/10/2002–4/7/2008. Input parameters: SLOW=30, FAST=10. System without exits, always in the market. Chart from TradeStation 8.

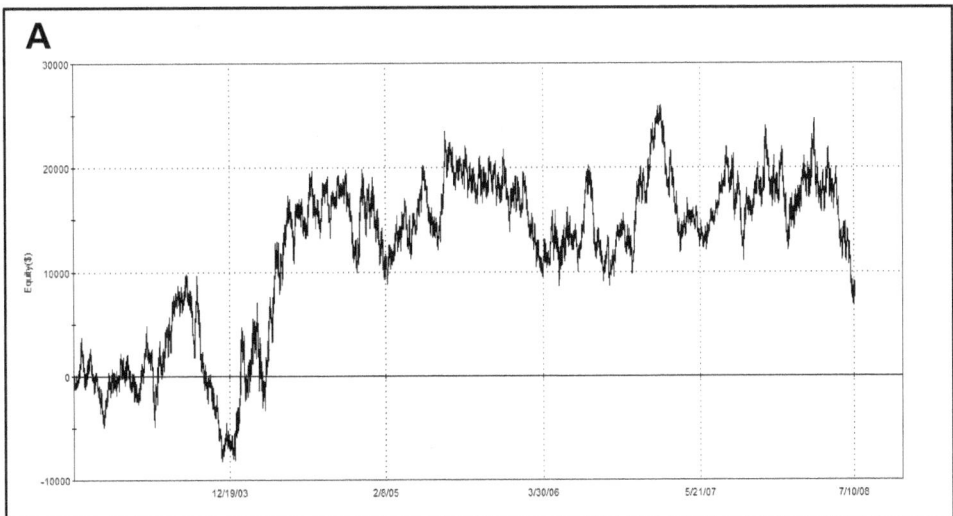

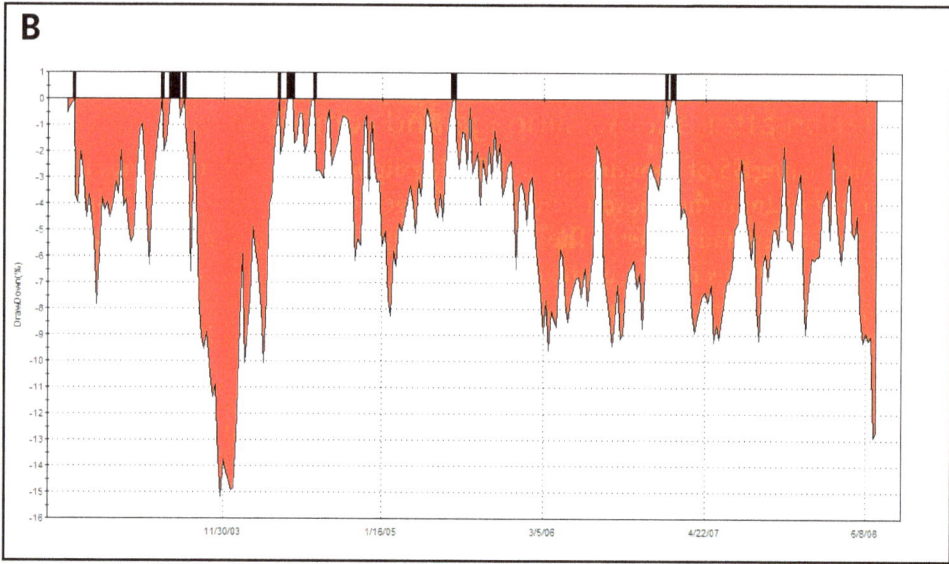

3.3 Variation of the input parameters: optimisation and stability diagrams

What does stability of a system's input parameter mean? A short theoretical excursion

Optimisation can be your best friend but also your worst enemy when you develop a trading system. The important point is that you always know what you are doing when you vary some of the system's input parameters. Keep in mind that every trading system is in some form an optimisation. When you select a system you compare it with others and choose it because it has shown a special behaviour in the past which convinces you that this special behaviour will hold in the future. Even if you do not adjust any of its input parameters, in rejecting other, maybe similar, trading systems you have essentially done this by optimising the input parameters afterwards with your computer.

The open question remains: at which point does the development and selection phase of a system end and the optimisation of your system start? Since it can never be completely separated, it is better to accept that every trading system is in some way an adaptation of the past and therefore is optimised. So the key question for you as a system developer is always: which parameter do you choose from your back-tests? Which settings are likely to continue to produce profits in the future in real trading? The answer to this question is different for each trading system but one rule holds true for all: the neighbourhood of your chosen system parameters must be nearly as profitable as your chosen system parameter and the bigger this profitable parameter range is the better. Murray Ruggiero, an experienced professional trading systems developer, writes about this topic [7]:

> *If you don't like the neighbouring numbers, you've got a problem, because odds are, you will wind up with the results of the neighbouring set of parameters.*

Let's have a look at an example (fig. 3.4) where we examine the hypothetical results of an imaginary system in order to select stable input parameters. On the right axis you find one input parameter of this hypothetical system which can be anything, a moving average, a distance of a stop or a profit target, a delay time, etc. As a function of this system parameter you find on the vertical axis the net profit in arbitrary units.

Figure 3.4: Choosing stable parameters for your trading system: Net profit as a function of one system input parameter in arbitrary units. Artificially generated result of a hypothetical trading system.

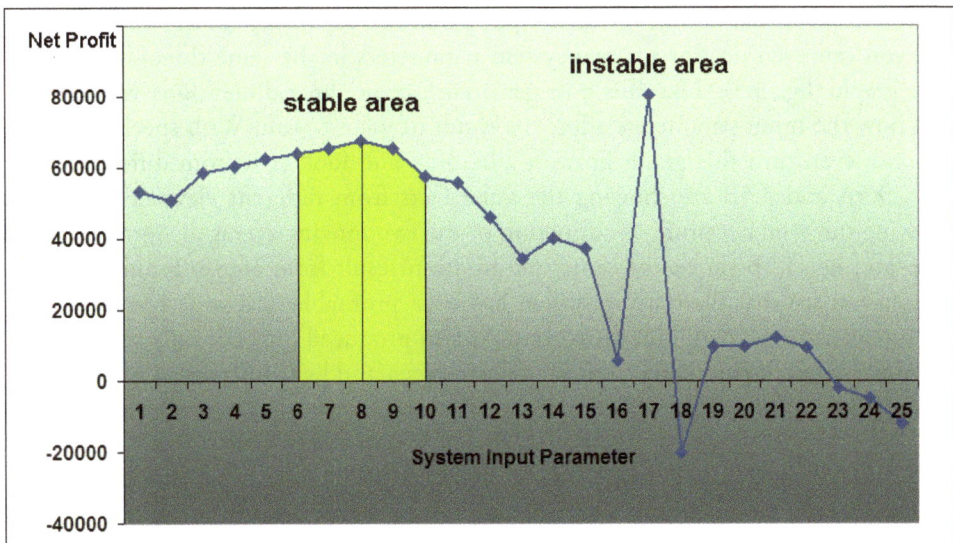

The best input parameter of this artificial trading system in terms of net profit would be 17. With this parameter, the system gained 80,000 units. But look at its neighbourhood. In the next neighbourhood, with parameter 16, the system's profit is poor (5,000 units) or with parameter 18 there is even a loss (–10,000 units). If your traded market only slightly changes in the future you will never be able to repeat this good profit which showed with parameter 17 in your back-test. So although in this hypothetical system 17 was the best parameter in the past, it is certainly not your best choice for the future.

If you, however, choose a parameter in the region between 4 and 10, e.g. 8, you are in safer territory. In that area your past net profit was not as high as your best fit parameter, but the parameters in the neighbourhood have similar profits to your chosen parameter. All gained profits are around 60,000 units. If the market changes in the future, it is likely that your trading system will still generate similar profits to those which it showed in the back-test with parameter 8 or with any other parameter between 4 and 10. So it is these broad plateaus of good (not necessarily the best!) parameters which you have to find.

Dependency of main system figures on the two moving averages

From theory back to reality. Let's check how our trading system LUXOR behaves when changing its two input parameters, including trading costs of $30 slippage and commissions per round turn. We want to see how the results of our trend-following system change when the lengths of the fast and slow moving averages are varied. We change the two averages in a wide range, the fast moving average length from 1 bar to 20 bars in steps of 1, the slow moving average length from 21 bars to 80 bars, also in steps of 1. A fast PC computes the necessary 1,200 system tests in about three minutes.

From these tests you can plot the total net profit as a function of the two varied input parameters. You can do this for each input parameter separately (as shown in fig. 3.4) but you can even do this for two system parameters in the same three-dimensional area graph (fig. 3.5). Like this you get a surface in three dimensions which show you how the input parameters affect the result of your system. With special software you can even turn this graph in every direction and look at it from different sides. Figs. 3.5A and 3.5B are showing the same facts from different views. Fig. 3.5A is showing the total net profit as a function of the two moving average lengths from the side, and fig. 3.5B shows the same optimisation result from above. From these two figures you see that the trading system has been profitable in a wide range of input parameter settings (dark blue areas) but has also produced losses or only small profits in other ranges of parameter settings (yellow, green and light blue areas).

Figure 3.5: Three-dimensional area diagrams for all trades of the system LUXOR. A: side view; B: top view. Net profit in US dollars as a function of the two input parameters: fast and slow moving average. Tested on British pound/US dollar (FOREX), 30-minute bars, 21/10/2002–4/7/2008, incl. $30 slippage and commissions per round turn. Diagrams generated with RINA 3D Smart View.

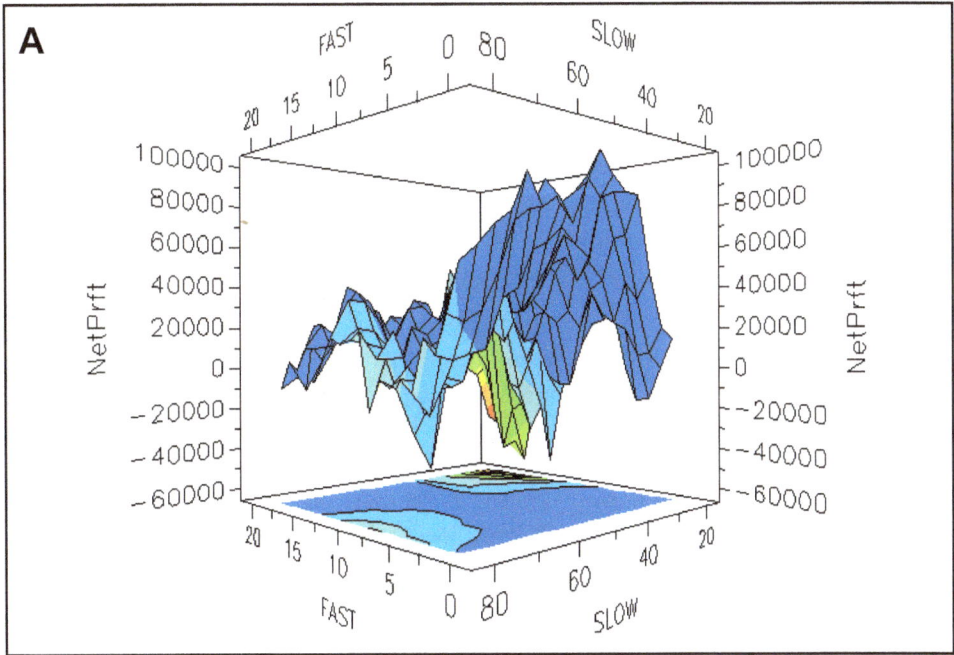

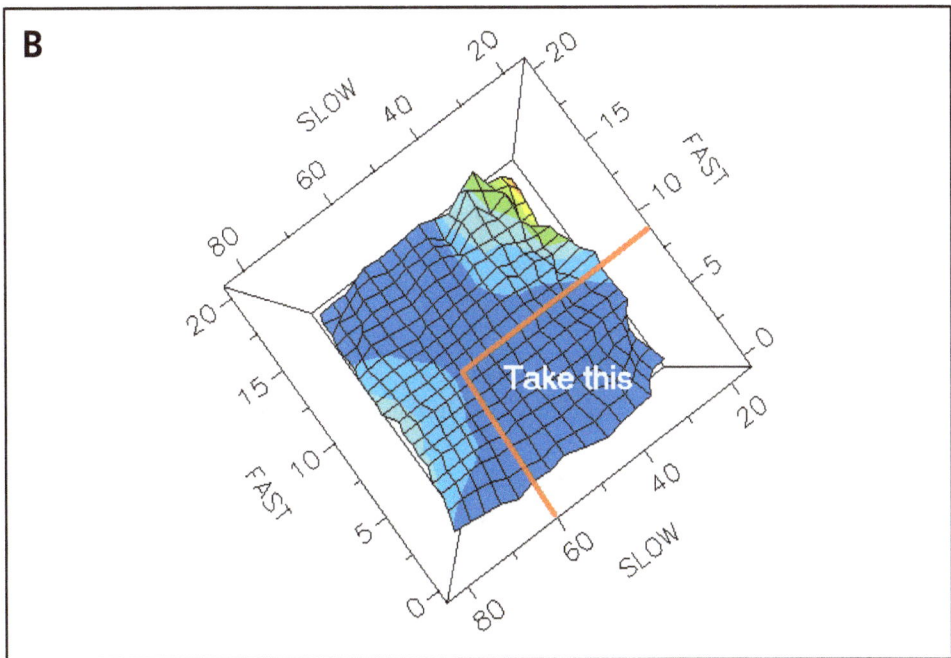

Of course we are looking for input parameters which produced a high net profit in the past. But as shown above in fig. 3.4 it is even more important for those system parameters that they have enough peer parameters in their near neighbourhood which were nearly as profitable as the chosen *best* ones. In our trading system which we have developed, so far the whole area in the lower right part (fig. 3.5B) seems at a first glance to fulfil this requirement. We'll now take this shorter area and have a closer look at it (figs. 3.6A–D). From these graphs you can see that the system stays stable against parameter variation in the chosen area. Although the total net profit varies in a relatively big range (between $20,000 and $100,000) it stays clearly positive for all selected input parameters. The best profits of nearly $100,000 are achieved in the region when the fast moving average is very small (< 3) and the slow moving average is between 30–50. This is also the area with the smallest maximum intraday drawdowns of about $15,000. Over all parameters the maximum intraday drawdown does vary quite a lot but never becomes excessive – it always stays below about $35,000.

Like the total net profit and the maximum intraday drawdown you can plot further important statistical figures as a function of the two input parameters (figs. 3.6C and D). If you do so you get further valuable insight into your trading system. If you watch, for example, the total number of trades of the system (fig. 3.6D) you can see a fact which holds true for many trend-following systems: the slower you make them to react (in our case the longer the look-back periods of the two moving averages are) the less trades you get. By changing the input parameters of the system you have the possibility of affecting some key attributes which allows you to adapt a system better to your trading style or to the requirements of a money management scheme in a bigger portfolio. Let's say you have many fast-reacting systems in your portfolio and need more slow-reacting components – you may achieve this by choosing longer look-back periods for the moving averages. If you need a faster-reacting system you make the input parameters smaller. We'll come back to this observation in our portfolio building section when correlations between different trading systems and their different time scales become important.

Interestingly, in our trading system, while the number of trades changes a lot with the system's input parameters, another trading figure, the average profit per trade, stays relatively stable (fig. 3.6C). It varies between $10 and $50 but mostly stays between $30 and $40, especially for all fast moving averages between 1 and 9 and the slower averages between 30 and 50.

From these results you can conclude that *good* system parameters will be an instantaneously reacting fast moving average (< 3) and a slow moving average between 30 and 50. Let's take the value "1" as input value for the fast moving average. It is clear that a one period moving average is not a real moving average, even if for the sake of simplicity we keep calling it a moving average. In fact the fast moving average becomes the closing price itself. For the slower average you can take any value between 30 and 50. We choose here 44 as an input value since it produces the highest total net profit and has a wide neighbourhood of profitable parameters.

You should always observe the behaviour of your system in the following months and if it turns out after a longer period of screening that the chosen parameters (1/44) are not the most stable choice then you must change them, for example to 3/30 (if these parameters proved to be more stable than your initial choice of 1/44). Such a parameter change is an example of a reoptimisation. You will find a more systematic approach to the topic of periodic reoptimisation and walk-forward optimisation in chapter 6. For the moment we stay with the parameters of 1 (fast moving average) and 44 (slow moving average) and we will take a closer look at the trading system's performance.

Figure 3.6: Three-dimensional area diagrams for all trades of the trading system LUXOR. Main system figures as a function of the two input parameters: fast and slow moving average. Tested on British pound/US dollar (FOREX), 30-minute bars, 21/10/2002– 4/7/2008, including $30 slippage and commissions per round turn. A: net profit; B: maximum intraday drawdown; C: average trade net profit; D: number of total trades generated. Diagrams generated with RINA 3D Smart View.

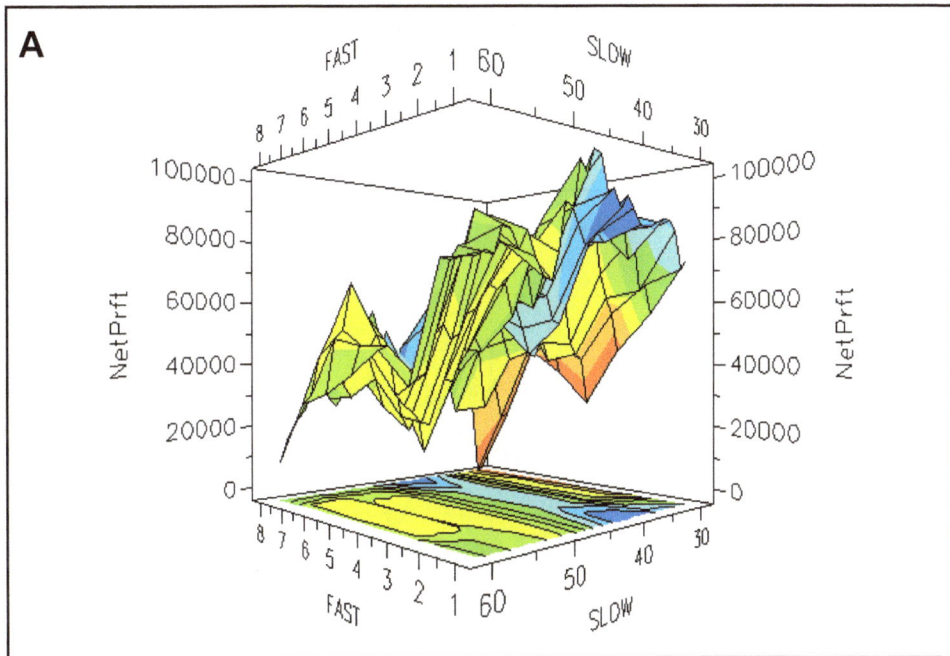

B

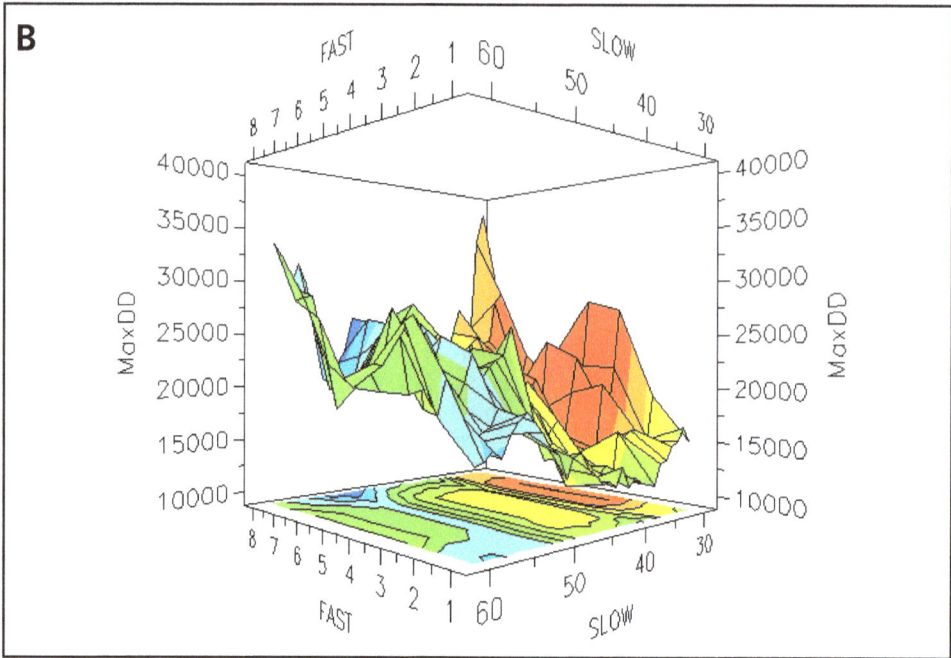

C

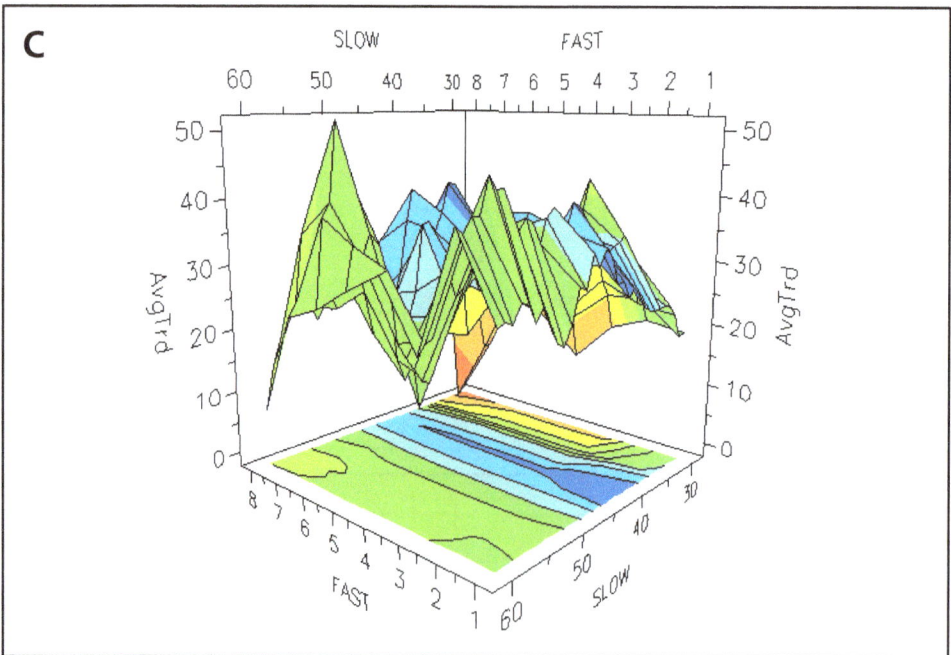

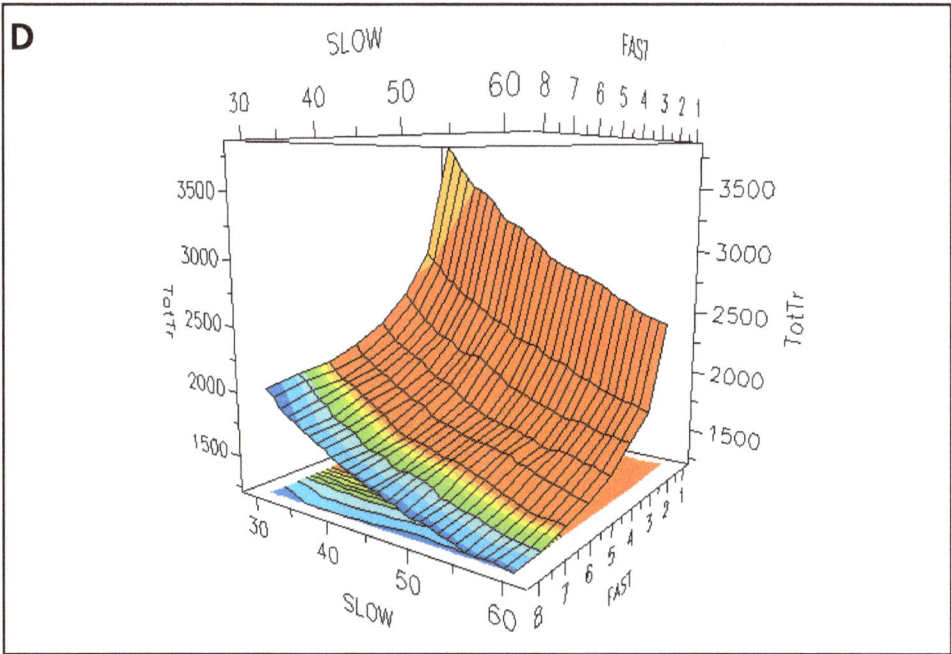

Result with optimised input values

With the fast moving average set to 1 bar (=closing price itself) and the slow moving average set to 44 bars you get a steadily growing equity curve (fig. 3.7A). This result is confirmed with the underwater equity curve which always quickly recovers after every drawdown (fig. 3.7B). The biggest drawdown happened in November 2003. It was, with 8%, only half as big as the drawdown of more than 15% which we got with the non-optimised input parameters (10/30).

Figure 3.7: Trading system LUXOR, tested on British pound/US dollar (FOREX), 30-minute bars, 21/10/2002–4/7/2008. Optimised input parameters in terms of net profit: SLOW=44, FAST=1. System without exits, always in the market, long or short. Back-test includes $30 slippage and commission. Chart from TradeStation 8. A: Detailed equity curve; B: Weekly underwater equity curve.

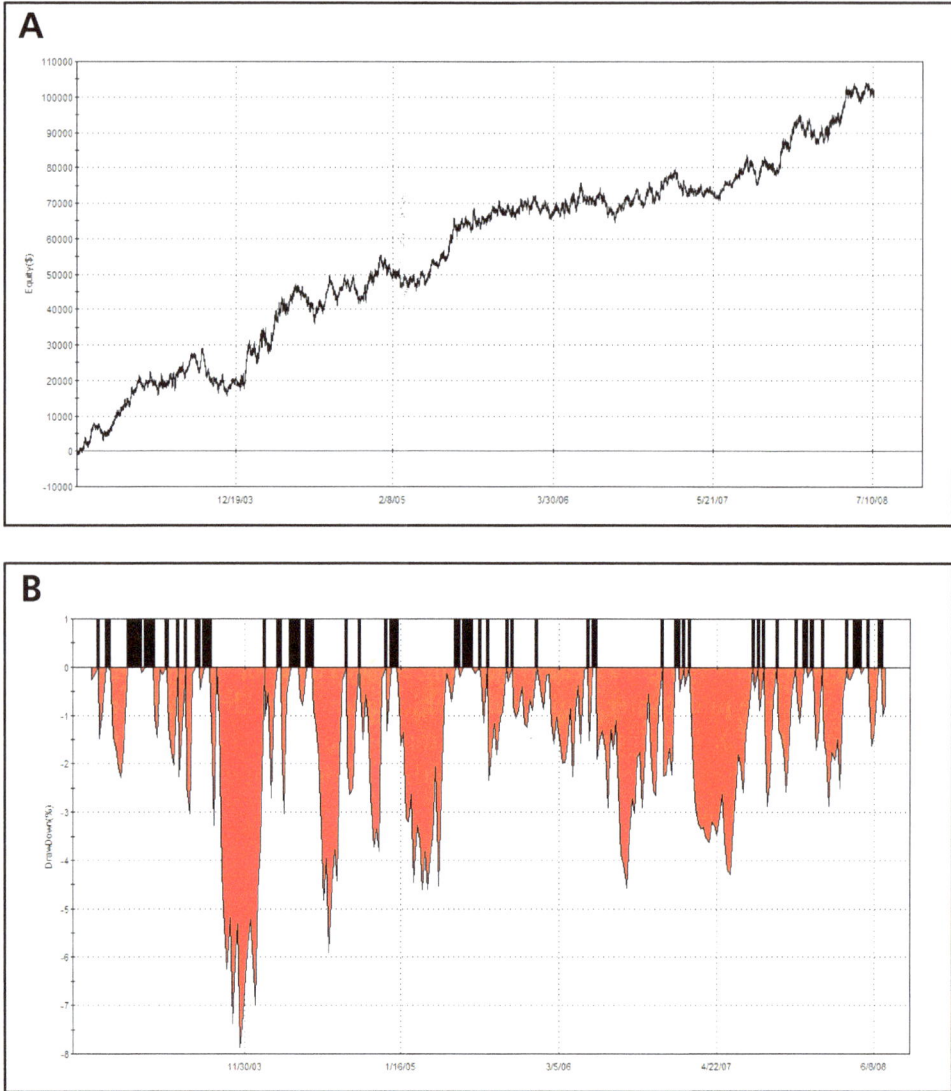

Table 3.2: Main system figures of the trading system LUXOR. British pound/US dollar (FOREX), 30-minute bars, 21/10/2002–4/7/2008. Input parameters: SLOW=44, FAST=1. System without exits, always in the market. Back-test includes $30 slippage and commissions per round turn.

	All Trades	Long Trades	Short Trades
Total Net Profit	$100,125	$73,888	$26,237
Gross Profit	$666,862	$347,323	$319,540
Gross Loss	($566,738)	($273,435)	($293,303)
Profit Factor	1.18	1.27	1.09
Total Number of Trades	2980	1490	1490
Percent Profitable	26.41%	28.26%	24.56%
Winning Trades	787	421	366
Losing Trades	2193	1069	1124
Avg. Trade Net Profit	$33.60	$49.59	$17.61
Avg. Winning Trade	$847	$825	$873
Avg. Losing Trade	($258)	($256)	($261)
Ratio Avg. Win:Avg. Loss	3.28	3.23	3.35
Largest Winning Trade	$5,428	$5,428	$4,418
Largest Losing Trade	($2,062)	($2,062)	($1,452)
Max. Consecutive Winning Trades	7	7	7
Max. Consecutive Losing Trades	24	18	21
Avg. Bars in Total Trades	24.69	25.61	23.77
Avg. Bars in Winning Trades	60.75	60.82	60.66
Avg. Bars in Losing Trades	11.75	11.75	11.76
Max. Drawdown (Intraday Peak to Valley)	($13,440)	($7,594)	($19,284)
Date of Max. Drawdown	26-Nov-03		

Although the overall return/drawdown ratio of the LUXOR system is acceptable a closer look at the system figures reveals that the system we have developed to this point cannot be traded yet (table 3.2). Although the system obviously shows a bias in the prices and the trading system is robust the average trade, with $33, is still not that profitable.

Furthermore, the system stays in the market 100% of the time because the exits are still missing. As a consequence the system is not useable in this state since the risks would be too high compared with the prospective returns. Therefore in the next two chapters we will further extend our trading system.

First we will look for useful intraday time filters in order to increase the system's profitability. The final section of this chapter will deal with adding the necessary exits.

3.4 Inserting an intraday time filter

In the past we have come across many master traders and profitable trading systems which exploit the different behaviours of financial markets during different phases within the trading day. There are traders and systems which are just successful in the afternoon with short-term breakout strategies and there are others which need their slow trend-following strategies running the whole night in order to make profits. The reason for the importance of the factor *time* in your trading strategies is simply that markets are controlled by people and people are constricted by their daily time schedule. Since the currency markets are trading 24 hours, the time of the day has a special importance for their behaviour. There will be differences if the big US traders are active or not, if it is night or day in Europe, in the US or in Asia. The daily FOREX volume clearly shows that the market activity changes a lot within each trading day. There are market phases of more activity and higher probability for profits and there are quiet market phases when nothing happens except accidental sideways movements with high market noise. As a consequence it is always worth examining how different time filters change the outcome of your trading system, especially when dealing with currency markets like the pound and dollar.[2]

Finding the best entry time

We now perform system tests in the following way. We take our LUXOR entry but we restrict the entry times to a short four-hour time window every day. We will shift the starting time of the window in steps of 30 minutes throughout the day in order to find the best window. (For the EasyLanguage Programmers: you have to add some lines into the LUXOR-code as shown above, Text 3.1, point 2, Time Window Filter.)

Fig. 3.8 shows the total net profit of the trading system as a function of the starting time of the four-hour time window. And the result is really significant! You see that the profit of our trading system highly depends on the chosen time window. When you start trading from 5pm until 3am Greenwich Mean Time (GMT) the trading system loses money, whereas it is able to gain high profits during GMT day time, especially in the morning between 8am and 12am.

[2] Time investigations are valuable for many other markets. Some of you might have read our article in Traders magazine [8] where we presented two short-term trading systems based on 5-minute and 20-minute intraday data for the European and US Stock Index Futures.

Figure 3.8: Total Net Profit as a function of the entry time of a four-hour time window. LUXOR system, tested on British pound/US dollar (FOREX), 30-minute bars, 21/10/2002–4/7/2008. SLOW=44, FAST=1. Calculation incl. $30 slippage and commissions per round turn. No exits are in place.

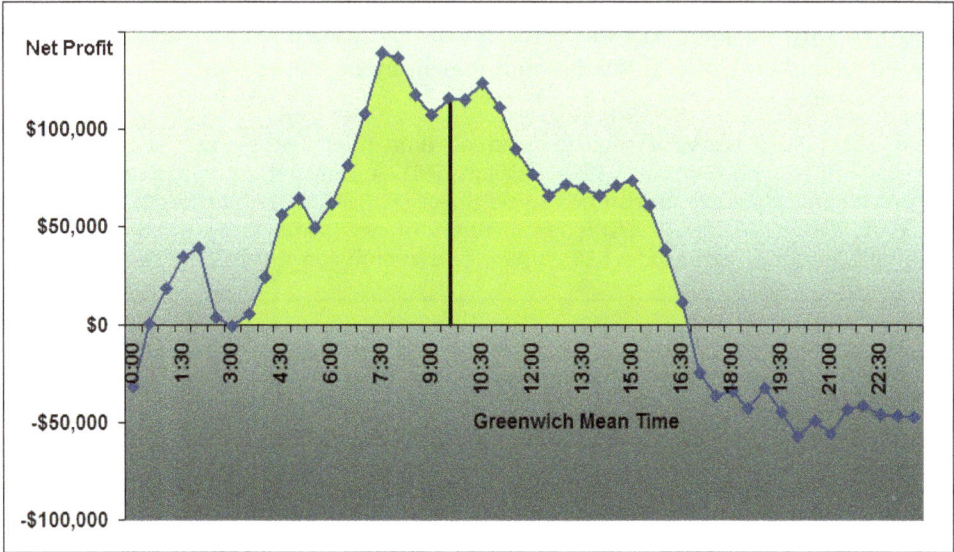

The highest net profit is earned when you take 7.30am as the starting point for your time window, and this means that you only allow entries and reversals from 7:30am until 11.30am. From our above discussion about stability and robustness of input parameters you know, however, that it is important that your chosen system parameter has a good and broad neighborhood. With this neighbourhood the trading system has the highest reliability of conforming to its back-test results in real trading. Therefore we take the starting time of the window right in the middle of the profitable parameter region at 9.30am, instead of the most profitable value at 7.30am. The chosen time filter means that we allow entries only between 9.30am and 1.30pm GMT. This is the time when the big volume from the US in the afternoon (GMT time) is still to come. It seems to be good for our trading system to enter a trend in the beginning of the day which later can be amplified by increasing volume from the US.

Result with added time filter

The detailed equity curve of our trading system seems not to have changed a lot because of the added time filter (fig. 3.9A). Instead, a look at the underwater equity curve reveals that the drawdowns within the five years of trading have increased from 8% before to 10% with the daytime filter. Furthermore, it now takes longer for our modified trading system to recover from these drawdowns. So what have we gained from our filter? You can evaluate the time filter impact with a closer look at the trading figures. If you look at the number of trades you see that they have been reduced dramatically by the inserted filter to 902, compared with nearly 3,000 trades which the system generated before.

Together with the fact that the total net profit slightly increased to $115,000, compared with $100,000 without the time filter, this leads to an important point for you when using this system:

The average profit per trade is now $128 (including $30 slippage and commissions) compared with the poor $33 which the system had gained before when trading was allowed around the clock. This is an improvement by a factor of four!

Figure 3.9: LUXOR system results with added time filter. Entries only allowed in the four-hour time window from 9.30am–1.30pm GMT. A: detailed equity curve; B: weekly underwater equity curve. British pound/US dollar (FOREX), 30-minute bars, 21/10/2002–4/7/2008. Optimised input parameters in terms of net profit: SLOW=44, FAST=1. Test without exits. Back-test includes $30 slippage and commission. Charts from TradeStation 8.

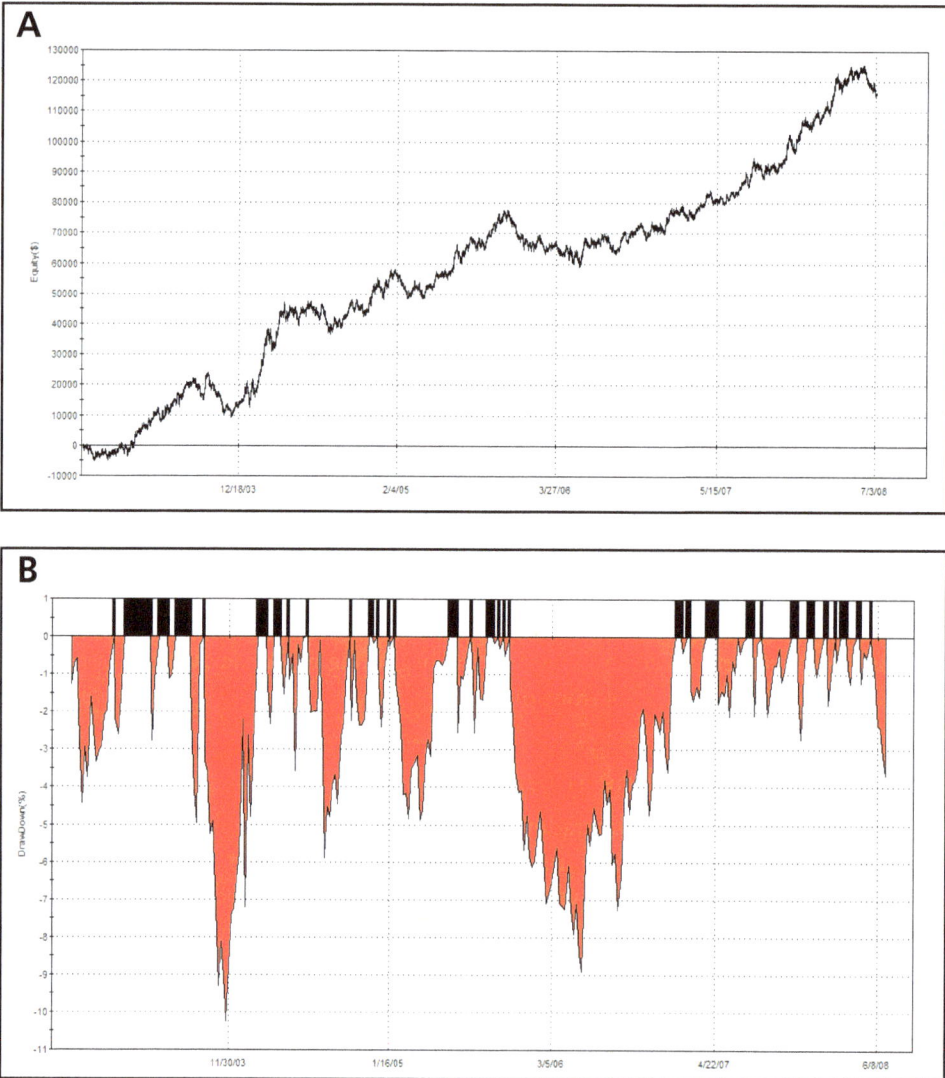

Table 3.3: Main system figures of the LUXOR system with added time filter: Entries only allowed in the four-hour time window from 9.30am–1.30pm GMT. British pound/ US dollar (FOREX), 30-minute bars, 21/10/2002–4/7/2008. Optimised input parameters: SLOW=44, FAST=1. System without exits, always in the market, long or short. Back-test includes $30 slippage and commission.

	All Trades	Long Trades	Short Trades
Total Net Profit	$115,502	$82,050	$33,452
Gross Profit	$428,864	$226,323	$202,541
Gross Loss	($313,362)	($144,273)	($169,089)
Profit Factor	1.37	1.57	1.2
Total Number of Trades	902	451	451
Percent Profitable	42.02%	44.79%	39.25%
Winning Trades	379	202	177
Losing Trades	523	249	274
Avg. Trade Net Profit	$128	$182	$74
Avg. Winning Trade	$1,132	$1,120	$1,144
Avg. Losing Trade	($599)	($579)	($617)
Ratio Avg. Win:Avg. Loss	1.89	1.93	1.85
Largest Winning Trade	$6,748	$6,748	$5,728
Largest Losing Trade	($2,531)	($2,531)	($2,442)
Max. Consecutive Winning Trades	6	7	6
Max. Consecutive Losing Trades	13	8	11
Avg. Bars in Total Trades	78.82	78.44	79.2
Avg. Bars in Winning Trades	116.73	113.29	120.66
Avg. Bars in Losing Trades	51.34	50.16	52.41
Total Slippage	$18,040	$9,020	$9,020
Total Commission	$9,020	$4.510	$4.510
Percent of Time in the Market	99.92%		
Max. Drawdown (Intraday Peak to Valley)	$18,894	$9,402	$17,378
Date of Max. Drawdown	24-May-06		

But in spite of these promising trade figures, the system still has some major weak points. As we already mentioned, the drawdowns have become slightly bigger – $18,900 maximum drawdown compared with $13,400 before. But this drawback and the fact that the trading system equity is not as steady as before are not the worst features.

The weak point of the trading system in its current state is simply that it is really dangerous since trade reversals are only allowed in the four-hour window between 9.30am and 1.30pm

GMT. If you get a reversal signal outside of this window, e.g. in the night at 1am GMT, since the market is closed the system cannot exit or reverse its position. Outside of your trading window, you have to stay in the market for the other 20 hours, regardless of what happens.

Of course the system is not tradable like this since the limitations and the risks of the system would be too high if you are forced to stay in the market for 20 hours irrespective of any developments during that time. We have to urgently change this situation and extend our trading system by adding exits. By adding exits we want to create not only a profitable trading system, but also one which can be controlled in terms of risk.

3.5 Determination of appropriate exits – risk management

Look at it this way: whether your trading system resembles a gunslinger shooting from the hip or a well-aimed sniper lying in ambush, knowing where your trades are heading could mean the difference between riding into the sunset or lying fatally wounded on a dusty street at high-noon. To stay alive you must know when to draw and when to run.

Thomas Stridsman [1]

Everybody knows that stops are necessary but nobody really likes them. Often you get the feeling that the stop has just thrown you out of the market before it turned in your direction and you missed the big move.

In this section we use statistical research to investigate exits quantitatively. In the course of all of our past statistical investigations it has become obvious that an exit can never be considered independently from the relative entry. It's important to be aware that the dynamics of the entry have a substantial influence on the dynamics of a useful exit or a reversal of your position. Imagine an entry into a quiet, not volatile market with low trading volume and compare it with an entry which was triggered during a phase of high activity, e.g. a news-breakout (fig. 3.10). In the first case it could be best to take profits at a close profit target as the market moves sideways without any direction. In the second case a wide stop and no profit target could be much better since these two exits give the trade enough room to develop. Every profit target or stop which is placed too close would throw you out of the profitable trade too early. The *best* exit in this case would be the end-of-day exit when the big trading volume has diminished and the breakout has obviously finished.

For this reason we don't recommend testing exits with artificially generated entries, e.g. with random entries or with entries taken at the opening of every trading day. We found that working with such random entries leads the statistical results into a wrong direction. The outcome is dominated by market situations which occur most of the time but which are not the typical ones applicable to your own, special market strategy.

Figure 3.10: The Dynamic of Exits. In the phase of low volume and low volatility different exits are needed than in the phase of increasing volume with the short breakout. Chart example was taken from Light Crude Oil, 5 minute, NYMEX from 22 August 2008. Chart and datafeed from TradeStation 8.

There are no universal optimal exits! If you are working with a different type of system or on another time scale you cannot transfer your existing exits to a different entry logic. Of course you can take such exits as a rough guide but you must spend time developing suitable exits for the different entry or time scale.

To find appropriate exits for the strategy developed above we take a small excursion into the field of statistics. We analyse the course of the single trades in order to determine useful stop-levels and profit targets. This analysis looks a little bit exotic at the beginning. As soon as you are familiar with it, however, you'll be rewarded with a good understanding of your trading system and its appropriate exits.

The concept of Maximum Adverse Excursion (MAE)

In order to find proper stop points for your system you should take a deeper look into the distribution of trades and examine each trade individually. When you do so, you will discover that there are similarities between them, but that every trade also has its own set of characteristics. These characteristics can be examined by using the Maximum Adverse Excursion (MAE) technique developed by John Sweeney less than ten years ago [9]. MAE is defined as the most intraday price movement against your position. In other words it's the lowest open equity during the lifespan of a trade. The MAE concept allows you to evaluate your systems' individual trades to determine at what dollar or percentage amount to place your protective stop.

Let's take a look at the MAE graphic of our trading system (fig. 3.11). This graph shows all 902 trades that are produced within the tested period. For each trade you can see the amount of drawdown that occurred in relation to the realised profit or loss. The winning trades are shown as green up arrows and the losing trades are represented as red down arrows. On the vertical y-axis of the MAE diagram you see the final profit whereas the horizontal x-axis shows the intraday drawdown of each trade.

Since we are using this graphic to determine where to place our stops we have put all the winning and losing trades on the same cluster graph. This means that although trades A and B in fig. 3.11 appear to be similar they are in reality quite different. Trade A had a drawdown of $2,400 and closed at a final loss of $1,000. Trade B, on the other hand, suffered an even bigger drawdown of $2,500 but recovered and managed to end with a gain of $1,000. Whether the dollar amount indicated along the y-axis is a profit or loss is determined by the colour and the direction of the small triangles. Keeping the trades clustered on the same graph makes it easier to figure out how much unrealised loss must be incurred by a trade before it typically does not recover. In this way the MAE graphic tells you when to cut your loss because the risks associated with the trade are no longer justified. This gives you a valuable indication of where to place your protective stop.

Figure 3.11: The MAE graph of LUXOR system. Green: winning trades, red: losing trades. System tested on British pound/US dollar (FOREX), 30-minute bars, 21/10/2002–4/7/2008, with entry time window 9.30am–1.30pm GMT. Input parameters SLOW=44, FAST=1. Without exits, always in the market, including $30 slippage and commissions per round turn. Diagram created with TradeStation 8.

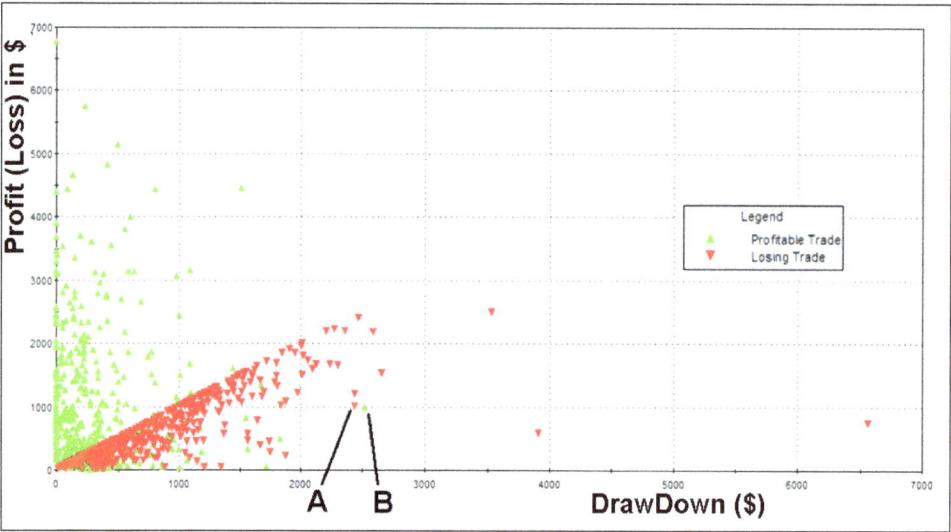

In order to decide where to put this stop we show the same MAE graph in percentage terms (fig. 3.12A). We switch to percentage terms since the percentage display gives a better adaptation to changing market conditions than fixed dollar values. Especially on markets with big point value changes the advantages of the percentage based calculation become obvious. In such conditions it is better to work with exits that are adapting to the current market value instead of staying fixed and inflexible.

Figure 3.12A: MAE graph in percentage terms. Green up arrows = winning trades, red down arrows = losing trades. Trend-following system British pound/US dollar (FOREX), 30-minute bars, 21/10/2002–4/7/2008, with entry time window 9.30am–1.30pm GMT. Input parameters SLOW=44, FAST=1. Without exits, always in the market, including $30 slippage and commissions per round turn. Diagram created with TradeStation 8.

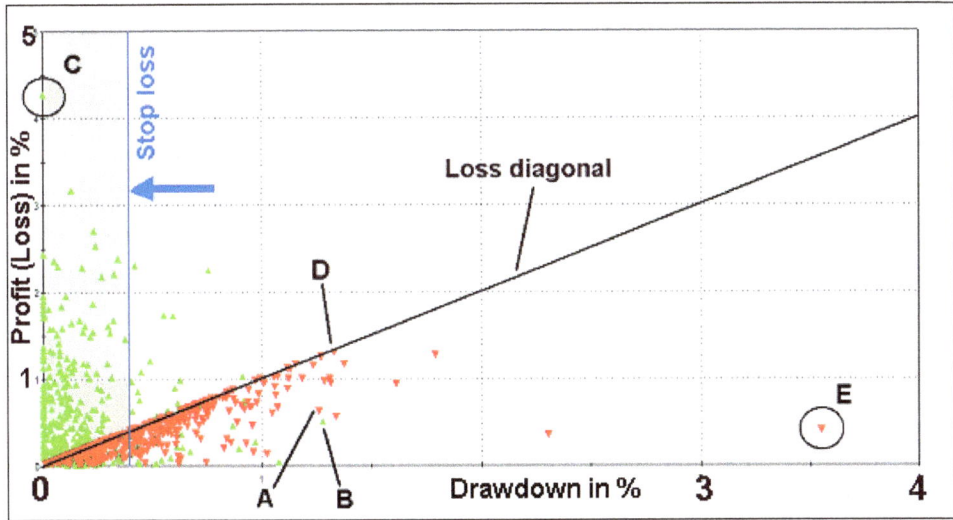

Figure 3.12B: Maximum Adverse Excursion graph in percentage terms after inserting a 0.3% stop loss into the system. LUXOR system tested on British pound/US dollar (FOREX), 30-minute bars, 21/10/2002–4/7/2008, with entry time window 9.30am–1.30pm GMT. Input parameters SLOW=44, FAST=1. Diagram created with TradeStation 8.

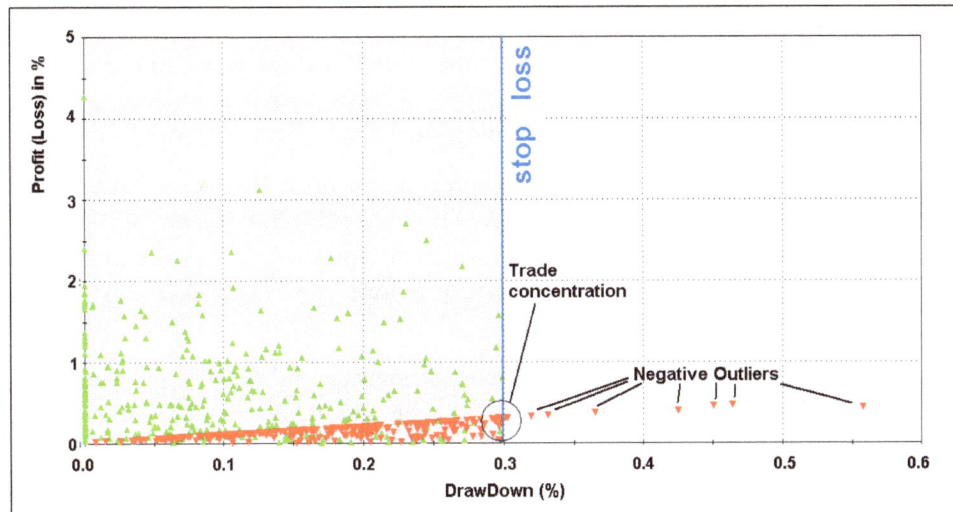

Let us briefly explain some trades from the MAE diagram in order to become more familiar with it. First you see that the relative positions of trade A and B explained above have changed. Trade A is now on a higher position in y-direction since the two trades took place in different times when the market was trading at a different level. Because the calculation is now based on percentage of the underlying market, the same dollar values usually mean different percentage values.

When watching all these 902 trades in the MAE diagram you can see some characteristics of the trading system. The first point is that on the left side of the diagram you find more winning than losing trades. This is clear since winning trades usually don't suffer such big drawdowns as losing trades. The *best* trades for you are obviously the ones which behave like trade C – trades that are profitable from the beginning without suffering any negative open equity in their lifetime and are placed on the far left side, close to the y-axis of the diagram (profit/loss axis).

Another interesting area of trades is what we call the *loss diagonal*. On this characteristic line you can find a lot of losing trades. Like trade D all these trades ended with a loss which represents their biggest drawdowns. On the other hand, trades like E also exist. This trade suffered a big drawdown of over 3.5% from the entry-point but recovered from this position to a final loss of only about 0.5%.

Now we want to place a protective stop loss at a certain distance (percentage of market value) away from the entry point in order to limit the risk of the trade. How does the MAE diagram help you to determine a good distance for this added stop?

Let us look how the MAE diagram helps to understand what an inserted stop loss does in your trading system.

The stop loss in the MAE diagram can be drawn as a vertical line. Such a stop loss theoretically cuts all trades that suffer a bigger loss from their entry than this set stop loss (fig. 3.12B). In the MAE diagram this means that the stop loss prohibits all the trades on the right of the 0.3% line and moves them to this line. This sounds good for all the losses (red points) that are made smaller by this stop. But think about all the winning trades. They are turned into a red spot, a loss of 0.3%, as soon as they reach the stop loss and never get the chance to become a winning trade.

We try to place a stop in an area that captures the majority of winning trades while simultaneously limiting the strategy's exposure to profit erosion. Obviously it is good to set a stop loss so as to cut as many trades which end on the loss diagonal as possible without affecting trades that end as winners, or at least those trades that recover from their lowest points.

So the question is what happens if you make the stop loss smaller than 0.6%, going to 0.4%, 0.3% or even 0.1%? Obviously you will then cut more and more trades that are ending on the loss diagonal and for which the stop loss does a good job in cutting them early enough. But the more you move your stop loss to the left side, the more trades you also cut which recovered from their biggest drawdowns or which even ended as winning trades.

Inserting a risk stop loss

In the MAE diagram you can see how all trades behaved and if there are any special points to consider when looking for a good place to set a proper risk stop loss. The MAE diagram can give you a hint that the *optimal* stop value is somewhere between 0.2% and 1%. However MAE does not tell you directly what the optimal value is to set this stop. For this reason we now look at the task from a different side by performing system tests in the following way. We add a risk stop loss into our trading system and vary its distance in reference to the trade's entry point in a wide range from 0.01% up to 1% in steps of 0.01%. At the time of writing the British pound was trading near US$2.00 and at this rate a 1% stop distance corresponds to 2 cents. Two cents are in other words 200 pips and mean $2,000 in your pocket. Therefore the fine 0.01% step means the 0.02 cents or 2 pips ($20 in your pocket) in these market conditions.

Figure 3.13: Ratio of total net profit/maximum intraday drawdown as a function of the stop loss distance in per cent. LUXOR system tested on British pound/US dollar (FOREX), 30-minute bars, 21/10/2002–4/7/2008, with entry time window 9.30am–1.30pm GMT. SLOW=44, FAST=1. Including $30 slippage and commissions per round turn.

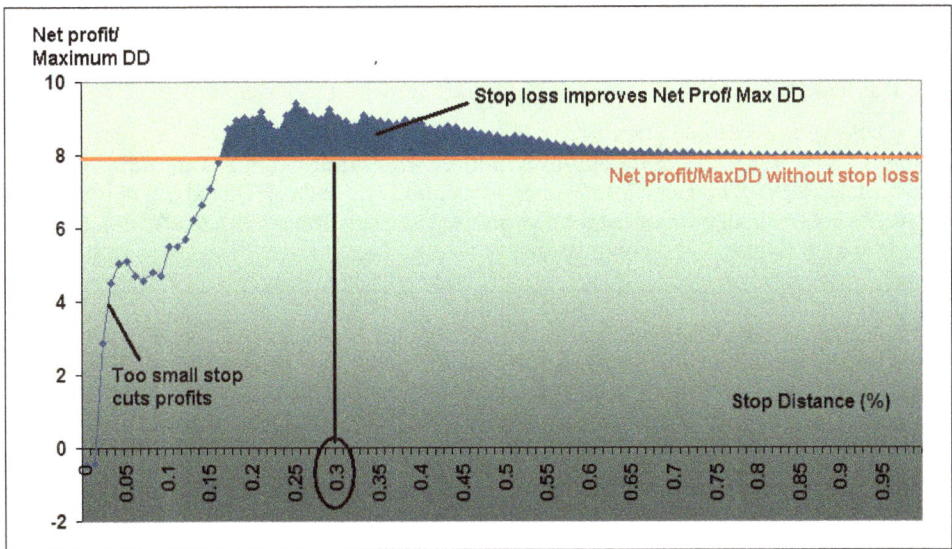

The tests give you important statistical figures for each stop level: net profit, maximum drawdown, biggest losing trade etc. You can draw diagrams of these figures dependent on the set stop loss distance. We do this here for the ratio of total net profit/maximum drawdown (NP/DD), see fig. 3.13. We do not take the total net profit alone because it does not tell you much about the system's risk, whereas the ratio NP/DD gives a meaningful estimate. Let's look at this ratio for all performed trades as a function of the stop distance. This graph tells you that stop loss points positioned too closely reduce the NP/DD ratio drastically. Obviously many trades are stopped out just at the beginning and the slippage and commissions do not allow gains with so little risk.

When increasing the distance more and more the system becomes profitable, but for all stop distances below 0.15% the NP/DD ratio is still decreased and stays below the ratio of the breakout-system without stop loss. However, if you set the stop futher away from the entry point and allow the trades more room to develop you get a nice improvement of the NP/DD. Any added stop in a broad range of values between 0.2–0.5% range increases the base system's return/risk ratio. Thus we can select a stop loss of 0.3% as a useful distance – this value is placed in the middle of this stable parameters region. The 0.3% corresponds to 60 pips or 600 US dollars with the British pound trading at US$2. It is important to mention that you cannot find a stop loss level that improves the overall net profit for every trading system or market. Usually profits are reduced by the boundaries which are imposed by the stop losses, especially in more choppy markets (e.g. in stock index futures like S&P 500 or FTSE 100).

Let's have a short look how the 0.3% risk stop loss affects the performance graphs of our trading system (figs. 3.14 A and B). The detailed equity curve seemed not to have changed too much. The nearly unchanged profitability of the trading system is confirmed by the system figures (table 3.4, left two columns). The total net profit is improved with the stop loss only slightly by less than 1% from $115,000 to $116,000, whereas the average trade net profit decreased a bit from $128 to $113.

So, the profitability of the trading system stays nearly unchanged with the inserted stop loss. But let's check if the risks of the system are now under better control.

Figure 3.14: A: detailed equity curve; B: underwater equity curve with 0.3% risk stop loss in place. LUXOR system tested on British pound/US dollar (FOREX), 30-minute bars, 21/10/2002–4/7/2008, with entry time window 9.30am–1.30pm GMT. SLOW=44, FAST=1. Including 30 $ slippage and commissions per round turn. Charts from TradeStation 8.

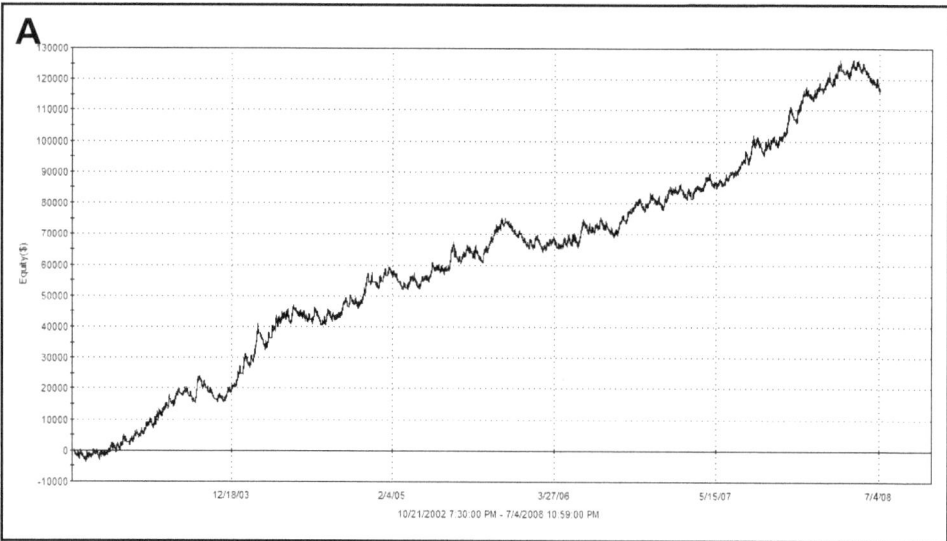

B

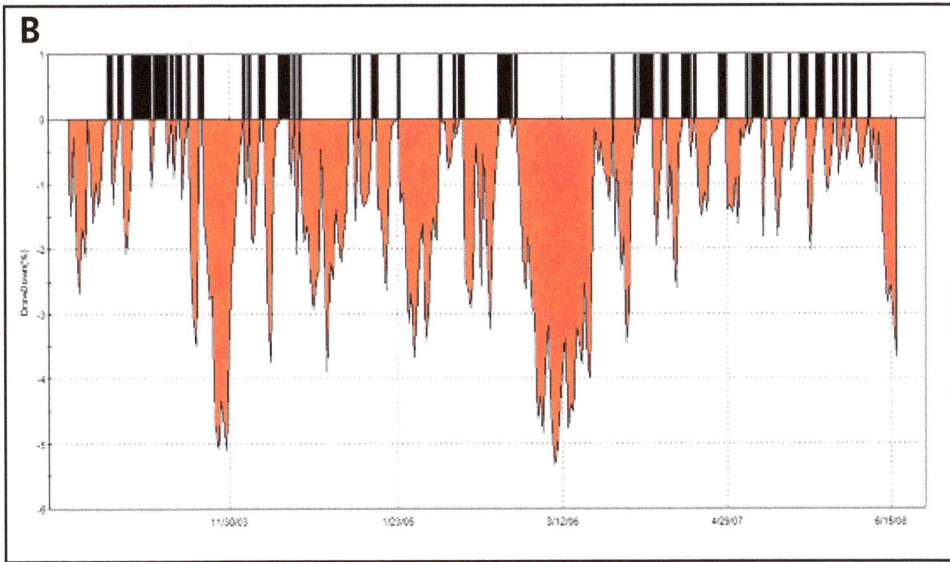

From the underwater equity curves you see that the maximum drawdown of the trading system is now reduced from 10% to 5% (compare fig. 3.14B with 3.9B). A look at the trading figures confirms this observation (table 3.4).

After inserting the risk stop loss the maximum intraday peak-to-valley drawdown is much reduced from $18,894 to $11,266. Even more importantly, the largest losing trade is now reduced to only $810 from over $2,500 when using the system without the stop loss in place. This significant reduction by nearly a factor of three helps you to control your risks, especially when trading the system with more than one lot in a bigger portfolio. You may ask why the biggest loss was not reduced to about $600, which corresponds to the 0.3% in today's market value, set by our stop loss. The reason was a gap which inhibited an execution of a trade at the exact stop price but at a US$250 worse price. Although such bad executions usually happen less than ten times within 1,000 trades, which is insignificant and well covered with the $30 slippage and commissions calculation, you have to keep in mind that this is always possible in general with every trade. Finally, we want to point out that the system's market exposure with the inserted stop was reduced for the first time. Whereas without any exit in place the system was in the market 100% of the time, this risk exposure is now reduced to 73%. The remaining 27% of the time while the system is not active can be used to invest the money somewhere else or to earn interest gains.

Adding a trailing stop

A trailing stop is a stop order which adapts to the current market price. In the case of a new long position it is initially set at a fixed percentage below the entry price. If the market price rises, the trailing stop price rises proportionately, but if the price falls, the trailing stop price doesn't change (fig. 3.15A).

Figure 3.15A: The principle of a trailing stop. Chart example from British pound/US dollar (FOREX), 30-minute bars, September 2008. Chart from TradeStation 8.

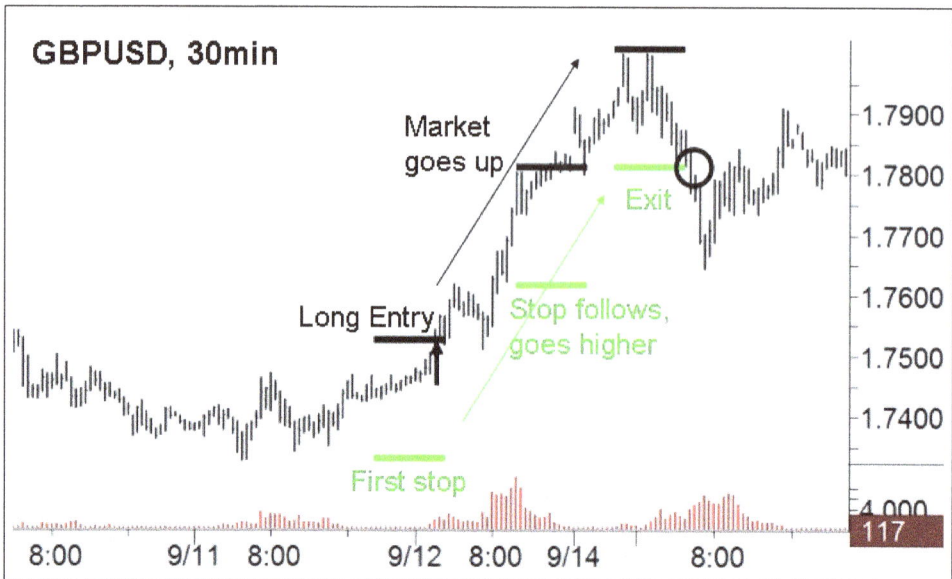

The trailing stop for short positions works analogously. This technique allows you to set a limit on the maximum possible loss without setting a limit on the maximum possible gain. Next we add such a trailing stop to our existing trading system. While looking for an appropriate trailing stop distance, we keep our initial risk stop loss of 0.3% in place. Whereas this initial risk stop is responsible for keeping the biggest losses under control, as outlined in the previous section, the now added trailing stop aims at keeping some more profit without losing it again.

If you add such a trailing stop and vary its distance from 0.01% up to 1.5% in steps of 0.01% you can plot the ratio of NP/DD as a function of the trailing stop distance (fig. 3.15B). Similar to the risk stop loss, tiny trailing stops cut the profits too much, since they don't give the trades enough room to develop. In particular, all trailing stop values below 0.2% lead to a disaster. However from 0.2 to 0.5% the results increase steadily and between 0.5% and 1% you find a broad region of trailing stops which increase the system's NP/DD ratio. If you set the trailing stops even wider then the ratio converges to the NP/DD ratio of the trading system without an added trailing stop. The stop distance becomes so big that fewer and fewer trades are affected by it.

It is worth mentioning that the NP/DD ratio (fig. 3.15B) is quite steady. Between 0.5% and 1% you find a broad region of values which lead to similar results. This increases the probability that the performed tests have a high predictive power for real trading. The trading figures (table 3.4, third column) reveal that a trailing stop of 0.8% (in the middle of the profitable area) leads to improvements, especially regarding profitability. The total net profit can be increased by the inserted trailing stop from $116,209 to $126,772 by nearly 10%. The average profit per trade increases by about the same percentage from \$113 to \$122. The risk figures are also slightly improved by the added trailing stop. The maximum drawdown of the trading system is further reduced from \$11,266 to \$10,292 and the percentage of time in the market is also now slightly lower (69.98%, compared to 73.56% before). With the two types of stops in place we will now check if inserting profit targets will further improve the trading system.

Figure 3.15B: Ratio of total net profit/maximum intraday drawdown as a function of the distance of an added trailing stop. Risk stop loss of 0.3% kept in place. LUXOR system tested on British pound/US dollar (FOREX), 30-minute bars, 21/10/2002–4/7/2008, with entry time window 9.30am–1.30pm GMT. SLOW=44, FAST=1. Including \$30 slippage and commissions per round turn.

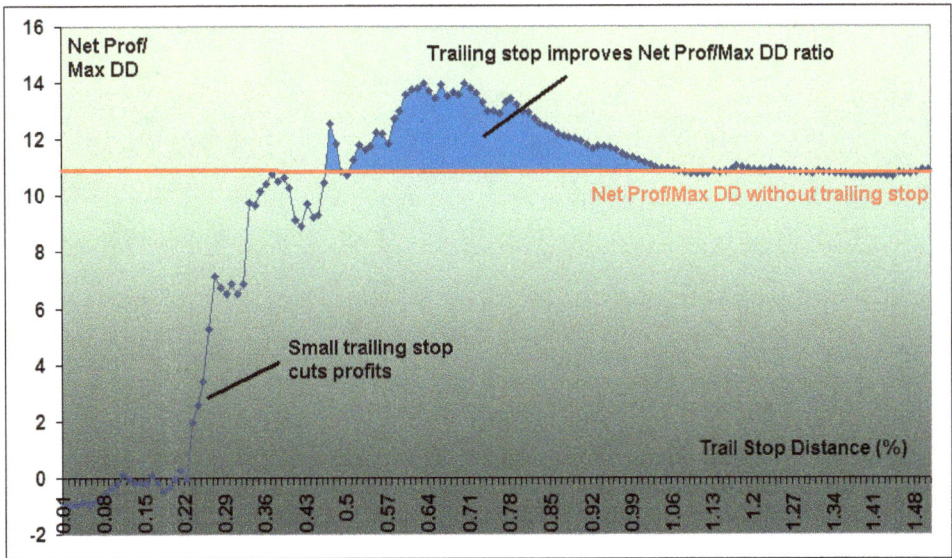

Looking for profit targets: Maximum Favourable Excursion (MFE)

John Sweeney's concept of MFE is complementary to MAE. MFE is defined as the most positive price movement for your position. It therefore corresponds to the highest open equity within the lifespan of a trade. Whereas MAE was useful to investigate your trades' drawdowns and to set a good stop loss, MFE reveals their run-ups and helps to find useful profit targets (fig. 3.16).

Like with MAE, the final profit (or loss) of the trades is shown on the vertical y-axis. Again winning and losing trades are drawn on this same axis with different colour (green points=winning trades, red points=losing trades). But in contrast to the MAE diagram, in the MFE diagram the horizontal x-axis represents the run-up, which means the highest profit a trade has had in its lifetime.

From the MFE diagram of the original trend-following system with the two exits in place (stop loss=0.3%, trailing stop=0.8%) you can spot the following features:

Figure 3.16: The MFE graph shows the realised profit/loss vs. run-ups of all trades. Green: winning trades, red: losing trades. LUXOR system tested on British pound/US dollar (FOREX), 30-minute bars, 21/10/2002–4/7/2008, with 0.3% risk stop and 0.8% trailing stop. Input parameters SLOW=44, FAST=1, including $30 slippage and commissions per round turn. Diagram created with TradeStation 8.

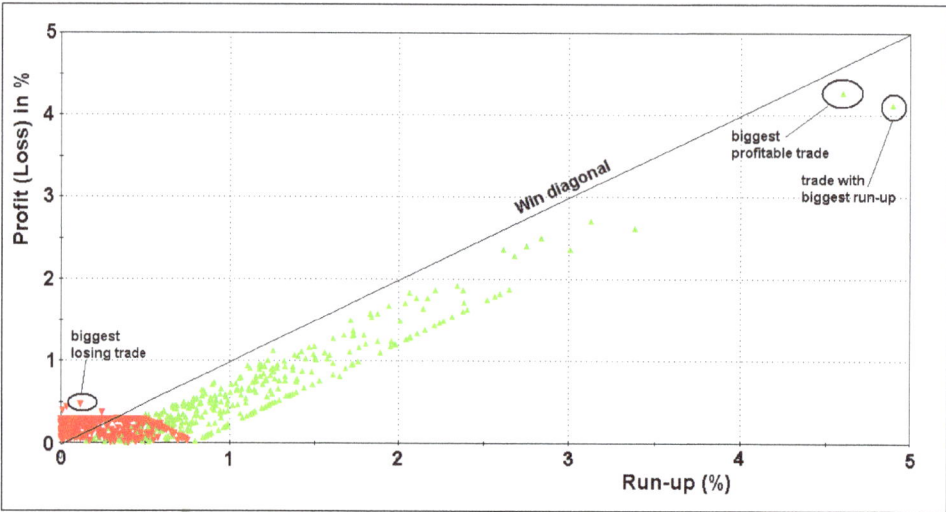

Most winning trades end near the win diagonal, which marks the points where a trade ended with the highest intraday run-up. The biggest profitable trade is a typical example. It had an intraday run-up of 4.5% and ended near this highest value with a final profit of just above 4%. Further, the MFE diagram shows the effect of the 0.8% trailing stop which we inserted in the last section: all trades that experienced a profit of more than 0.8% were kept profitable – the trailing stop makes sure that the highly profitable trades cannot completely reverse their direction. The MFE diagram also reveals that the losing trades (red points) stay mostly on the far left side. This means that they usually had only small run-ups.

These findings suggest that profit targets cannot be that effective for our trend-following system with the two stops already at work. If a losing trade never comes into a big profit and if winning trades don't significantly change their direction then a profit target will not be helpful. Inserted profit targets cannot find a point to skim profits out of the market before it turns.

Let's verify if these findings can stand further computer tests. We take our basic breakout system with the two stops and add a profit target. The target closes each trade immediately if a profit of x percent of the market value is reached (fig. 3.17). The figure shows that profit targets placed too closely, like stops that are too small, reduce the overall profits of the trading system. The closer you set the profit target the worse it gets. Only a small region of quite big profit targets around 2% (=4 cents or 400 pips conditions or $4,000 for one contract, with the pound trading at $2) lead to a profit bigger than our system with just the stops and no target in place. If you place the targets even higher than 2.5% away from the entry point you finally reach the result of the base system. The MFE diagram shows that this area of high profits can only be reached by less than 10% trades. Therefore profit targets to exit a trade are only of small use for our entry set-up on the British pound/US dollar FOREX market.

Figure 3.17: Ratio of total net profit/maximum intraday drawdown as a function of the distance of an added profit target. Risk stop loss of 0.3% and trailing stop of 0.8% are kept in place during tests. LUXOR system tested on British pound/US dollar (FOREX), 30-minute bars, 21/10/2002–4/7/2008, with entry time window 9.30am–1.30pm GMT. SLOW=44, FAST=1. Including. $30 slippage and commissions per round turn.

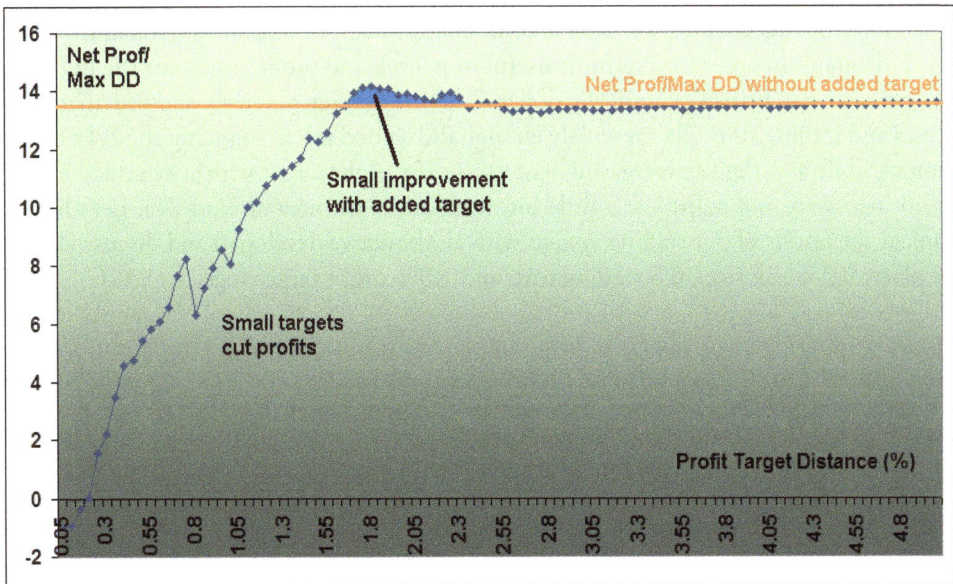

The tests confirmed what the MFE diagram showed: it is not possible to predict how far the breakout will lead the market. Therefore, except with targets between about 1.8% and 2.4% away from the entry point, it is better not to set any profit targets but just let the market run as far as it goes. Again, like with the stop loss, this conclusion may not hold true for other markets with the same trading system or for the British pound/US dollar FOREX on other time scales with completely different entry set-up. One example where profit targets are more rewarding is stock index futures, where changes in trend direction happen more often. Furthermore, profit targets become more valuable if they are set to significant points, e.g. at supports and resistances, gaps etc., where the market is more likely to turn. Another reason why profit targets are useful will be discussed at the end of this chapter in a short section on money management.

Summary: Result of the entry logic with the three added exits

You can determine your stop and profit target levels in your trading system alone with classical optimisation tests, as shown in figs. 3.13, 3.15B, and 3.17. Such optimisations show you optimal stop and target levels and give you valuable information about the stability of the optimal parameters we found. However, such diagrams do not show you how the final net profit and drawdown have emerged. You cannot see from such graphs if one single highly profitable trade or a hundred small winners are responsible for the total net profit of your trading system. This missing valuable information about the distribution of all your trades is only provided by the MAE/MFE diagrams. They show you in one single chart all the trades' intraday run-ups and drawdowns. In this way the MAE/MFE method provides useful additional information about your trading system and complements the optimisation graphs.

Therefore, in this chapter we used a combination of optimisation graphs and MAE/MFE diagrams in order to determine useful stop levels and profit targets for the LUXOR system. For the British pound/US dollar FOREX market our tests showed that stop losses and trailing stops placed widely enough did a good job in reducing the risks of the system while also slightly increasing its profits. The profit target which we added finally is not necessary and helps just a little bit, if placed in the area around 2%. Let's have a look at the results of our trading system with all the above developed and discussed exits in place: 0.3% risk stop, 0.8 trailing stop and 1.9% profit target (figs. 3.18A–C).

Figure 3.18: LUXOR system with all three exits in place: 0.3% risk stop, 0.8% trailing stop and 1.9% profit target, tested on British pound/US dollar (FOREX), 30-minute bars, 21/10/2002–4/7/2008, with entry time window 9.30am–1.30pm GMT. SLOW=44, FAST=1. Including $30 slippage and commissions per round turn. A: detailed equity curve; B: end of month equity curve; C: average profit per month. Charts created with TradeStation 8.

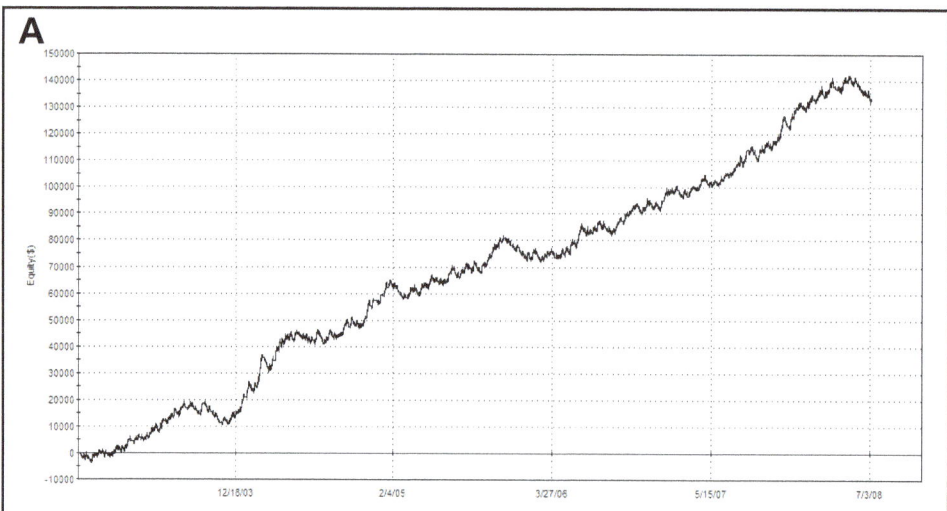

B

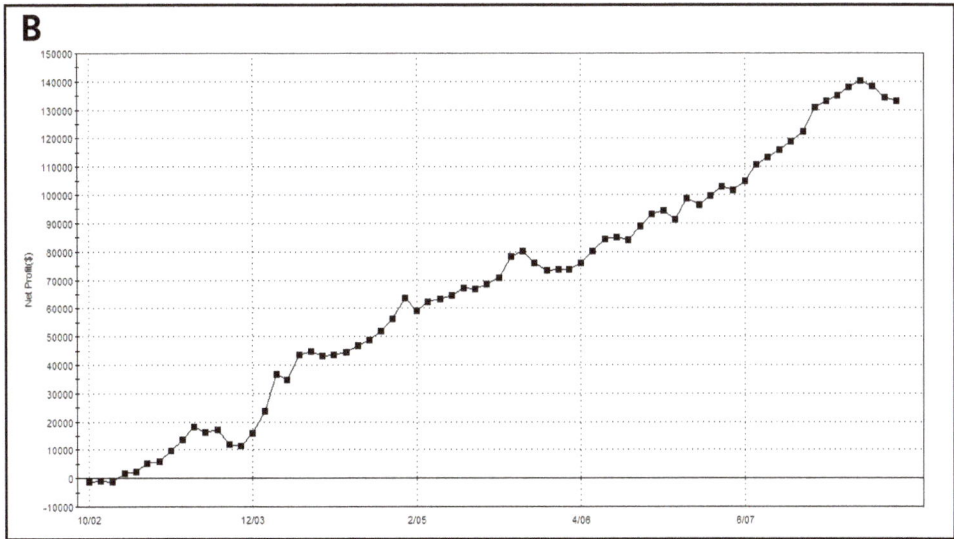

C

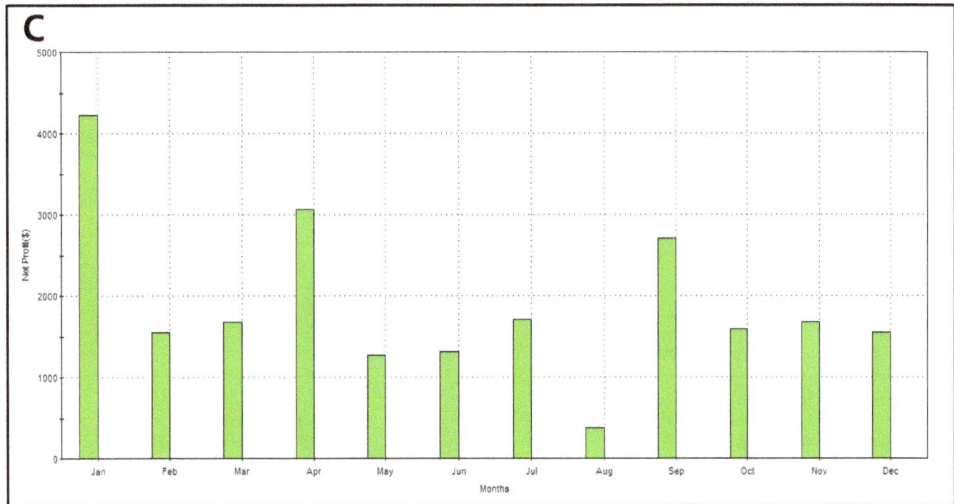

The detailed equity curve seems not to have changed a lot if you compare it with the equity curve without added exits (fig. 3.19A). It just looks a bit steadier with fewer and less sharp drawdowns. The biggest drawdown is now 6% (compared with 10% with no exits in place) and the system always quickly recovers to new equity highs within some weeks. The longest recovery period from any drawdown was six months. This is also confirmed with the end of month equity curve which plots the account value of the traded money once per month. If you sort the profits by different months from January until December you can see that the trading system was profitable in all months (fig. 3.18C), which is another proof for its reliability.

Table 3.4: How additional exits change the result of the LUXOR system; change of trading figures of the system tested on British pound/US dollar (FOREX), with one exit added after another, 30-minute bars, 21/10/2002–4/7/2008, with entry time window 9.30am–1.30pm GMT. SLOW=44, FAST=1. Including $30 slippage and commissions per round turn.

	Without Exit	With Stop Loss 0.3%	With Stop loss 0.3% and Trail Stop 0.8%	With Stop loss 0.3% and Trail Stop 0.8% and Profit Target 1.9%
Total Net Profit	$115,502	$116,209	$126,772	$132,590
Gross Profit	$428,864	$399,440	$405,347	$414,533
Gross Loss	($313,362)	($283,232)	($278,576)	($281,944)
Profit Factor	1.37	1.41	1.46	1.47
Total Number of Trades	902	1025	1040	1051
Percent Profitable	42.02%	34.34%	35.38%	35.20%
Winning Trades	379	352	368	370
Losing Trades	523	673	672	681
Avg. Trade Net Profit	$128	$113	$122	$126
Avg. Winning Trade	$1,132	$1,135	$1,101	$1,120
Avg. Losing Trade	($599)	($421)	($415)	($414)
Ratio Avg. Win:Avg. Loss	1.89	2.7	2.66	2.71
Largest Winning Trade	$6,748	$6,748	$7,510	$3,900
Largest Losing Trade	($2,531)	($810)	($810)	($810)
Max. Consecutive Winning Trades	6	5	6	6
Max. Consecutive Losing Trades	13	12	12	12
Avg. Bars in Total Trades	78.82	52.81	49.47	46.79
Avg. Bars in Winning Trades	116.73	108.74	100.75	93.42
Avg. Bars in Losing Trades	51.34	23.56	21.39	21.45
Percent of Time in the Market	99.92%	73.56%	69.98%	66.70%
Max. Drawdown (Intraday Peak to Valley)	($18,894)	($11,266)	($10,292)	($10,292)
Date of Max. Drawdown	24-May-06	24-Feb-06	24-Feb-06	24-Feb-06
Total Slippage and Commission	$27,060	$30,750	$31,200	$31,530

Left column: system without exits
Second column: system with 0.3% risk stop loss
Third column: system with 0.3% risk stop and a 0.8% trailing stop
Right column: system with 0.3% risk stop, 0.8% trailing stop and 1.9% profit target

These findings are also underlined with the trading system's figures calculated with all the exits in place (table 3.4, right column). One remarkable point is that the 1.9% profit target reduced the largest winning trade from $7,510 to $3,900, but at the same time did not reduce the overall total net profit.

How exits are affected by money management

The risk and money management of a trading system or of a whole portfolio of systems and markets can never be separated completely. The two components are highly dependent on each other. Therefore it is essential that your money management strategy is integrated into an overall approach to system design and development. Money management does not exist in a vacuum but is based on proper pre-calculated exits within your applied risk management schemes for every single trading system. In this section we will show the interplay of the two components on the practical example of our trend-following trading system LUXOR.

Fig. 3.19 shows the profits and losses of all generated trades of the system. Whereas in fig. 3.19A you see the result of the trading system without added exits, fig. 3.19B shows the trades with the following exits in place: a profit target of 1.9%, a risk stop loss of 0.3% and a trailing stop of 0.8%.

Figure 3.19: Scatter graph of profits for all generated trades of the LUXOR system. Tested on British pound/US dollar (FOREX), 30-minute bars, 21/10/2002–4/7/2008, with entry time window 9.30am–1.30pm GMT. SLOW=44, FAST=1. Including $30 slippage and commissions per round turn. A: without added exits; B: with 0.3% risk stop loss (red line), 1.9% profit target (green line) and 0.8% trailing stop. The exits act like borders for the trade distribution. Graphs created with TradeStation 8.

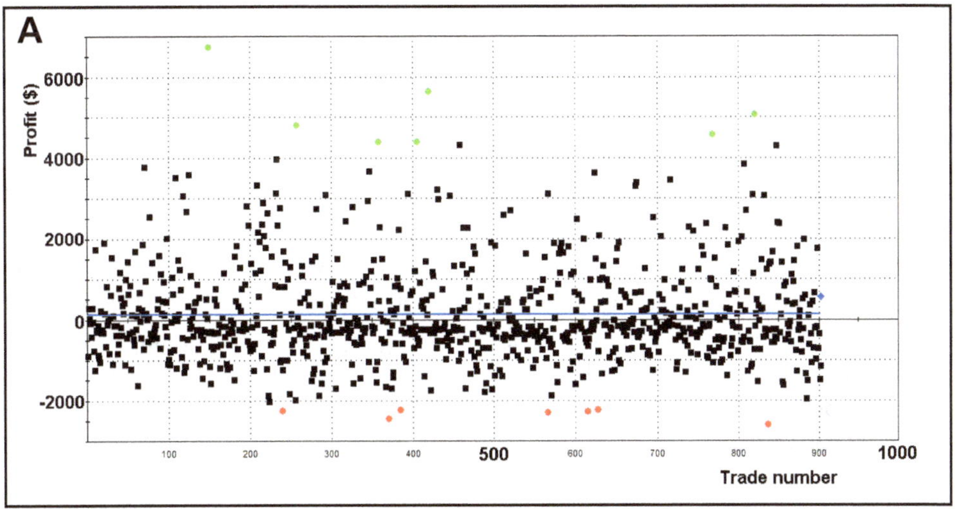

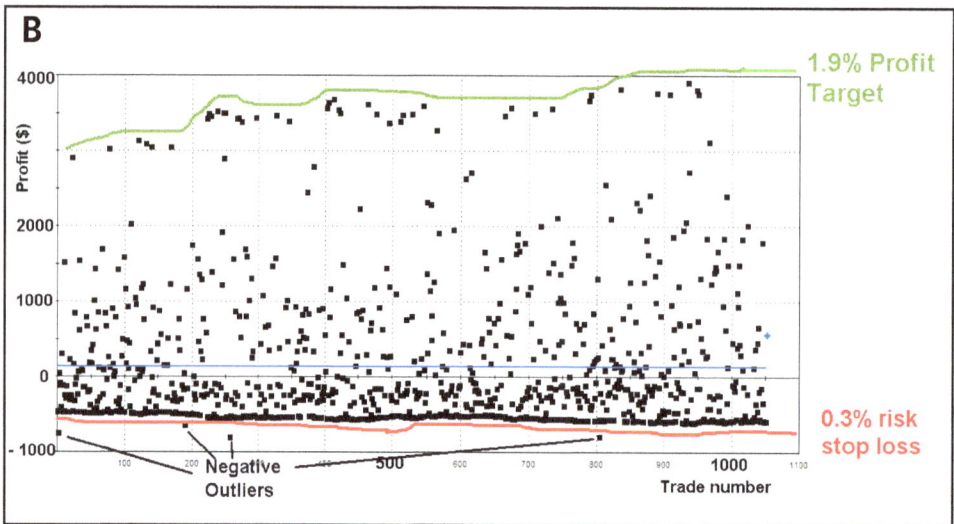

In contrast to the MAE/MFE graphs the scatter graphs show on the horizontal axis just the number of each trade. There is no more display of any drawdowns or run-ups that a trade has had within its lifetime. We start here with this simpler demonstration since it can show more clearly the effects of the applied exits. When you compare the scatter graphs of the generated trades without and with exits some interesting impacts of the exits become apparent.

The first point is that the difference between the biggest winning trades and the biggest losing trades becomes smaller with added exits. Whereas without any exits the trades are widespread between losses of over $2,000 and gains of over $6,000 they are pressed closer together by applied profit target and stops to an interval between about -$500 (largest losses) and $4,000 (largest gains). The dark cloud of trades which somehow looks like a swarm of bees seems now to be captured between the ground (stop loss) and a roof (profit target). The two borders are not straight lines since we are using percentage based exits instead of fixed dollar exits. These dynamic types of exits adapt themselves to the point value of the traded British pound/US dollar market.

Concerning the stop loss you can see that not all of the trades near this line are really situated between the 1.9% profit target and the 0.3% stop loss. Four negative outliers lead to higher losses than the pre-calculated 0.3% since the stop loss is sometimes over-rolled by occurring gaps. As mentioned above the biggest losing trade is therefore about 0.4% ($810) instead of 0.3% ($600). Keep in mind that in the reality of trading, especially when dealing with higher lots in non-liquid markets, bigger losses than your pre-calculated ones can always happen. They will not harm you much, however, if you consider them in advance and if your trading system is stable enough to produce the results which you have calculated nearly 100% of the time – like in the case we show here.

In contrast to the permeable behaviour of the initial stop loss you find no trades above the 1.9% target line. Because the target is chosen very far away from the entry point only few trades are able to reach it and no trade manages to pass it by using a market gap. So the scatter graphs show the effects of the 0.3% risk stop loss and the 1.9% profit target.

But what about the 0.8% trailing stop which is also in place? Whereas the primitive scatter graphs do not show the effect of the trailing stop, it can be made visible in the MFE diagram (fig. 3.20). The MFE scatter graph shows how the trailing stop (marked blue) affects both some of the losing trades (red points, left side) and some of the winning trades (right side). The trailing stop follows trades which have a big run-up and pulls the stop with a distance of 0.8% behind them in order to keep their profits. The diagram shows that this stop is highly effective in most cases and was only over-rolled by a negative outlier trade in one case. On the left side of the MFE graphic you see again the effect of the risk stop loss with the four outliers mentioned above.

Figure 3.20: How the Exits prepare for Money Management. MFE diagram of all trades. How risk stop loss and trailing stops affect the trade distribution and make trades more calculable. Graph created with TradeStation 8.

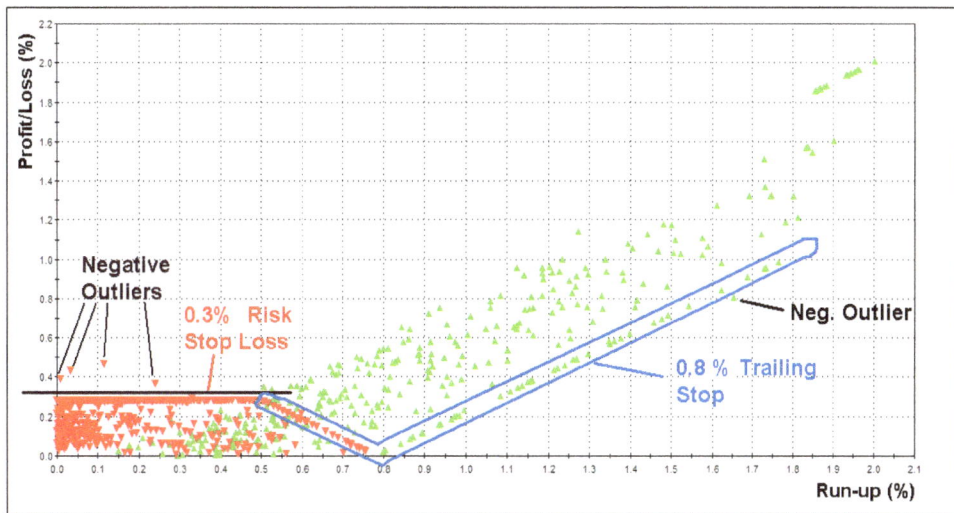

The added exits make the risks of the LUXOR trading system more calculable. Although you do not know if the initiated position will be a winning or a losing trade, after having added the exits you know that it is likely in the area between a 0.3% loss and a 1.9% win. You cannot tell this for sure, since there are some outlier trades which cannot always be stopped by your exits exactly at the pre-calculated values, but you can have fairly high confidence. This knowledge is useful in order to determine how much money you can spend on the next trade if you want to risk a certain percentage of your trading capital. This is an important step in order to apply a money management scheme which helps you to enhance your returns (see chapter 7).

3.6 Summary: Step-by-step development of a trading system

In this chapter we have shown in the example of the GBP/USD currency pair how to develop a new trading system step-by-step (fig. 3.21). Every trading system starts with an idea and a sound logic. The idea for our trading system LUXOR was taken from the STAD TradeStation Development Club but there are many other good sources of ideas including books, the internet and seminars. Once you have found the idea, you have to test it and change it according to your needs. Therefore you should somehow transfer the idea into an algorithm, a sequence of rules, which you can apply to historic market data. During this test process you will find new ideas and you will face new problems, e.g. how to program your code correctly and how to handle weak points of your software.

Although this process is time-consuming it is valuable since you get a detailed knowledge of your trading system. This knowledge is a key factor for your success when applying your system, since confidence and trust in your trading system is the most important factor. If you don't trust your system, you will stop trading it when the first drawdown occurs. So all the tests – with and without slippage and commissions, with and without exits, with optimisations and stability tests – are later rewarded with a good expertise about what you are doing and why you are doing it. In this way you come up with a trading system that contains a reliable risk management and prepares you for money management since you get a better estimation of the outcome of the trades.

Figure 3.21: Step-by-step development of a trading system. From an idea to a final system including entries, exits, trading costs, etc.

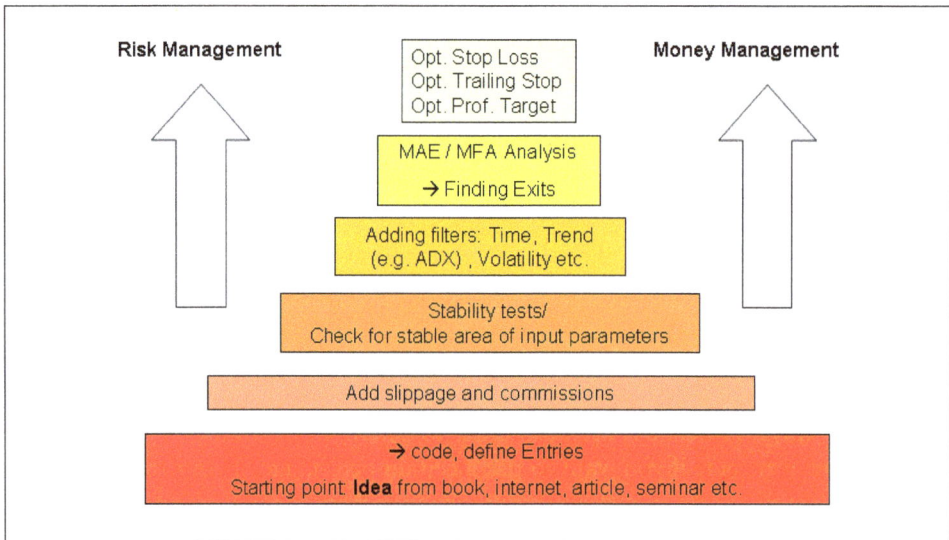

4

Two Methods for Evaluating the System's Predictive Power

"Once you have a system, the biggest obstacle is trusting it."

Tom Wills

IN ORDER TO check the robustness of the LUXOR trading system we now perform the following two reliability tests.

4.1   Timescale analysis. We keep the system's input parameters unchanged while we change the bar length of the tested market.

4.2   Monte Carlo analysis. Changing the order of the performed trades gives you valuable estimations about expected maximum drawdowns.

Whereas Monte Carlo analysis is a well-known tool for anyone who has had experience with the evaluation of risks, timescale analysis is a new method which we have not seen in any publications so far. We find it a useful tool which can be easily performed with any standard software package that allows the bar compression of the used price data to be changed.

4.1 Timescale analysis

Changing the compression of the price data

In order to perform a test we need to have data that was not used during the building and the development of the trading system. This data is called *out-of-sample data*. The simplest way to get such out-of-sample data for your trading system is just apply it to the same market and the same data but to change the timescale. Although in this way the new timescale is not really different, its price structure changes a lot within diverse timescales. Therefore many valuable trading systems which work well on one timescale fail completely on another scale in the same market.

As far as the trading system LUXOR is concerned, for timescale analysis, you first develop and test a trading system step-by-step on one timescale, like we did on 30-minute data. You develop the entries, you add trading costs, then through optimisation and filtering you will arrive at a complete system with stops and profit targets. Then you just take this whole trading system and apply it like it is to the same market on different timescales. With today's software platforms like TradeStation 8, such system tests can be performed easily.

You keep all your applied strategies on the chart while changing the symbol properties: in this case you are changing the bar length from 30 minute to any other, for example 5-minute, 10-minute, 120-minute, daily, etc. If you perform such a change you see that the chart and the indicators which you use for signal generation look similar, although you are working on different timescales (fig. 4.1). Since the indicators, in our case the two moving averages, are calculated on the basis of the chart bars, it does not matter too much if the bars are calculated every 5 minutes, 30 minutes or 120 minutes. But although the properties of some indicators look similar, the market in fact behaves differently when looking at its different timescales in more detail. Keep in mind that on the 5 minute scale you watch the price data over five years much more closely than on larger timescales like the 120 minute timeframe.

Whereas in the 120-minute timescale 120 bars mean half a month of price data, the same amount of bars on a 5-minute timescale just contains half a day (fig. 4.1).

Figure 4.1: British pound/US dollar FOREX on different timescales: A: 5-minute bars; B: 30-minute bars; C: 120 minute bars. Chart examples from July 2008. The two moving averages like all other parameters for signal generation are kept the same while changing the timescale of the chart. Each of the three figures shows about 100–150 bars.

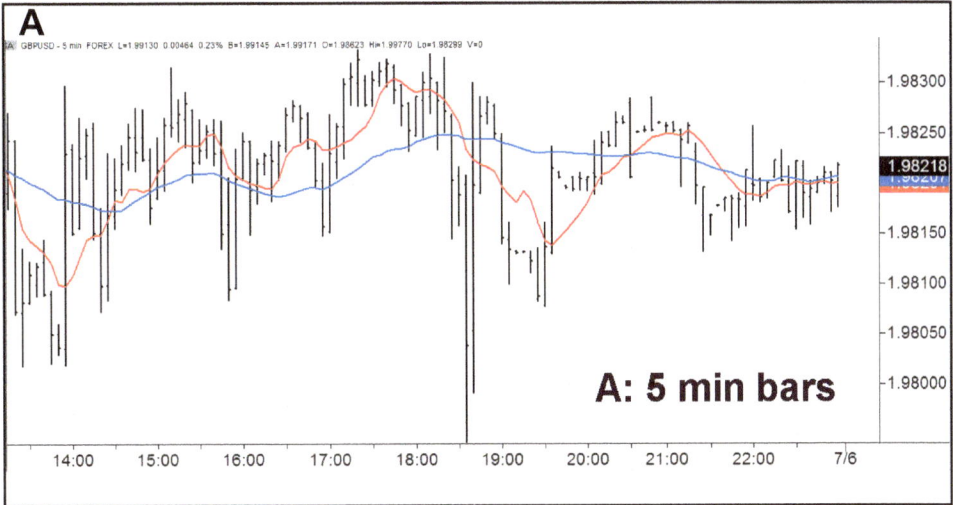

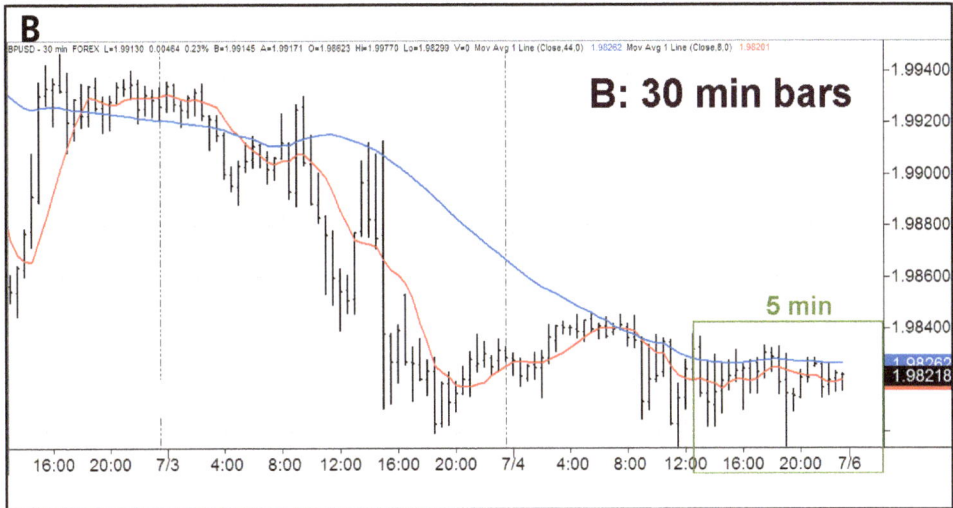

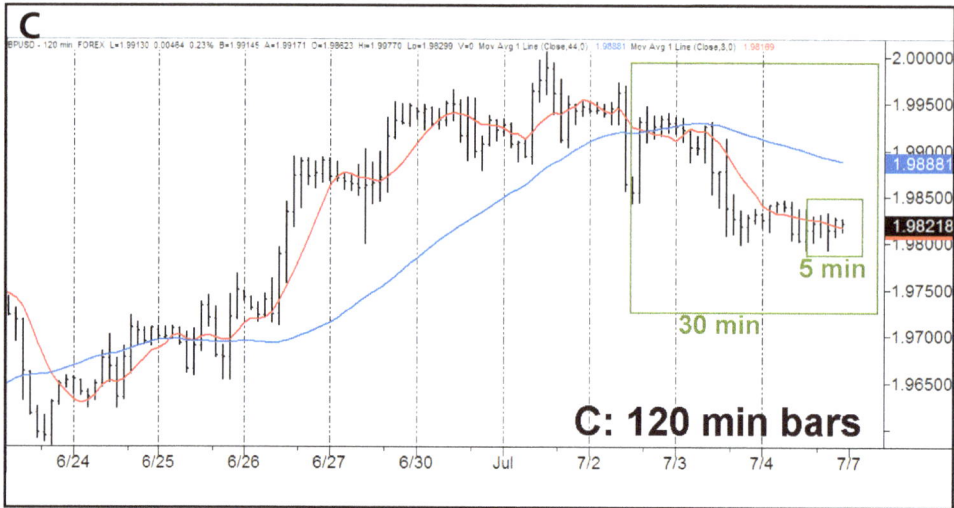

LUXOR tested on different bar compressions

It is fascinating to check how a trading strategy changes on different timescales regarding its important system figures and equity lines. Let's do such a timescale analysis for the LUXOR trading system. As you remember LUXOR was developed on 30-minute data of the British pound/US dollar FOREX market. Let's have a look at the equity lines on different timescales (fig. 4.2). You see from these curves that our developed system logic gains steady profits on all the different timescales, starting from 5-minute up to 180-minute bar calculations.

Figure 4.2: Detailed equity curves from system tests on different timescales – from 5-minute up to 180-minute bar calculations. Trend-following system British pound/US dollar (FOREX), 30-minute bars, 21/10/2002–4/7/2008, with entry time window 9.30am–1.30pm GMT. SLOW=44, FAST=1. All three exits in place: 0.3% risk stop, 0.8 trailing stop and 1.9% profit target. Including $30 slippage and commissions per round turn.

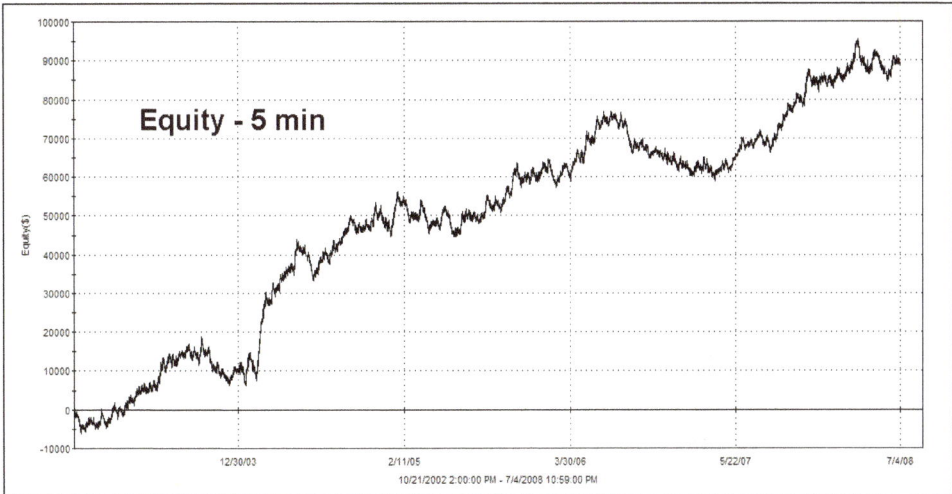

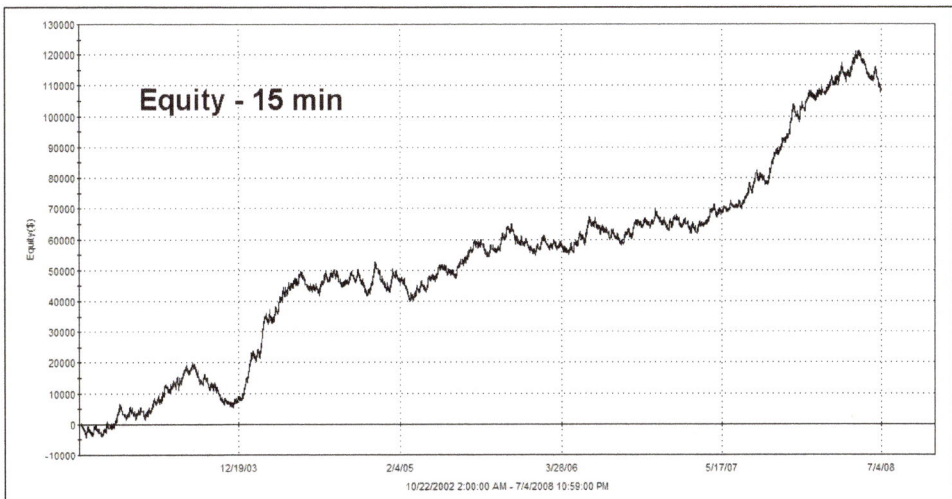

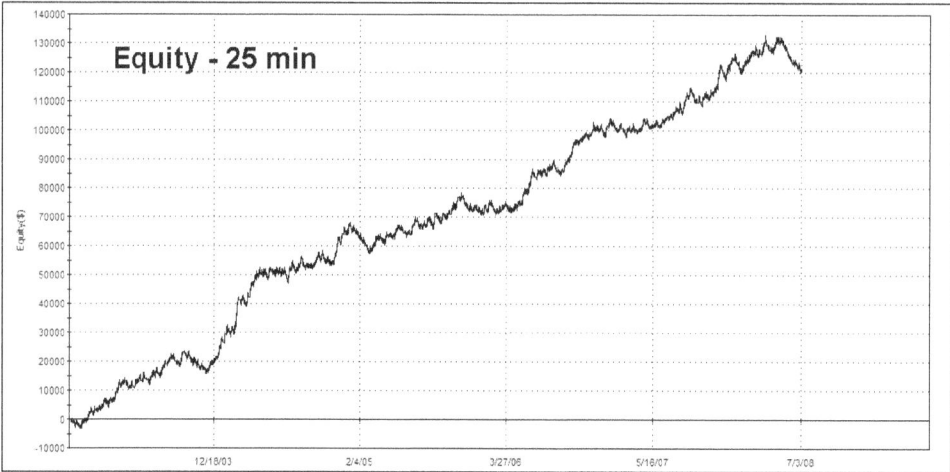

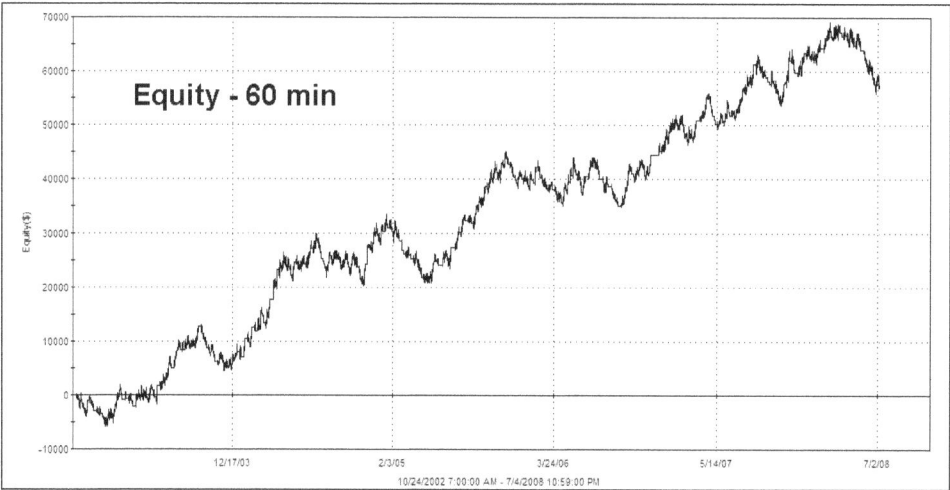

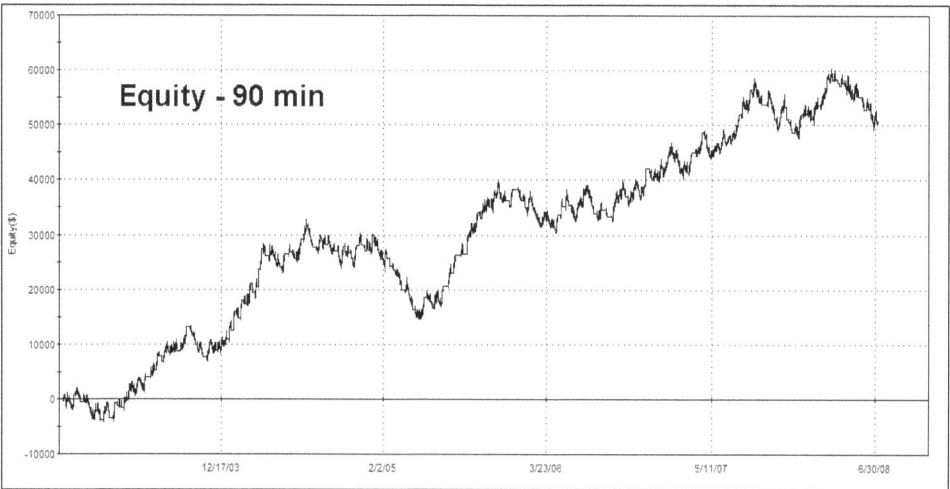

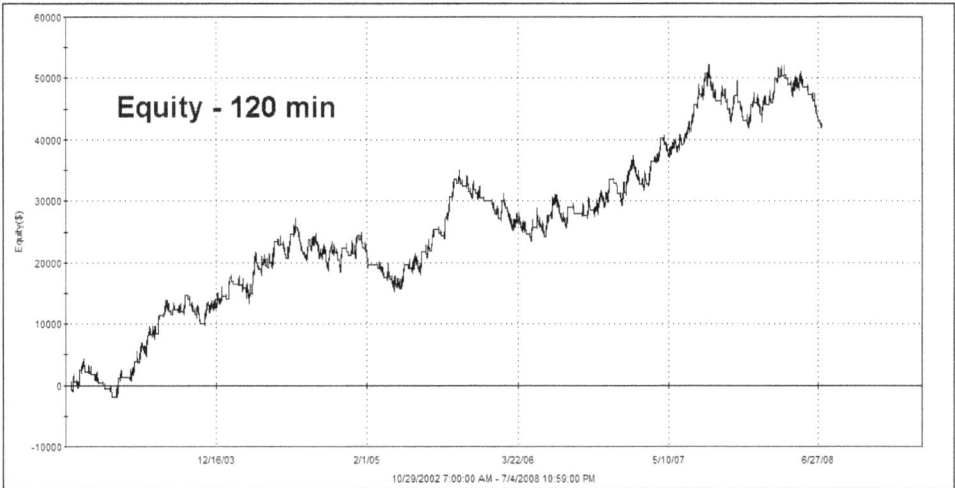

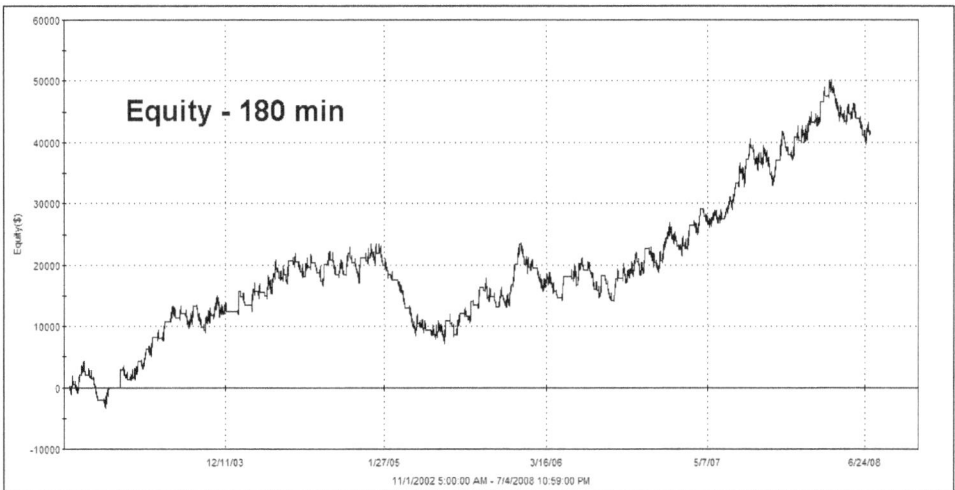

Although the trading system makes profits on all the different timescales, the shapes of the equity curves with their drawdown phases appear a bit different.

Net profit and maximum drawdown dependent on the traded bar length

We'll now have a closer look at the trading system's behaviour by comparing important trading figures as a function of the chosen bar lengths.

When plotting the total net profit and the maximum intraday drawdown of the trading system for the test period as a function of the chosen timescale, some interesting features are revealed (fig. 4.3). You see a broad region of bar lengths between 5 and 35 minutes which all produce relatively similar good returns with similar low drawdowns. The 30 minute timescale is the most profitable but it is well placed in an area of other useful timescales. However, you should pay attention to the fact that at about 40 minutes the profit decreases quite a lot. As a consequence of this graph it could be even safer to use the LUXOR system on smaller timeframes like 20 minutes or 25 minutes where you also have good results but you are further away from the less profitable timescales. As you can see when you go down to the small timescales, like 1-minute bars, the system is not profitable any more. For larger timescales above the most profitable region of 5–35 minute bars the gained total net profit goes further and further down until it diminishes completely for bar lengths above 210 minutes.

Figure 4.3: Timescale analysis. Total net profit and maximum drawdown as a function of the bar length. Trend-following system British pound/US dollar (FOREX), 30-minute bars, 21/10/2002–4/7/2008, with entry time window 9.30am–1.30pm GMT. SLOW=44, FAST=1. All three exits in place: 0.3% risk stop, 0.8 trailing stop and 1.9% profit target. Including $30 slippage and commissions per round turn.

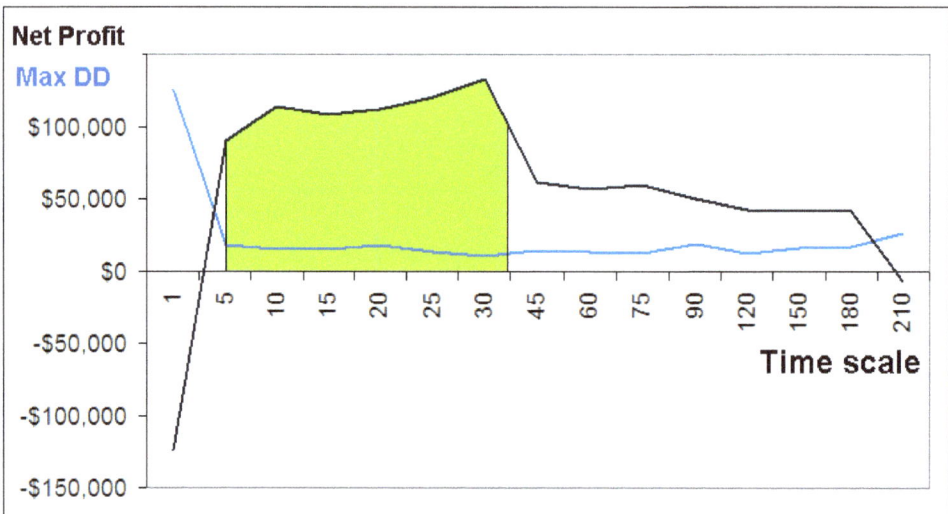

Explanation for the time dependency of the system

What are the reasons for the system's total net profit time dependency?

To understand this you need to remind yourself that the total net profit of a trading system is the number of all trades multiplied with the average profit per trade (fig. 4.4). For example let's say that you have a trading system which generates 1,000 trades. In this case an average profit per trade of $100 leads to a total net profit of $100,000 (1,000 × $100).

Figure 4.4: The total net profit of a trading system is the product of two factors: number of trades and average profit per trade.

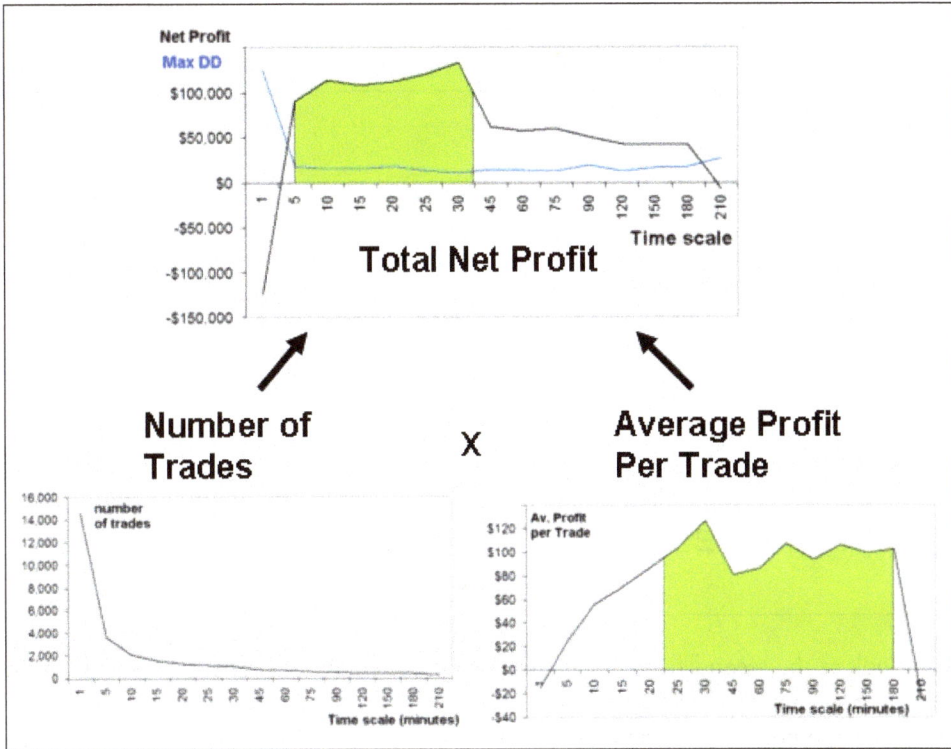

Therefore to understand the total net profit of a trading system, you must investigate the two factors which contribute to it: number of trades and average profit per trade. If you first look at the number of trades which are generated within the test period 2002–2008 you see that it strongly depends on the selected timeframe (fig. 4.5). The smaller you set the timeframe, the higher is the number of generated trades. On a 1-minute scale our trading logic generates over 14,000 trades in the five years whereas on a 210-minute basis only 210 trades are generated. In other words: on a 1-minute basis you get more than 2,000 trades per year or ten trades per day whereas on a 120-minute basis you only get about 40 trades per year, which means about one per week. This is plausible because on a smaller time scale you have many more bars for calculation, as discussed above (see fig. 4.1).

Figure 4.5: Timescale analysis. Number of generated trades as a function of the bar length. Trend-following system British pound/US dollar (FOREX), 30-minute bars, 21/10/2002–4/7/2008, with entry time window 9.30am–1.30pm GMT. SLOW=44, FAST=1. All three exits in place: 0.3% risk stop, 0.8 trailing stop and 1.9% profit target. Including $30 slippage and commissions per round turn.

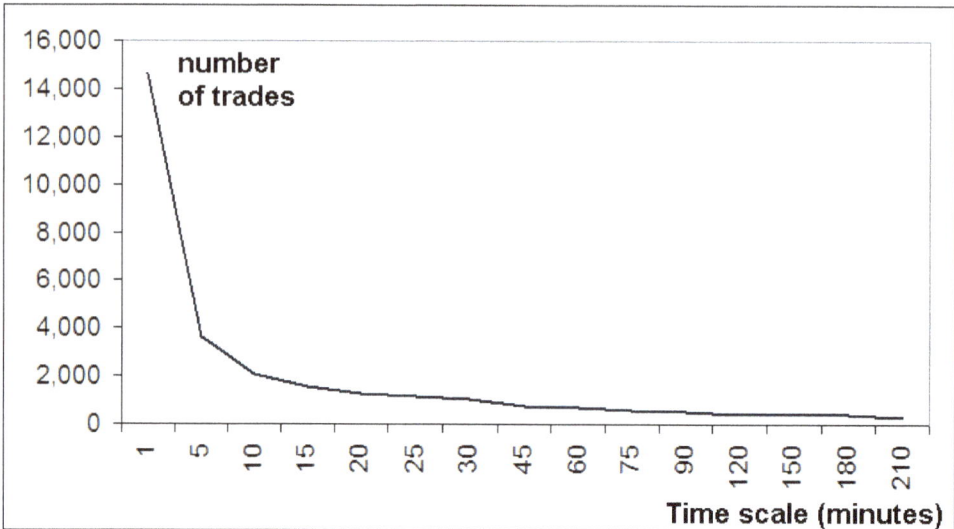

Let's look at the second factor in the calculation of total net profit; the average profit per trade as a function of the selected timescale (fig. 4.6). You see that the smaller the timescale chosen, the smaller the profit per trade you get. The worst situation appears on the 1-minute timescale, where the profit per trade becomes negative. It seems that the statistical noise is too high within the small timescales of 1-minute to 5-minute bars. Too many arbitrary movements take place there which are difficult to exploit systematically with our trading system. Furthermore, trading costs and slippage matter more on the small timescales. If you stay away from the small bar lengths and set them to values between 25 and 180 minutes then the system produces an average profit per trade between $80 and $120 (green area in fig. 4.6). This is really a remarkable result since you have to keep in mind how much the market structure changes when varying the timescale in this big range.

Figure 4.6: Timescale analysis. Average profit per trade as a function of the bar length. Trend-following system British pound/US dollar (FOREX), 30-minute bars, 21/10/2002–4/7/2008, with entry time window 9.30am–1.30pm GMT. SLOW=44, FAST=1. All three exits in place: 0.3% risk stop, 0.8 trailing stop and 1.9% profit target. Including $30 slippage and commissions per round turn.

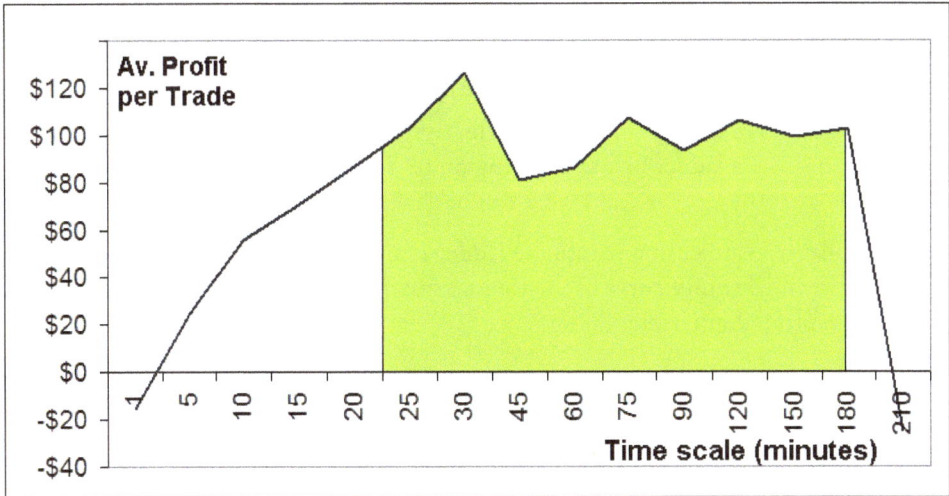

From the variation of the total number of trades and average profit per trade depending on the selected bar length you can conclude how the total net profit varies with changing timescale. On the short timescales the total net profit suffers from a too low profit per trade. But already with timescales longer than five minutes the low average profit per trade can be compensated with the higher number of trades and leads the trading system to a high total net profit with low maximum drawdown. If you increase the timescale further, above 40 minutes and more, the total net profit becomes lower and lower since less and less trades are generated while the single trade profit does not increase. As a consequence our trading system works best in the medium timescales between 10 and 35 minutes.

Now what do all these findings mean for the predictive power of our trading system? The trading system which was developed and optimised on the 30 minute timescale shows promising results under variation of the timescale. From these results with the proven stability you can draw the conclusion that the trading logic has a good chance of standing up to further out-of-sample data tests and can be profitable in real trading.

4.2 Monte Carlo analysis

"What is the last thing you do before you climb on a ladder? You shake it. And that is Monte Carlo simulation."

Sam Savage, Stanford University [10]

Nearly everybody has heard of it, but nobody uses it. Many people are afraid that Monte Carlo analysis is such a complex method that in order to understand it you must be a professor in mathematics. However the truth is that it is not that difficult and it should be used by everybody who wants to do more than just to look at the gained equity lines of system back-tests.

The principle of Monte Carlo analysis

But what does Sam Savage mean when he says that Monte Carlo analysis is just a technique to shake a ladder before climbing on it? To understand his sentence you first must know what the ladder is and what can be shaken on it.

As you probably assume, in our case the ladder is a trading system. Fig. 4.7 shows this ladder, the detailed equity curve of the trading system LUXOR, with all filters and exits applied as explained in chapter 3.

Figure 4.7: Detailed Equity Curve of system LUXOR. Tested on British pound/US dollar (FOREX), 30-minute bars, 21/10/2002–4/7/2008. With entry time window 9.30am–1.30pm GMT. SLOW=44, FAST=1. All three exits in place: 0.3% risk stop, 0.8% trailing stop and 1.9% profit target. Including $30 slippage and commissions per round turn. Calculation based on one contract basis, results incl. $30 slippage and commissions per trade. Chart created with Market System Analyzer (see www.adaptrade.com).

This detailed equity curve represents all the 1,051 trades performed by the trading system within the test period 21/10/2002–4/7/2008, one after another in a chronological order.

Now let's shake the ladder as following: you keep all these 1,051 trades (e.g. trade 1=$120 win, trade 2=$90 loss, trade 3=$445 win … trade 1,051=$150 loss) and you put them into a new order. Fig. 4.8 shows an example of how you do this with a trading system that contains six trades: each of the six trades is kept but put into a new position.

Figure 4.8: The principle of Monte Carlo analysis: A trading system which contains six trades is shaken – this means that the positions of the six trades are exchanged accidentally.

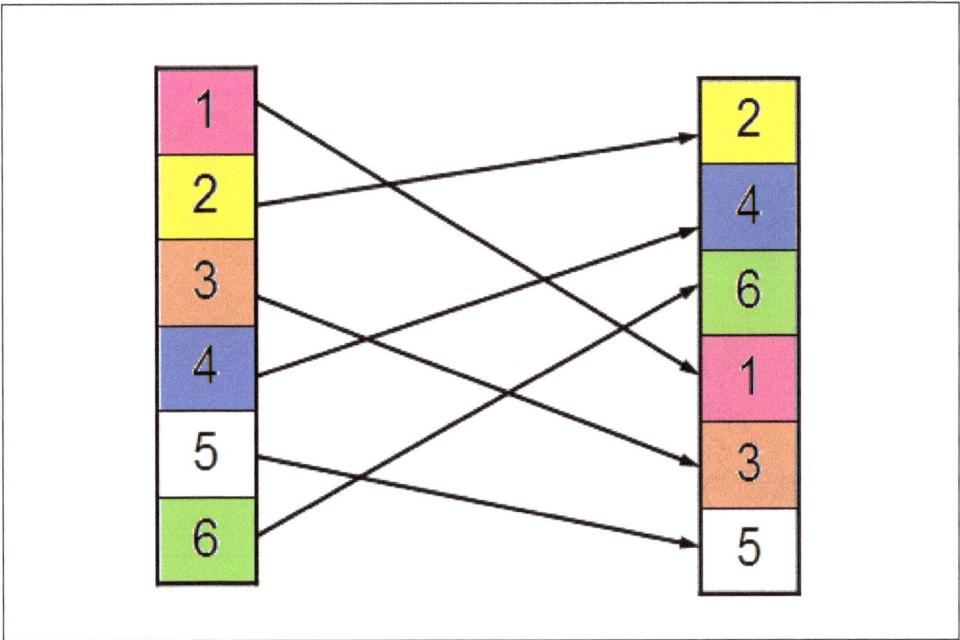

You can do it in the same way with every arbitrary number of trades. The new positions of the trades are determined randomly. For example, in our system trade 1 is now in position 842, trade 2 in position 66, trade 1,051 in position 980 etc. The important point is that every trade still exists like before – no trade is deleted and no trade is added. This permutation method is called *selection without replacement*.[3]

Exchanging the order of the performed trades

The above example suggests that the final outcome of all trades must stay the same, independent of whatever new order the trades are placed in. Since the sum of your trades stays the same all new equity curves must reach the same amount in the end. But since the trades are now in a new order, the shape of the new equity lines and especially the occurring drawdowns become different (fig. 4.9).

---

[3] Another possible permutation method is selection with replacement, which will be used later in chapter 9.6. The advantage of a selection without replacement is that it exactly duplicates the probability distribution of the input sequence, whereas selection with replacement may not. The drawback to selection without replacement is that the randomly sampled trade sequences are limited to the number of trades in the input sequence. Thus if you have a short sequence of trades (e.g. less than 50 trades), this may limit the accuracy of your calculations. The first method is similar to random selection with replacement with the advantage that the final list of trades will have the same statistical properties as the original list. The second method introduces more randomness into the trade sequence, which may be preferable if the expected trades in the future will likely be different than those of the original sequence.

Figure 4.9: Blue: detailed equity curve; Black: 15 permutations of the trades sequence (shaken trades). Trend-following system LUXOR British pound/US dollar (FOREX), 30-minute bars, 21/10/2002–4/7/2008. Calculation based on one contract basis, results including $30 slippage and commissions per trade.

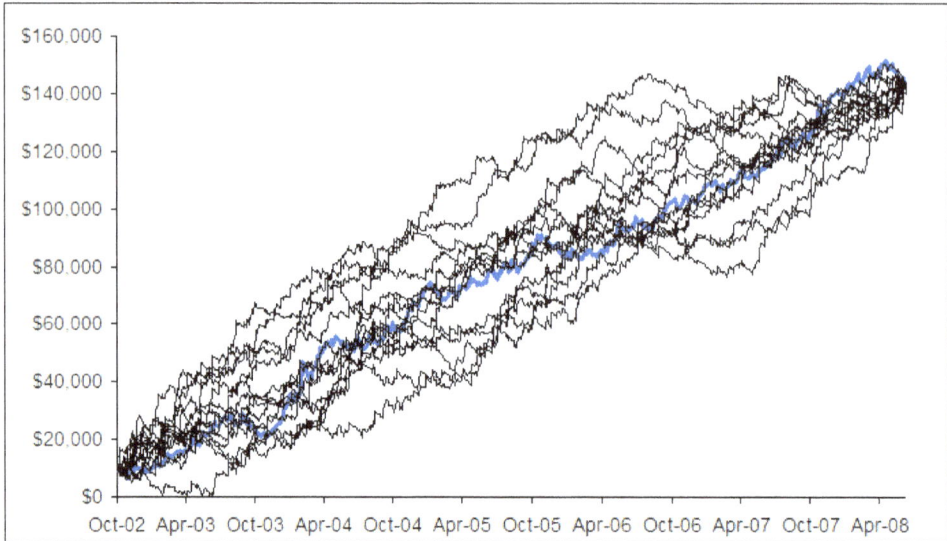

This figure shows the original trade sequence (thick blue line) and 15 permuted trade sequences (thin black lines). All the permutated equity curves have the same starting and ending points because we did not add or remove any trades but just changed the order of their appearance. The change of the trade orders leads to the effect that between the equity curves there are big variations with different drawdown phases that occur at different times.

Probabilities and confidence levels

Now that you have grasped how your trading system can be shaken, we need to bring ahead the understanding of Monte Carlo analysis just one step further. You can do this sampling not only 15 times but many more times. In fact with 1,051 different trades you have 1,051! = 1,051 × 1,050 × 1,049 × 1,048 × ... × 3 × 2 × 1 possible permutations, an unbelievable high number![4] Bear in mind that even the apparently small number of 200! (200 × 199 × 198 × ... × 3 × 2 × 1) is bigger than the number of all the atoms that exist in the complete universe! The job of calculating all these different possibilities cannot even be done by fast computers within a reasonable time. For these practical reasons in Monte Carlo analysis you chose *only* some hundreds or thousands of such arbitrary trade sequences randomly. The results are sorted and from this classified list probabilities for each result can be assigned. The following simple example will demonstrate how to determine such probabilities:

---

[4] The first trade you can put on 1,051 different positions, the second trade has 1,050 positions left, the third trade 1,049 positions and so on: 1,051 × 1,050 × ... × 2 × 1 possibilities.

Consider flipping a coin 1,000 times and estimating the amounts of heads and tails. If the coin is built completely symmetrically (which is not possible in real life but used by mathematicians who do statistical calculations) then you can call this coin fair. While it is likely that the number of heads and tails with such a fair coin will be close to 500, it is also unlikely that they will both be exactly 500. What is far more likely is that the number of heads will fall in some range around 500. Instead of getting a head exactly 500 times and tails exactly 500 times you get a Gaussian distribution of values around 500 (fig. 4.10). This leads us to the introduction of a *confidence level* and *confidence interval*.

These values describe the distribution of the experimentally gained data around the true parameter (in this case 500). The confidence level (95%) says how likely it is that the true parameter of 500 is placed within the confidence interval around your estimation. For the Gaussian distribution, which is applicable for this ideal experiment, you can be 95% sure that the value 500 is accurate within 3.1%. This means that with 95% probability you will throw between 469 (500 times -3.1%) and 531 times (500 times +3.1%) ahead from the 1,000 trials.

Figure 4.10: Gaussian distribution of probabilities for flipping a coin 1000 times. You can tell with 95% confidence that the coin falls to heads between 469 and 531 times. Figure created with MATLAB.

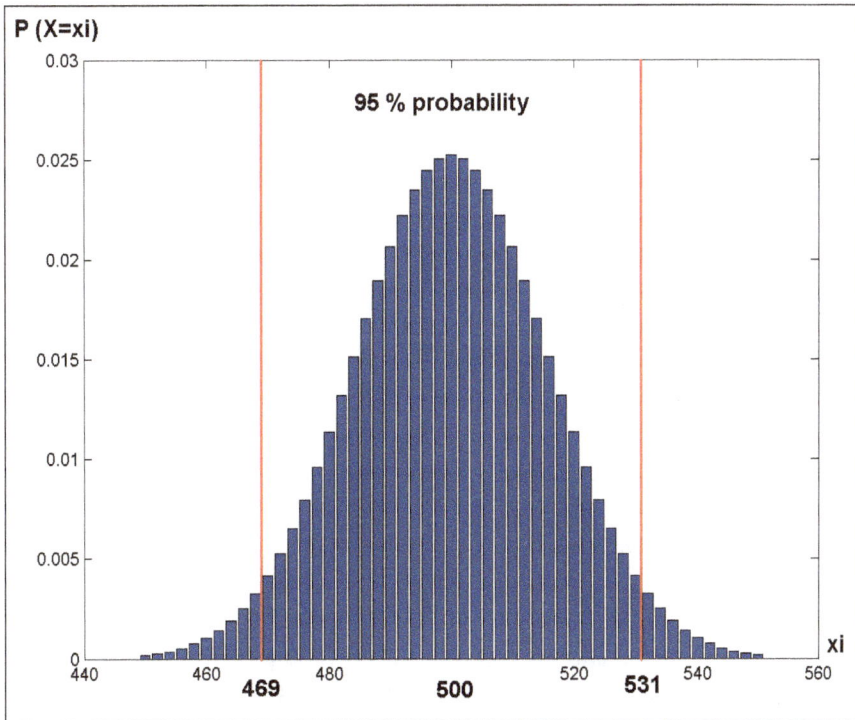

These confidence levels (e.g. 95%, 99% confidence etc.) are used in Monte Carlo analysis.

Performing a Monte Carlo analysis with the LUXOR trading system

Let's look at the concrete example of a Monte Carlo analysis of our trading system LUXOR (table 4.1).

Table 4.1: Monte Carlo analysis of 5,000 permutations with worst case maximum drawdown and average drawdown as a function of confidence level. Trend-following system LUXOR British pound/US dollar (FOREX), 30-minute bars, 21/10/2002–4/7/2008. Calculation based on one contract basis, results including $30 slippage and commissions per trade. Calculation performed with Market System Analyzer.

Test period:	21/10/2002–4/7/2008	
Market	GBP/USD, 30-min bars	
Costs:	30$ Slipp. + Comm.	
Number of samples for Monte Carlo analysis	5000	
Total Net Profit	$132,589.50	
Final Account Equity	$142,589.50	
Total Number of Trades	1,051	
Number of Winning Trades	370	
Number of Losing Trades	681	
Largest Winning Trade	$3,900.00	
Average Winning Trade	$1,120.36	
Largest Losing Trade	($810.00)	
Average Losing Trade	($414.01)	
	Worst Case Max. Drawdown	**Worst Case Average Drawdown**
ORIGINAL SYSTEM	($10,292)	($1,976)
MONTE CARLO results at 60% confidence	($12,321)	($2,006)
MONTE CARLO results at 70% confidence	($13,222)	($2,040)
MONTE CARLO results at 80% confidence	($14,325)	($2,090)
MONTE CARLO results at 90% confidence	($16,136)	($2,176)
MONTE CARLO results at 95% confidence	($17,908)	($2,259)
MONTE CARLO results at 99% confidence	($21,364)	($2,308)

Looking at the top of the table you see that most of the trading system figures stay the same for all different confidence levels. This is clear from our above discussions. During the performed type of Monte Carlo analysis you just change the order of the trades when shaking them but you do not cancel or add any trades since in our case we chose the method *selection without replacement.* So most of the trading figures, like average trade, total net profit, total number of trades, final account equity, biggest winning trade, biggest losing trade, average winning trade etc., stay the same when you perform your 5,000 permutations.

The most important aspect of Monte Carlo analysis is the estimation of expected drawdowns. The Monte Carlo analysis is a tool which checks for possible worst case scenarios. It looks for the worst drawdowns which can happen in the lifetime of your trading logic. In our case the trading system has a maximum drawdown of $10,292 and an average drawdown of $1,976 (table 4.1). The performed Monte Carlo analysis tells you, with 99% confidence, that the worst case drawdown of our trading system will not exceed $21,364 and usually average drawdowns will be in the range around $2,000. So by bringing all trades into different order 5,000 times with 99% confidence the worst case drawdown will not become bigger than $21,364.

Although this number is more than double the drawdown of the original system, $21,364 maximum expected drawdown is not more than the average profit per year ($22,000 = $132,000/6 years). This value is acceptable for a single trading system. But still our calculation means that if you start the system for the first time you have to be prepared that there is a 1% chance of facing a $21,000 drawdown before making any profits. Keep in mind that 99% confidence is a quite high level. If you look at lower confidence levels, your expected worst-case drawdowns and average drawdowns get remarkably lower.

Limitations of the Monte Carlo method

If you want to estimate the real risks which are hidden below the results of your performance table, Monte Carlo analysis is the right method. But when drawing conclusions from Monte Carlo calculations you still must keep in mind the assumptions on which they are based and their limitations. The dangerous point is that for the Monte Carlo analysis you take the trades from the trading logic as you get them from your back-tests. But what if this trading logic is only curve fitted and over-optimised? The Monte Carlo analysis cannot see this! Since it just takes the trades of your system (which might be over-fitted) it usually shows a good result if the back-test is good. On the other side it shows bad results only if the back-test is bad.

So Monte Carlo analysis is only useful when applied correctly and not to over-fitted trading systems. And still, even if it is applied correctly, you need to be careful in its interpretation. Sometimes things on the markets take place which cannot be avoided:

> *"And some events are beyond the model's ability to predict them. The brainy sorts at Long-Term Capital Management, the hedge fund that imploded during 1998, employed sophisticated probability models. But those models failed dramatically during a financial calamity that was triggered by a default in Russia. That's a warning that this high-tech planning is not foolproof. My concern is that people are using Monte Carlo as a certainty test. It isn't. It's a probability test."* [10]

More than two decades later we know that the crisis in 1998 was rather small compared to what happened in 2000 and 2008, and could not be predicted by any mathematical models.

Keep in mind that in Monte Carlo analysis the following assumption is used: returns of markets follow a Gaussian, normal distribution like the perfect flipping coin (fig. 4.10). However the reality in the financial markets is different! Fig. 4.11 shows the daily changes of the British pound in US dollars within the last 20 years. Although the general behaviour of the markets can be described by the Gauss model, there are some days with huge percentage changes that are outside the Gaussian curve.

Such days are impossible to predict and the Monte Carlo analysis which is based on the Gaussian distribution reaches its limits. To get more reliable results for such extreme scenarios you have to choose more realistic distributions than the Gaussian distribution, leading to more complex mathematical models which go beyond the scope of this book.

Figure 4.11: Daily changes of the British pound vs. US dollar in percent from August 1988– August 2008. Biggest gain was 2.8%, biggest loss 3.3%. The Gaussian distribution cannot describe the daily changes exactly, especially for large gains and losses (encircled areas). Figure generated with MATLAB, data taken from TradeStation 8.

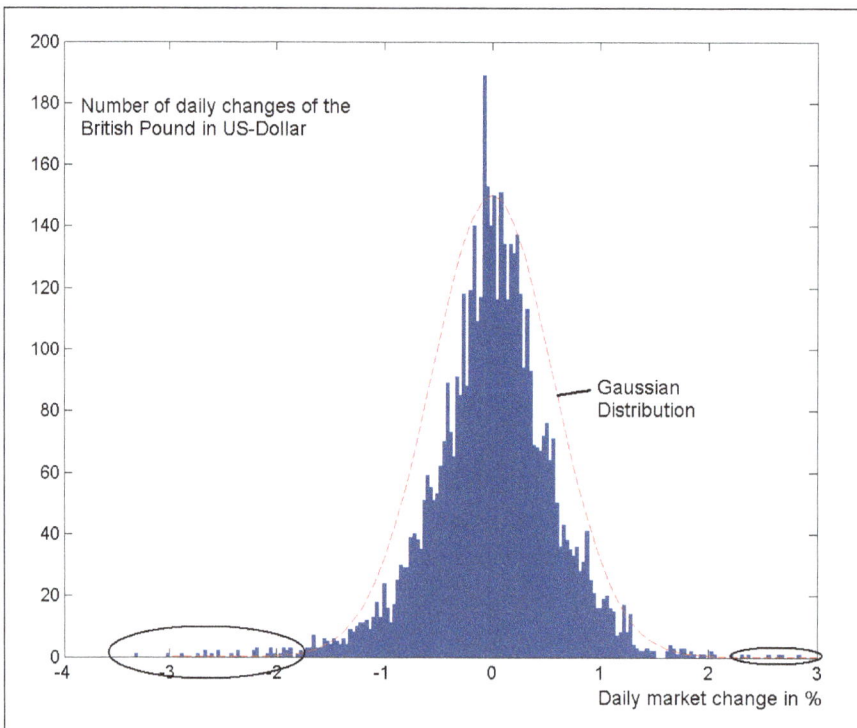

5

The Factors Around Your System

MANY TRADERS BELIEVE that the system code is what counts in becoming a successful trader. In fact the code is the **least** important thing since there are many other factors around a trading system. These factors are discussed in this chapter.

If you are a systematic trader you have probably already had the following experience. You develop a trading system by accident after some time-consuming research. Its back-test results look promising and its logic seems sound. You decide to start to trade it but the real performance is not as good as you expected. Your trading system still contains a slight upward bias in real trading but it is far away from the bright results which your tests showed. Why does this happen? Are there any ways to avoid this and to be sure that the back-test results will hold in real trading? Although we do not want to arrive at a final answer to these questions in this chapter we will try to pinpoint the main traits of this topic. The argument is complex and unfortunately there is no room for a short and easy formula that the reader can adhere to without leaving a critical standpoint. We focus therefore on the question of how much predictive power your trading system needs to have for the future and we try to find out which factors the trading system's predictive power depends on.

Most of the theoretic base of this work is provided by David Aronson's book, *Evidenced-Based Technical Analysis* [2]. We take it here as our main reference and we will look at the topic from a practical point of view with real examples of trading systems.

5.1 The market's long/short bias

When developing trading systems the market mood is a key factor. It is different if the market under scrutiny was in an upward, sideways or downward trend within the test period. In the bull market 1995–2000 many trading systems performed the best on the stock markets and futures like FTSE 100, S&P 500, Nasdaq etc. which had a long bias. When the market turned down after 2001 these systems went bust. While they had been able to gain huge profits between 1997 and 2000 they met harsh difficulties during the bear market in the years that followed.

The trend is your friend?

We'll discuss this long/short bias of a market here on the example of the British pound/ US dollar FOREX (fig. 5.1). As you can see the market shows an overall upward trend in the test period. Whereas the pound was trading at $1.50, it became stronger against the dollar and in summer 2008 traded at around $2. If you now develop a trading system which goes long in the year 2002 and stays long until July 2008, you will have earned more than $50,000 with one contract (fig. 5.2). But as you can see the trading equity (= the gained money) of this simple system behaves exactly the same as the traded market itself.

As you can imagine every only-long trading system with a similar result to this is almost useless. Since the market itself has an upward bias it is no big achievement of an only-long trading system to gain money. On the other hand every system which enters only on the short side and has not lost any money within the test period 2002–2008 can be a useful trading logic for the future. It will probably earn money as soon as the market goes sideways or even reverses into a downward trend.

As you see from the underwater equity curve (fig. 5.2B) the only-long system, although it has good returns, is very risky. It stays in the market 100% of the time and therefore suffers huge drawdowns. Moreover the system needs nearly two years to recover from its biggest losing period.

Figure 5.1: British pound/US dollar (FOREX), weekly bars, 1/7/2002–4/7/2008. A long entry signal is placed on 21/10/2002.

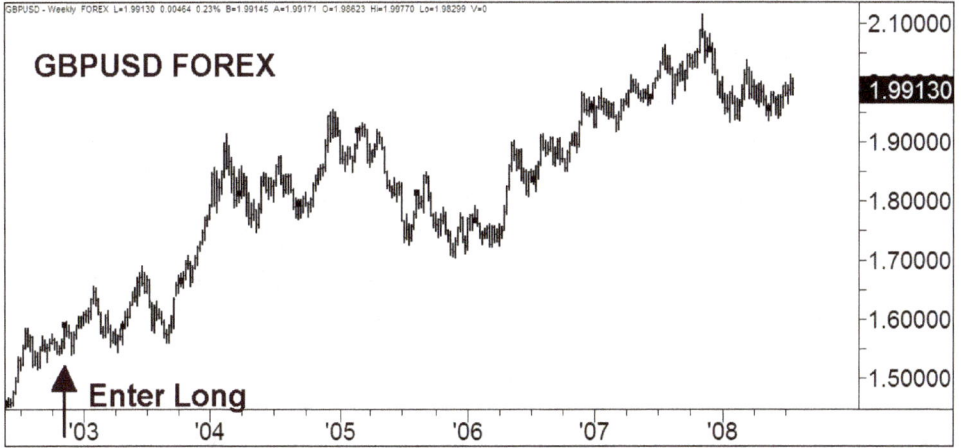

Figure 5.2: Only long trading system for British pound/ US dollar (FOREX), 1/7/2002–4/7/2008. A long entry signal is placed on 21/10/2002 and the system stays in the market all the time. A: detailed equity curve; B: underwater equity curve showing all drawdowns.

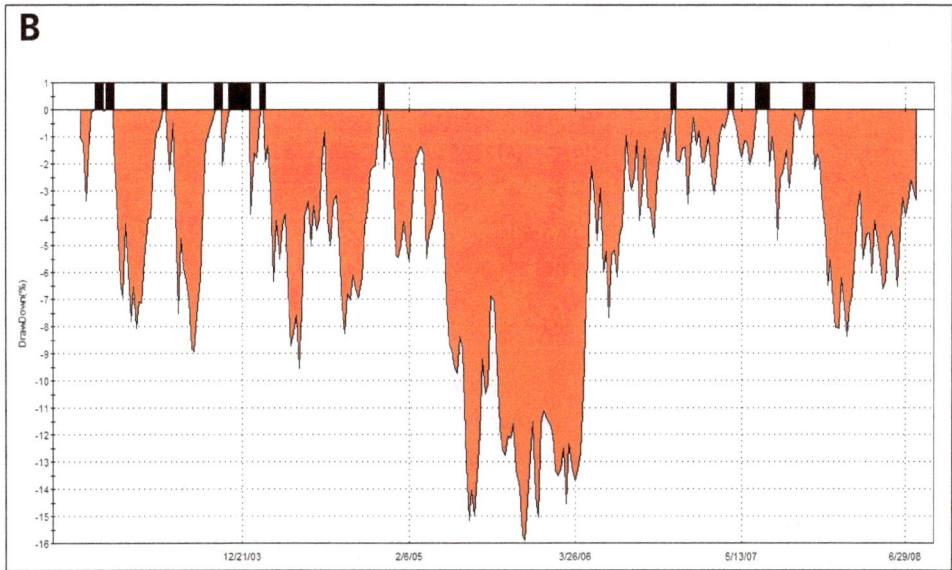

Consequences for system development

When developing a trading system you can compare its long side with this only-long system, as the minimum result to achieve. You know how much of the profit was earned simply by the market trend and the additional achievement of your trading logic compared with this market bias. The most important figure of your system tests is thereby the total percentage of time your trading system has been in the market. Only if the system was in the market 100% of time is the market bias 100% important. If you trade, however, a system which is only seldom in the market, let's say only 10%, the market bias becomes less important. Another reason to keep the time in the market low is to decrease the risk and exposure as discussed in chapter 3.5 when we talked about exits and risk management.

What other conclusions can you draw as a systematic trader or system developer from the long/short bias of markets? When you look at the trading systems which we present here you can see that most of them have a similar amount of short and long trades. Although in some cases (stocks and stock index futures) markets crash more quickly than they go upwards, we tend to build the systems without long or short bias. Most of our systems (like LUXOR) have a similar amount of long and short trades, although their profitability in a long or short direction may be different because the market has shown an uptrend. Since you do not know if this uptrend will continue in the future, your system is more stable and less adapted to this market bias if it produces the same amount of long and short signals.

5.2 Out-of-sample deterioration

David Aronson stated a fact which we absolutely agree with from our own experience in systems' evaluation [2]:

> "Market behaviour is presumed to be a combination of systematic behaviour (recurring patterns) and random noise. It is always possible to improve the fit of a rule to a given segment of data by increasing its complexity. In other words, given enough complexity, it is always possible to fashion a rule that buys at every market low point and sells at every market high point. This is a bad idea. Perfect timing on past data can only be the result of a rule that is contaminated with noise. In other words, perfect signals or anything approaching them almost certainly means the rule is, to a disturbing degree, a description of past random behaviour (i.e. overfitted). Overfitting is manifested when the rule is applied to the test data segment. There, its performance will be worse than in the training data. This is because the legitimate patterns found in a training set recur in the test set, but the noise in the training set does not. It can be inferred that profitability in the training set that does not repeat in the testing set was most likely a consequence of over-fitting."

This is a meaningful description of the concept of degrees of freedom as depicted more formally in Chapter 2. In this chapter we will have a look at a real example of such an over-fitted system.

A Bollinger Band system with logic and code

Bollinger Bands were first introduced by John Bollinger in the early 1980s and have since become popularised and investigated extensively [17]. Bollinger Bands consist of three price levels, the first being a simple moving average (middle line). An upper and lower band is then calculated based on a specific number of standard deviations above and below this central line (fig. 5.4 A and B). These can be used to trigger long and short entry signals.

We will stay at this point with the pound/dollar FOREX market from 2002–2008 (Datafeed = TradeStation) to test a Bollinger Band system. We optimise all its main six input parameters for the entry and exit points on daily data within the training period between 30/04/2002 and 1/3/2006 (fig. 5.3). Please note that this Bollinger Band system allows a different optimisation of its input parameters concerning the long and the short side. For the upper and the lower Bollinger Band the length of the moving averages and their distance from the entry point can be varied. So you have four input parameters which you can optimise for the entries. Furthermore we insert two variable, percentage-based exits, which can be optimised as well: a risk stop loss and a profit target.

Figure 5.3: British pound/US dollar, 30/04/2002–4/7/2008. The Bollinger Band trading system is optimised in six parameters within the training data range (30/04/2002–28/02/2006). Afterwards the results of this trading system are checked in the test data range (1/3/2006–4/7/2008).

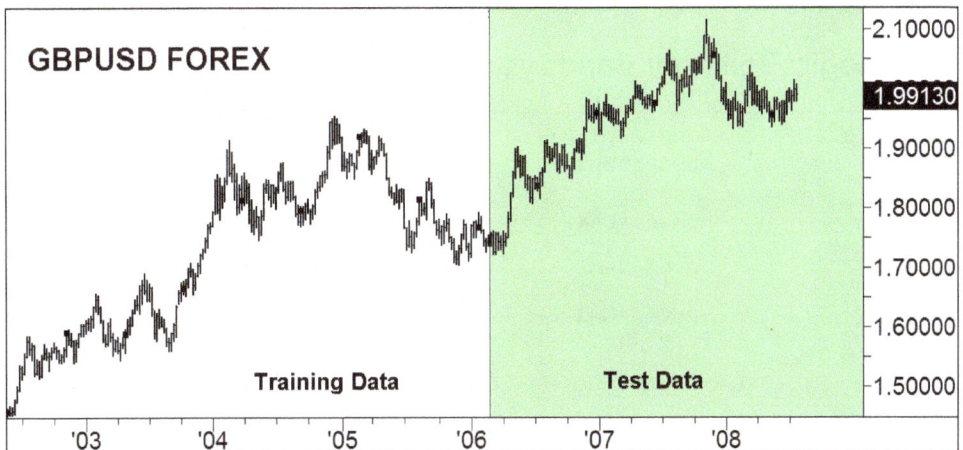

Figure 5.4A: Entry and exit logic of a Bollinger Band breakout system. Four parameters in the entry logic and two parameters in the exit logic can be optimised.

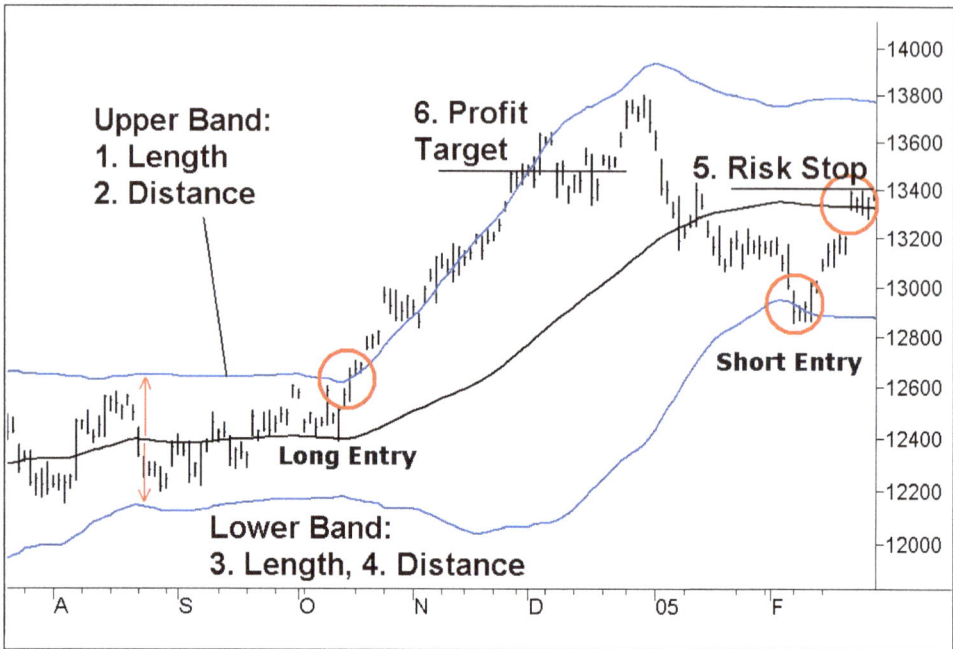

Figure 5.4B: EasyLanguage Code of a Bollinger Band breakout system with entry and exit logic. Four parameters in the entry logic and two parameters in the exit logic can be optimised.

Entry logic: Bollinger Band system

```
inputs:              LengthUp(18),
                     NumDevsUp(2),
                     LengthDn(20),
                     NumDevsDn(2);

vars:                UpperBand(0),

                     LowerBand(0),
                     Price(0);

Price = (O+H+L+C)/4 ;

//UpperBand = BollingerBand( Price, LengthUp, NumDevsUp ) ;
//LowerBand = BollingerBand( Price, LengthDn, -NumDevsDn ) ;
UpperBand = BollingerBandFC( Price, LengthUp, NumDevsUp ) ;
LowerBand = BollingerBandFC( Price, LengthDn, -NumDevsDn ) ;

if CurrentBar > 1 and High crosses under UpperBand then
     Sell Short ( "BBandSE" ) next bar at UpperBand stop ;
```

```
if CurrentBar > 1 and Low crosses over LowerBand then
    Buy ( "BBandLE" ) next bar at LowerBand stop ;

Exit Logic:

(for both long positions/short positions)

1) Place an initial stop loss x % below entry price (Opt value:
x =1.9)
2) Place a profit target z % above entry price (Opt value: x
=4.8)
```

Optimising the Bollinger Band system

If you optimise all these six input parameters together with an optimisation criteria focused on the highest net profit on daily data of the pound/dollar FOREX market in the period from 30/04/2002–28/2/2006 you get the following result (fig. 5.5).

Figure 5.5: Bollinger Band system for British pound/dollar (FOREX), daily, all six input parameters optimised for maximum total net profit, 30/04/2002–28/2/2006. A: detailed equity curve; B: underwater equity curve showing all drawdowns.

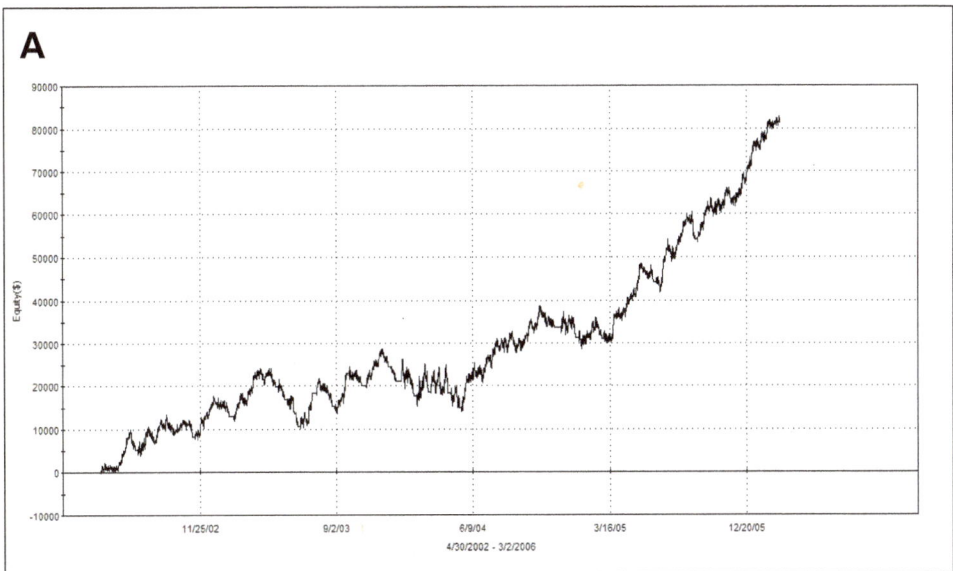

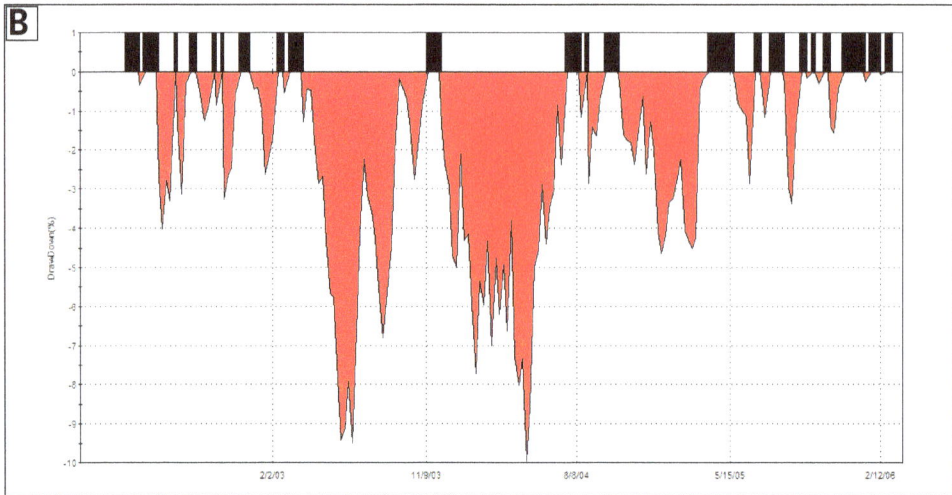

As you can see the gains of the system are steady. The drawdowns are not tiny (about 10%) but the system's profitability is high. The trading system performs nearly as many short trades as long trades and so the long/short bias of the underlying market is under control, although the trading system has high market exposure, with it holding a position in the market 89% of the time.

Out-of-sample result

Now let's see what happens if you apply the optimised trading logic to test data on which no optimisation has taken place. In this test period of two years from 1/3/2006–4/7/2008 you keep the same input parameters as you found in the training period (fig. 5.6).

As you can see the system has completely lost its bright performance. The smoothly increasing equity curve of the training period transformed itself into a directionless sideways movement. The steady equity curve of the training set suffers a big drawdown at the beginning of the test set, from which it needs nearly a two-year recovery period.

These obvious observations within the equity line are confirmed with the system report (table 5.1). Whereas within the training period the system has a total net profit of $78,000, it was only $379 in the test period. From the big average profit per trade of $1,131 in the training period, only $10 is left in the test period. Even the biggest intraday drawdown was worse in the small test period: $20,000 in the test period compared with $14,000 in the training period.

Figure 5.6: Detailed equity curve of Bollinger Band system for British pound/ dollar (FOREX), daily, training and test period. All six input parameters optimised for maximum total net profit within the training period 30/04/2002–28/02/2006. Test period from 1/3/2006–4/7/2008.

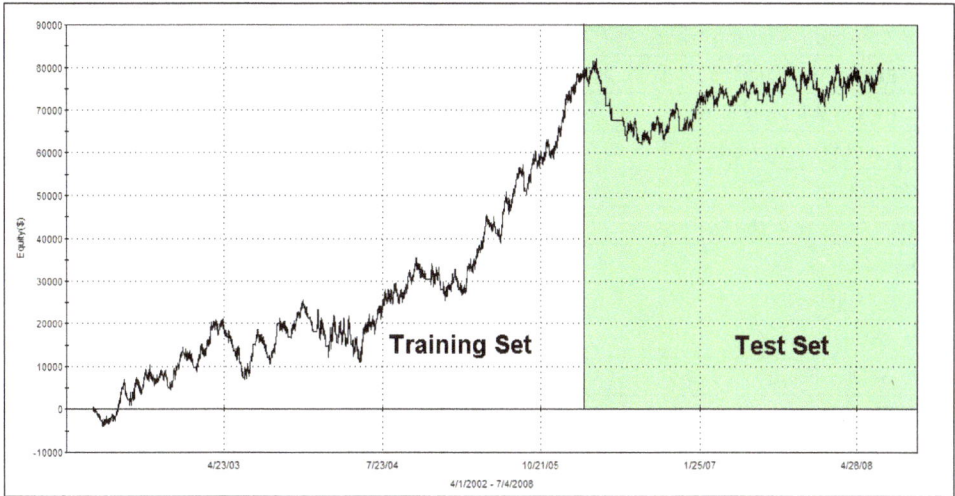

Table 5.1: Bollinger Band system for British pound/US dollar (FOREX), daily, training and test period. All six input parameters optimised for maximum total net profit within the training period 30/04/2002–28/2/2006. Test period from 1/3/2006–4/7/2008.

		TRAIN		TEST
Test period from		30/04/2002		01/03/2006
until		28/02/2006		04/07/2008
	All Trades		All Trades	
Total Net Profit		**$78,050.50**		**$379.00**
Gross Profit		$150,638.50		$53,000.00
Gross Loss		($72,588.00)		($52,621.00)
Profit Factor		2.08		1.01
Total Number of Trades		69		36
Total Number of Long Trades		30		16
Total Number of Short Trades		39		20
Percent Profitable		63.77%		47.22%
Winning Trades		44		17
Losing Trades		25		19
Avg. Trade Net Profit		**$1,131.17**		**$10.53**
Avg. Winning Trade		$3,423.60		$3,117.65
Avg. Losing Trade		($2,903.52)		($2,769.53)
Ratio Avg. Win: Avg. Loss		1.18		1.13

	TRAIN	TEST
Largest Winning Trade	$8,348.00	$6,409.00
Largest Losing Trade	($3,658.00)	($3,884.00)
Max. Consecutive Winning Trades	4	4
Max. Consecutive Losing Trades	4	6
Avg. Bars in Total Trades	13.88	15.42
Avg. Bars in Winning Trades	15.52	20.71
Avg. Bars in Losing Trades	11	10.68
Trading Period	3 Yrs, 11 Mths	2 Yrs, 4 Mths, 8 Dys
Percent of Time in the Market	**89.17%**	**85.13%**
Time in the Market	3 Yrs, 5 Mths, 27 Dys	2 Yrs, 2 Dys
Longest Flat Period	14 Dys	30 Dys
Max. Equity Run-up	$83,593.50	$19,428.00
Date of Max. Equity Run-up	28/02/2006	06/12/2007
Max. Equity Run-up as % of Initial Capital	83.59%	19.43%
Max. Drawdown (Intraday Peak to Valley)		
Value	($14,664.00)	($20,091.00)
Date of Max. Drawdown	18/05/2004	10/08/2006

Reasons for the out-of-sample deterioration

We suggest the following reasons and discuss their possible contribution:

A: The trading logic generates less than 100 trades, therefore the results are not statistically significant.

We conducted the same experiment with the same trading system on a 30-minute basis. There the system generated 3,000 trades in the training period and got a similar out-of-sample deterioration. So although 69 trades of the daily system are not enough to be statistically significant, the results shown here are typical and the low number of trades is certainly not the main reason for the system deterioration.

B: The system was published at the beginning of 2006 and the trading logic has been adopted by too many traders which destroyed its performance.

This explanation is believed by some traders who have found a new trading system or just an interesting idea. They believe that when their trading system is published the performance will suffer since other traders will immediately adopt the logic. Since many people now trade this system its good performance could diminish because of increasing slippage at first, and later because of a changing market structure since more and more people change their trading style towards the successful system. System developers try to prevent this from happening with their trading systems by hiding them in a strongbox for some years and not showing them to anybody until they lose their predictive power anyway. David Aronson writes about the topic of system disclosure in his book:

> This rationale also lacks plausibility. Even when numerous traders adopt similar rules, as in the case with futures trading funds that employ objective trend-following methods, reduced rule performance seems to be due to changes in market volatility that are not related to the usage of technical systems.

In other words: although everybody knows that trend-following methods work they do still continue to work, so the disclosure of the system is not a big reason for its success or failure. Furthermore, this system has been open to the public since the day John Bollinger developed it, which was a long time before 2006.

C: The market dynamics within the training data range is different from the one in the test data range.

In our opinion this can be one part of the explanation for deterioration. We'll discuss this extensively in the next section.

D: The system has been adapted too much to market noise within the training period, i.e. curve over-fitting.

The process of optimisation favours a set of rules which fit the training data better than the test data. Let's assume that the training data, like all real market data, consists partially of recurrent patterns (predictable data) and random noise (unpredictable data). Now you take a trading system and you adapt it to this data which is partially random and partially contains a special pattern. If your trading system is simple enough but has a sound logic with valid rules, it is able to capture some parts of the recurrent predictable patterns but does not adjust itself to the market noise. In this way the trading system keeps a certain amount of predictability for the future. If you, however, add more and more rules to this system it adjusts itself more and more to the existing noise. At a certain point the system becomes over-fitted and loses its predictability for the test period, or for the future, since the noise will be different. This is probably the most important aspect of the sample deterioration and we will investigate it with a step-by-step case study in the final section of this chapter.

You can also draw another conclusion from this thesis: all artificial market data, produced with computers by random processes, only consists of noise and are therefore useless for trading system development. If you develop a trading system based on this noisy data it will have no predictive part if applied to other data showing a different type of noise. What your trading system is trying to detect are the patterns which repeat themselves. These patterns are mainly produced by human behaviour like greed, fear and exaggeration and not by random, artificial mathematical processes.

5.3 The market data bias

Expanding the training period

Now the Bollinger Band trading system is optimised within a much longer training period of daily data from 1986-2006 (fig. 5.7). Afterwards the results are checked within the test data range which is the same as above, from 1/3/2006-4/7/2008 (fig. 5.8).

As you can see, the result in the out-of-sample area (Test Set) is now positive and much better than in the test above with the optimised parameters from the short training range. A closer look at the trading figures confirms this observation (table 5.2). You now get a total net profit of $16,757 in the test range and a good average trade net profit of nearly $600. Please note that the average monthly return within the test range is $591, which is even higher than the average monthly return of the long test data range of $321. However the risk of this trading system is still quite high, with a maximum drawdown of $16,939. This is nearly as much as the total net profit earned in the test period. We can summarise that the result of this out-of-sample test for the Bollinger Band system with the longer training period is much better than the one which had the shorter training period.

Figure 5.7: British pound/US dollar, 03/03/1986–4/7/2008. The Bollinger Band trading system is now optimised within the long training data range 1986–2006. Afterwards the results of this trading system are checked in the test data range (green). See the shorter training range 2002–2006 which was used above.

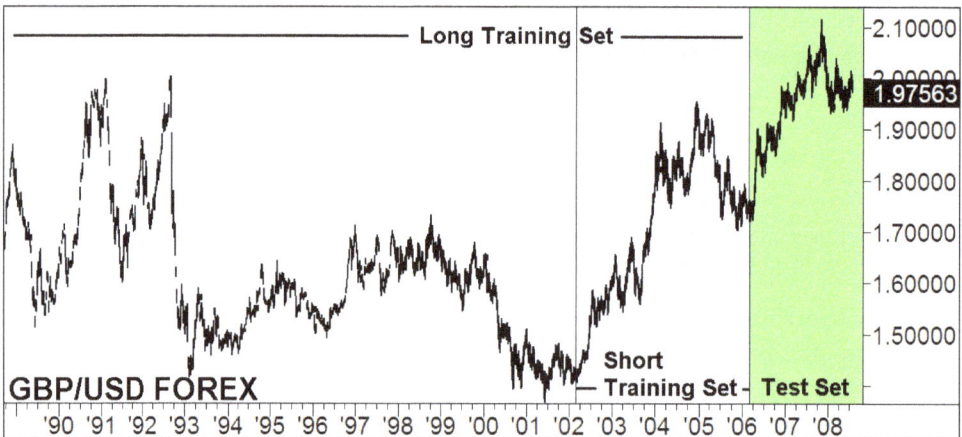

Figure 5.8: Bollinger Band system for British pound/US dollar (FOREX), daily, training and test period. All six input parameters are now optimised for maximum total net profit within a longer training period of 20 years: 03/03/1986–28/2/2006. Test period is kept the same, from 1/3/2006–4/7/2008. A: detailed equity curve; B: underwater equity curve showing all drawdowns.

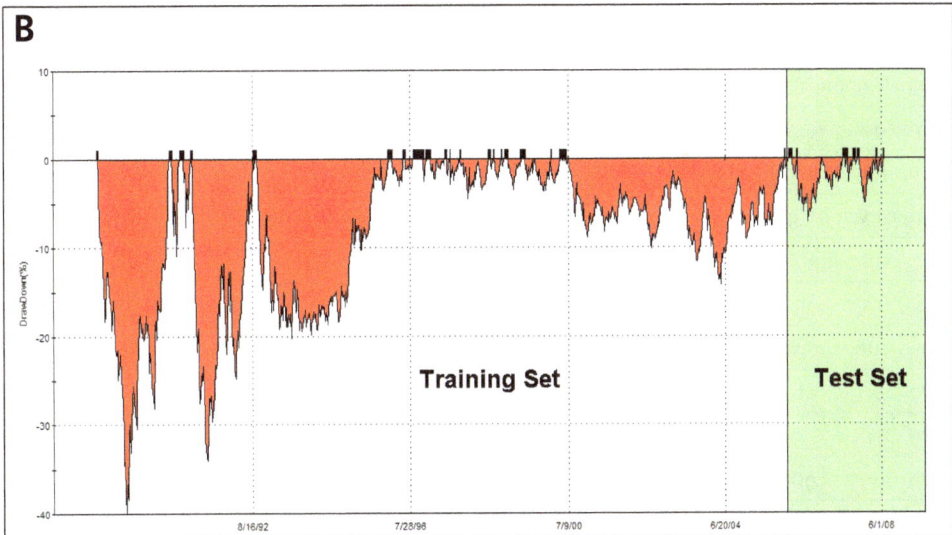

Table 5.2: Bollinger Band system for British pound/US dollar (FOREX), daily, training vs. test period. All six input parameters are now optimised for maximum total net profit within a longer training period of 20 years: 03/03/1986–28/2/2006. Test period is kept the same, from 1/3/2006–4/7/2008.

	TRAIN	TEST
Test Period from	03/03/1986	01/03/2006
until	28/02/2006	04/07/2008
Total Net Profit	$175,737.50	$16,757.00
Gross Profit	$367,121.50	$44,964.00
Gross Loss	($191,384.00)	($28,207.00)
Profit Factor	1.92	1.59
Total Number of Trades	149	28
Total Number of Long Trades	74	14
Total Number of Short Trades	75	14
Percent Profitable	63.76%	64.29%
Winning Trades	95	18
Losing Trades	52	10
Even Trades	2	0
Avg. Trade Net Profit	$1,179.45	$598.46
Avg. Winning Trade	$3,864.44	$2,498.00
Avg. Losing Trade	($3,680.46)	($2,820.70)
Ratio Avg. Win: Avg. Loss	1.05	0.89
Largest Winning Trade	$27,750.00	$5,578.00
Largest Losing Trade	($20,050.00)	($8,132.00)
Max. Consecutive Winning Trades	8	5
Max. Consecutive Losing Trades	5	3
Avg. Bars in Total Trades	34.8	22.61
Avg. Bars in Winning Trades	29.67	22.56
Avg. Bars in Losing Trades	45.42	22.7
Annual Rate of Return	5.12%	6.59%
Avg. Monthly Return	$321.61	$591.59
Std. Deviation of Monthly Return	$4,363.12	$2,723.27
Return Retracement Ratio	0.09	0.35
RINA Index	28.23	5.86
Sharpe Ratio	0.1	n/a

	TRAIN	TEST
K-Ratio	3.3	2.12
Trading Period	19 Yrs, 11 Mths, 27 Dys	2 Yrs, 4 Mths, 4 Dys
Percent of Time in the Market	99.96%	99.42%
Time in the Market	19 Yrs, 11 Mths, 24 Dys	2 Yrs, 4 Mths, 1 Dy
Longest Flat Period	n/a	n/a

	TRAIN	TEST
Max. Equity Run-up	$187,179.50	$29,301.00
Date of Max. Equity Run-up	28/02/2006	16/11/2007
Max. Equity Run-up as % of Initial Capital	187.18%	29.30%

	TRAIN	TEST
Max. Drawdown (Intraday Peak to Valley)		
Value	($39,750.00)	($16,939.00)
Date of Max. Drawdown	02/07/1991	08/08/2006

Conclusion: How to choose your training data

The results of our trading system during the test period are more similar to the results of the longer training period of 1986–2006 than the results of the shorter training period from 2002–2006. Although you cannot see this from the chart of the GBP/USD itself, the market data has a different behaviour during the different years of the test. This behaviour manifests itself in volatility, in trend duration, in a different frequency of breakouts or patterns etc., which affects the *best* parameters of the Bollinger Band system in the different training periods.

The conclusion is that it's advisable to make the training period as long as possible. Since a longer period contains much more data, there is a higher probability that within this longer data range there are some periods which behave similarly to your test data range and therefore train your system better. The longer you make the training period for your trading system the better your chances for similar results in the out-of-sample tests and later in real trading. On the other hand, keep in mind that this rule is only valid if your market data contains a lot of different market phases. If you choose a market which is always in an upward trend (like the Long Gilt from 1980–2000) you can train on it any trading system with a long-entry bias but it will be of no use when the market changes its bullish behaviour. If you are aware of this however, and you are careful in choosing the right training data, you can avoid having to adapt your trading system to such market biases.

5.4 Optimisation and over-fitting

Step-by-step optimisation of the LUXOR system

We now switch back to our trading system LUXOR which we presented in chapter 3. When optimising a trading system the first point you must be sure of is that the trading logic is based on an idea which is concrete and profitable. For the trading system LUXOR we have already shown that the logic seems to be sound and profitable and additionally we have performed some stability tests with it. We now take this system and perform a step-by-step optimisation of its six input parameters. First we optimise the slow moving average, second the fast moving average, then the time window filter before we finally optimise the three applied exits one after another: risk stop loss, trailing stop and profit target (fig. 5.9).

Figure 5.9: Step-by-step optimisation of the six input parameters of the LUXOR system. 1. Slow moving average, 2. Fast moving average, 3. Time window filter, 4. Risk stop loss, 5. Trailing stop, 6. Profit target. Chart example from British pound/US dollar, 30 minute, FOREX from 26 December 2007.

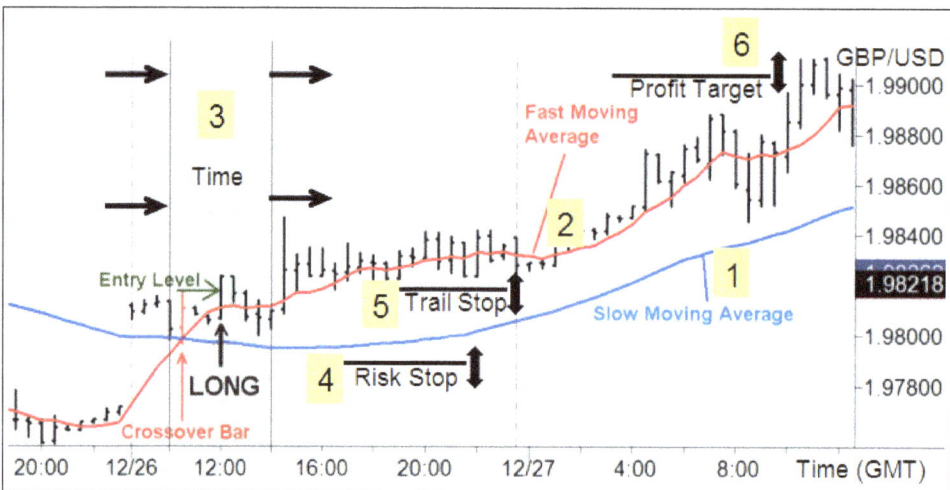

To perform our tests we again use British pound/US dollar FOREX data but we return to the intraday 30 minute timescale. On this timescale we have nearly six years of intraday data available, from 21/10/2002–4/7/2008. From the above discussion of market data bias you know that it's advisable to use as much data for the training period as possible. However, you must still have a big enough amount of data left for testing your strategy out-of-sample. As a compromise we use the period from 21/10/2002–28/02/2007 for training/optimisation and afterwards we check how the optimised system performs within the subsequent test period of more than one year from 1/3/2007–4/7/2008.

Results depending on the number of optimised parameters

If you look at the equity lines during the training periods you can see that they improve more and more with the optimised parameters. Starting from a directionless equity line when no parameters are optimised the equity curve becomes more enticing as more input parameters of the trading system are optimised. This is not surprising since the system better adapts to the training market data the more degrees of freedom it has. Now the main question is how the trading system behaves within the test data area, depending on the number of optimised parameters. When no optimisation took place (i.e., the system operated with a slow moving average based on 30 bars and a fast moving average of 10 bars, no time filter and exits in place) the result within the test data is negative (fig. 5.10A).

If you now optimise the first parameter (slow moving average set to 40) for total net profit in the training range the system result is much improved in the training region, however the equity curve of this optimised system improves only slightly in the test data range (fig. 5.10B). If you look at the trading figures (table 5.3) you can see this result confirmed.

Table 5.3: System figures for training and test area after optimisation for total net profit of one parameter after another. The optimised values are different from the gained values in chapter 3 since the optimisation period is shorter now, not the complete data range as before.

Tested symbol:GBPUSD 30 min	TRAIN REGION: 21/10/2002–28/2/2007						
Parameter number	0	1	2	3	4	5	6
Additional optimised values	no	slow moving average=40	fast moving average=2	time window: 9:30a.m.-1:30 p.m GMT	Risk stop loss: 0.47%	trailing stop: 0.67%,	profit target: 2.25%
Total Net Profit	$17,961	$58,018	$58,449	$67,921	$80,827	$84,352	$90,240
Avg. Trade Net Profit	$12	$51	$33	$118	$127	$125	$133
Max. Drawdown (Intraday Peak to Valley)	($18,032)	($27,644)	($14,122)	($17,884)	($12,693)	($12,199)	($12,108)
	TEST REGION: 1/3/2007-4/7/2008						
Parameter number	0	1	2	3	4	5	6
Additional optimised values	no	slow moving average=40	fast moving average=2	time window: 9:30a.m.– 1:30 p.m GMT	Risk stop loss: 0.47%	trailing stop: 0.67%,	profit target: 2.25%
Total Net Profit	($12,569)	($9,736)	$18,038	$37,324	$25,062	$25,875	$25,464
Avg. Trade Net Profit	($27)	($26)	$34	$200	$126	$124	$122
Max. Drawdown (Intraday Peak to Valley)	($16,820)	($17,613)	($8,089)	($10,097)	($8,448)	($9,970)	($9,970)

For example, the total net profit within the test data range improves only from -$12,569 to -$9,736 and the average trade from -$27 to -$26 after optimisation of the first parameter. This means practically no change. If you optimise the second important parameter for the trading system's entry, the fast-moving average (to a value of 2), then you can see a further improvement within the training set. But now the improvement within the test data range is even bigger than for the training area. This is underlined with the system figures, e.g. the average trade within the test region improves from -$26 to a positive value of $34. This is even better than the value within the training region ($33).

If you now insert a third parameter into the trading system and optimise it (to a value of 9.30am–1.30pm) a dramatic change occurs. The system's results improve greatly within both the training region and the testing region. Please note, however, that the result in the test region improves more than in the training region. For example, the average profit per trade becomes $200 in the testing period against $118 in the training period. We can summarise that for the first three input parameters every optimisation of the trading system within the training period also leads to an improvement in the testing period. Sometimes the improvement in the testing period is smaller (like with parameter 1: slow moving average), sometimes it is even bigger than in the training period (like with parameter 2 and 3: fast moving average and time filter). If you now continue the optimisation of the trading system within the training period by adding suitable exits you get some really interesting findings.

Adding more optimised parameters in the training period can improve results in that area, but these additional parameters will not improve results in the testing period any more.

This out-of-sample deterioration cannot be seen directly from the equity curves (figs. 5.10C–5.10G). All equity lines keep steadily growing within the test regions with every added optimised system parameter, and drawdowns stay low. However, if you have a closer look at the system's report you see that in fact some hidden worsening takes place in the trading system (table 5.3). The average profit per trade decreases from $200 to $126 after the optimised risk stop loss is inserted and stays in the area between $120 and $125 after inserting the next exits, trailing stop and profit target. There is similar behaviour for the maximum intraday drawdown. While the inserted risk stop loss reduces the drawdown from $10,097 to $8,448, the additional exits increase the drawdown again to nearly $10,000.

Figures 5.10 A–G: System LUXOR for British pound/US dollar (FOREX) training and test period. Training period 21/10/2002–28/2/2007 (white), test period 1/3/2007–4/7/2008 (green). One input parameter is optimised after another. A: no optimisation. B: slow moving average: optimised value = 40. C: fast moving average: optimised value = 2. D: time window: optimised setting 9.30am–1.30pm GMT. E: risk stop loss: optimised setting = 0.47% F: trailing stop: optimised setting = 0.67%. G: profit target: optimised setting = 2.25%. The optimised values are different from the gained values in chapter 3 since the optimisation period is shorter now, not the complete data range as before.

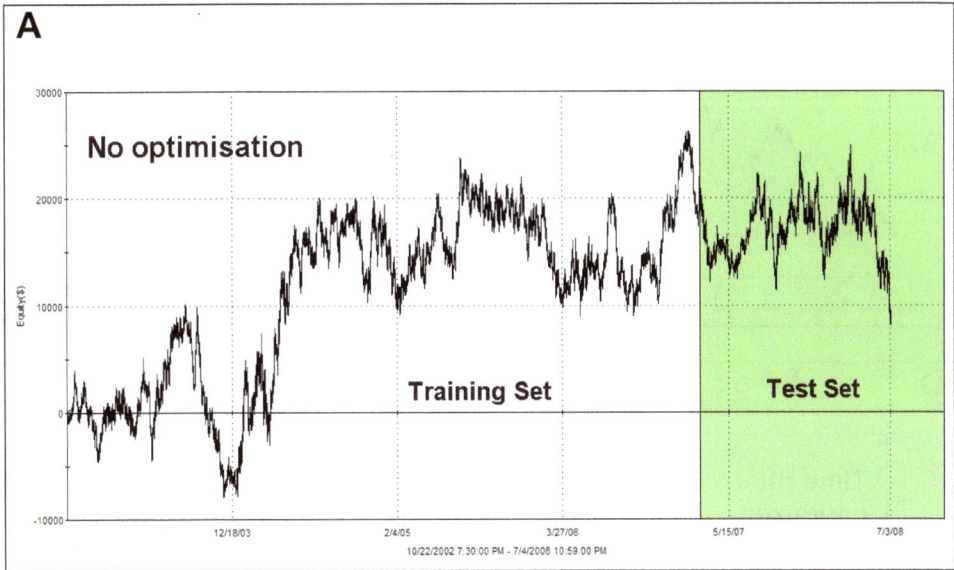

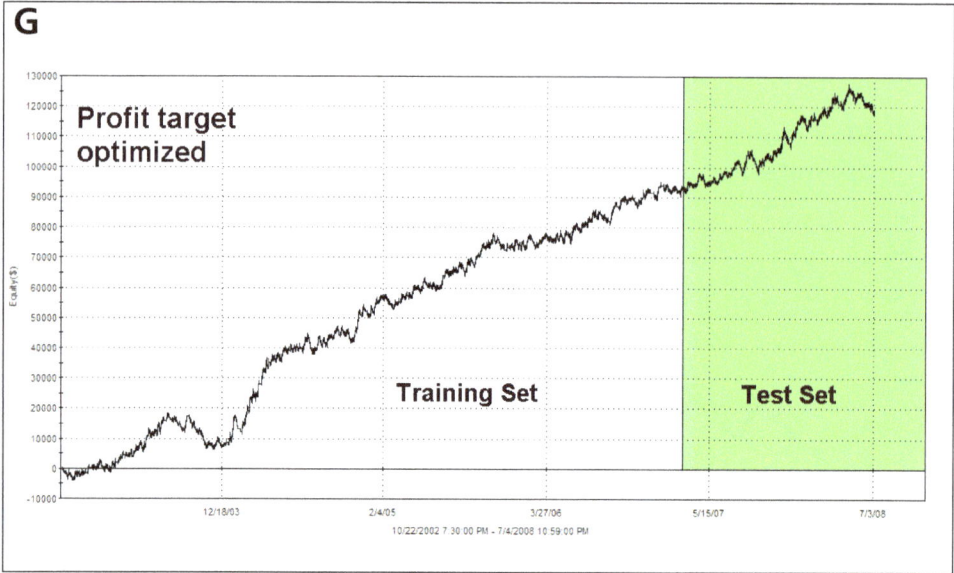

The behaviour of the trading system within the different stages of optimisation for training and test area can be seen best when you plot trading system figures against number of optimised input parameters. If you do this for the total net profit you get a good insight of what happens during the different stages of system optimisation (fig. 5.11). The figure reveals how the total net profit within the training range (blue line) steadily increases with every added optimisation parameter, whereas the performance within the test range (green line) changes with increasing system complexity. With only a few parameters being optimised the net profit in the test range increases with every additional parameter, reaching its high with the third parameter (time window filter) and then being reduced with the fourth optimised parameter (risk stop loss). It then cannot be made bigger again with further optimised parameters.

Figure 5.11: Finding an optimal rule complexity for system LUXOR for British pound/US dollar (FOREX) training and test period. The system's input parameters are optimised for maximum total net profit, from left to right, one after another, within the training period 21/10/2002–28/2/2007 (blue line = training results). Then results are checked in test data range 1/3/2007–4/7/2008 (green line = test results).

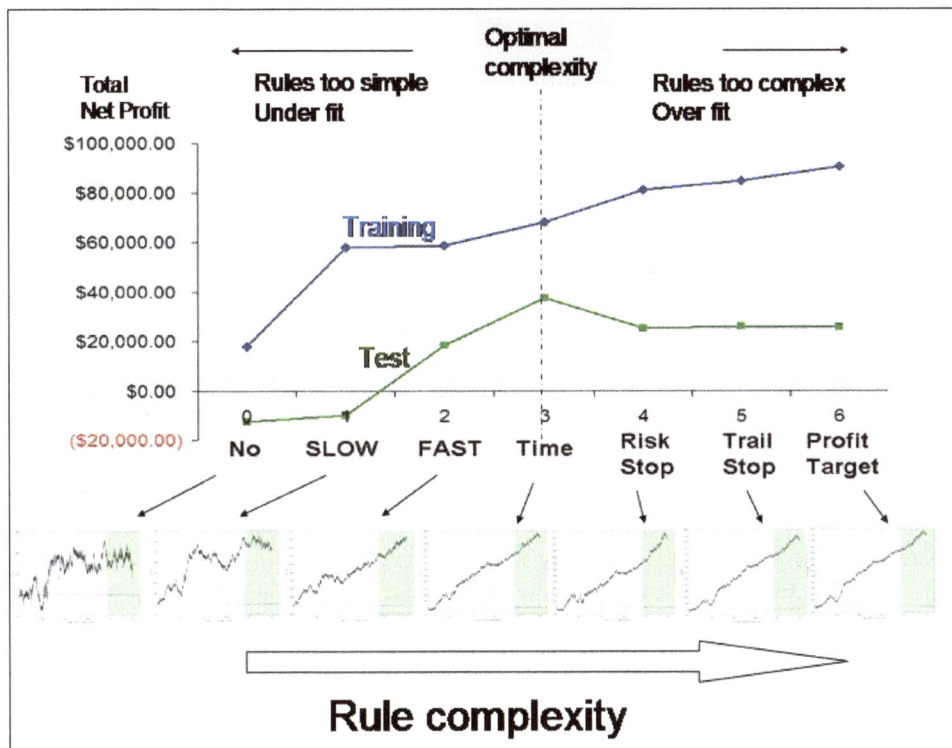

The meaning of the trading system's complexity

How can you now interpret this behaviour of the trading system?

Let's start within the diagram (fig. 5.11) from the left side when no system parameter is optimised. There the trading system has a low complexity, since the applied rules are quite simple and not optimised at all. If you start to optimise the first parameter the system's performance changes markedly. The raw and simple trading logic used so far can easily be made better. Interestingly when not many optimised parameters have been introduced the behaviour within the test range sometimes changes more than within the training range. The change can be much worse, but it can be better than the improvement that takes place in the training range. The reason for this behaviour is that a system that has only been optimised a little reacts sensitively to parameter changes because there are not many parameters in place yet. The rule complexity and the predictability for your test set is low.

Furthermore, keep in mind that much of what happens in different market phases and areas is accidental and also depends on the market sample bias. It can be that the out-of-sample data period is more friendly to our trading system logic in a certain stage than the training data period. With further parameters being optimised or added the changes in the system's reaction become smaller but still performance improves in the out-of-sample test data range. With the first three parameters being optimised our trading system reaches an important point: it reaches its optimal complexity.

From this point on every further optimised parameter (risk stop, trailing stop, profit target) decreases the system's performance in the test region although the results still improve in the training region. You now have the situation of curve over-fitting. Every new optimised parameter improves the fit of the system to the training area but what happens here is more an adjustment to the existing market noise than an improvement in predictive capability. Thus the net profit within the test region does not become bigger with further optimised parameters but instead it decreases from the fourth parameter onwards. You now again have an out-of-sample deterioration.

It should be remembered that although the results in the out-of-sample area cannot be improved any more with these exits, they still have an important function. As discussed in chapter 3.5 when talking about risk management, every stop loss leads to a better control of risk. We see the valuable function of the stops when we look at the largest losing trades which take place in the testing region – the added stop losses decrease this figure drastically from $2,631 to $1,023 (not shown in table 5.3). Another figure which improves with inserted exits is the time the system stays in the market, which goes down from 100% to about 80%. With exits in place the outcome of trades is more predictable and this helps you to include the trading system into a bigger portfolio and to apply position sizing methods.

5.5 Rule complexity explained with polynomial curve fitting

Interpolating data points with polynomial functions

You have just seen how a trading system's predictive power for the future changes with the number of rules which are involved in the strategy. In our system these rules have been the fast and slow moving average, the highly effective intraday time filter and finally the three exits we added. You have seen that a simpler trading system has more predictive power than a more optimised one. We can state that this result was not just gained by accident but it is well founded on statistical rules. We will explain these rules now with a short discussion on interpolating data points with polynomial functions.

Let's assume that you have ten data points as your sample data (fig. 5.12).

Figure 5.12: Ten points of sample data, generated with a sine function and random distances from it. Curve generated with MATLAB.

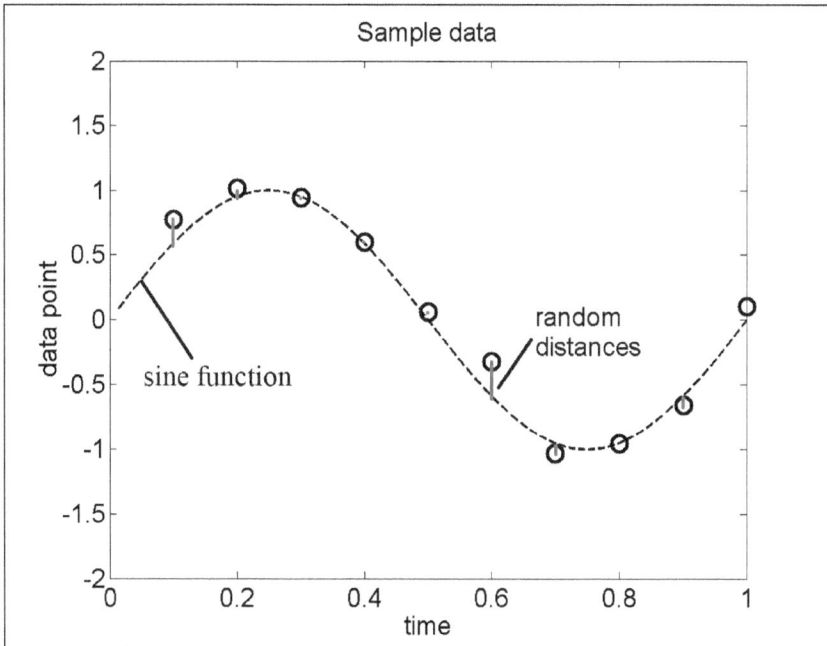

In our case the ten points were not chosen randomly but with a combination of a rule and random behaviour. We took a sine function which is a normal oscillation and placed the ten points around the sine function with randomly taken distances. Here these are just mathematical points but as a trader you can imagine that these values could also be the prices of any financial markets, for example values of a tick chart of the FTSE 100 future or any stock you like. Thus our data point simulation is an approximation for financial markets in the way that you assume that the markets have a certain order or direction (at least during special times or events) but that around this order you have lots of random behaviour and market noise.

To interpolate these ten data points as well as possible you can use mathematic polynomial functions with different complexity. The higher the order of the polynom, the greater its complexity becomes. The easiest polynomial function (degree = 0) is a constant (fig. 5.13).

Figure 5.13: Approximation of the ten data points with a polynomial function of degree = 0, a constant with value = 0. Curve generated with MATLAB.

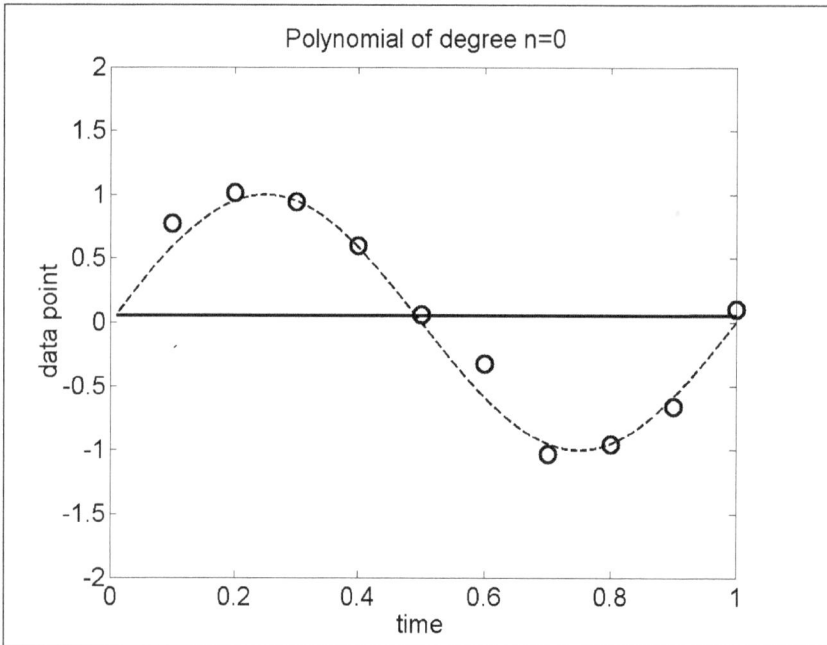

You see that this horizontal function touches some data points, but other points are a long way from it. The next higher complexity level is to interpolate the 10 data points with a linear function, which is a polynomial of degree 1 (fig. 5.14). In the picture of a trading system this line could be a simple trend line. Since the results of the constant and the linear function are rather poor fits to the 10 data points, we have to increase the adaptive function's complexity. The second order polynomial seems to give a quite good fit to the data points (fig. 5.15). This curve reaches more data points and comes quite close to all points, although not all are reached exactly. If we increase the degree of the polynomial function to 3, we already have a very nice fit to the data points and when we go to a much higher order of polynomial (degree = 9) we obtain a 100% fit to the training data (figs. 5.16 and 5.17). The polynomial of degree 9 passes exactly through each data point.

Figure 5.14: Approximation of the ten data points with a polynomial function of degree = 1, a linear function. Curve generated with MATLAB.

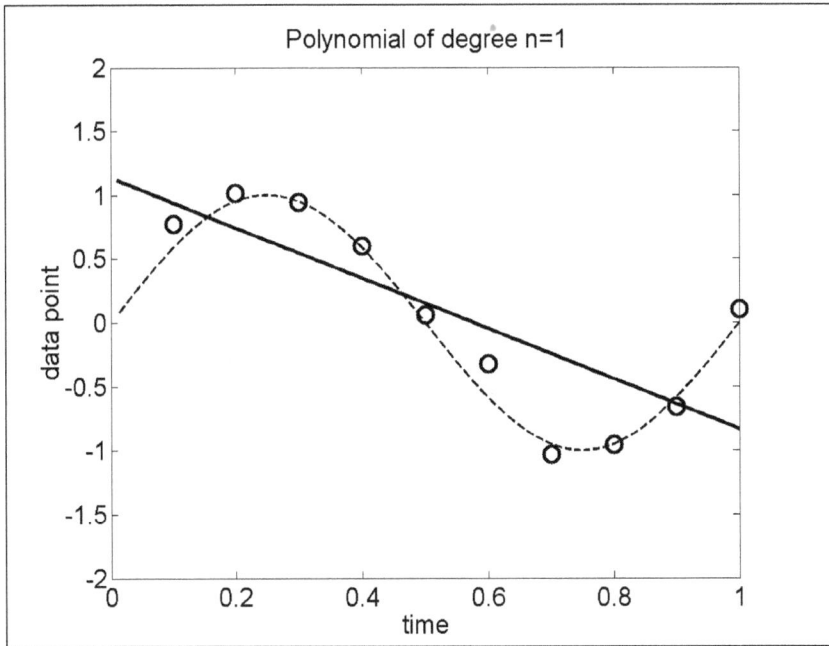

Figure 5.15: Approximation of the ten data points with a polynomial function of degree = 2, a parabolic function. Curve generated with MATLAB.

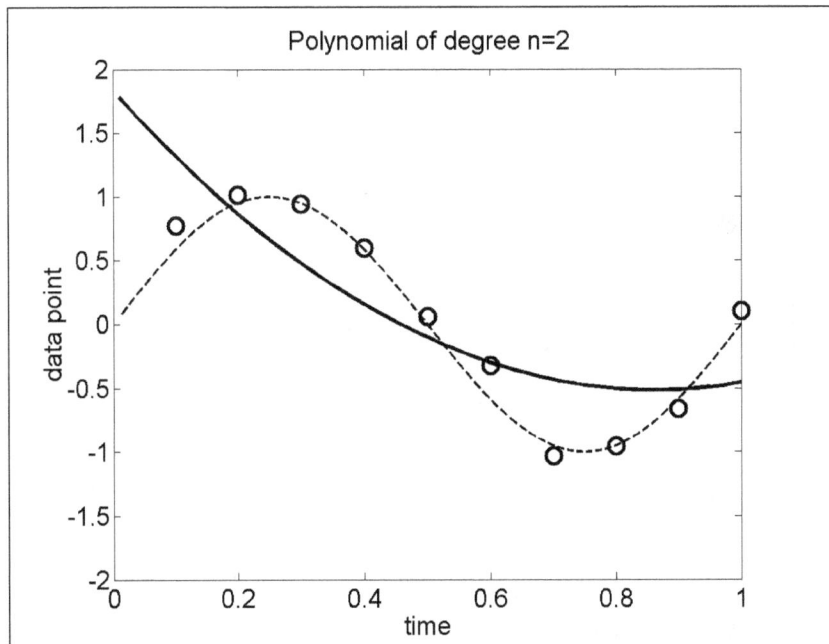

Figure 5.16: Approximation of the ten data points with a polynomial function of degree = 3. The fitness to the data points increases but also the complexity of the function. Curve generated with MATLAB.

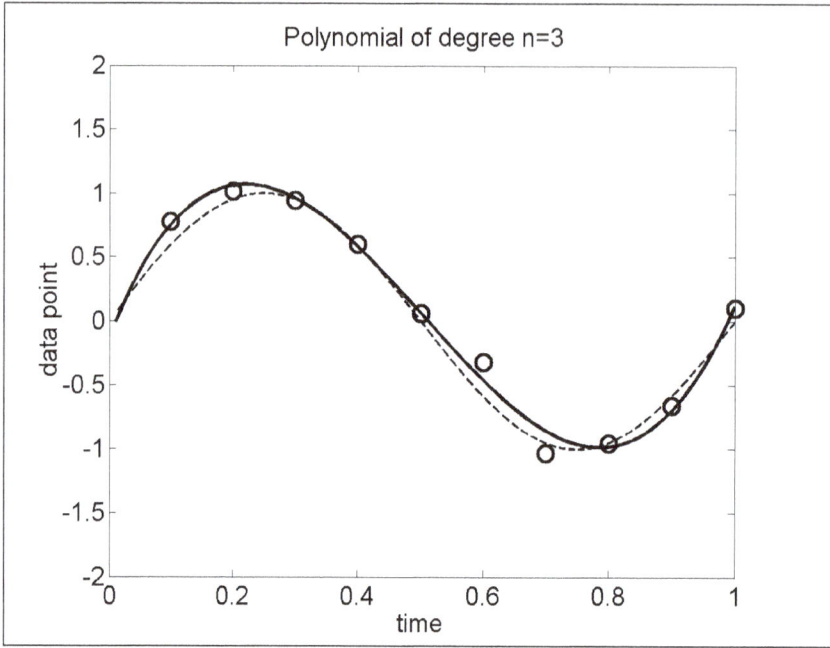

Figure 5.17: Approximation of the ten data points with a complex polynomial function of degree = 9. Curve generated with MATLAB.

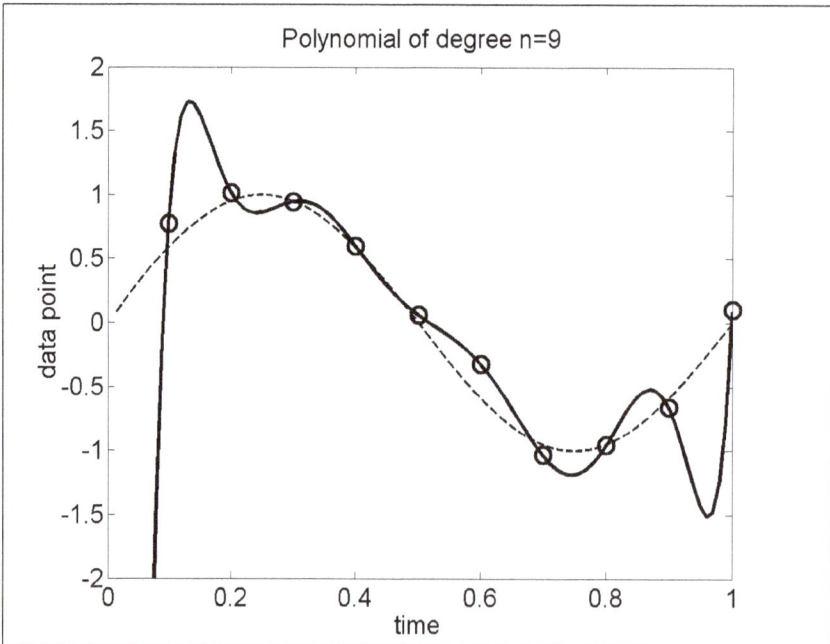

You can also plot the results of these graphs in a table (table 5.4). There you see how the average error of the fitness function becomes smaller with a higher degree of polynomial. Whereas the polynomial of degree 0 has a big standard deviation from the ten data points (5.39), the 9th degree polynomial nearly reaches the points without any error (0.0003).

Table 5.4: Average error of fit to data points (standard deviation) as a function of the degree of the polynomial. The higher the degree of the polynomial, the better its fit to the data points, but the higher its rule complexity becomes.

Degree of Polynomial	Average error of fit to data points (standard deviation)
0	5.3932
1	2.1863
2	1.6583
3	0.057
4	0.0555
5	0.046
6	0.0407
7	0.0407
8	0.0256
9	0.0003

If you have a closer look at the result of the 9th degree polynomial fit, you can see that the fitted curve oscillates wildly and gives a poor representation of the chosen sine function with the data points randomly around it. This 9th degree polynomial could stand for a very complex trading system with many components added until you have got a perfect fit of the trading logic to your market data.

But what are the conclusions which you can draw from these fitness functions and what is the predictive power of the different polynomials for the future?

Predictive power of the different polynomials

Let's see what happens if we add further data points by letting the sine function continue into the future (fig. 5.18). You can see that the polynomial of degree 0 continues to go sideways with the sine function. Thus this simple function has quite a poor the predictive power the future , but it is worth mentioning that it stays exactly the same as the result of the back-test of the ten data points.

Figure 5.18: Predictive capability of the polynomial of degree = 0 for unseen test data. Curve generated with MATLAB.

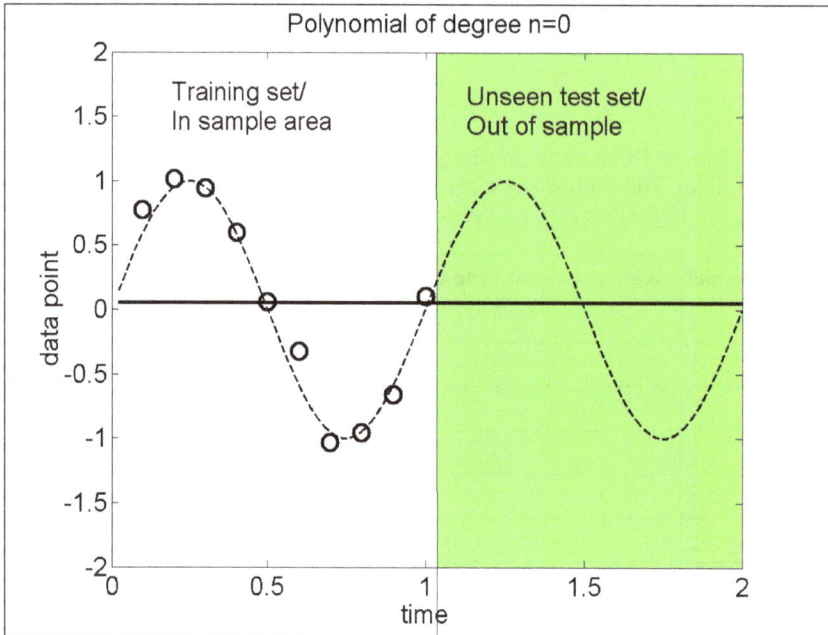

Figure 5.19: Predictive capability of the polynomial of degree = 9 for unseen test data. Curve generated with MATLAB.

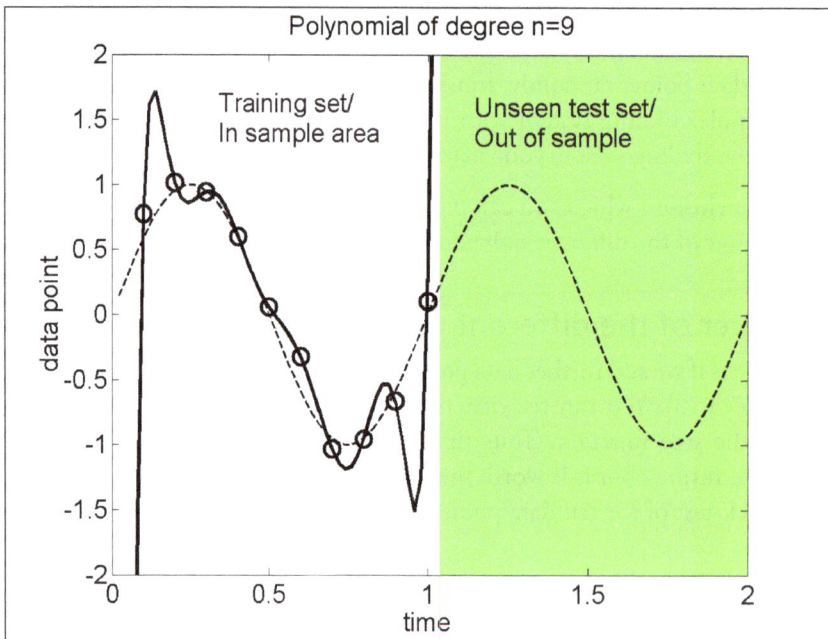

In contrast to this simple approximation of the training data set, let's have a look at the the polynomial of degree 9 (fig. 5.19). Obviously this complex polynomial (or trading system) does not have any predictive power for the future! The well curve fitted complex function misses the new points completely.

You might expect the best solution somewhere in between these two extremes. But this is not true. In fact no polynom of degree higher than 0 is a good approximation for the data points which are placed near a sine curve. All polynoms (even with degree 1) grow quickly away from the horizontal line around which the sine function oscillates. Thus all polynoms, except the polynom of degree 0, are useless for making predictions! Although the polynom of degree 0 is poor it is the only robust one.

What is the way out of this situation? Does it mean that you must stop trading system development completely and look at the trend of the markets with simple lines?

Conclusions for trading system development

What you have seen in this example is that markets cannot be approached with pure mathematical methods. But this does not mean that all trading systems must be of zero complexity.

Our mistake here was that we tried to approach a periodic sine function with a non-periodic polynomial function. In this way, we forced our algorithm to adapt to a situation for which it is not built. The polynomial function was not suited to the function we were trying to use it for because it is not the correct approximation for a periodic environment. The idea of periodicity was missing. The conclusion for you as a system developer and trader is that you must first have an idea of the market! Only when you have this can you start to code your idea and only like this will you get a code that makes sense.

Just as it is useless to approach periodic functions with polynomials, it is useless to approach trendless markets with trend-following methods or to approach markets with no volatility with break-out systems. We know that this leads into further conflicts since markets are steadily changing, but using ideas and experience is the best approach you can take.

Further consequences of these tests are that once you have a simple, robust logic with a proper risk management in place, you can stop your system development process. It is often better to use just one or two indicators, or only the price itself, rather than several combined indicators. Adding more and more rules will just increase the adaptation of your trading system to past market data, but it will not increase its predictive power for real trading. Therefore it is better to save your time and invest it otherwise, for example in adding a money management scheme or by diversifying your strategy with further simple but robust systems within a portfolio.

5.6 Example of a simple, robust trading system

As the last chapters show, the more parameters a trading system has, the less robust it is.

In this chapter we present the opposite of a curve-fitted system: an example of a system which consists only of a few parameters. And with these few parameters it is quite stable – over decades and in various different markets.

Since this strategy is so simple and robust, you will find it well documented in the literature in several books, e.g. the one from Jay Kaepell, *Seasonal Stock Market Trends*, from 2009 [25].

Besides being simple, this system is based on a coherent idea. As just pointed out in the last chapter, this is the most important requirement for a trading system, to give it a higher chance to maintain its back-tested returns in real application in the future.

Here comes first the idea and then following is an example of a possible implementation with trading rules.

Idea

The beginning-of-month (BOM) effect refers to a phenomenon that says that prices rise more on the first few days of the new month than on the other days of the month. For example, in the S&P 500 from 1928–2018, you can see the average return achieved on each different day of the month (fig. 5.20).

Figure 5.20: Average profit in percent on different days of the month, S&P 500 index from 1/1/1928–31/12/2018. At the beginning of each month the profits are high – the sum of the first four trading days is about 4%. On the other side the rest of the month from day 5 to 30, the profits add up to zero. Chart created with Excel.

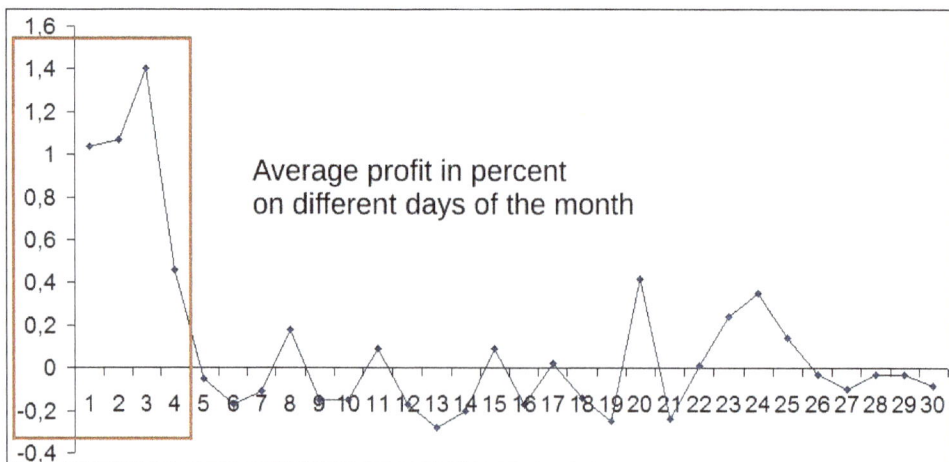

The chart shows that each of the first four days on average is profitable. On these four days every day brings on average about 0.5–1.5% return, whereas the rest of the month the average sum of the returns is about zero. So according to this evaluation, nearly all performance in the S&P 500 stock market can be gained just on the first four days each month – together about 4% each month on average.

Reasons for the BOM effect could, for example, be an increased cash flow at the end of the month, since salaries, pensions, etc., will then become due. However, with private individuals barely sustaining the market, the reasons are more likely to be those of large investors seeking to improve their balance sheets by switching funds or selling sub-funds. This is also called *window dressing*. Whatever the final reason could be, the effect is there and can be exploited with the following simple trading approach.

Trading rules

- Entry: Buy a stock market index every last trading day of each month on close.

- To avoid bear markets: do not enter when the market (on the month end) closes below the 40-day moving average.

- Exit: 1. Stop Loss: exit when the market drops below the 40-day moving average, exit on close of any day.

- Exit: 2. Time exit: Exit at the end of the fourth trading day, on the close of this day.

Some example signals within a daily chart of the S&P 500 index are displayed in figure 5.21 A and B.

Figure 5.21: Implementation of the beginning of month system with two different software platforms. A: chart created with TradeStation 9.1, data from TradeStation. B: chart created with AmiBroker, data from Norgate.

Displayed is the S&P 500 index end of 2017, beginning of 2018. Entry: each last day of the month on close. Exit: A simple moving average (green) acts as exit and as filter for entries. Second exit: time based, four days after entry, always on market closing price of the day.

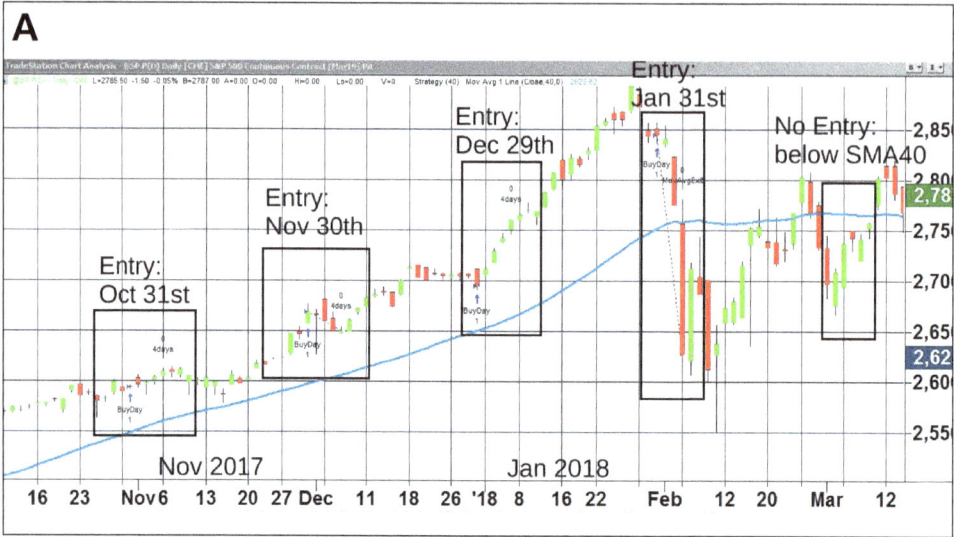

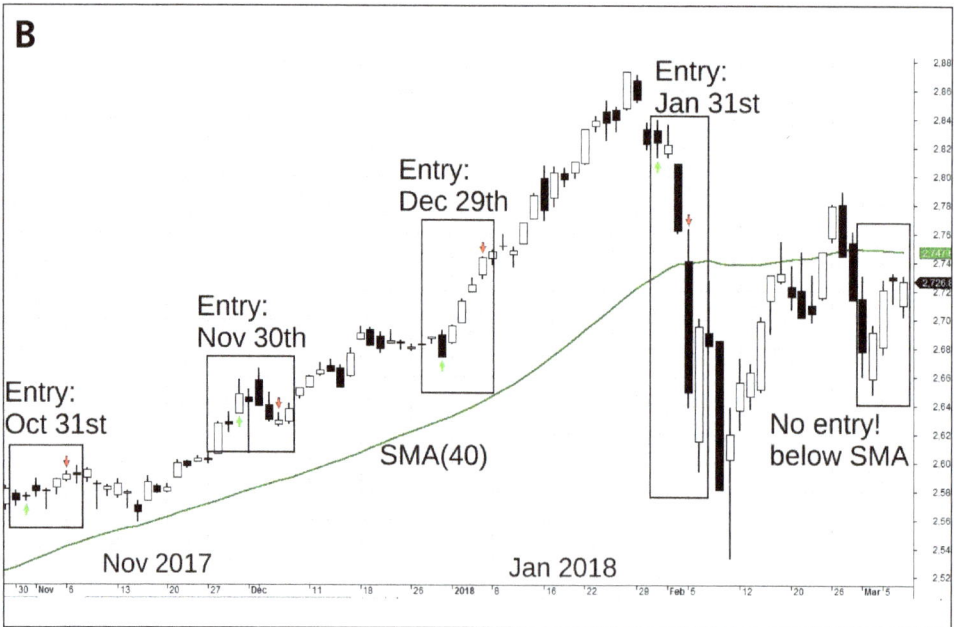

As you can see from the above figures, which show the trading logic, there is a simple moving average in place. This moving average has two functions: on the one hand it should prevent an entry in a bearish market phase and on the other hand it should act as a stop loss on an end-of-day basis.

The following figures 5.22 A and B and table 5.5 show the result which you get in Tradestation (9.1) when you apply this simple trading logic to end-of-day data of the S&P 500 Index (here symbol: @SP.P, means S&P 500 Pit data), including $40 slippage and commissions per round turn. The code of this system, for your own experiments, can be found in Appendix 4 and 5.

Figure 5.22: Beginning of Month System (BOM), applied to the S&P 500 Index with Tradestation 9.1, including $40 slippage and commissions per round turn. A: equity curve. B: underwater equity curve, showing the maximum drawdowns.

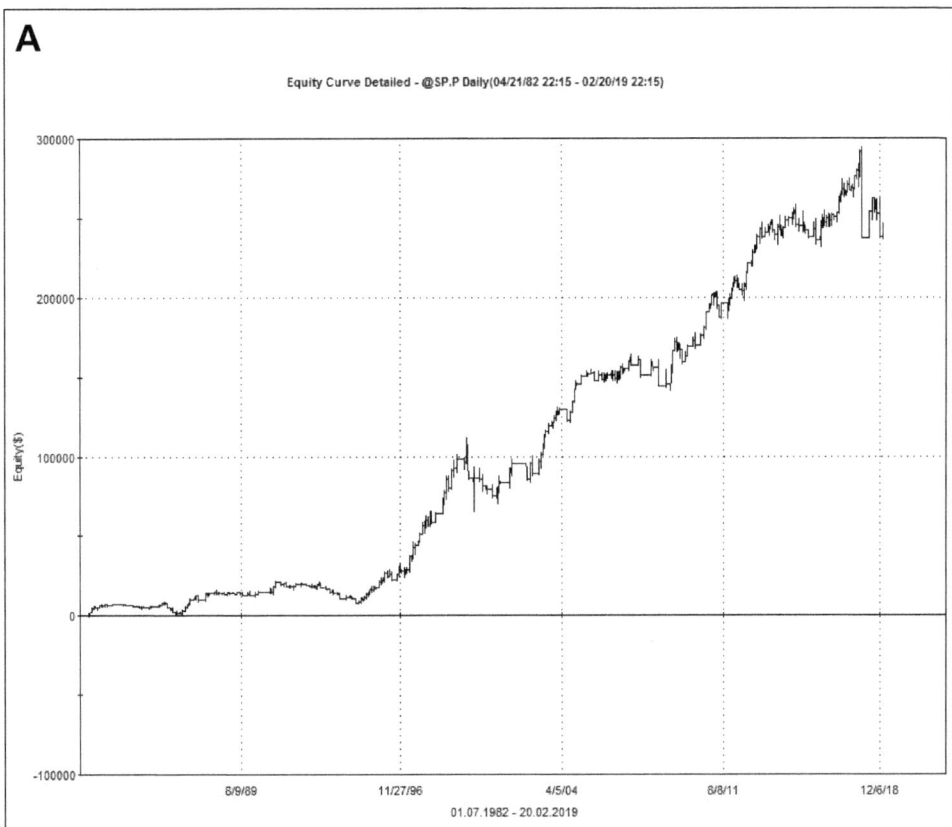

Figures and data from TradeStation.

B

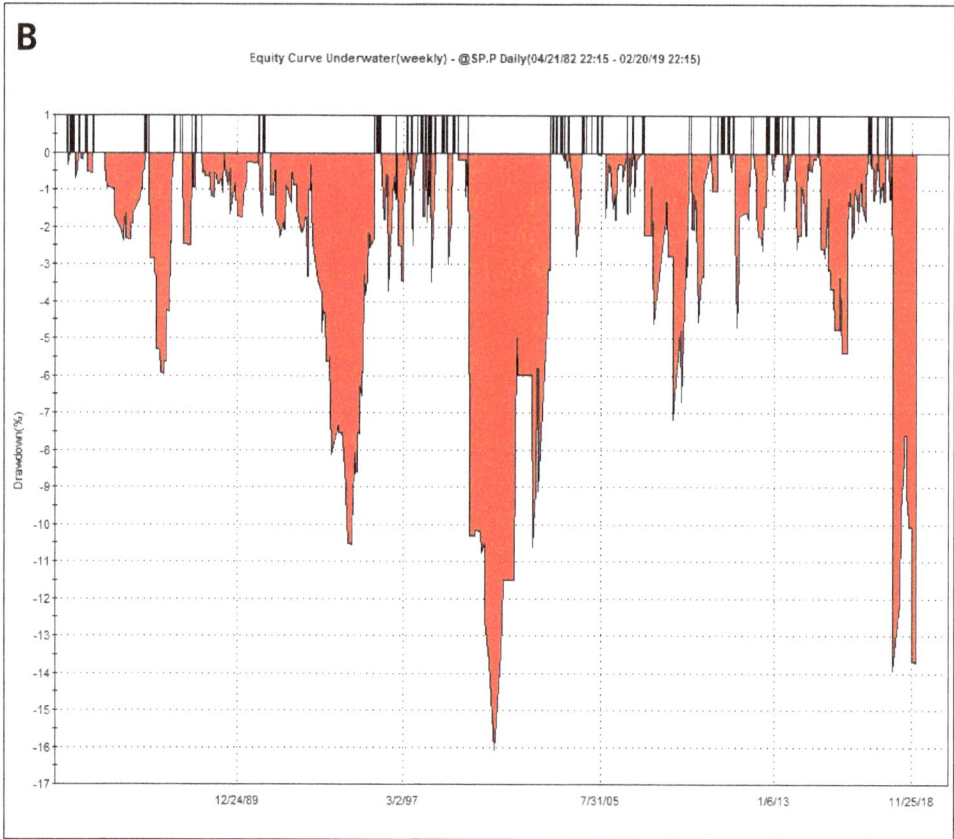

Equity Curve Underwater(weekly) - @SP.P Daily(04/21/82 22:15 - 02/20/19 22:15)

Table 5.5: System figures (TradeStation performance summary). Beginning of Month System (BOM), applied to the S&P 500 Index, including $40 slippage and commissions per round turn

All Trades			
Total Net Profit	$244,477.50	Profit Factor	1.70
Gross Profit	$595,087.50	Gross Loss	($350,610.00)
Total Number of Trades	269	Percent Profitable	61.34%
Winning Trades	165	Losing Trades	104
Avg. Trade Net Profit	$908.84	Ratio Avg. Win/Avg. Loss	1.07
Avg. Winning Trade	$3,606.59	Avg. Losing Trade	($3,371.25)
Largest Winning Trade	$16,635.00	Largest Losing Trade	($54,565.00)
Max. Consecutive Winning Trades	8	Max. Consecutive Losing Trades	5
Avg. Bars in Winning Trades	5.00	Avg. Bars in Losing Trades	4.31
Avg. Bars in Total Trades	4.70		
Max. Shares/Contracts held	1	Account Size Required	$54,565.00
Return on Initial Capital	244.48%	Annual Rate of Return	3.38%
Return Retracement Ratio	0.06	RINA Index	721.64
Trading Period	36 yrs, 7 Mths, 20 Dys	Percent of Time in the Market	11.42%
Max. Equity Run-up	$295,170.00		
Max. Drawdown		**Max. Drawdown**	
(Intraday Peak to Valley)	($58,065.00)	**(Trade Close to Trade Close)**	($54,565.00)
Net Profit as % of Drawdown	421.04%	Net Profit as % of Drawdown	448.05%
Max. Trade Drawdown	($54,525.00)		

As you can see, this primitive system seems to be profitable. We don't want to go into the details of this test now however – since various evaluations will follow.

From now on we switch our analysis software from TradeStation to AmiBroker. Of course you could do the same, following tests as well with Multicharts, TradeStation, WealthLab or any other platform.

We switch to AmiBroker because of the possibility of a better datafeed. AmiBroker allows easy importing of data from various data vendors. In the following we use Norgate Data (norgatedata.com).

The Norgate end-of-day datafeed is quite impressive. It provides high-quality data with long histories – for the Dow Jones Industrial Average the data goes back to 1896 and for the S&P 500 index back to 1928! But also in many other stock indices, especially in the European and Asian markets, their data rows are long and clean.

Furthermore, Norgate Data is one of the few data vendors in the world who can supply data as a basis for system tests that are free of survivorship bias, which will become important later in this book in chapter 9 when we develop systems on portfolios of stocks.

Optimisation of the main parameter of the system

We stay with the S&P 500 index, but now we have data that starts in the year 1928.

Let's perform an optimisation of one parameter of the BOM system on this index (fig. 5.23).

Figure 5.23: CAR/MDD (Compound annual return/Maximum system drawdown) of the BOM System as a function of the length of the moving average. The moving average is the main system parameter – it acts as entry filter and stop at the same time

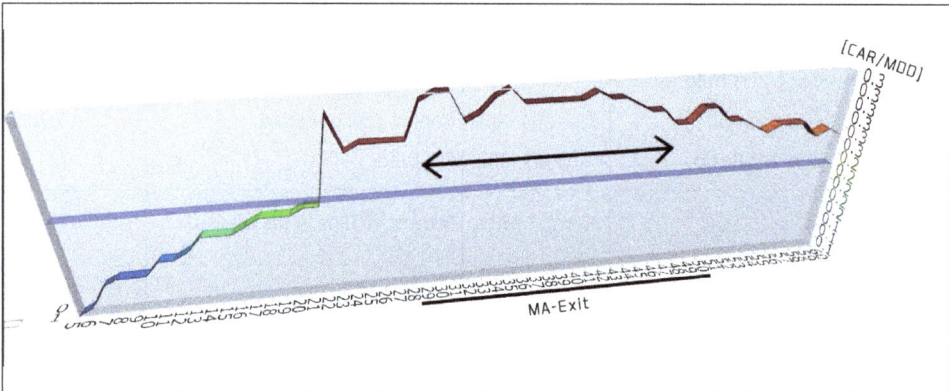

Optimisation on S&P 500 daily data from 1/1/1928–31/12/2018 with AmiBroker.

Concerning a good return/risk ratio (indicated by the CAR/MDD ratio), you find the best values of the moving average with lengths between 30 and 50. Let us stay in the middle at around 40 days.

All the following markets are tested with this same parameter (SMA length = 40) with AmiBroker on end-of-day data from Norgate.

The complete free AmiBroker code can be found in Appendix 5.

Results

Let us start the presentation of the results with the well-known S&P 500 index (fig. 5.24).

Figure 5.24: Results of the BOM system on the S&P 500 index, tested on daily data 1/1/1928–31/12/2018. All calculations include $40 slippage and commissions per round turn. Back-test performed with AmiBroker on Norgate Data

Figure 5.24A: Equity curve

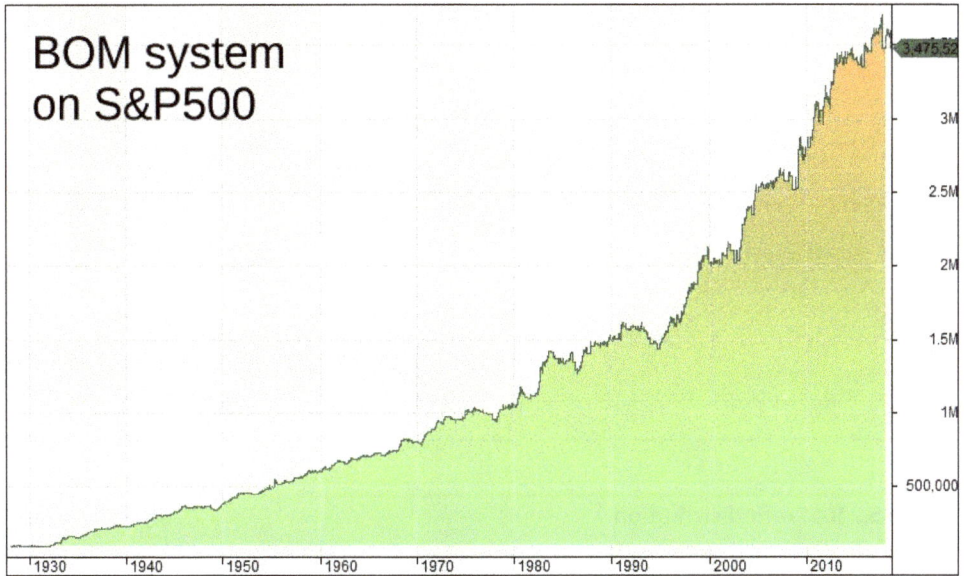

BOM system on S&P500

Figure 5.24B: Underwater equity curve

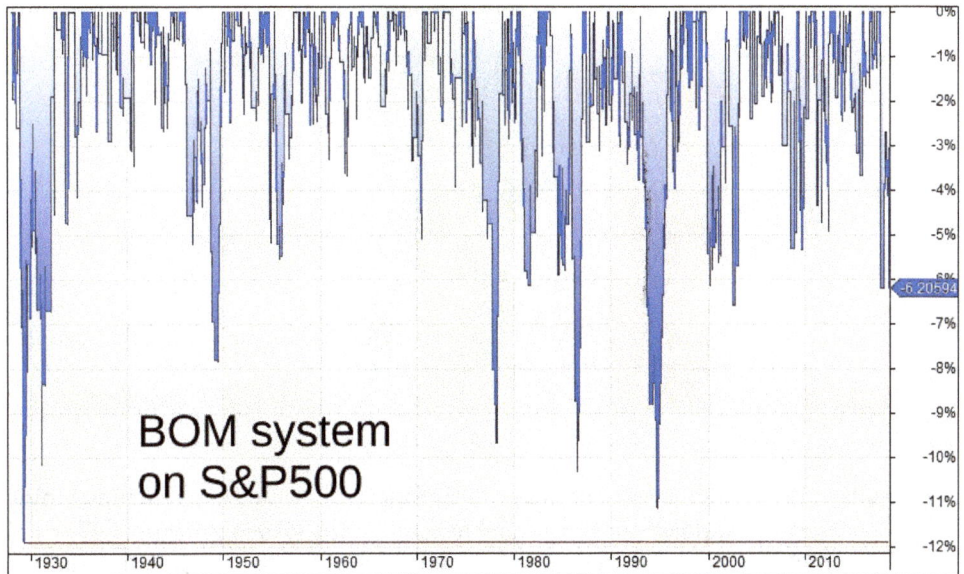

BOM system on S&P500

Figure 5.24C: Logarithmic equity curve

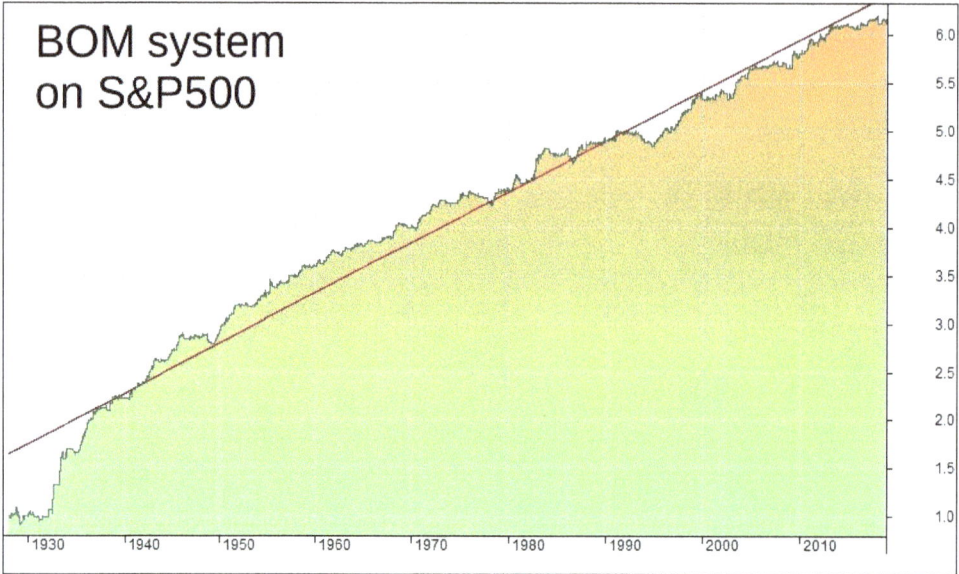

Figure 5.24D: Profit distribution

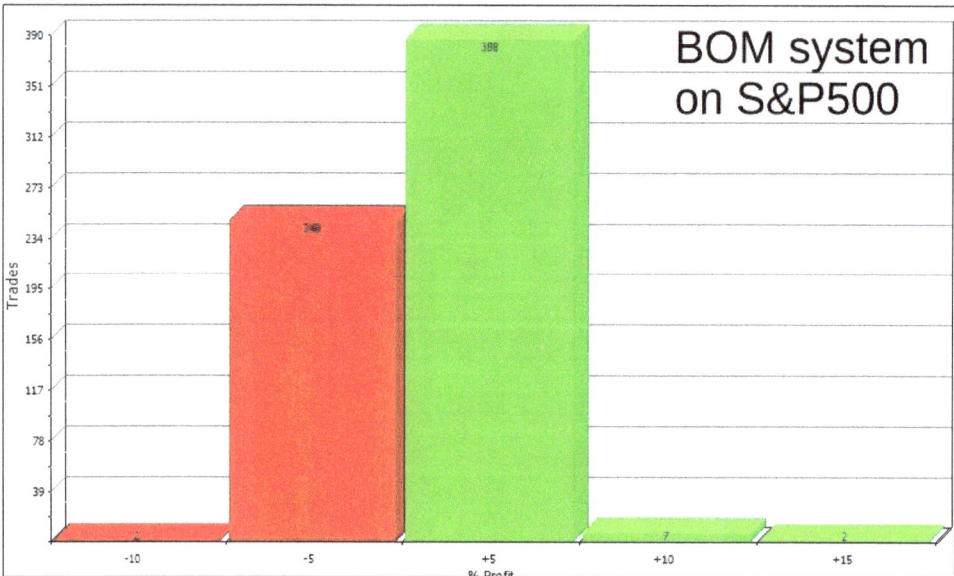

The results show the high stability of this primitive approach, which has been functioning for almost a century and has survived several recessions. The system generates 647 trades of which 61.3% are profitable (table 5.6). The average trade net profit is 0.57%. The system gains an average profit of about 4% per year.

Please note, however, that the BOM strategy is only invested in the market four days a month. The other 26 days you have your money freely available and can deploy it elsewhere. Therefore the risk-adjusted return is significantly higher.

Particularly noteworthy are the low declines of the system, of only 11.9% over such a long test period (fig. 5.24B).

Please note that on long-term tests we also show logarithmic representation of the charts (fig. 5.24C). Since gains are reinvested the equity curves of a profitable trading system grow exponentially and therefore the log charts show better how the performance changes across different decades.

In the end, it is worth taking a look at the distribution of profits and losses of each trade (fig. 5.24D). Because the holding period is only four days maximum and the 40-day line acts as an emergency stop on an end-of-day basis, the greatest losses are limited to typically –5%. On the other hand, typical profits are usually in the 5–10% range. The system generates its steady profits by the fact that the number of profitable trades is significantly higher than the number of loss trades due to the plausible trading logic.

Let's have a look at the results of different other markets, tested with the same parameters like the above shown S&P 500 without any further optimisations or adjustments (fig. 5.25A–Z).

Figure 5.25A–Z. Results of the BOM system on different stock indices with same system parameters, tested on daily data. All back-tests performed with AmiBroker on Norgate data include $40 slippage and commissions per round turn.

Figure 5.25A: BOM system on DJ Global

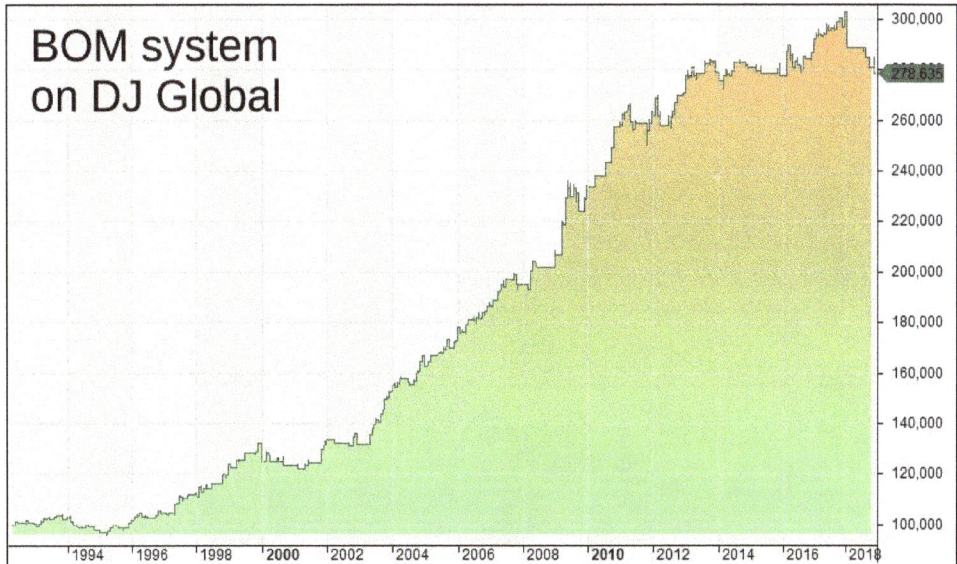

Figure 5.25B: BOM system on DJ Global ex US

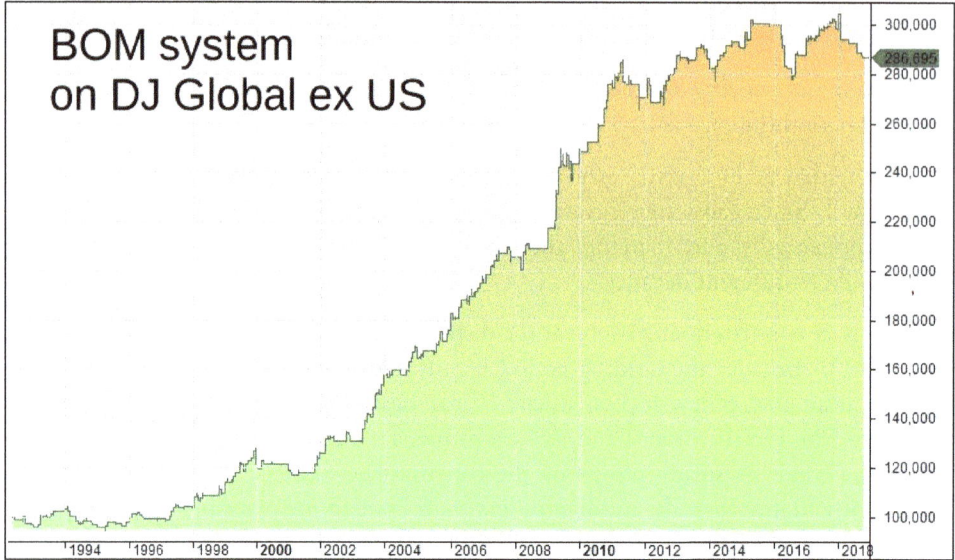

Figure 5.25B: BOM system on DJ Global ex US

Figure 5.25C: BOM system on S&P 500

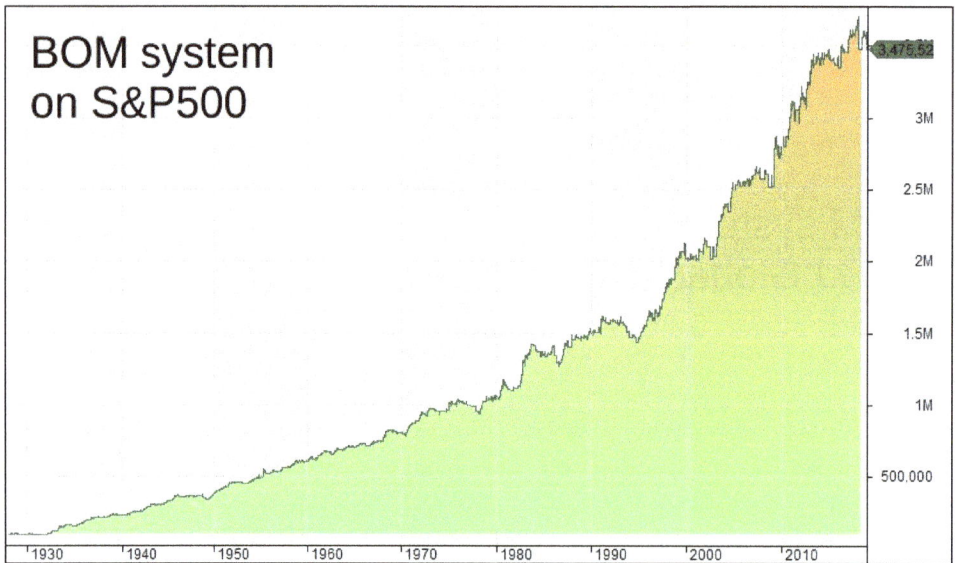

Figure 5.25C: BOM system on S&P 500

Figure 5.25D: BOM system on Nasdaq 100

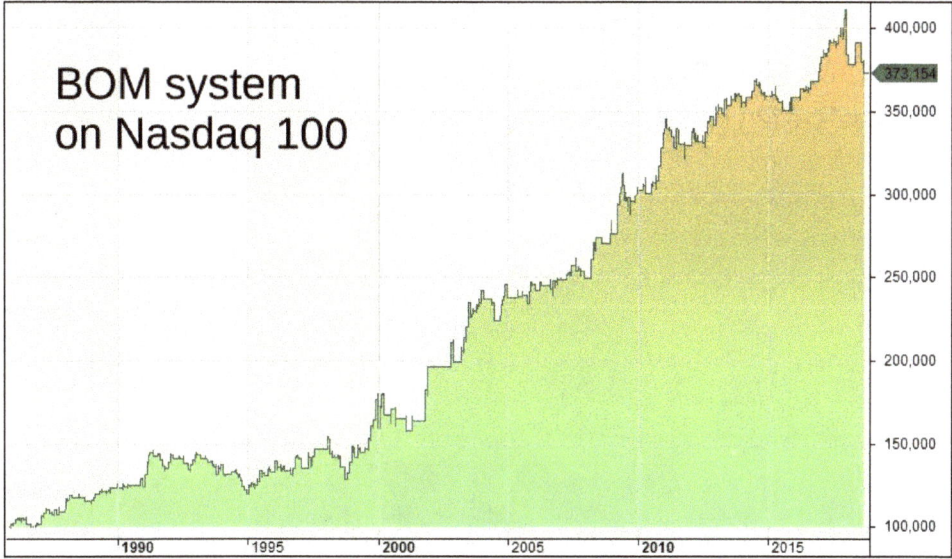

BOM system
on Nasdaq 100

Figure 5.25E: BOM system on Dow Jones

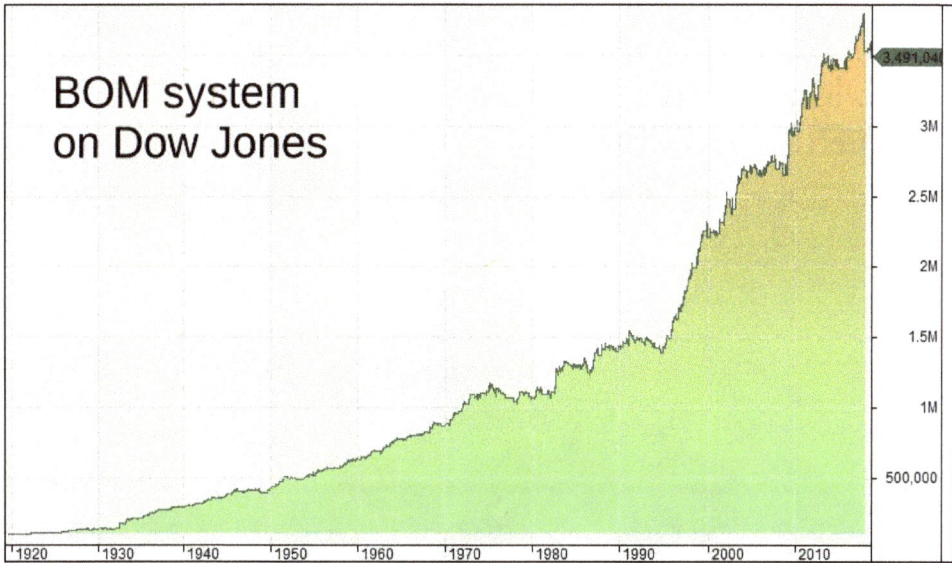

BOM system
on Dow Jones

Figure 5.25F: BOM system on S&P 1500

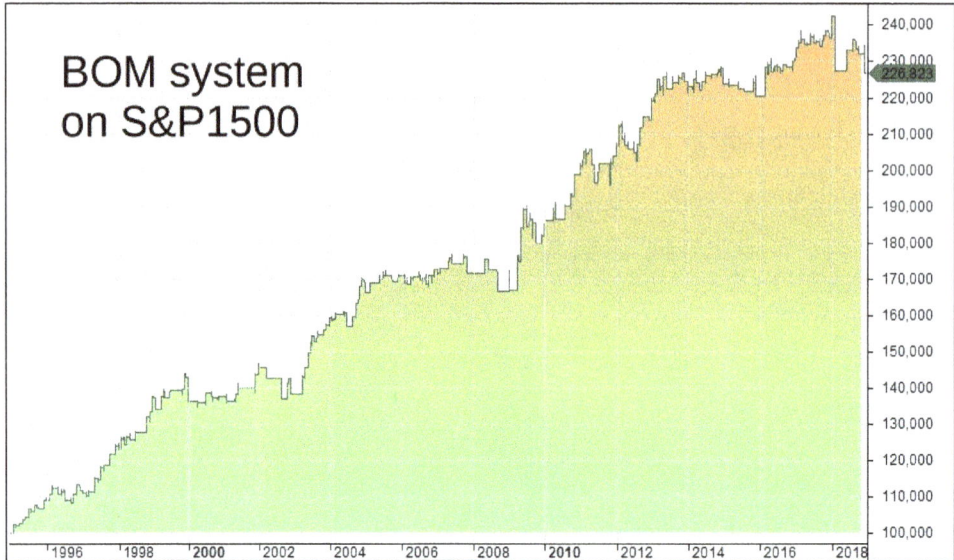

Figure 5.25F: BOM system on S&P 1500

Figure 5.25G: BOM system on Russell 2000

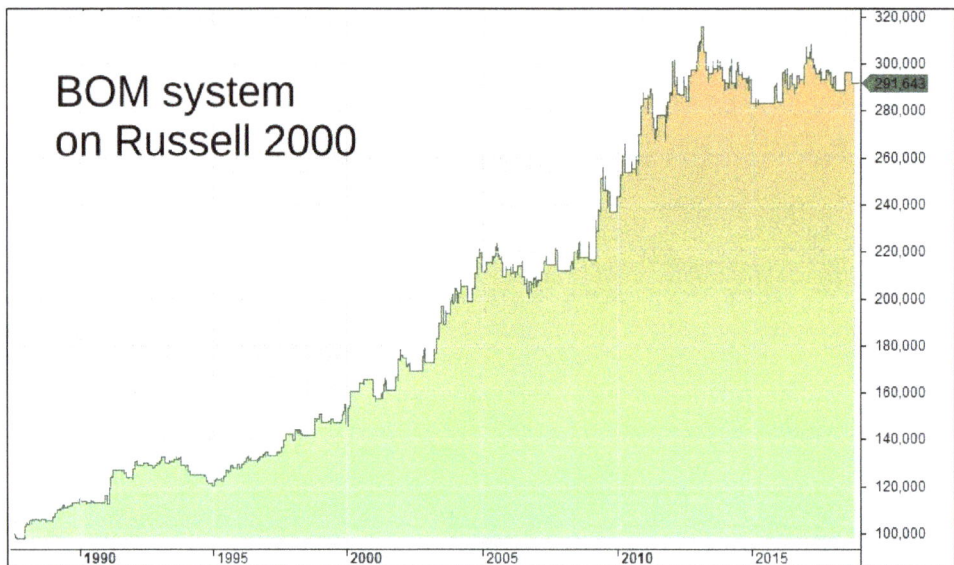

Figure 5.25G: BOM system on Russell 2000

Figure 5.25H: BOM system on EuroStoxx 50

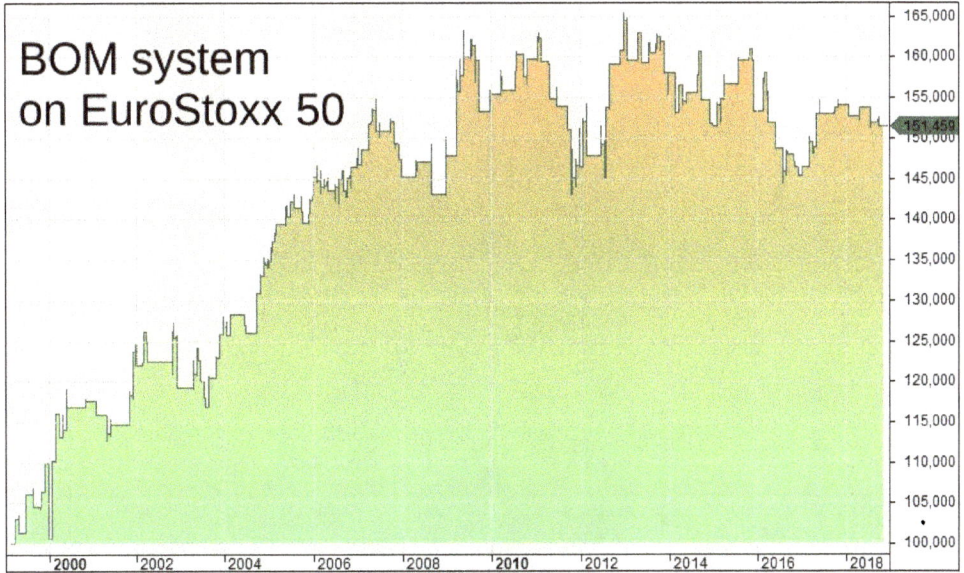

Figure 5.25I: BOM system on FTSE100

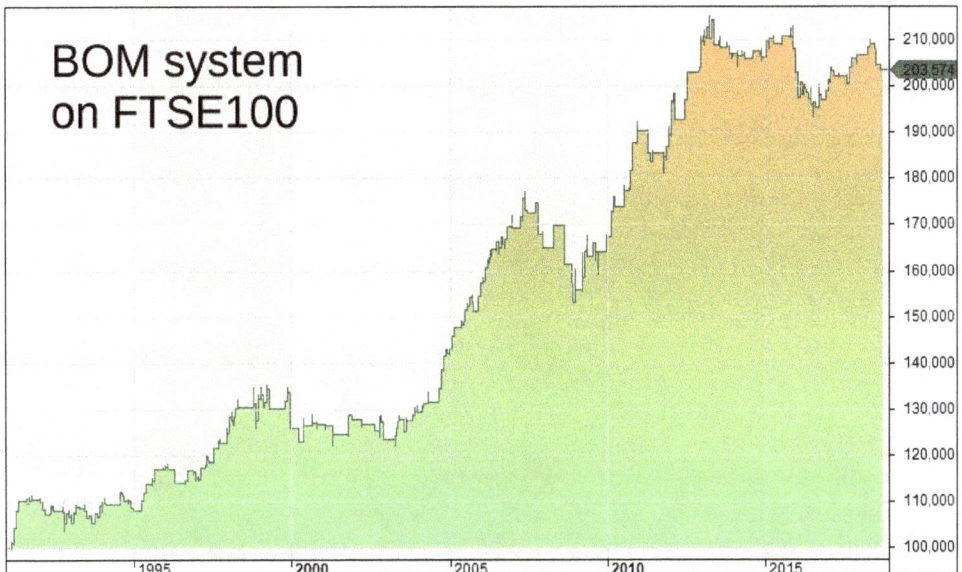

Figure 5.25J: BOM system on DAX30

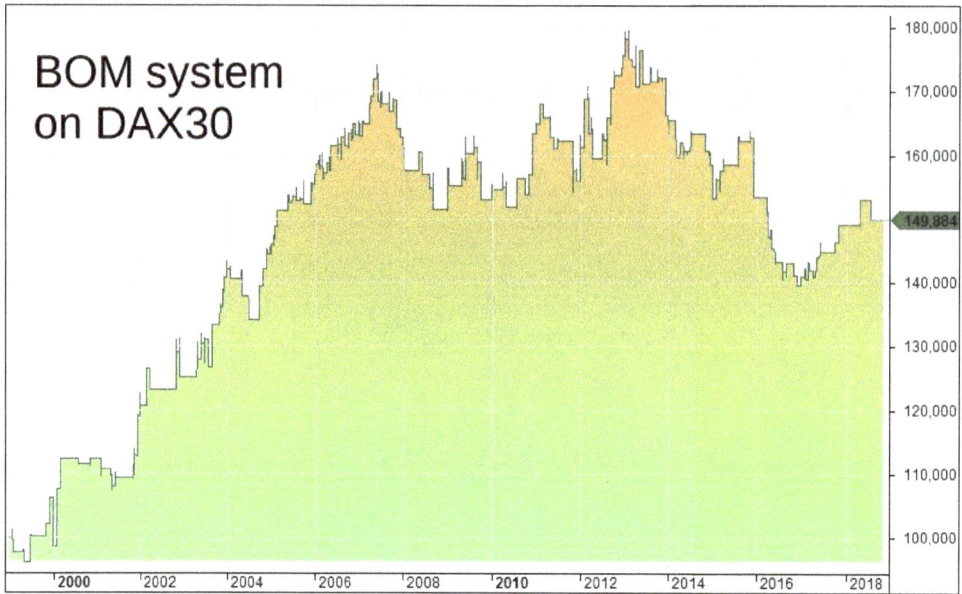

Figure 5.25K: BOM system on CAC40

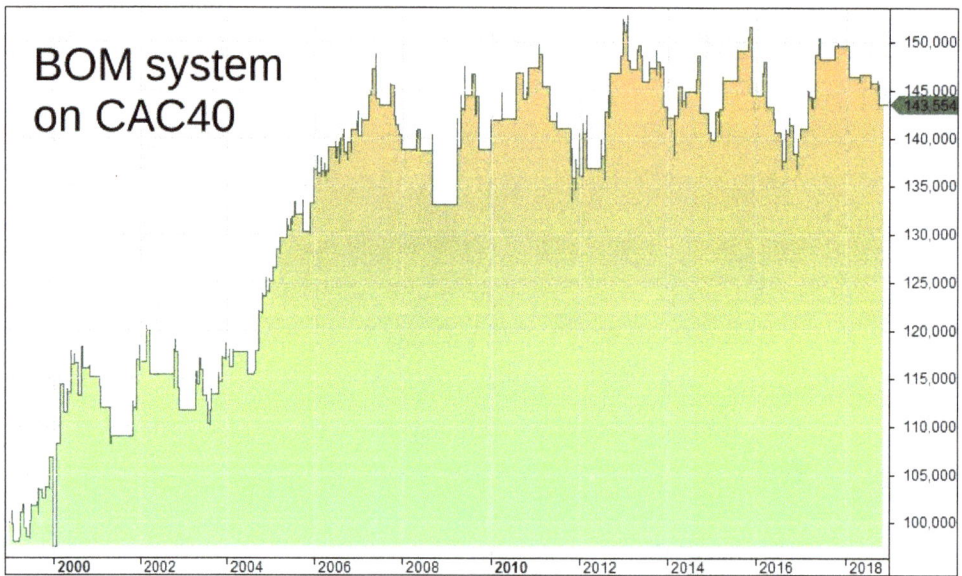

Figure 5.25L: BOM system on IBEX35

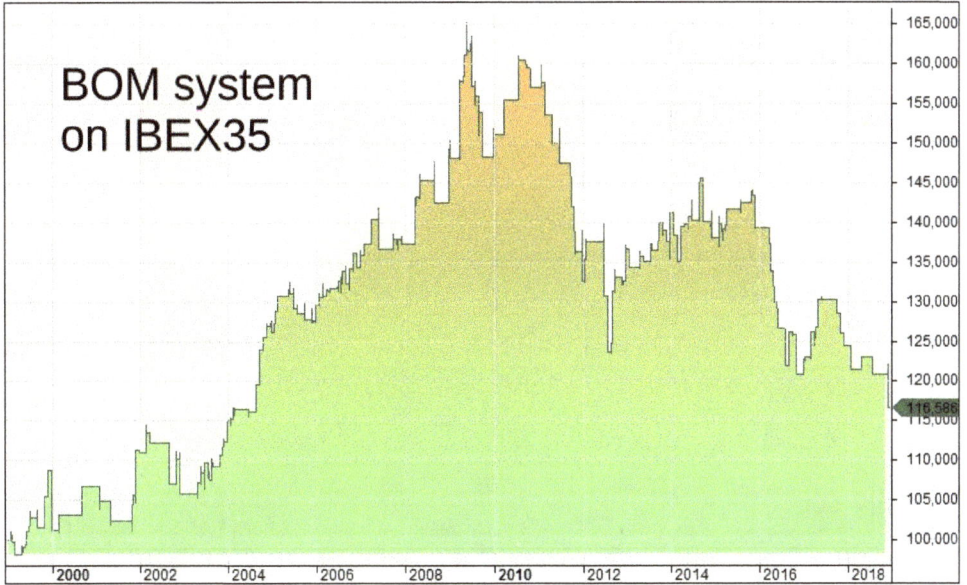

BOM system
on IBEX35

Figure 5.25M: BOM system on FTSE MIB

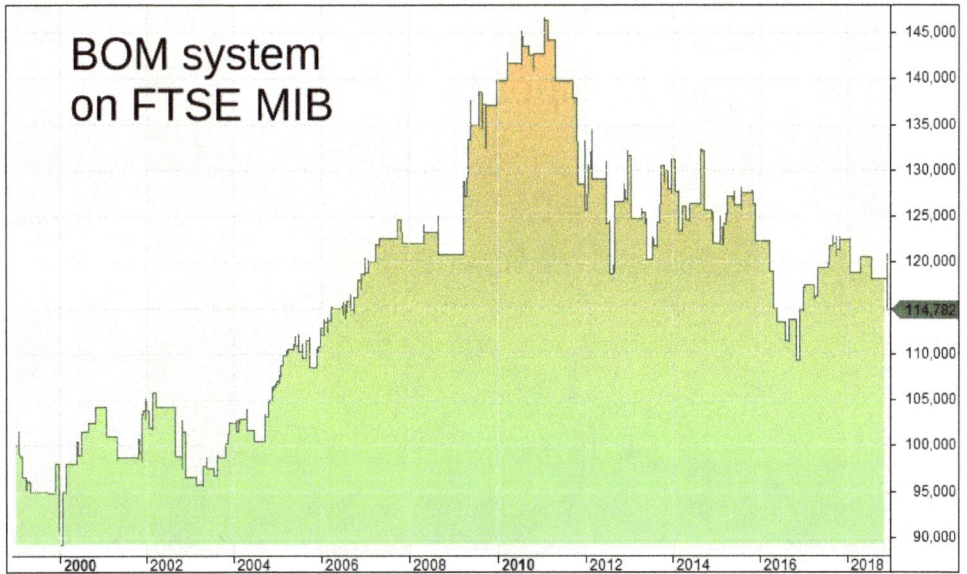

BOM system
on FTSE MIB

Figure 5.25N: BOM system on Russian RTS

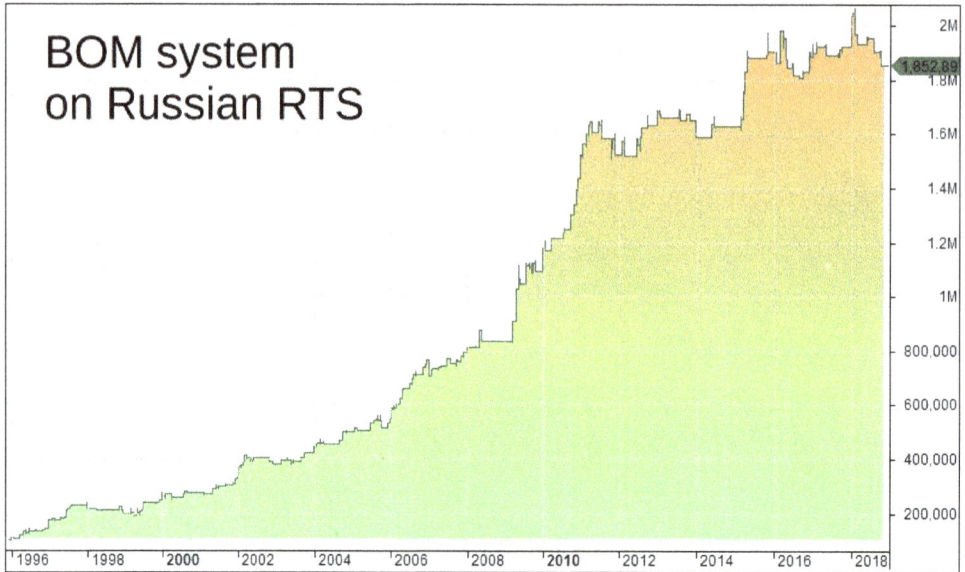

Figure 5.25O: BOM system on Shanghai Composite

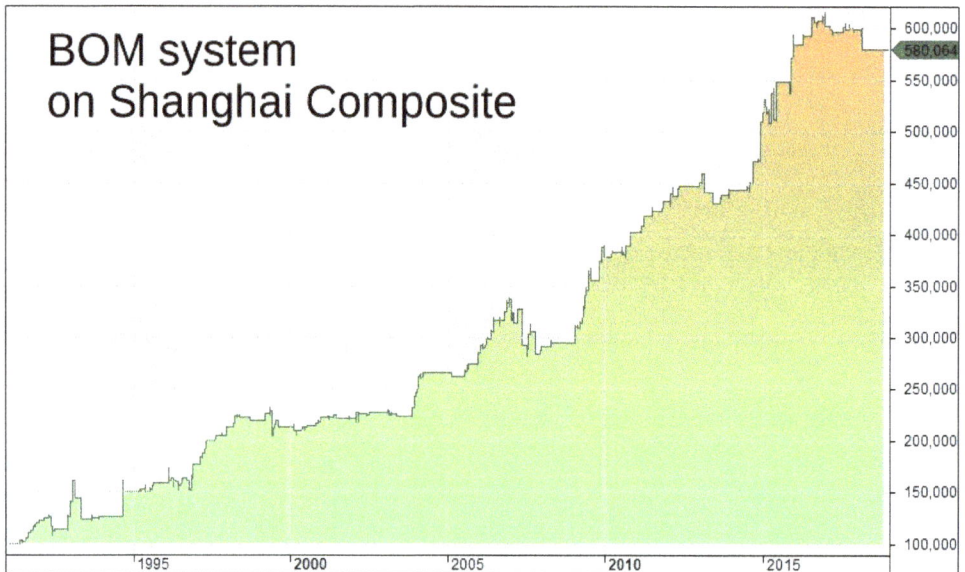

Figure 5.25P: BOM system on Hang Seng

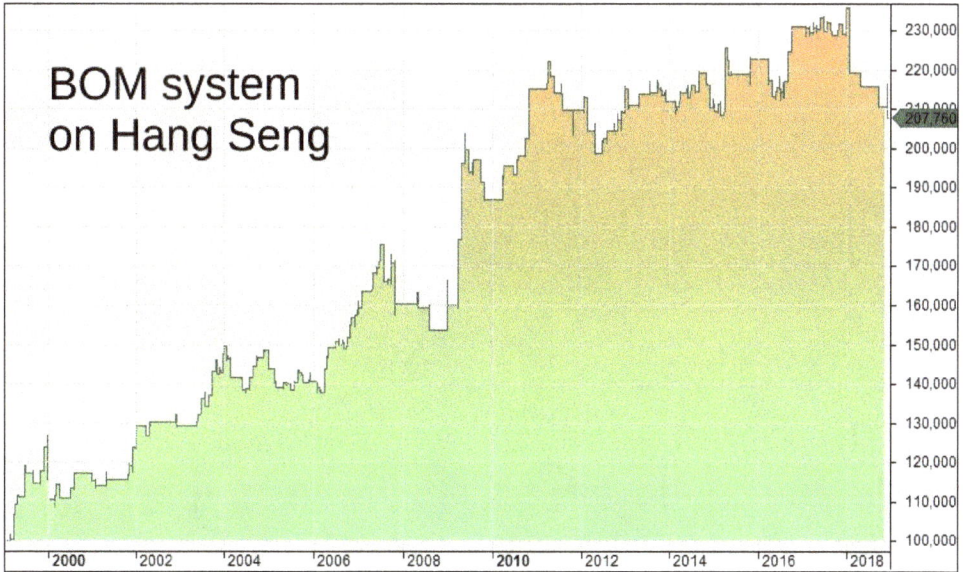

BOM system
on Hang Seng

Figure 5.25Q: BOM system on FTSE China 50

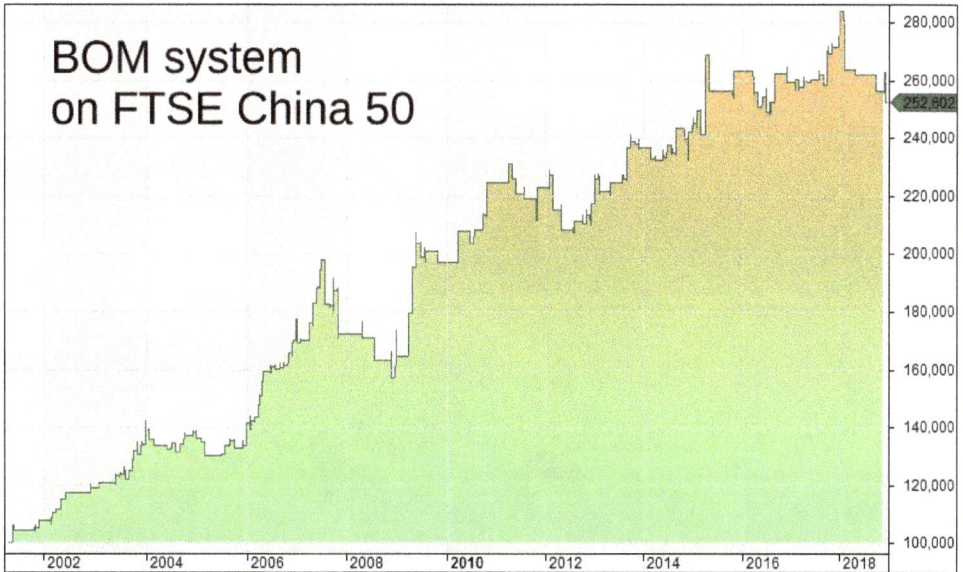

BOM system
on FTSE China 50

Figure 5.25R: BOM system on Nikkei 225

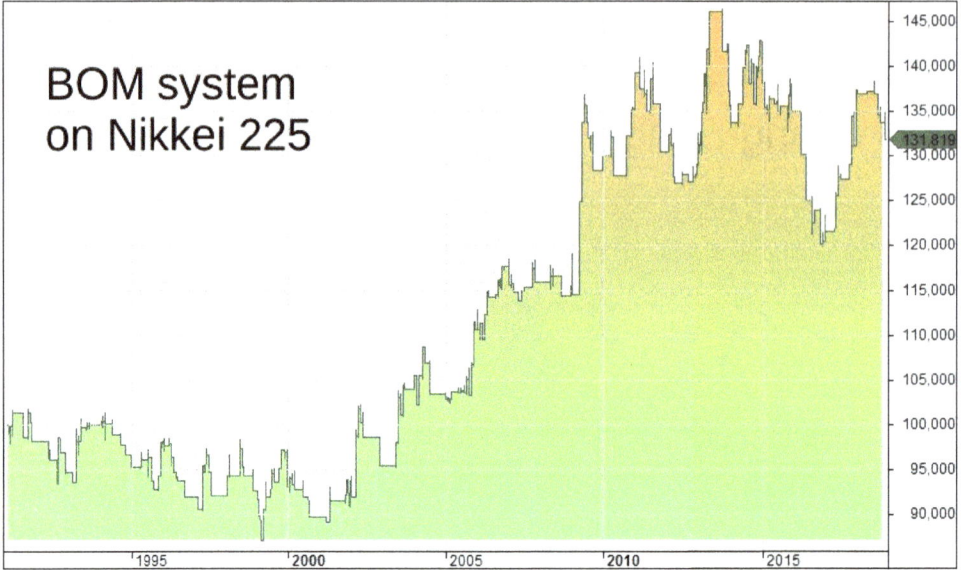

Figure 5.25S: BOM system on Straits Times

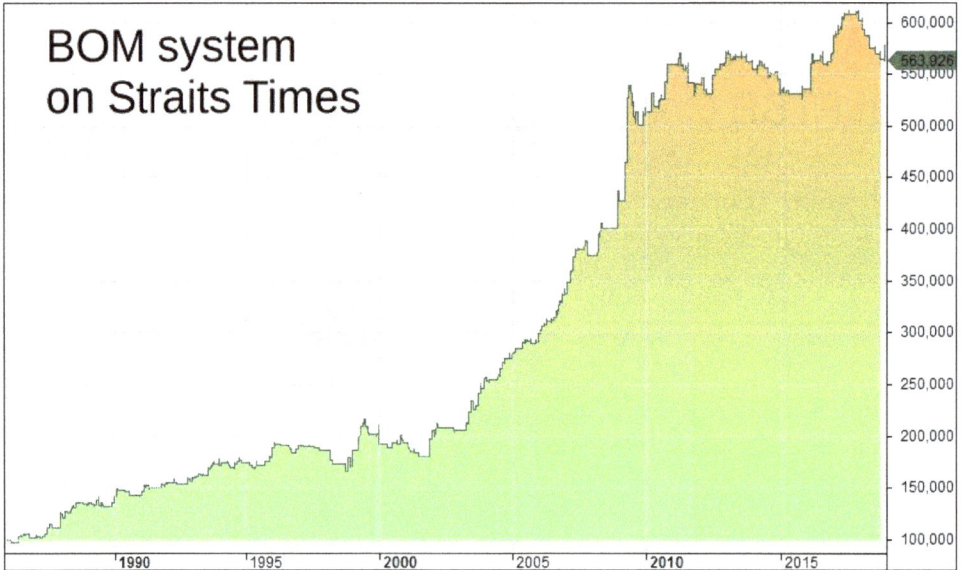

Figure 5.25T: BOM system on CNX Nifty 50

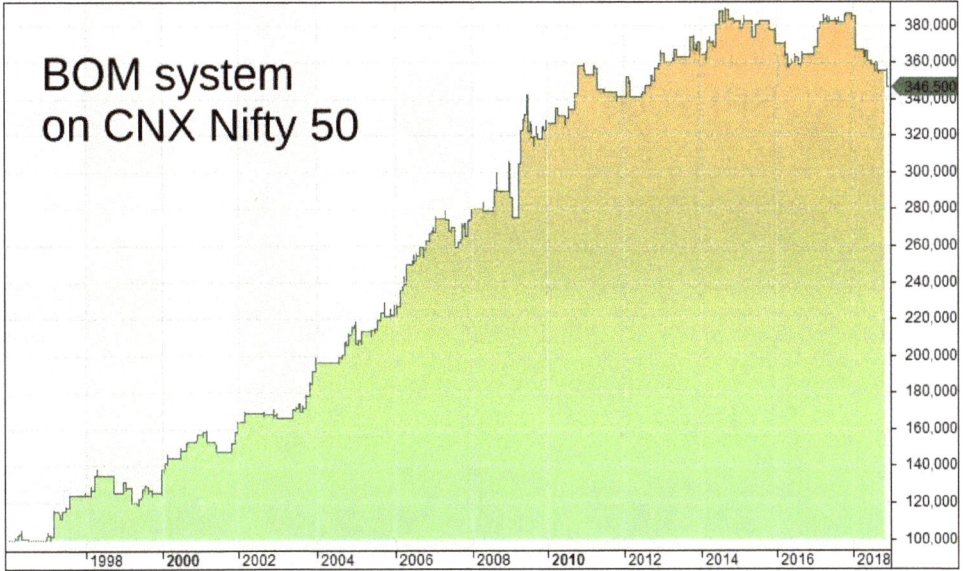

Figure 5.25U: BOM system on BSE Sensex 30

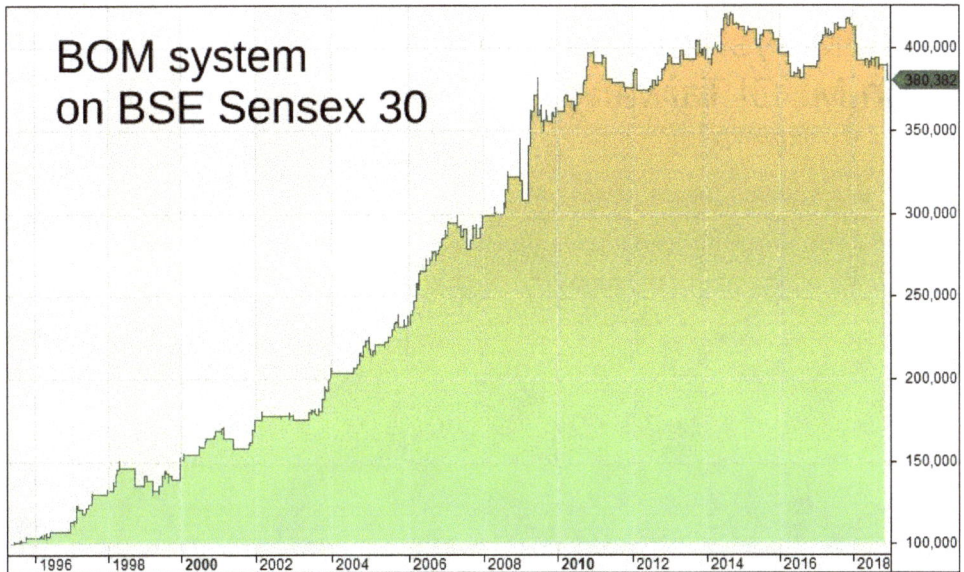

Figure 5.25V: BOM system on KOSPI 200

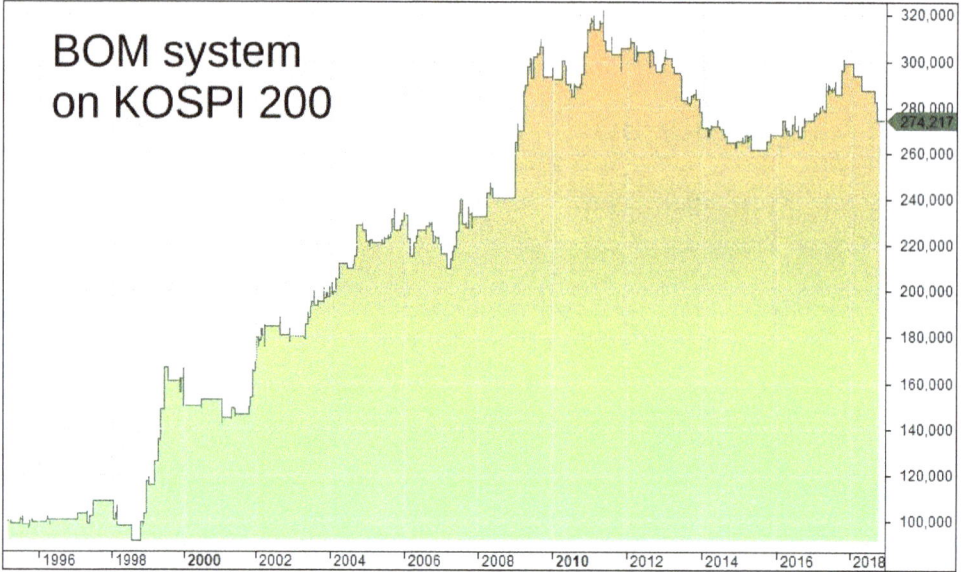

Figure 5.25W: BOM system on MSCI Taiwan

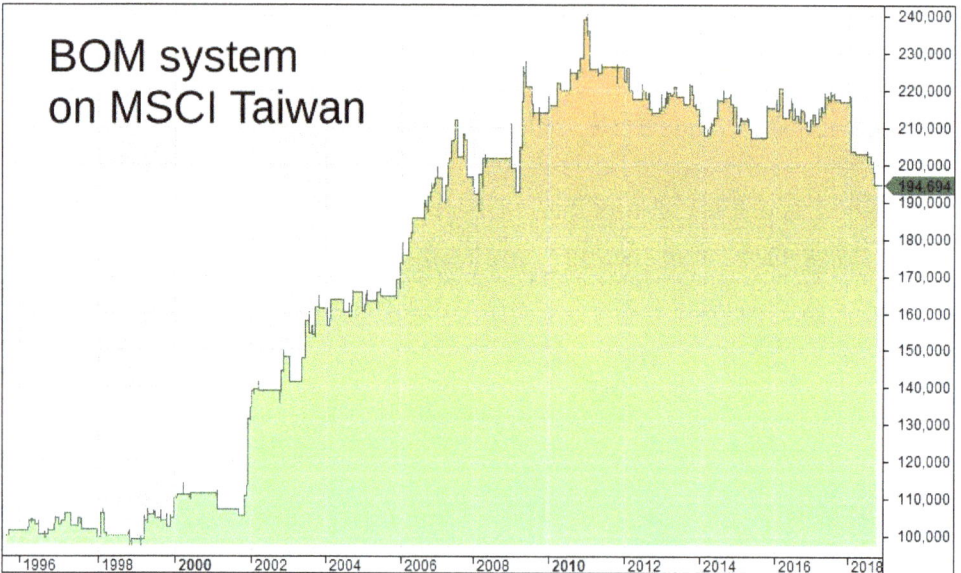

Figure 5.25X: BOM system on All Ordinaries 500

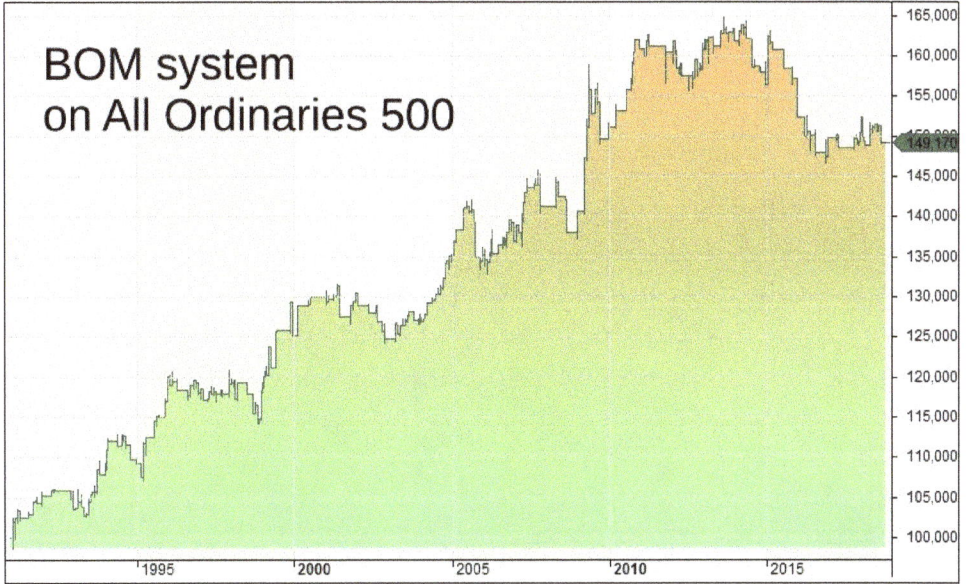

Figure 5.25Y: BOM system on Mexico IPC

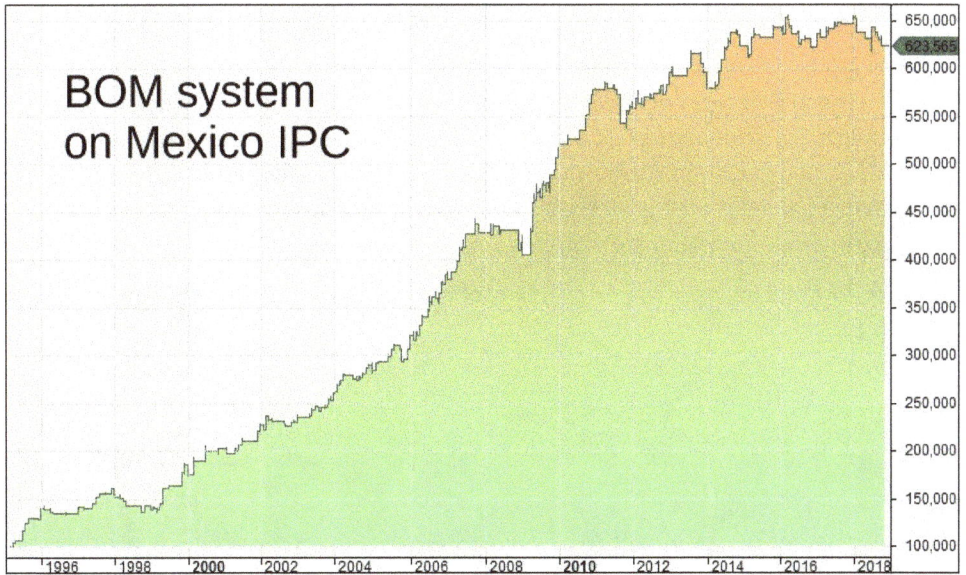

Figure 5.25Z: BOM system on Bovespa

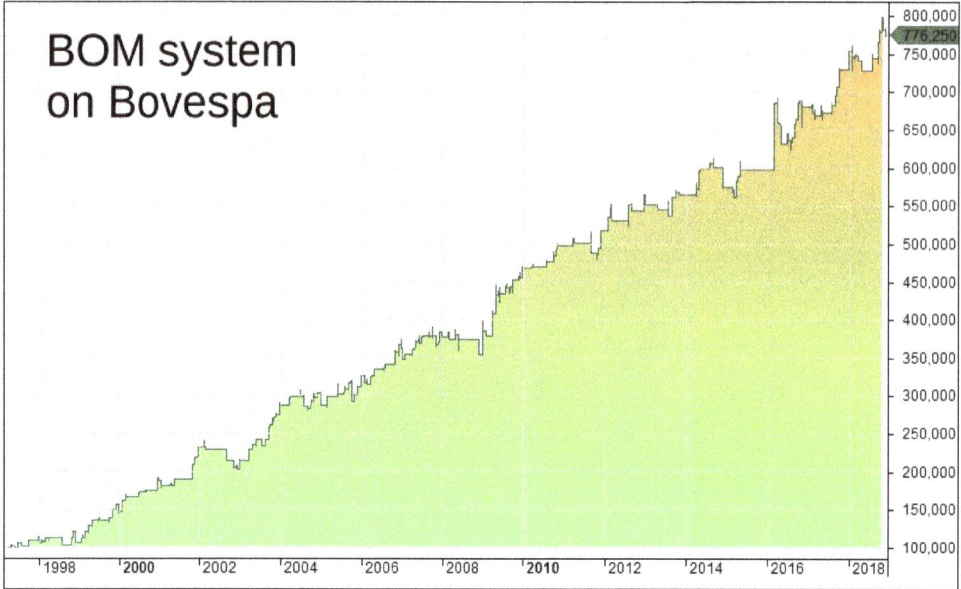

The strategy works on many different stock indices with the same parameters.

Please note, however, that within the last ten years a small performance decay took place in some markets. An explanation for this is the fact that performances around the world vary depending on the real upward behaviour of the individual stock markets: in those countries where total stock returns are positive in recent decades (like US, FTSE 100, China and other countries) the statistics look better. The point is, however, that performances are also positive even in those countries like Italy and Spain where total stock returns in recent years are negative.

In the following table you find an overview of our performed tests on the single markets (table 5.6).

Table 5.6: Main figures of the BOM system on different stock market indices

	Index	Region	Symbol (Norgate)	Data since	# Trades	% profitable	Avg. Profit per Trade (%)	Annual Return (%)	Risk Adj. Return %	Max Sys DrawDown (%)
A	Dow Jones Global	World	$W1DOW	01/04/1992	206	63.1	0.51	3.9	34.51	-8
B	Dow Jones Global ex US	World	$W2DOW	01/05/1992	193	60.6	0.56	4.03	38.78	-9.5
C	S&P500	USA	$SPX	01/01/1928	647	61.3	0.57	3.97	37.66	-11.9
D	Nasdaq 100	USA	$NDX	01/11/1985	251	56.9	0.57	4.05	36.82	-17.7
E	Dow Jones	USA	$DJI	01/09/1919	690	62.4	0.53	3.64	35.22	-12.6
F	S&P1500	USA	$SP1500	01/01/1995	188	61.7	0.45	3.47	30.21	-6.6
G	Russell 2000	USA	$RUT	01/08/1987	239	57.3	0.47	3.46	30.92	-10.6
H	EuroStoxx 50	Europe	$STOXX50	01/03/1999	134	59.7	0.34	2.11	22.28	-12.65
I	FTSE 100	Great Britain	$FT100	01/01/1991	192	60.42	0.39	2.57	25.85	-13.6
J	DAX	Germany	$DAX	01/01/1999	141	57.4	0.32	2.04	20.14	-22.3
K	CAC40	France	$CAC	01/01/1999	142	59.1	0.28	1.82	18.07	-10.9
L	IBEX35	Spain	$IBEX	01/01/1999	134	54.4	0.14	0.77	8.23	-29.4
M	MIBTEL	Italy	$FTSEMIB	01/01/1999	132	55.3	0.14	0.69	7.48	-25.4
N	Russian Trading System	Russia	$RTS	01/12/1995	151	68.87	2.06	13.48	135.1	-20.07
O	Shanghai Composite	China	$SSEC	01/02/1991	167	61.7	3.08	6.5	71.15	-23.65
P	Hang Seng	China	$HS	01/02/1999	137	56.2	0.58	3.74	36.57	-14.5
Q	FTSE China 50	China	$XINO	01/05/2001	124	62.1	0.8	5.38	52.92	-20.58
R	Nikkei 225	Japan	$N225	01/02/1991	178	51.1	0.18	0.99	10.72	-18.1
S	Straits Times	Singapore	$STI	01/01/1986	236	59.8	2.27	5.38	51.25	-16.8
T	CNX Nifty 50	India	$NIF	01/01/1996	165	60.6	0.79	5.55	51.03	-13.8
U	BSE Sensex 30	India	$SEN	01/05/1995	169	65.68	0.82	5.8	52.97	-13.39
V	KOSPI 200	Korea	$KO	01/03/1995	160	55.63	0.69	4.32	43.42	-18.7
W	MSCI Taiwan	Taiwan	$TWMSCI	01/09/1995	159	50.94	0.46	2.9	29.93	-19.02
X	All Ordinaries 500	Australia	$XAO.au	01/01/1991	202	54.9	0.21	1.44	13.52	-11
Y	IPC	Mexico	$MXX	01/03/1995	177	62.71	1.07	7.98	72.63	-15.45
Z	Bovespa	Brasilia	$BVSP	01/04/1997	144	66	1.51	9.88	99.2	-15.4

One of several possible ideas to further improve this already profitable system is to select each new month only the market that has shown the greatest strength over the last 12 months, which is about 252 trading days.

All you need to do for this is to add the following line into your AmiBroker Code and apply it to the above portfolio of the 26 stock indices:

```
Position Score = 100 + Ref(ROC(C, 252),-1);
```

(For the programmers: Adding the value of 100 just makes sure that the results are positive. It does not change the ranking.)

With this line the trading system logic checks every new month which market has been the strongest within the last year. Of course it rolls the lookback period forward each new month. In this way the strategy adapts itself to changing market conditions and reacts automatically on worldwide fundamental changes. If only your portfolio of tradable indices contains enough different geographic regions and markets.

Like this you combine the strength of momentum strategies with the idea of the beginning of month effect. And in this way you minimize exposure to low performance market phases like the Italian S&P MIB or the Spanish IBEX and automatically spend more time in the strongest markets.

You can see the result of this simple rotation in fig. 5.26 and table 5.7.

Figure 5.26: Results when you always choose the strongest market (over the last 252 days = 1 year) for the beginning of the month trade. A: equity curve; B. underwater equity. Back-test performed with AmiBroker on Norgate Data includes $80 slippage and commissions per round turn. Backtesting period 01/01/1995–31/12/2018.

Figure 5.26A: equity curve strongest

Figure 5.26B: underwater strongest

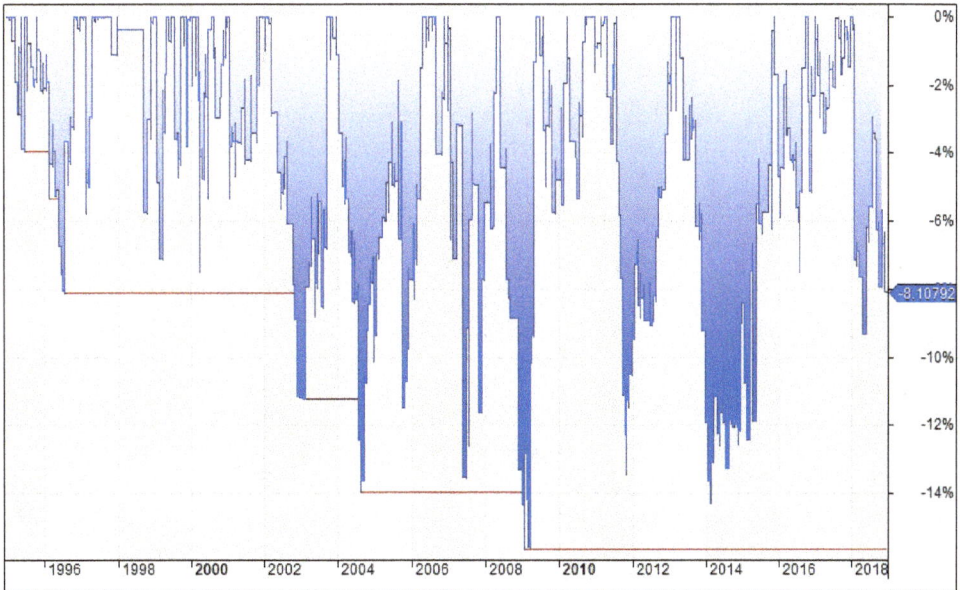

Table 5.7: System figures: You always choose the strongest market (over the last 252 days = 1 year) for the beginning of the month trade. Back-test performed with AmiBroker on Norgate Data includes $80 slippage and commissions per round turn. Backtesting period 01/01/1995–31/12/2018.

Initial capital	100000
Ending capital	716270.71
Net Profit	616270.71
Net Profit %	616.27%
Exposure %	16.34%
Net Risk Adjusted Return %	3772.55%
Annual Return %	**8.55%**
Risk Adjusted Return %	52.32%
Transaction costs	21360
All trades	**267**
Avg. Profit/Loss	2308.13
Avg. Profit/Loss %	0.79%
Avg. Bars Held	4.7
Winners	**156 (58.43 %)**
Total Profit	1679565.02
Avg. Profit	10766.44
Avg. Profit %	2.78%
Avg. Bars Held	5
Max. Consecutive	9
Largest win	45915.54
# bars in largest win	5
Losers	**111 (41.57 %)**
Total Loss	-1063294.32
Avg. Loss	-9579.23
Avg. Loss %	-1.99%
Avg. Bars Held	4.27
Max. Consecutive	5
Largest loss	-55672.77
# bars in largest loss	5
Max. trade drawdown	-55672.77
Max. trade % drawdown	-10.7
Max. system drawdown	-102686.92
Max. system % drawdown	**-15.66%**

You get a compound annual return of more than 8% with a maximum drawdown of about 15% – for such a simple system, which is only invested in the market four days per month.

Please note that these are the results without using any leverage!

If you are an experienced trader you could use CFDs, options or futures to trade this strategy. You would just need to hold your position for the first four trading days each month. If you take care of your position size and stop loss, the profitability of this simple strategy would generate easily double-digit profits. (Keep in mind that drawdowns would increase accordingly.)

The above result could be further optimised. For example, if you choose 50 days instead of 40 for the moving average which acts as entry filter and exit, the results would become better – you would get nearly 10% annual return in the back-test.

However, this chapter is not intended to show how best to optimise. We just wanted to give you an example of a robust trading system which works on several markets over many decades and therefore fits with the topic of the previous chapter about rule-complexity and over-fitting.

Strategy evaluation

Positive
- Simple
- Can be traded without much effort
- Good results in various markets
- Robust strategy without much optimisation
- No big drawdowns
- There are fundamental reasons why it works
- Little market exposure (four days) – in the rest of the month other strategies could be traded

Negative
- Only one signal per month
- Slight performance decay within the last ten years

Further ideas
- Select each month the market with biggest relative strength (rotating)
- Trade with leverage – experienced traders could use futures to increase profits

6

Periodic Reoptimisation and Walk-forward Analysis

6.1 Short repetition: normal, static optimisation

W E ARE GETTING closer to real-life trading. This chapter explains the important topic of periodic reoptimisation of the system parameters with walk-forward analysis (WFA).

Figure 6.1: Equity curve of system LUXOR for British pound/US dollar (FOREX) training and test period, 30-minute data. Training period 21/10/2002–28/2/2007 (white), test period 1/3/2007–4/7/2008 (green).

Let's first remind ourselves of the normal optimisation process which we set out in chapter 5. In order to optimise your system you take a fixed training data set (in sample data) and then you apply the system to previously unseen data: this is the *test set*, or *out-of-sample data* (fig. 6.1). In our example the training data set was about four years and four months, from 21/10/2002–28/2/2007 and the test set was one year and four months from 1/3/2007–4/7/2008.

Obviously this well-known procedure of optimising your trading system on a special market has some disadvantages. You only have one in-sample and one out-of-sample area. The out-of-sample test range is usually the most recent data. The more data you have in the training set the more efficiently you can train your system to different market conditions (compare with chapter 5.2). Further, keep in mind that this normal optimisation process can work well for sound trading systems for a certain time. But be aware that over a longer period of time the market structure could change. In such a case you will need to adapt the trading system as well. A purely static approach with the input parameters fixed forever will fail sooner or later. Since there is no system code which can work forever you have to change your system parameters from time to time. These are good reasons to look at more dynamic optimisation methods.

6.2 Anchored vs. rolling walk-forward analysis (WFA)

If you take the above example but make the optimisation window bigger and bigger you arrive at an anchored WFA. The optimisation is anchored since it always starts at the same point of time (fig. 6.2A). This is the simplest form of WFA. It usually works best, like the static optimisation we examined above, when the tested market keeps its personality within the tested sample.

Figure 6.2A: Anchored walk-forward analysis. For every new optimisation run the in-sample optimisation window starts at the same point of time but its length is subsequently increased. The unseen out-of-sample data follows.

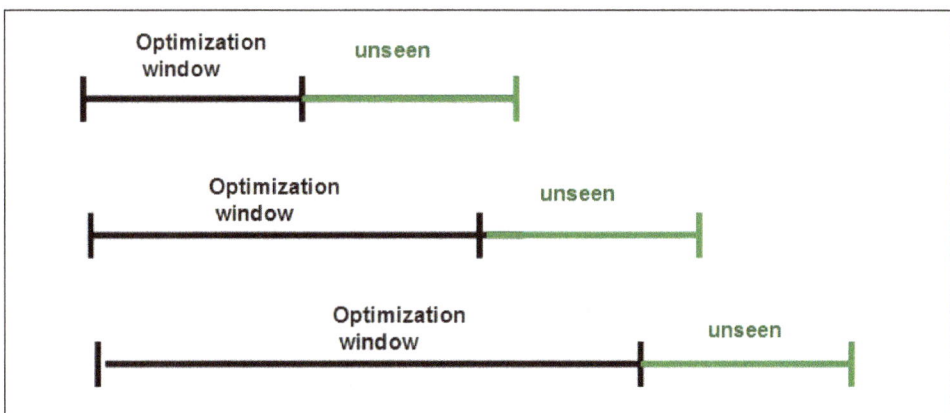

However, as you know, markets and their personalities can be complex. Sometimes a market will show an equity curve that has some very profitable and some not-very-profitable intervals within the tested data ranges. If a market appears to have such a changing personality then the anchored WFA may be not the best method. In these cases it is necessary to perform an optimisation method which better adapts to changing market conditions, the rolling WFA (fig. 6.2B). The rolling WFA is particularly appropriate for short-term intraday systems.

Figure 6.2B: Rolling walk-forward analysis. Shifting in-sample optimisation window = 1 year and shifting unseen out-of-sample data = the 3 following months.

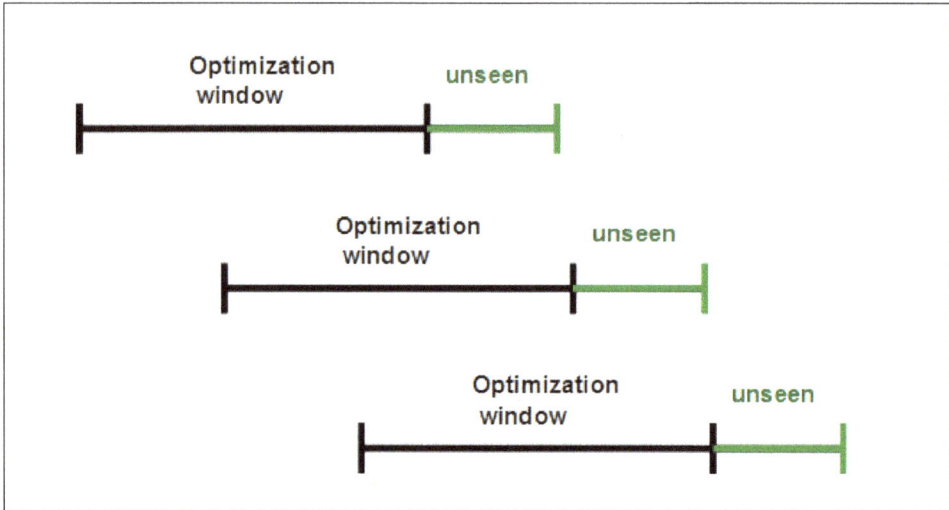

The better adaptation of the rolling WFA may mean it is more appropriate, and may yield results that walk forward better, in live trading than results obtained from an anchored WFA.

6.3 Rolling WFA on the LUXOR system

Periodic optimisation of the two main system parameters

Let's try the rolling WFA on the LUXOR system with 30-minute data of the pound/dollar pair. So instead of optimising the code's input settings within a fixed test data range, we now have to do a rolling reoptimisation of the two main system parameters, the fast and slow moving average. As seen in chapter 5.4, the system is most reactive on these two moving averages that trigger the entry signals. During this reoptimisation process, we keep all other system parameters (time filter and the three exits) constant with the values gained in chapter 3. We optimise the two moving averages in periods of one year and shift this optimisation period three months further with every new run (fig. 6.2B). To complete the WFA and to check its results we apply the optimised values to the unseen data ranges. In this way we see how our periodically optimised system walks forward.

With the rolling WFA we have a training set which is not static as before but which is moving forward as the time goes by. In our case we use one-year in-sample optimisation periods which move forward every three months. With each new optimisation you get two new optimal moving average values. For example, during the optimisation period between November 2002 and November 2003 you get an optimal fast moving average length of 3 bars and an optimal slow moving average length of 21 bars. If you shift the optimisation period by three months to February 2003 until February 2004 the parameter's best values change to 1 (fast) and 39 (slow) for the moving averages. (Of course a moving average of length 1 is just the price itself.)

If you shift the optimisation window by three months again (now from May 2003 until May 2004) the two input parameters change again to 1 (fast) and 21 (slow) which is shown in (table 6.1). So instead of the static optimisation you now have 19 optimisation runs for the two main input parameters within the training period. Please note that these 19 optimisation runs use nearly the whole market data range for both optimisation and for testing. Remember that the static optimisation from chapter 5.4 just could use a small part of about one year of the data for the out-of-sample test. So you now get a much more detailed test of your trading system on much more data – not by having more data available (you still only have the six years from 2002–2008) but by using it in a cleverer way.

Table 6.1: Periodic reoptimisation of the trading system LUXOR on 30-minute data of the GBP/USD FOREX pair. The gained best parameters are applied subsequently to out-of-sample areas of three-month test data.

Training Set				Test Set	
Training Start	Training End	Fast Moving Average	Slow Moving Average	Test Start	Test End
1-Nov-02	1-Nov-03	3	21	1-Nov-03	1-Feb-04
1-Feb-03	1-Feb-04	1	39	1-Feb-04	1-May-04
1-May-03	1-May-04	1	21	1-May-04	1-Aug-04
1-Aug-03	1-Aug-04	1	21	1-Aug-04	1-Nov-04
1-Nov-03	1-Nov-04	1	27	1-Nov-04	1-Feb-05
1-Feb-04	1-Feb-05	1	27	1-Feb-05	1-May-05
1-May-04	1-May-05	2	33	1-May-05	1-Aug-05
1-Aug-04	1-Aug-05	1	15	1-Aug-05	1-Nov-05
1-Nov-04	1-Nov-05	1	15	1-Nov-05	1-Feb-06
1-Feb-05	1-Feb-06	1	15	1-Feb-06	1-May-06

Training Set				Test Set	
1-May-05	1-May-06	1	15	1-May-06	1-Aug-06
1-Aug-05	1-Aug-06	5	48	1-Aug-06	1-Nov-06
1-Nov-05	1-Nov-06	2	39	1-Nov-06	1-Feb-07
1-Feb-06	1-Feb-07	1	39	1-Feb-07	1-May-07
1-May-06	1-May-07	1	39	1-May-07	1-Aug-07
1-Aug-06	1-Aug-07	6	21	1-Aug-07	1-Nov-08
1-Nov-06	1-Nov-08	1	24	1-Nov-08	1-Feb-08
1-Feb-07	1-Feb-08	1	24	1-Feb-08	1-May-08
1-May-07	1-May-08	1	24	1-May-08	1-Aug-08

If you plot the two optimised input parameters as a function of the start of the optimisation window you see their change within the five years (fig. 6.3). Please note that the two optimised parameters change rather slowly – an important aspect for the gained out-of-sample test results, which we will discuss now.

Figure 6.3: Change of the optimal parameters for the fast and slow moving averages as a function of the shifting one year optimisation period. During the tests the following other parameters are kept in place: entry time window 9.30am–1.30pm GMT, exits: 0.3% risk stop, 0.8% trailing stop and 1.9% optimised for trading system LUXOR on 30-minute data of the GBP/USD FOREX pair.

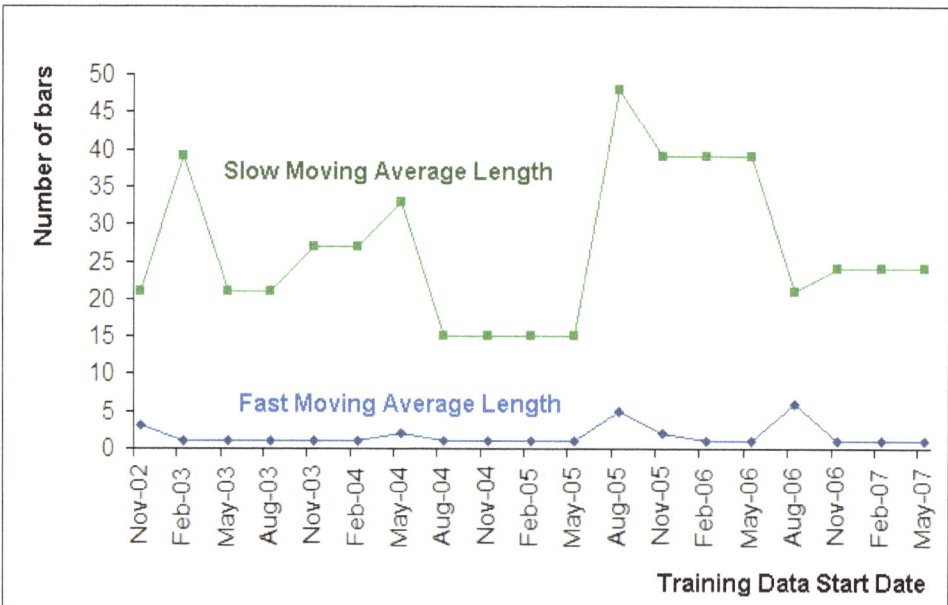

Out-of-sample test result

Let's apply the trading system with these optimised parameters to the unseen data. In table 6.1 you can see that the optimal parameters 3 (fast) and 21 (slow) which have been gained in the first one-year optimisation window between 1 November 2002 and 1 November 2003 are applied to the subsequent three months from 1 November 2003 until 1 February 2004 of unseen data. The optimal parameters for the subsequent optimisation period (February 2003 until February 2004: fast moving average = 1 bar, slow moving average = 39 bars) are applied to the unseen data between 1 February 2004 and 1 May 2004 and so forth for all the other 17 periods. In this way you get a complete out-of-sample test of the trading system applied to previously unseen data. The result is shown in fig. 6.4.

Figure 6.4: Out-of-sample test for the periodically optimised values. System LUXOR for British pound/US dollar (FOREX) 2/11/2003–4/7/2008. During the tests the following other parameters are kept in place: entry time window 9.30am–1.30pm GMT, exits: 0.3% risk stop, 0.8% trailing stop and 1.9% optimised for trading system LUXOR on 30-minute data of the GBP/USD FOREX pair.

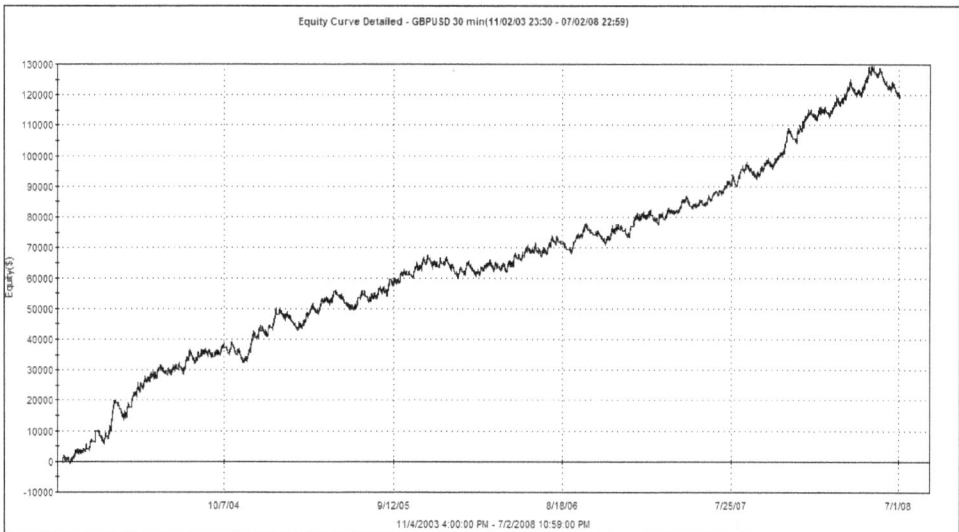

The total net profit is slightly higher and the maximum drawdown lower than with the originally developed system. This is an astonishing result since this equity line is a 100% out-of-sample test for the two main input parameters, the fast and slow moving average. The explanation for this result can partially be given by fig. 6.3 and table 6.1. There you can see that the two moving averages have had little need to change during the five years within the different optimisation windows. In other words the market conditions have not changed a lot and the system was fast enough to adapt to the changing market conditions which have led to these profitable results.

Conclusion

The 30-minute data of the GBP/USD pair is a proper example of a periodic reoptimisation working with the chosen optimisation window (1 year) and shifting period (every three months). Please note, however, that the right selection of this reoptimisation window and period is a complex topic of which you should be aware. The periodic walk-foward optimisation is one of the most powerful tools available today, but like every method it has its pitfalls and needs to be applied correctly. As with every optimisation the settings of an appropriate walk-forward analysis depend on the number of variables in your trading system.

As we saw in chapter 5, the fewer rules your system contains, the more robust your strategy will be in real trading. A trading system with too much complexity leads to too much adaptation of your system to the data and therefore to curve over-fitting. This rule, which was found in normal optimisation with one training data and one test data set, can be transferred to the periodic reoptimisation. However, with the periodic reoptimisation you have the advantage that your out-of-sample data range (the test data) is bigger and therefore an over-fitted system with too much complexity usually fails in the walk-forward analysis more often than it does during the static system tests. Because of this you can trust your system more when it passes the WFA than normal static back-tests.

6.4 The meaning of sample size and market structure

One point which is relevant during every optimisation process and especially of periodic reoptimisation is the question of how to choose your optimisation period. Do you re-optimise every day, every two weeks or every year? Your computer, with its limited power, may give an answer to this question but there are still other points there to investigate, one of which is the market's inherent attributes, which we call *market structure.*

In our LUXOR system we had a rolling optimisation period of one year and a subsequent out-of-sample test period of three months. These chosen settings proved to be appropriate for our system/market combination. But what are good settings for other systems and markets? What if you work with daily data, with 10-minute data or with 1-minute data?

On a TradeStation forum we recently found a double-edged comment about this topic:

> *The problem is that if you use an inadequate sample size then your system is much more likely to get blindsided by price patterns that haven't been previously observed when you implement it. Adequate sample size is the cheapest insurance a system trader can get. Unless a system is tested on an adequate sample of historical data, it is statistically impossible for it to walk forward reliably, no matter how good the test result looks. No amount of post-processing, analysis, walk-forward runs, out-of-sample testing or anything else can compensate for an inadequate historical data sample. If you sampled half a year of hourly wind speed data in Florida during a season when*

no hurricanes (or even any severe local thunderstorms) hit, you might come away with the impression that you had gathered a representative sample of Florida wind speeds.

Let's illustrate what this statement means. Fig. 6.5 shows an artificial market as a function of time. As you can see our market is built in such a way that it has phases of slower and faster oscillations. In this case the structure of the market is a special oscillation or frequency. Of course markets can have hundreds of other typical attributes like opening gaps, trending behaviour, over-bought areas, etc. The fast and slow oscillation here is just a representation for a changing market structure.

Figure 6.5: The market changes as a function of the time. Every market has its special structure, frequency, trends etc.

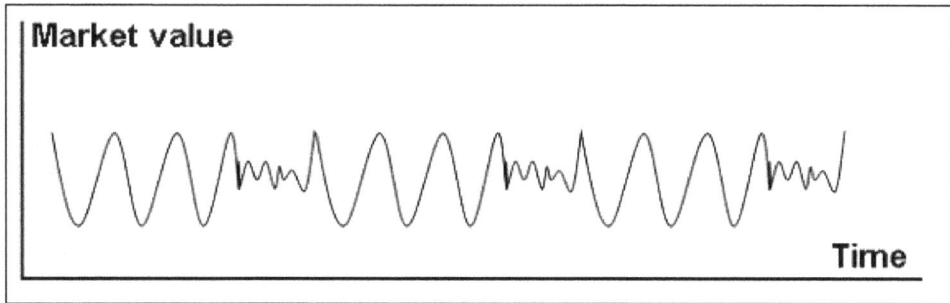

Figure 6.6: Optimisation window fits to the market structure. Ideal case: unseen data is same as data in optimisation window.

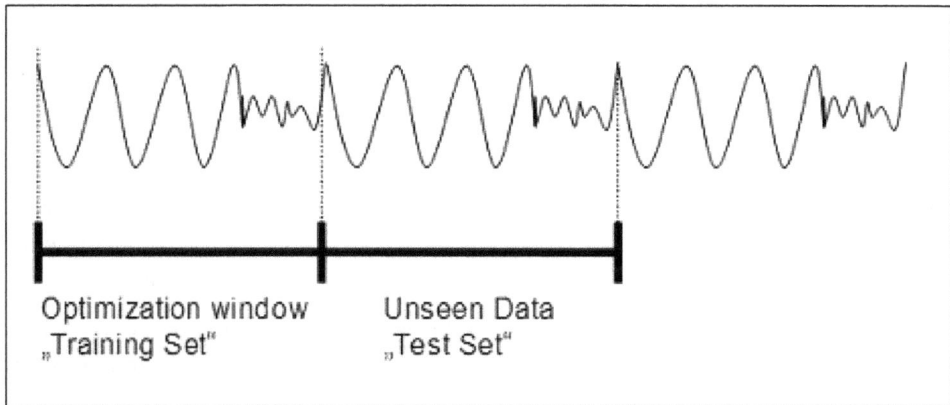

Figure 6.7: Data in the optimisation window has a different structure than the unseen data. Worst case optimisation window.

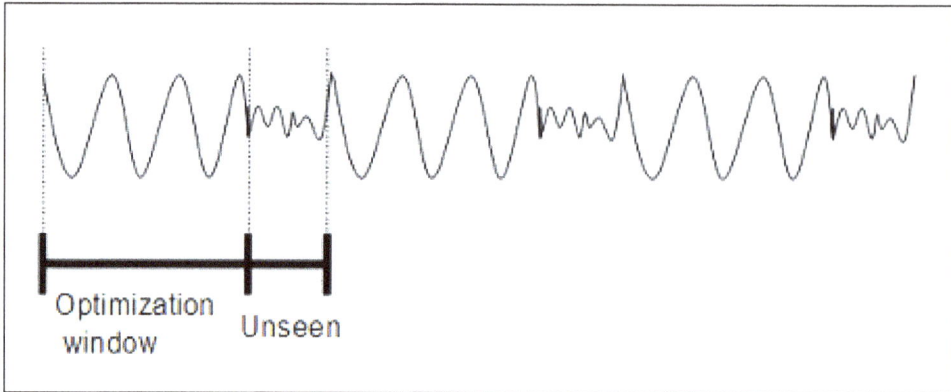

When you now apply your rolling WFA with shifting optimisation window and window of unseen out-of-sample data you can have the two extreme situations as shown in figs. 6.6 and 6.7. The optimisation window can catch a part of the market which contains all the information of the market (fig. 6.6) or it can be chosen in such a way that it just captures an area of market data which is completely different to the price structure which will follow (fig. 6.7). Obviously when doing WFA you will never have one situation or the other but always a mixture in between. What is ultimately suitable can only be discovered through a series of tests in order to gain the necessary experience of different scenarios.

Imagine that you run walk-forward tests on the S&P 500, FTSE or DAX with different out-of-sample exclusion percentages and stress test coefficients on that same short sample of data, in order to get a quantitative idea of the number of walk-forward run and out-of-sample exclusion percentages that work best when walk-forward analysing your system. And let's also assume that you're unlucky enough that everything you run passes all the logical tests for reliability above the accepted threshold and comes out looking OK. Unlucky, you say? Sure, because you can slice and dice your data until your computer goes obsolete but you'll still never *see* the occasional market breakdown that occurs in the stock markets once in 20 years. That's because you're attempting to draw a set of complex statistical inferences out of a pathetically inadequate sample of data.

The longer your sample, the higher the probability that it contains most of the conditions it's likely to encounter in the future. It is human nature to want to curve fit a beautiful system to a short sample of data, but remember that sample sizing is a complex topic. There are high-risk but valid systems that trade very frequently, that may have a shelf life – the interval between reoptimisations – of a day or two and that might look at relatively short histories of data in n-tick or minute range timeframes. To a limited degree, data bars exhibit fractal properties. In other words, 20 years of daily data consists of about 5,000 bars. A year of 15-minute cash session bars also consists of about 5,000 bars. Both charts will exhibit similar patterns of trends, support and resistance, consolidations, double-bottoms, channel breakouts and other manifestations of the dynamic interaction of the group psychology of bulls and bears.

But does this mean that a year's worth of 15-minute data is equivalent to 20 years of daily data? No, it doesn't. The probability of recording a crash in six months' of data would not be any better if its sampling interval were three minutes instead of 60 minutes or daily bars. Be careful with short data samples regardless of timeframe or trading frequency. If your optimisation window is short, it is more likely you will miss important data outside of the window. You will be generalising on limited historical data, and this will lead to a weaker potential for predicting the future.

7

Position Sizing Example, Using the LUXOR System

STEADY MONEY IS not made by mysterious super trading systems, it is made by proper money management of average trading systems.

7.1 Definitions: money management vs. risk management

In order to understand what money management really means, its relation towards risk management is essential. Thus we first of all want to work out the different meanings of the two terms.

Risk management (RM)

Within a single trading system the simplest form of risk management is the control of the distance between the entry and the exit. As a practical example see in chapter 3.5 how different stops and targets are added to an entry logic and how this changes the risk figures like maximum drawdown, average losing trade and largest losing trade. This step is the first in risk management and it is the implementation of the quantified risk values into your trading strategy. The second level of RM is the permanent measurement of risk during active trading. By screening your trading systems regularly, e.g., every month, you have to check if they continue to behave in reality as calculated during testing. You have to watch carefully if markets change concerning point value or volatility: this could affect your calculated risk figures and can mean that adjustments are necessary.

Money management (MM)

Money management (also called *position sizing*) describes how to use your existing trading capital in the most efficient way and it provides answers to the following basic questions:

1. What percentage of the available funds should be totally invested?

2. What percentage of the available funds is it possible to risk in the next trade in a special market?

3. What leverage and market exposure should be chosen?

The success of a trading strategy is highly dependent on correct money management. With appropriate money management techniques the existing capital should not only be maintained but increased in an optimal way. With prudent money management the loss of a single trade is limited in such a way that even if the trade goes wrong often, there is trading capital remaining to try many additional successive similar trades. All MM schemes have one thing in common: they only work on the basis of a trading system with a positive expectancy. Although a proper MM decreases the lot size in unfavourable phases it can only make gains if the system comes back and shows a profit factor higher than 1 in the long run. Whether the profit factor is 1.5 or 1.001 is not that important. As long as it is higher than 1 and the system makes steady profits a good MM can improve the results of your trading system. You do not need to have an extraordinarily profitable trading system to gain money. In the long term it's enough to have a stable strategy with a positive expectancy and proper money management.

From the above definitions of risk management and money management it is obvious that the two processes cannot be separated but they are highly dependent on each other (fig. 7.1).

Figure 7.1: The interaction of money and risk management. The goal of money management is to maximise your profits. The goal of risk management is to minimise your risks. The two different processes are connected with each other.

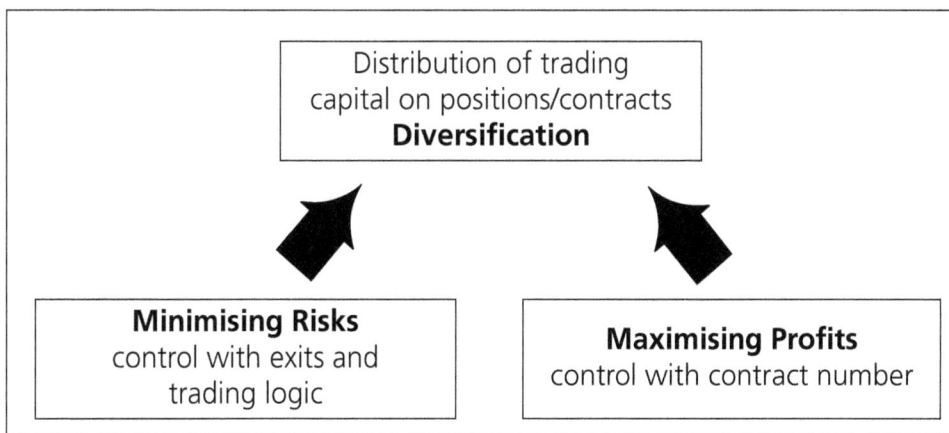

The distance of your initial stops and therefore the risk of your trading system is important for the determination of the number of lots you can trade. On the other hand the distribution of your trading capital is important in deciding how much you can risk in a single trade in a single market.

7.2 Application of different MM schemes

It is time to go from theory to reality and check how MM affects the results of our trading system LUXOR on the pound/dollar FOREX pair within the last five years. To keep things comparable we again work with 30-minute data. All computer tests in this chapter are calculated with $30 slippage and commissions per round turn.

You have probably heard about lots of different MM approaches like Kelly formula, Optimal F, Profit Risk Method, Martingale, Anti-Martingale etc. We do not want to indulge in an overview of all these methods with their pros and cons here. Instead we will choose only a few of them which we have found useful in our experience for real applications.

Reference: The system traded with one lot

Let's start with the result of the LUXOR trading system developed in chapter 3, calculated with one fixed lot and a starting account equity of $100,000 (fig. 7.2). This equity curve is the simplest method of position sizing. It can be called *fixed size money management*, which means in other words that you simply choose the number of shares or lots which are used for each trade. The main purpose of this approach is to provide a good baseline for comparison with more sophisticated money management methods which we will now expound.

Figure 7.2: Detailed equity curve. Traded with one fixed lot. Starting account size = $100,000. LUXOR system British pound/US dollar (FOREX), 30-minute bars, 21/10/2002–4/7/2008, with entry time filter and exits in place. Including $30 slippage and commissions per round turn. An area with a recent small drawdown is encircled as a comparison for the following MM schemes. Chart created with Market System Analyzer.

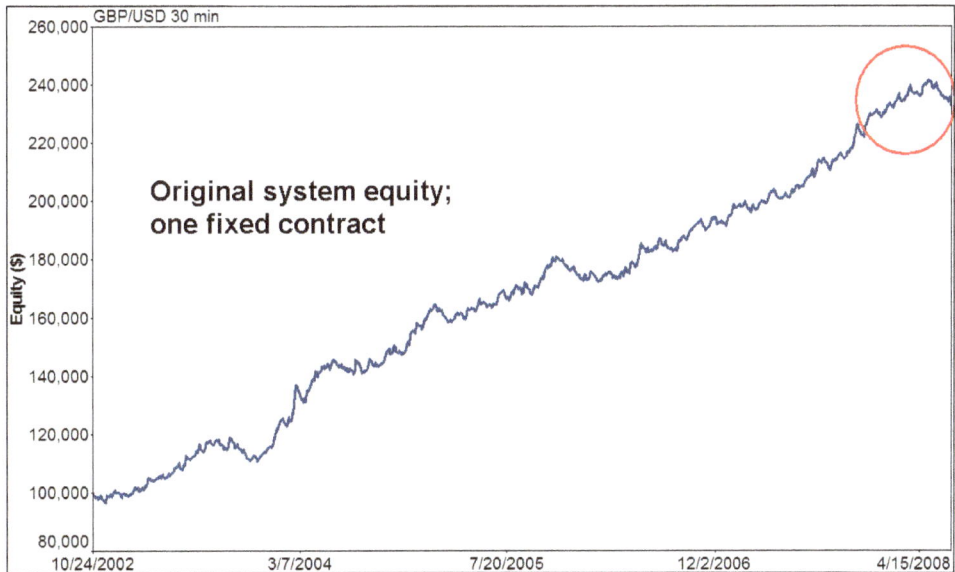

Maximum drawdown MM

This method was used and described by Larry Williams [11]. The basic idea of this MM scheme is derived from risk management: you want to be sure you have enough equity in your account to withstand the worst-case drawdown the account has had in the past. At least, you would need enough equity to cover the size of the worst-case drawdown plus the margin requirement. This means that in order to trade one lot, you would need as a bottom line the one-lot margin requirement plus the worst-case one-lot drawdown. Larry Williams recommended, in order to make his MM a bit safer, to take 150% of the worst-case drawdown plus the margin for the first lot. Each subsequent lot is then added when the equity increases by 150% of the worst-case drawdown. This should ensure that you have enough equity to avoid losing everything even if the worst-case drawdown repeats itself. Let's see what this simple MM scheme does with our trading system (fig. 7.3).

Figure 7.3: 150% maximum drawdown MM by Larry Williams. Upper blue line: equity curve. Lower black area: number of traded lots. Starting account size = $100,000. Trend-following system British pound/US dollar (FOREX), 30-minute bars, 21/10/2002–4/7/2008, with entry time filter and exits in place. Including $30 slippage and commissions per round turn. An area with a recent drawdown is encircled. Chart created with Market System Analyzer.

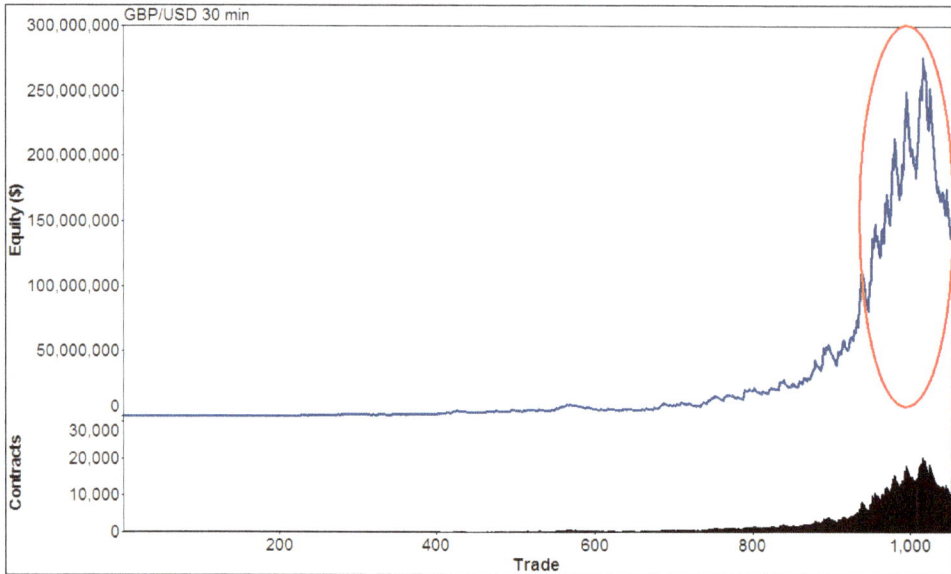

Instead of $120,000 profits without money management the system can now reach a final profit of $137m with the applied MM scheme! But be careful. First of all the high number of 15,000 lots is not realistic. If you traded that much you certainly could not keep the same back-test result as with trading one lot. Even in the very liquid currency markets, such a high trading volume would change the market and lead to worse fills. Another point is the high risk of your trading system with the increased profits. Please note that the drawdown after the equity peak of $276m is $139m bigger than the left profit. So the higher gains have the price of higher risks. Let's see how other MM methods perform.

Fixed fractional MM

Fixed fractional MM was developed by another trader and book author, Ralph Vince, at around the same time as Larry Williams' maximum drawdown scheme [12]. Ralph Vince's method is also known as fixed risk position sizing because it risks the same percentage or fraction of the account equity on each trade. For example, with an account value of $10,000 a fixed fractional MM of 2% means that you want to risk a maximum of $200 per transaction.

But how do you set this risk of $200 in real trading? Let's check what this means with the example of our trading system and the pound/dollar. To answer this question we must go back to our previous findings, the strong interaction between risk and money management, and to chapter 3 where we looked for exits.

We found an optimal stop loss value of 0.3% for the pound/dollar. With the pound/dollar trading at $2.00 the 0.3% stop loss would mean a risk of $600 for one lot (0.3% × $2.00 × 100,000) and this approach has not yet taken into account the slippage and the fact that even in the back-test the biggest loss was much bigger ($810). So obviously there is a dilemma. You cannot trade the pound/dollar currency pair with a $10,000 account equity with that 0.3% initial stop loss and a risk of 2%. The way out is to make changes to your money management or your risk management. You have to choose one of the following two possibilities:

1. Change of risk management: you set a tighter stop to lower your risk per trade.

2. Change of money management: you increase the account equity or you increase the risk.

There is a possibility that option one directly affects the trading logic. From all our findings about stops and profit targets we know that the trading system performance suffers with stops that are too tight. From the discussion in chapter 3 you have seen that trades need enough room to develop. Tight stops remove this room and can turn a profitable strategy into a losing strategy. Since we do not want to change this risk management it means we must change our money management (possibility two) and set the initial account value higher. Doing this is much easier to calculate but means in practice that you must have enough funds available. That's one reason why single traders very seldom use MM schemes and why bigger funds are more successful in the long run.

Let's calculate how much should be the minimum account. We want to risk 2% of our account with the next transaction. Since our risk with one lot is chosen by the preset stop loss of the trading system ($600), this means that the account must be at least $30,000, when trading one lot at this risk ($600 is 2% of $30,000). We take double this value to be sure not to conflict with our risk settings. So we trade one lot with $60,000. With a starting account value of $100,000 this means that one lot is allowed per transaction until the account value has reached $120,000 (= 2 × $60,000). The third lot can be traded when the account reaches $180,000 and so on. Please note that when the account equity decreases, the number of traded lots also has to be lowered accordingly. The result of this MM is shown in fig. 7.4A. You see that while the equity curve (blue line) is growing, more lots can be added (lower black area), until the highest account value of $790,000, reached in May 2008, when 14 lots are traded. When trading with so many lots the trading system comes into a drawdown phase (red encircled) which then leads to a bigger drawdown. Please note how this drawdown phase is huge compared with the original trading system traded with one fixed lot since now the drawdown is amplified by the 14 lots.

It is worth finding out what happens when we increase the risk per transaction more and more, to 5%, 10% then even to 30% (figs. 7.4B–D). As you can see the biggest equity point reached in May 2008 gets dramatically higher and higher. Whereas the fixed fractional MM with 2% risk reaches a biggest equity peak of $790,000, the MM with 5% risk reaches over $22m, the MM with 10% reaches $981m and the MM with 30% risk reaches over $6bn!

But as you know, trees do not grow to the sky and the high profits have a high price. With the 30% fixed fractional MM finally only $538m is left from the $6bn reached before. So the suffered drawdown from the equity peak of over $6bn was ten times higher than the final profit! The more aggressive the MM that is chosen, the higher the equity peak, but the bigger the drawdown which the equity curve suffers thereafter. The fixed fractional MM scheme works like an amplifier of the gains but also of the losses. You see again from this simple example, as with the above shown maximum drawdown MM, that although an aggressive MM seems to be attractive at the first glance because it promises big profits, the risks behind it quickly become too high.

Figure 7.4: Applying fixed fractional MM. The aggressiveness of the MM is increased from 2%, 5%, 10% up to 30%. Upper blue line: equity curve. Lower black area: number of traded lots. Starting account size = $100,000. Trend-following system British pound/ US dollar (FOREX), 30-minute bars, 21/10/2002–4/7/2008, with entry time filter and exits in place. Including $30 slippage and commissions per round turn. An area with a recent drawdown is encircled. Charts created with Market System Analyzer.

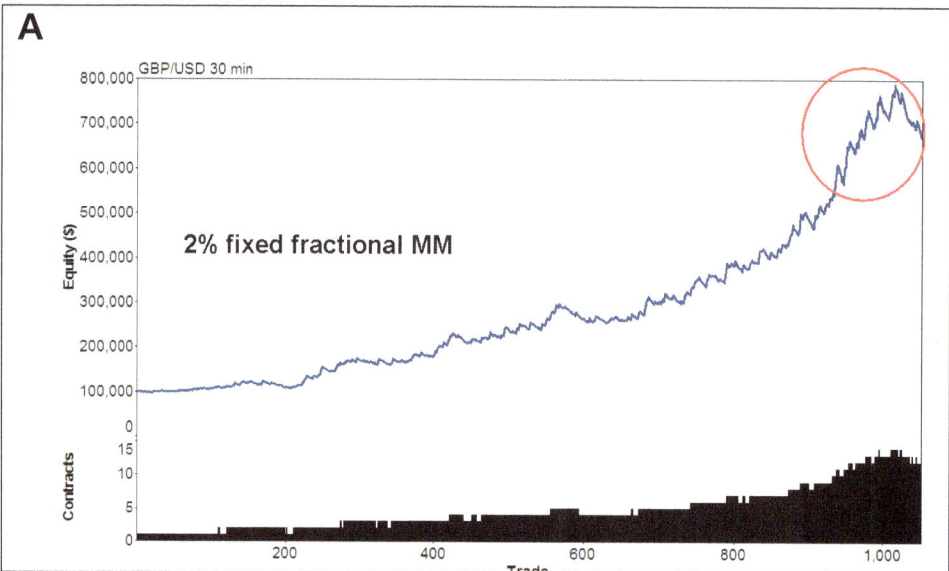

B

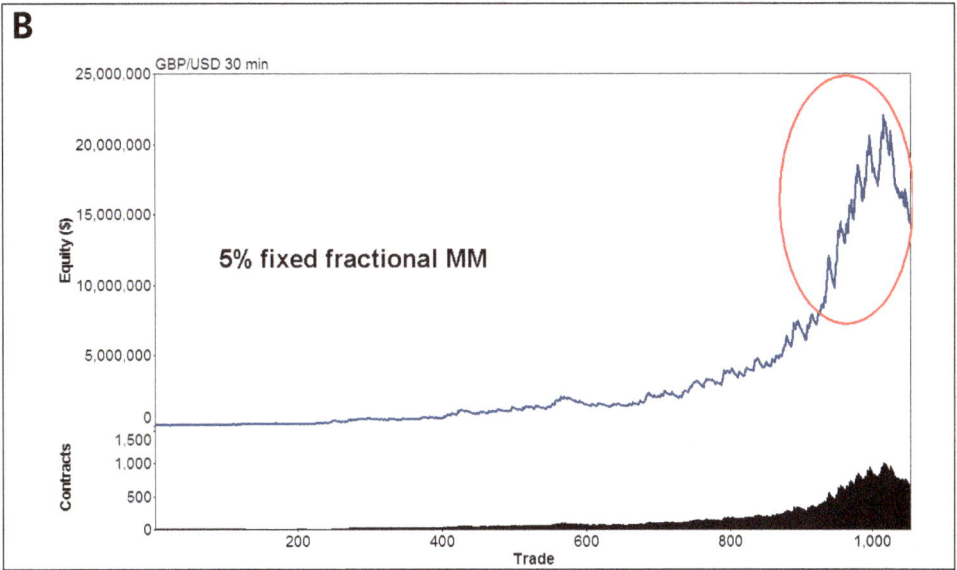

GBP/USD 30 min

5% fixed fractional MM

C

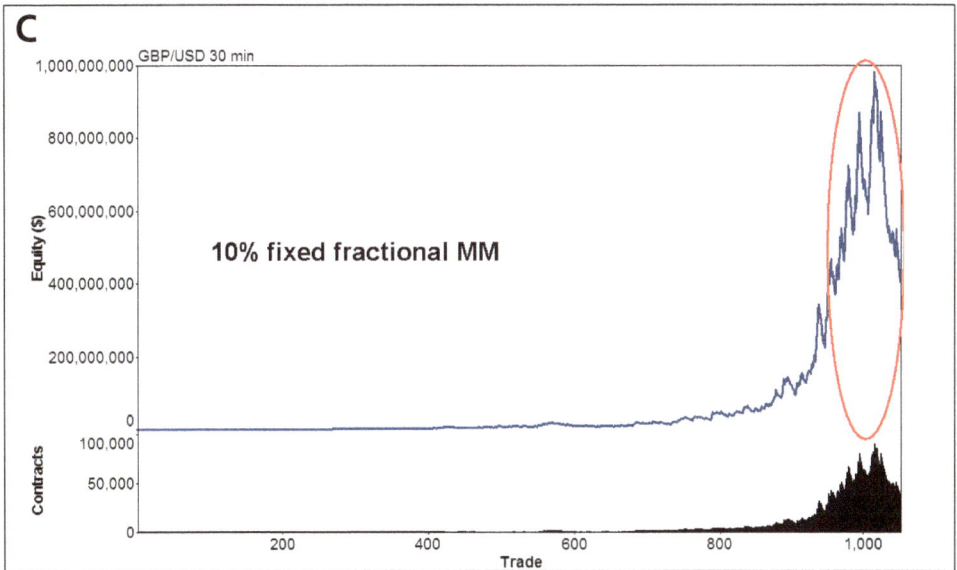

GBP/USD 30 min

10% fixed fractional MM

D

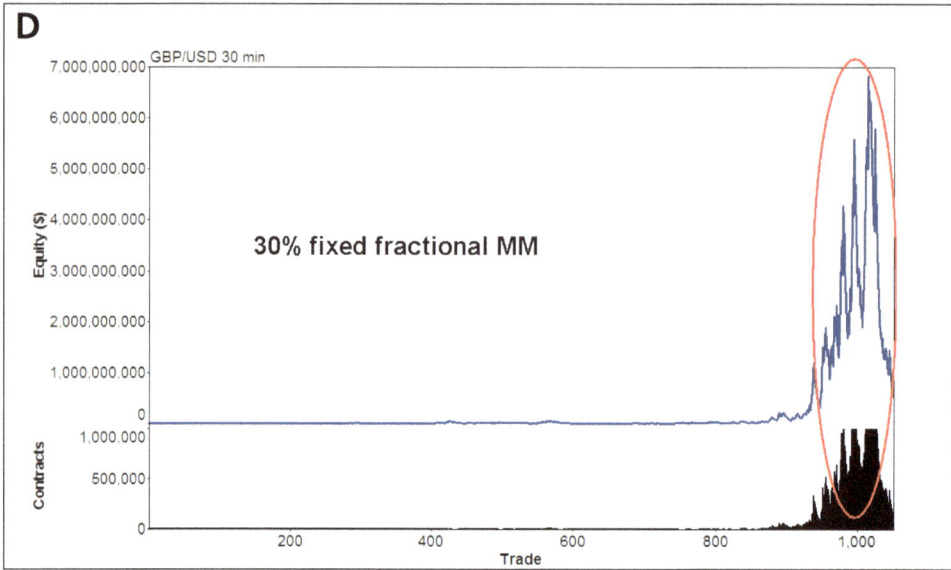

So let's see if there are more conservative methods out there.

Fixed ratio MM

Fixed ratio MM was first introduced by Ryan Jones in his book *The Trading Game* in 1999 [13]. In the fixed ratio position sizing the key parameter is the *delta*. This delta is the dollar amount of profit per traded unit to increase the number of units by one. A delta of $10,000 means that if you're currently trading one lot you would need to increase your account equity by $10,000 to start trading two lots. Once you get to two lots, you would need an additional profit of $20,000 to start trading three lots. Then, trading with three lots, you would need an additional profit of $30,000 to start trading four lots and so on. The base to calculate the number of traded lots in fixed ratio position sizing is the following equation:

```
N = 0.5 × [((2 × N₀ - 1)² + 8 × P/delta)⁰·⁵ + 1]
```

N is the traded position size, N_0 is the starting position size, P is the total closed trade profit, and delta is the parameter discussed above. As the mathematicians know $x^{0.5}$ means the square root of x.

A few points are worth mentioning. The profit P is the accumulated profit over all trades leading up to the one for which you want to calculate the number of lots. As a consequence the position size for the first trade is always N_0 because you start with zero profits (P = 0). Please note that the account equity is not a factor in this equation, so changing the starting account size will not change the number of traded lots. Neither is the trade risk a factor in this equation – if trade risks are defined for the current sequence of trades, they will be ignored when fixed ratio position sizing is in effect. All that matters is the accumulated profit and the delta. The delta determines how quickly the lots are added or subtracted.

Ryan Jones' position sizing rule leads to a MM scheme which is a bit more conservative than the fixed fractional MM by Ralph Vince which was shown above. You can simply compare the two MM schemes as following (fig. 7.5):

Ralph Vince, fixed fractional lots = constant * account-size
Ryan Jones, fixed ratio lots = constant * squareroot(account-size)

So in contrast to the above situation with fixed fractional MM where the number of traded lots is linearly increased with the account size, with the fixed ratio MM the number of lots is increased like a square root function. This MM type is a bit more agressive in the beginning, but becomes more conservative and slower with more gained trading capital.

Figure 7.5: Fixed Ratio vs. Fixed Fractional MM. As trading capital increases, the fixed ratio MM increases the number of lots more slowly, with a square root function, than the fixed fractional MM, which works linearly.

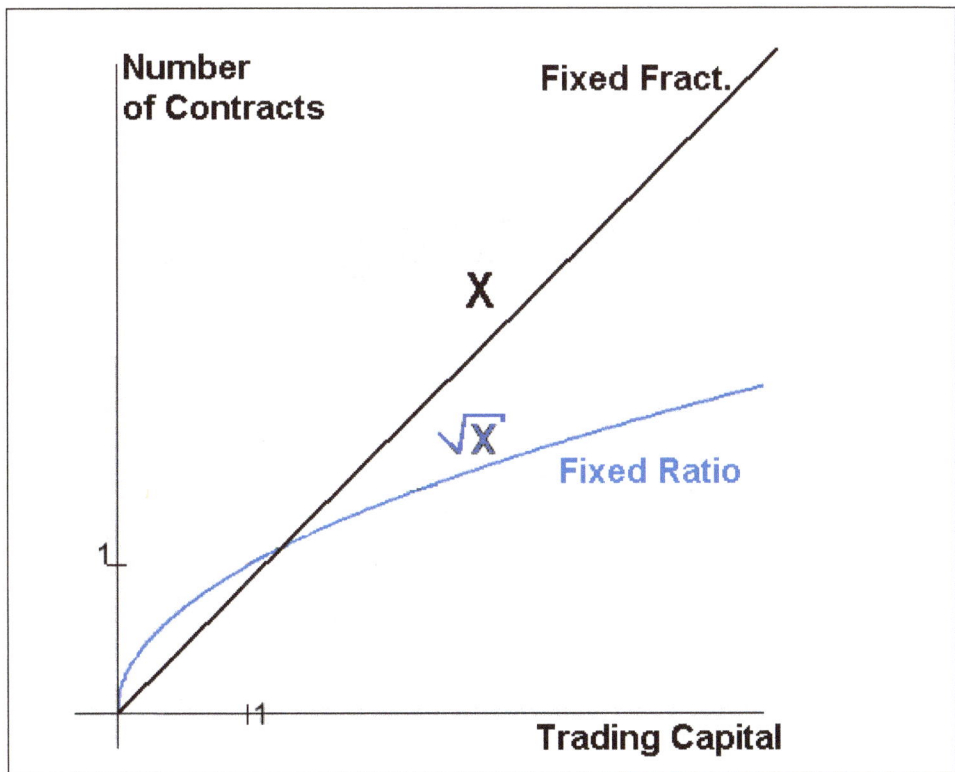

To see how fixed ratio MM works let's start with a delta of $100,000. This means that you can add the second lot only after your account value has increased by another $100,000–$200,000 (fig. 7.6A). Obviously this MM is very slow and not much different from just trading one lot all the time so let's make it a bit more aggressive. (figs. 7.6B and C).

Figure 7.6: Applying fixed ratio MM. The aggressiveness of the MM is increased from A to C. Upper blue line: equity curve. Lower black area: number of traded lots. Starting account size = $100,000. LUXOR system on British pound/US dollar (FOREX), 30-minute bars, 21/10/2002–4/7/2008, with entry time filter and exits in place. Including $30 slippage and commissions per round turn. An area with a recent drawdown is encircled. Chart created with Market System Analyzer.

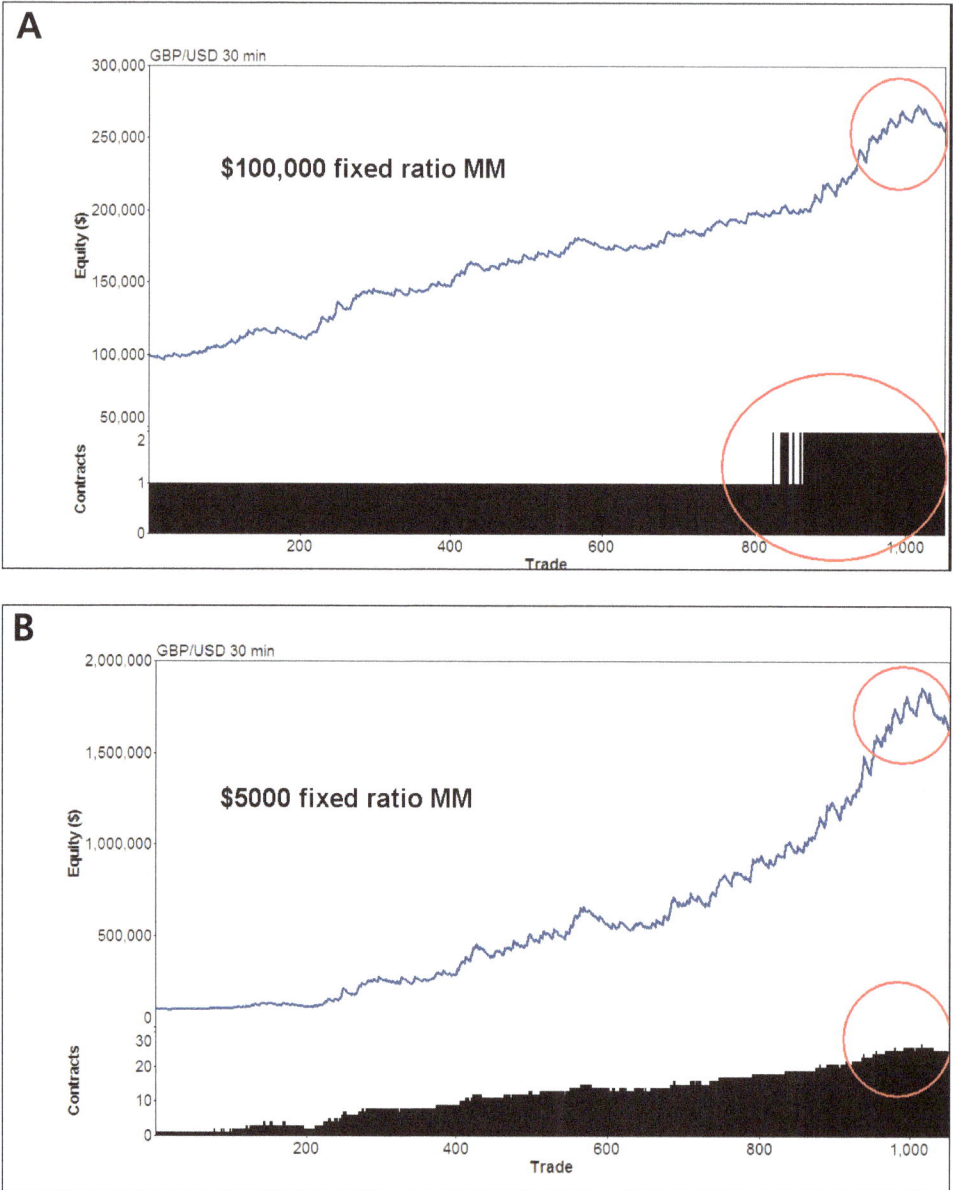

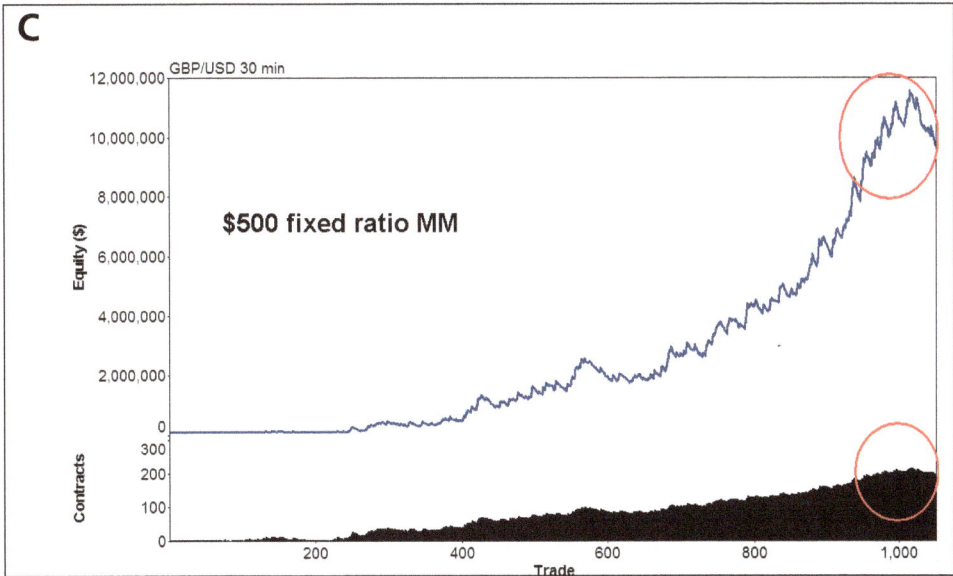

As with the fixed fractional MM the more aggressively you increase the lot size, the higher equity peaks you can reach, but also the bigger drawdowns you get in phases where the trading system shows some weakness. Compared with the fixed fractional MM the fixed ratio MM shows a better return/risk ratio as you can see when you have a closer look on the delta=$500 fixed ratio MM (fig. 7.6C). There you see that the equity high is $11.5m and the drawdown is about $1.8m. Although the drawdown is still excessive, the return/drawdown ratio is, with 6.4 in this example, better than the comparable 5% fixed fractional MM where you have an equity peak of $22m but then a drawdown of $8m leading to a return/drawdown ratio of 2.8.

7.3 Monte Carlo analysis of the position sized system

Position sizing increases your profits. But with the profits the risks also become higher. To get a better idea of how big the risks become we do a Monte Carlo analysis of the LUXOR system after position sizing and compare its results with the situation when no MM is applied (table 7.1).

Table. 7.1: System figures without (green) and with money management (yellow). LUXOR system on British pound/US dollar (FOREX), 30-minute bars, 21/10/2002–4/7/2008, with entry time filter and exits in place. Including $30 slippage and commissions per round turn.

	One Fixed Contract		$5,000 Fixed Ratio MM	
Test period:	21/10/2002–4/7/2008		21/10/2002–4/7/2008	
Market	GBP/USD, 30-min bars		GBP/USD, 30-min bars	
Costs:	30$ Slipp. + Comm.		30$ Slipp. + Comm.	
Number of samples for Monte Carlo analysis	5000		5000	
Max Number of Contracts	1		27	
Minimum Number of Contracts	1		1	
Average Number of Contracts	1		12	
Total Net Profit	$132,590		$1,528,499	
Starting Account value	$50,000		$50,000	
Final Account Equity	$182,590		$1,578,499	
Total Number of Trades	1,051		1,051	
Number of Winning Trades	370		370	
Number of Losing Trades	681		681	
Largest Winning Trade	$3,900		$90,144	
Average Winning Trade	$1,120		$13,737	
Largest Losing Trade	($810)		($15,418)	
Average Losing Trade	($414)		($4,860)	
Monte Carlo analysis Results	Worst Case Max. Drawdown	Worst Case Average Drawdown	Worst Case Max. Drawdown	Worst Case Average Drawdown
ORIGINAL SYSTEM	($10,292)	($1,976)	($229,560)	($26,115)
MONTE CARLO RESULTS AT 90% CONFIDENCE	($16,136)	($2,176)	($295,316)	($29,168)
MONTE CARLO RESULTS AT 95% CONFIDENCE	($17,908)	($2,259)	($340,234)	($30,588)
MONTE CARLO RESULTS AT 99% CONFIDENCE	($21,364)	($2,308)	($446,064)	($33,182)

This table shows that the $5,000 fixed ratio MM trades up to 27 lots simultaneously. This MM leads to a total net profit of over $1.5m, compared to the $132,000 when trading one fixed lot. The price for the higher gain is higher risk. The MM increases the largest losing trade to $15,418 (from $810) and the maximum drawdown to $229,560 (from $10,292). The Monte Carlo analysis reveals that the worst case drawdown which can happen with 1% probability (since with 99% it is avoided) is now $446,064 (from $21,364).

7.4 Conclusion

The type of MM to select depends on the risks which you are prone to take. MM works like an amplifier of your trading logic, independently of which method you chose for position sizing. If it is properly adjusted then it will increase the profits of your trading system, but never forget that the risks are increased too – even with the best MM. In order to increase profits and at the same time keep the risk low it is advantageous to combine different systems and markets. You will find some ideas about this topic in the following chapter.

Part III

Systematic Portfolio Trading

So far this book has dealt with single trading systems only.

Once you have got some robust trading systems, the question arises of which trading systems to use on which markets and especially how to combine them in a useful way.

This final section of this book deals now with the question of how to construct portfolios.

The following two possibilities are discussed:

1. How to combine different trading systems and markets to construct portfolios (chapter 8).

2. How to use one strategy and apply it to huge portfolios of stocks (chapter 9).

Chapter 8 is taken from the first edition and has been updated, while chapter 9 is completely new. With the inclusion of this important new chapter on trading portfolios of stocks, we have responded to the wishes of many readers who said they missed this topic in the first edition.

8

Dynamic Portfolio Construction

T$_{\text{HIS CHAPTER DEALS}}$ with the question of how to combine different trading systems and markets to construct portfolios.

The topic is too large to provide a complete overview in this book, but on the following pages and in appendices 1–3 we have provided some practical tips from our own experience.

8.1 Introduction to portfolio construction

Even if many traders are aware of the notion that trading a portfolio of multiple systems on the same asset, or the same system on multiple assets, or both, smooths the overall equity line, few traders test and optimise a system with this perspective in mind. One motive for this in the past may have been that the most common technical analysis packages did not allow traders to produce a portfolio equity line easily. Nowadays things have changed and many software houses offer products that allow traders to test a multi-market, multi-systems portfolio.

A list of the main available software for portfolio trading

The following list is only a small selection which are the most important concerning this book.

AmiBroker (AmiBroker.com)

AmiBroker is a technical analysis and trading system development platform, with advanced real-time charting, portfolio back-testing/optimisation and scanning capabilities. AmiBroker's robust system development environment allows the trader to find market inefficiencies, code the system and validate it using powerful statistical methods including the walk-forward test and Monte Carlo simulation. AmiBroker allows you to trade directly from charts or programmatically, using an auto-trading interface to various brokers and data services.

MultiCharts (MultiCharts.com)

MultiCharts is a complete trading software platform for professionals:

- It comes with high-definition charting, support for nearly all data feeds and the main brokers, dynamic portfolio-level strategy back-testing, EasyLanguage support, interactive performance reporting, genetic optimisation, market scanner, data replay, and plenty of strategies and indicators.

Wealthlab (www.wealth-lab.com)

A dedicated software platform for back-testing and auto-trading:

- It supports daily/intraday strategies, portfolio level testing and optimisation – best for back-testing price based signals (technical analysis), C# scripting – software extensions supported – data feed handling, strategy execution, etc.

Market System Analyzer (www.adaptrade.com)

This is cheap and smart software that can do whatever you need in the way of portfolio testing. It allows you to import system report data from TradeStation in Excel format, even if you need to do it for every single stock or future in the portfolio (and this is quite time-demanding). It performs equity line crossovers, Monte Carlo analysis, trade dependency and portfolio analysis.

The role of correlations

Even though there are dozens of portfolio-building software programs available, the inclination to consider a single equity is still deeply rooted among traders. Nothing could be more wrong: with all the trading systems' intricacies set aside, a mediocre system optimised on a bunch of assets will be likely to produce a reasonable portfolio equity line. This should always be kept in mind when you scan different assets' prices with a newly-built trading system because what you are doing makes no sense if not included in a multi-market perspective. This is why we believe that approaching quantitative trading with a focus on a portfolio of assets, should they be stocks, futures, mutual funds or any other instrument, is a key element in surviving in the long run.

Today there is a deep flaw in the difference between what commonly-accepted financial theory predicates about portfolio construction, and what you can do with an average technical analysis software in practice.

Modern portfolio theory is built on the premise that in order to build an efficient portfolio you need to consider the correlations among the different assets. The more uncorrelated the assets the more efficient the portfolio, because if a position is losing, another position on a diverse asset will make money, dampening the overall effect on the portfolio equity line. The backbone of modern portfolio theory relies on the assumption that you cannot forecast the markets so that a systematic trader, who believes exactly the opposite, becomes confused on how to approach the topic.

Correlation is indeed a pivotal question for a systematic trader because if, for example, you are using the same system on different markets and this system is trend-following, it is clear in order to have two different positions – one losing and the other winning – you need to have some markets that trend and other markets that stay choppy (a situation that often occurs). But let's assume that you are trading multiple assets with two different systems, one trend-following and the other counter-trend. In this case you do not need all markets to be trending to have an upward sloping portfolio equity line. Some markets can trend and others can zig-zag with no definitive trend, and notwithstanding the overall portfolio will be profitable.

Let's move the reasoning a step ahead: let's assume that we have both trend-following systems (prone to exploit trending markets) and counter-trend systems (prone to exploit choppy markets) applied over the same markets. How does correlation fit into this picture? It seems that a sane reply would be simply that when it boils down to building a real portfolio with real trading systems the complex traditional theory totters and it shows how difficult it is to move from a pure theoretical world to the everyday life of a systematic trader.

Another critique of a portfolio approach based on correlation among assets is that correlation is not a stationary measure of the relative behaviour of two different assets. By stationary we mean that a form of correlation is not bound to last forever, economics change correlations among assets, so that presuming that in one year's time correlation will be the same as today could be fatal. Let's take the example of oil: economies were much more dependent on oil during the 1973–74 and 1979 shocks than during the 2008 bubble. So inflation perspectives during the 2008 bubble were much less imperative than 30 years earlier because Western economies were much less dependent on oil. The unfixed character of correlations is a controversial area that theoretical portfolio construction seems not to consider in an appropriate way.

Publications and theoretical tools

Among academic papers there is a shortage of good publications about portfolio construction with an algorithmic approach. One author that tried to fight against this situation is Thomas Stridsman. He wrote two inspiring books, *Trading Systems That Work* and *Trading Systems and Money Management*, where even without arriving at a final conclusion he tried to address all the relevant topics of portfolio construction properly. The rest of the technical literature on trading systems is almost silent on this approach. So, at this point it is impossible to go ahead with the sure support of an authoritative author and we need to navigate in uncharted waters.

Traders are often accused of being brutal and unfortunately we belong to this category. This is why our approach to portfolio construction is based on a practical approach that starts from a simple consideration: a trader, even a sophisticated one, should always be in control of what he does. We often meet professional traders, both private and institutional, that employ theoretical tools they do not fully understand or that they do not properly dominate. This is harmful when you come to real trading because markets are merciless. A trader, when using a trading system, needs to have total control of all its nuances. To employ complicated tools that require much time to be explored and understood is out of the reach of an average trader and portfolio manager. Time is short, markets are running all day long and you need to have a quick grasp of what to do without delving into complicated statistical problems.

Portfolio trading in practice

A sound approach to portfolio trading is something that is based on sound and prudent premises. Better, on sceptical premises. Scepticism in quantitative trading is the best rule you can apply since it lowers risk. It is hard to have doubts about everything but if you get accustomed to it you will arrive at the conclusion that there are just a few tenets that are really safe for a trader. We will now review some hard-earned lessons we have gained through experience:

The more the better

It would be unwise to dictate rules for the trading systems development field that should be abided only by traders who have huge programming and statistical skills or simply by professional traders that are backed by a powerful IT department. If you do not know how to make money in a discretionary way, every moderately good trading system (even a properly tested moving average crossover system) will be a better solution than merely following your gut feeling. Sometimes it can seem that to be a successful system trader you need to be a rocket scientist, though this is not the case at all. If you do not know how to make money in a discretionary way, whichever sound trading system you use will allow you to have an edge against the market.

It is useless to wonder if it is better to use a simple profitable moving average crossover system carefully optimised on a portfolio or a complex breakout and counter-trend system optimised with a detailed walk-forward analysis if you are only able to have the first one. You can only trade with the tools and systems available to you and not with the tools and systems you would have in an ideal world. Time is money and sometimes it could be more rewarding to trade with a simple system rather than spending years developing a more complex system that is beyond your reach. A situation that often recurs in this business is the very sophisticated would-be trader that decade after decade keeps improving his system without ever applying it with real money, since it was not yet accomplished. Perfectionism is not a good quality in trading systems' development.

A price series is a price series and nothing more than a price series

A trading system should produce good results on a price series and not forcedly on a precise number of other price series. Thomas Stridsman argues that he usually tests a system over 30–60 markets along 20 years and he wants it to perform moderately well on at least two-thirds of all markets (see [1]). We think that this is a sophisticated approach and we agree with it, but we have encountered only a few trading systems that were successful on all markets. In many cases systems usually work with the same efficiency on futures that belong to the same category: bonds, currencies, stock indexes, cereals, etc. As stated above, there is not a clear recipe for success and you can only trade with the systems you have at your disposal today. If your systems work on all the markets you will trade on all the markets, but if they just work on three different markets they should not be discarded just for this reason.

We know what happened today, but we have no means of knowing what will happen tomorrow

Cancel every estimate from your dictionary when you build a trading systems portfolio. There are some authors that claim that you need to figure out your estimated portfolio return and variance in order to decide money management, systems and markets selection. This is the wrong approach because the very reason we are using trading systems is because we do not know how to predict the future and neither the expected average returns and variance can be estimated.

If we limit risks, profits will take care of themselves

We cannot control the profit of a position which we entered without the support of an estimate. What we control is the risk; that is the difference between the entry price and the stop loss. This is what we need to analyse in order to protect our capital.

This is a defensive approach to systematic portfolio trading and it must be clear that it does not exclude, once properly researched, other portfolio composition methodologies. As should be clear from the book, a trader should assess all the trading methodologies and tools the industry provides, but it is always prudent to apply only those methodologies that he can fully control and understand. The four points above are a kind of bottom line in systematic portfolio trading.

In the literature about trading systems there are really few ideas on how to compose a portfolio; that is, which markets to trade and which systems to apply to which markets. Usually in our business, where there is a lack of information about a specific topic it means that some gold nuggets are hidden somewhere. Portfolio composition is one such area that for years has not been able to overcome some useless ideas such as the Wilder's Commodity Selection Index or other more sophisticated approaches full of estimates, the origins of which nobody knows.

Let's look at some practical ways to build a systems portfolio. These approaches are real ones and have been applied either by us or by the best trading systems developers we have met in the last decade. We will not delve into the intricacies of each one because this would take us too far away from our path. Whichever method you decide upon, please test it carefully before trading. In this chapter we will pinpoint some hints about pros and cons you will encounter with every portfolio construction method.

Unfortunately we do not have a definite word about this subject: we believe that portfolio composition method can often depend on which systems you are adopting and, overall, it will be affected by whether you are trading many markets with the same systems, many markets with many systems or one market with many systems.

Total vs. partial equity contribution

Once the system is tested against a basket of stocks and futures, and results are moderately positive on almost all the markets, the pivotal question will be whether to trade all the markets or to trade just those instruments where the system was best performing and discard the others. If you just follow this path, you will surely have the best historical equity line you ever saw, but you will probably go bust after a few trades. The common tenet here is that you need to trade all the markets because you do not know what will happen tomorrow. The futures that were the best performing could become choppy or the underperforming futures could become volatile and it may be easier to make money on them. Obviously there is no way for you to pretend you know which futures will be volatile tomorrow. Everybody would agree with this tenet. But before sticking to it without discrimination it is better we understand that it relies on some basic premises.

The first premise is that it assumes we just have a unique trend-following system or we just have a unique counter-trend system but not both of them. Only with one of these systems would we be worried if the market becomes respectively too choppy or too trendy. The second premise is that we need to apply the same system to all the same markets and not, for example, a counter-trend system to a traditionally choppy market and a trend-following system to a traditionally volatile market. If instead of having a single system to trade all the markets we have two different systems to trade all the markets this is surely a step ahead. We remind readers of our number 1 principle: the more the better. To arrive at a unique conclusion without specifying how many systems we have is impossible because we still need to make clear what the starting point is. If you just have a trend-following trading system it will be prudent to trade all the markets because you are not able to know in advance which market will trend and which market will be in congestion. If you have a trend-following system and a counter-trend system you can prudently trade all the markets or even apply the trend-following system to the traditionally volatile markets and the counter trend to the traditionally choppy markets. This second solution is obviously more hazardous than the first but there are additional tools that can lower the risk.

Partial equity contribution

Another solution would be to test the systems on all the markets and then choose a fixed fraction of the best performing markets according to the broad category to which they belong: cereals, energies, currencies, stock indexes, bonds, etc. This portfolio is a kind of compromise between the total contribution and the all markets choice and it is neither too aggressive nor too defensive. This method could be the golden middle.

8.2 Correlation among equity lines

As we have seen, this is one of the sacred topics of portfolio trading: look for those markets that are negatively correlated and trade them. In this way you can smooth the resulting portfolio equity line. The premise of this approach is always that you need to have the same system, set with the same inputs, on all the markets. If you trade a trend-following system and a counter-trend system the logic would require you to trade the same market in order to be sure that, whether it is trendy or choppy, you have a tool at your disposal that will fit the market situation and will make more money than the other one you trade. But there is a lot more in store for this approach. Nobody understands why you should check correlations on the price series instead of on the equity line itself. If you are a systematic trader you will not build your portfolio considering the price correlation among the assets, but you will only watch the equity lines and the correlations among them. If equity lines are growing it means that the systems are suitable to trade that market, if they are decreasing you would be better off to stop them.

Correlation among assets varies according to the economic situation. These changes take a lot of time to shape but once they take root they go ahead for years. So there is no reason not to exploit them. What we believe is that equity lines are the most suitable indicators for checking correlations among systems and among markets. More precisely when we quote equity lines, "we want to measure the inter-correlations of daily equity changes among the different market systems" [12]. Price series themselves would be more important in terms of correlation if we were to manage assets using just fundamental analysis – their role in this case would be paramount in terms of asset allocation. It is not by accident that most platforms still use a correlation matrix based on monthly equity lines to calculate correlations among the different markets. As far as we are concerned, we would advocate the use of a shorter measure of correlation in order to minimise drawdown (weekly correlation or some form of averaging and smoothing of daily correlation). In our experience it is difficult to find negative correlations among futures' monthly equity lines and even a negative correlation coefficient that amounts to -0.2 is really interesting in order to lower the portfolio drawdown (fig. 8.1).

Figure 8.1: Matrix of linear correlations among monthly equity lines of one of our portfolios traded with real money.

	BO	C	CL	FGBL	GC	JY	QM	SF	SM	TY	US	W	S	EC
BO		(0.2465)	0.0845	0.0971	(0.0162)	0.2678	0.2458	0.2354	0.1481	(0.0178)	0.0081	0.5000	0.4830	0.0962
C	(0.2465)		(0.0218)	(0.0334)	0.0944	(0.1478)	(0.1656)	0.1085	0.0349	0.1350	0.1129	0.0315	0.4600	0.0082
CL	0.0845	(0.0218)		0.0502	(0.0024)	0.1159	0.5514	0.1630	0.0755	(0.0019)	0.0158	0.0920	(0.0345)	0.0691
FGBL	0.0971	(0.0334)	0.0502		(0.1612)	(0.0187)	0.1421	0.2673	0.1600	0.3054	0.1733	0.0439	(0.0551)	0.0000
GC	(0.0162)	0.0944	(0.0024)	(0.1612)		(0.0351)	0.0462	0.0285	0.1195	(0.0360)	(0.0838)	0.0437	0.1981	0.2711
JY	0.2678	(0.1478)	0.1159	(0.0187)	(0.0351)		0.1819	(0.0304)	0.0971	(0.1208)	(0.0050)	0.2806	0.2511	0.1176
QM	0.2458	(0.1656)	0.5514	0.1421	0.0462	0.1819		0.2274	0.1419	(0.0835)	(0.1079)	0.1026	0.0669	0.1926
SF	0.2354	0.1085	0.1630	0.2673	0.0285	(0.0304)	0.2274		0.0704	0.0075	0.0089	0.1198	0.2008	0.1664
SM	0.1481	0.0349	0.0755	0.1600	0.1195	0.0971	0.1419	0.0704		(0.0880)	0.0172	0.0498	0.2007	0.2108
TY	(0.0178)	0.1350	(0.0019)	0.3054	(0.0360)	(0.1208)	(0.0835)	0.0075	(0.0880)		0.3063	0.0197	0.0159	(0.2185)
US	0.0081	0.1129	0.0158	0.1733	(0.0838)	(0.0050)	(0.1079)	0.0089	0.0172	0.3063		0.0841	0.0363	0.0100
W	0.5000	0.0315	0.0920	0.0439	0.0437	0.2806	0.1026	0.1198	0.0498	0.0197	0.0841		0.4674	0.0616
S	0.4830	0.4600	(0.0345)	(0.0551)	0.1981	0.2511	0.0669	0.2008	0.2007	0.0159	0.0363	0.4674		0.2080
EC	0.0962	0.0082	0.0691	0.0000	0.2711	0.1176	0.1926	0.1664	0.2108	(0.2185)	0.0100	0.0616	0.2080	

As you can see there is no negative correlation lower than -0.30. By the way, this is a portfolio multimarket multisystem dating to May 2008. The average starting period is 2001–2002 when electronic markets were launched, but many trading systems – on FGBL (German Bund Futures) for example – are much older. The more uncorrelated asset seems to be the 10-year Treasury Bill (TY) which has a negative correlation with at least seven other equity lines out of 14 (50% of the markets). The second most uncorrelated are GC (Gold) and JY (Japanese Yen). The most correlated asset is Wheat which has no negative correlation with any other. In second place, Eurodollar (EC), Swiss Franc (SF) and Soybean Meal (SM) have a negative correlation just one market out of 14.

The most common way to compose a portfolio with a matrix of correlation among equity lines is to attach more weight to those price series that are uncorrelated with the others in order to smooth the portfolio equity line. In the example of fig. 8.1, Eurodollar, Swiss Franc and Soybean Meal would be the price series with the lowest number of contracts to be traded, while Gold and Treasury Bills should be weighed more than any other asset.

8.3 A dynamic approach: equity line crossover

Every trader is haunted by the obsession of the possible failure of the systems he is trading. This is the psychological burden systematic traders need to withstand in order to achieve success.

A common way to gauge a system's failure is drawdown, or a multiple of the drawdown. We believe that, even if the drawdown figure is important, it is not the key element in evaluating the performances of a trading system. If you do not pretend that subsequent trades are dependent on preceding ones, drawdown is just one of the possible sequences of losing trades a system can encounter. Moreover, drawdown is the direct misfortune a trader can encounter in their job and it would be inappropriate to use drawdown, or even worse a multiple of it, as a final threshold before stopping a system.

Our idea is, why not use a dynamic approach that indicates to the trader when the system starts faltering? And, overall, why not adopt a general objective approach that indicates not only which systems are stopped because they are out of synchronisation with the market, but also which ones to activate because they start to be in synchronisation with the market?

What we would like is to set criteria for discarding a system when it starts to lose money, but also criteria for activating a dormant system when it fits the current market conditions. The idea is to trade a system when the equity line crosses over the 15–30 period moving average of the equity line itself and stop trading with a system when the opposite is true (fig. 8.2).

Figure 8.2: The blue line is the 30-period moving average and the red line is the 1-period equity line. At point A there was a down crossover and trading was stopped. At point B there was an upward crossover and trading was resumed.

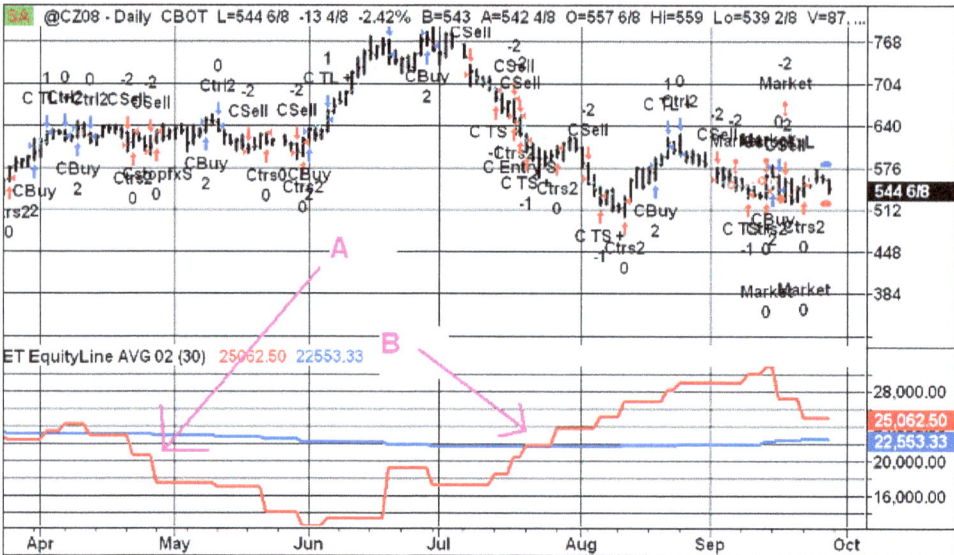

The same crossover rule could also be applied to the whole portfolio of systems as a second security measure after being applied to the single system. In this case it would be proper to distinguish between a portfolio of daily systems (it would not be advisable to exit a trade on a daily trading system simply because the portfolio equity line dropped below its average) and a portfolio of intraday trading systems.

In our experience, it is not a sure thing that this equity line crossover approach will work equally well on all systems and all markets. If the system is a good one, if it does not have too many rules and if it is properly optimised and equally properly re-optimised at periodic intervals, it is likely that the equity line crossover approach will never encounter a downward crossover. So if the system is too good, applying this approach will never improve the overall system results. However, applying the equity line crossover to the whole portfolio of systems with a whole portfolio equity line is a tool that can help the trader prevent the nightmare of the *black swan* when everything goes wrong.

Usually the equity line crossover is a dynamic tool that reduces the risk more effectively than the use of the simple drawdown. Moreover, the simple drawdown rule or a multiple of it has no corresponding contrary rule to activate a dormant system, whereas our proposed security rule can give this indication.

8.4 How to transform an average system portfolio into a profitable one: the case of LUXOR

With all these thoughts, let's have a look at the equity curve of the LUXOR trading system. This strategy was given just as a simple example ten years ago, but the early good performance led to over-confidence of some users who tried to over-optimise it or added new variables. Instead of further optimising and keeping this system absolutely as it was, it was better to use a moving average crossover on the equity line and switch it off (fig. 8.3).

Figure 8.3: Equity curve of the LUXOR trading system with 24-month moving average (black) from 21/10/2002–04/07/2018. See part II of this book where you find its development. Left side: system development area (21/10/2002–04/07/2008). Right Side: out-of-sample area. Tested on GBPUSD, 30-minute data with TradeStation.

After its development the system continued to perform in a similar way for a certain time out-of sample, but then started to move sideways. You can see that a two-year moving average does a good job here. It lets the system equity run in its profitable phase and catches a useful moment after some drawdown (October 2011) to switch it off.

Although this simple shutdown mechanism seems to work on this example, the question is whether it can be generally applied to any other trading system.

This type of quick system evaluation certainly works only in cases when your strategy has a sufficient trade frequency! Don't try to build an equity-line based switch for a case when your trading logic produces few signals. The outcome then depends too much on chance. With the LUXOR system you got 3,765 trades between 21/10/2002–04/07/2018, about 235 trades per year, so the trade frequency is quite high.

The 2-year moving average on the equity line means in this case that your decision to switch off the system is based on about 400–500 signals. This might be a statistically relevant figure to use a simple moving average of some years as a switch here.

In the next chapter of this book, you will find a completely different system to this short-term LUXOR: a Bollinger Band applied to daily data on stocks (chapter 9). For that longer-term system you could never decide only after two years if you could switch off the system or not. You would rather have to wait decades to get enough statistically relevant data to have a chance for a serious decision.

The whole topic of when to switch off a system is still hotly debated in the professional world and we assume that these debates will continue for a long time.

But if you handle this challenge just a bit better than the average trader, it can turn your strategy portfolio into a success.

8.5 Dynamic portfolio composition: the walk-forward analysis activator

Let's look at an example on an intraday trading system which is put under periodic optimisation every three months inside a process of walk-forward analysis. If during the three-month periodic reoptimisation the system has a walk-forward efficiency ratio of more than 50% then it is traded in real time and conversely if the walk-forward efficiency ratio goes under 50% then the system is momentarily stopped. In this way we can decide which trading systems in our trading systems' farm are to be applied and which ones are to be suspended. Fabrizio Bocca classifies all his systems in relation to the walk-forward ratio every three months and then he allocates his trading capital to those systems that have the highest rank.

Figure 8.4: this is an example of how a trading systems' farm could be ranked through WFA. On the right corner there is a column denominated RCD where the WFA results are condensed in a comprehensive index. If the index is positive the trading system is traded with real money, if it is negative (zero in the column) is it deactivated.

N.	Trading System	MM	P16 Months	PI 12 Months	MI 13 Years	PI Years	RCD
1.	Euro Rev Br	15	0,183	8,443	12,729	10,422	9,314
2.	Open Week Bund	30	1,338	2,054	10,262	17,404	8,300
3.	Bund Kagi Daily	30	6,039	1,826	7,837	11,500	6,797
4.	Gold Kagi Daily	30/15	-1,000	2,069	6,349	11,016	5,110
5.	Euro Nightmare	15	5,951	4,314	4,135	7,210	5,067
6.	Bund Big Deep	30	4,193	6,540	3,477	2,690	4,193
7.	Dax Castle	15	0,235	1,237	3,832	9,649	3,807
8.	TBond DBZ	30	1,754	1,918	4,918	4,510	3,612
9.	Mazzle Dax	15	2,983	3,871	2,564	4,044	3,250

N.	Trading System	MM	P16 Months	PI 12 Months	MI 13 Years	PI Years	RCD
10.	TBond Kagi Daily	15/30	3,954	1,682	2,525	5,966	3,217
11.	Crude Oil Multi	30	0,387	-0,477	2,013	3,318	1,407
12.	Fib Castle	15	-1,000	-0,034	1,122	4,302	1,151
13.	Big Deep US						0,000
14.	Vit Daily Bond US						0,000
15.	Open Week Dax						0,000
16.	Open Week Spmib						0,000

8.6 Largest losing trade/largest losing streak/largest drawdown

Another way to compose a portfolio of different markets and systems would be to normalise risk by the largest losing trade or drawdown. This is one of the most popular approaches. In this way the system with the highest losing trade, largest losing streak or largest losing drawdown will have the lowest number of contracts allotted to it and conversely the system with the smallest losing trade, losing streak or losing drawdown will have the highest number of contracts allotted. Obviously the loss figures on which this method is based make sense only if you do not consider WFA, otherwise these loss figures will vary with every WFA you periodically make. Moreover if you adopt this approach with largest losing streak or largest losing drawdown then you must believe that trade dependency has some value since otherwise it would be difficult to believe that the trade sequence will repeat itself in the future exactly as it did in the past. If the trade sequence varies drawdown will also vary. As for the use of the largest losing trade, you need to consider that a theoretical test will never encompass mistakes and slippages and in our experience these are the best candidates to be the largest losing trades. In any case, the largest losing trade, being precisely just one trade, has a low statistical significance but many traders use it because it is easy to grasp and apply. We have nothing against it, but – as with everything – it should be regarded with caution and the drawbacks it entails should be kept in mind.

9

Trading a Portfolio of Stocks

Fʀᴏᴍ ᴏᴜʀ ᴇxᴘᴇʀɪᴇɴᴄᴇ there is a common rule of thumb for most trading systems. The more signals a system produces, the less profitable it is! Or from the other side, the best trading systems with the highest profits per trade usually don't give entry signals every day in every market phase. Instead their signals occur rarely, maybe only one time per month, per year, etc., dependent on the system logic and the chosen timescale. This means that with the more profitable systems you will have long periods without any signals. Periods when you just sit like a fisherman for many hours, waiting for the fish to bite into the fishing line.

One way to lower such waiting times is to combine different trading systems, as shown in the previous chapter 8. There we demonstrated the effects of correlation between different systems and markets and how to benefit from diversification. With more systems and more markets, you can reduce the time to catch a *fish*.

In this chapter we present a completely different approach to getting enough signals – just with one trading system.

All you have to do is to give this one trading system a sufficient number of stocks with enough possibilities to monitor at the same time. If your trading strategy has more choices every day, the chance becomes higher that it will generate an entry signal. However, you will never know in advance on which stock your next signal will occur. Instead the trading system tells you what and when to buy, and when to sell.

Although it looks a bit complex at the first glance, it is not.

We explain how it works in this chapter, step-by-step with the example of a proven system. We start with a short repetition of the Bollinger Band system (chapter 9.1). In order to get a better feeling for this system, we'll first apply it to some single stocks of the current Dow Jones Index (chapter 9.2).

Before you are ready to back-test a complete portfolio of stocks you have some points to consider. One such point is certainly the data. In order to get accurate back-test results, it is indispensable to test on the right universe of stocks in a correct way. With this we mean that your database must contain not only the stocks that are in your tested universe (e.g. in the S&P 500 index) today, but also the stocks that had to leave this universe before. Otherwise your back-tests have a *survivorship bias*. This is an important topic, which we discuss in chapter 9.3.

Now you are prepared to start the in-depth development of your trading system on a portfolio of stocks. We guide you through this development process on the example of the S&P 500 stock universe (chapter 9.4) and will repeat some of the basic methods which we used on a single symbol test already, but now on a portfolio: Monte Carlo analysis (9.5) and walk-forward analysis (9.6).

After this, we apply the Bollinger strategy to further challenging portfolios of stocks with the same parameters: Nasdaq 100, S&P 1500 and the Australian stock market (9.7).

In the section thereafter (9.8) we show a small position management example of five Nasdaq 100 stocks within a portfolio. This is to demonstrate how such a management could look in real trading.

The next section tries to answer the basic psychological question of many traders: Why is it so difficult to let your profits run and cut your losses short (9.9)?

Finally we show some methods for implementing trading systems like the Bollinger Band strategy in your daily trading business (9.10).

We again want to underline that our Bollinger breakout system is just an example chosen for educational purposes – like all the other trading strategies presented in this book.

It shall serve you as a starting point for your own system development projects. Feel free to use it and to change it for your personal needs. Therefore, we provide the associated AmiBroker code for you at the end of this book (Appendix 5).

All figures in this chapter were generated with AmiBroker, unless mentioned differently.

9.1 Modifications when applying a Bollinger Band system to stocks

You know the Bollinger trading logic already from chapter 5.2. where we applied it on FOREX data.

In this chapter we'll use the Bollinger system to trade portfolios of stocks. Before we start, let us quickly repeat the idea of Bollinger Band strategies when used to trade breakouts (fig. 9.1).

In phases when the market (in this case the Netflix stock) moves sideways and the volatility drops, the Bollinger Bands become narrower. It is a situation where market participants are unsure about the further development and stay on the sidelines. Such phases form the base of succeeding bigger movements. The longer the indecisive phase takes, the stronger the subsequent breakout.

The reason for this breakout is that the participants in the preceeding inactive market become afraid to miss the starting train and want to jump in. Like this, they amplify the new trend.

In the shown example of Netflix, an upside breakout above the upper Bollinger Band (thick green line for stocks) is impulsive, even creating an upside-gap. After the breakout the Bollinger Bands quickly follow the trending price. Like this, the lower Bollinger Band (thick red line for stocks) can be used as a natural adaptive exit trigger.

When applying the Bollinger system to stocks, some modifications compared with FOREX and futures are necessary.

The first and main point is that we only want to allow long signals when trading stocks. Trading the short side is generally possible, but needs its own special measures which would be beyond the scope of this book.

Secondly, we use daily data for the following practical reasons: Daily data is easy to handle in back-testing and has advantages in application in real trading. It also generates a suitable amount of trading signals which are manageable in your daily business. You check the signals after the close of one day and apply the orders before the open of the next day.

The third reason to modify the original Bollinger strategy is that stocks in general behave differently than futures or currency (FOREX) markets. Stocks, especially small stocks, tend to be 'choppier' than complete market indices. Each piece of news on a stock, every fundamental change, or just a big order from a fund, has an impact on the stock price. The smaller the stock and its traded volume, the bigger are the changes and the more difficult it is to trade.

Furthermore, keep in mind that with Bollinger Band breakouts you have a momentum type of system. Your goal here is to capture big moves on volatile stocks.

For all these reasons, it is necessary to look out for different parameters of the Bollinger Band system when trading stocks (fig. 9.1).

Figure 9.1: Daily chart of Netflix with simple moving average (SMA) and Bollinger Bands, June 2016–May 2017. To trade stocks long only, both the upper and lower Bollinger Bands are shifted one full standard deviation upwards. New entry (thick, green line) and exit (thick, red line). Compare with the symmetric old entry and exit distances (thin green and red line) used in long/short systems for FOREX (fig. 5.4A) and for futures (appendix, fig. A1.1)

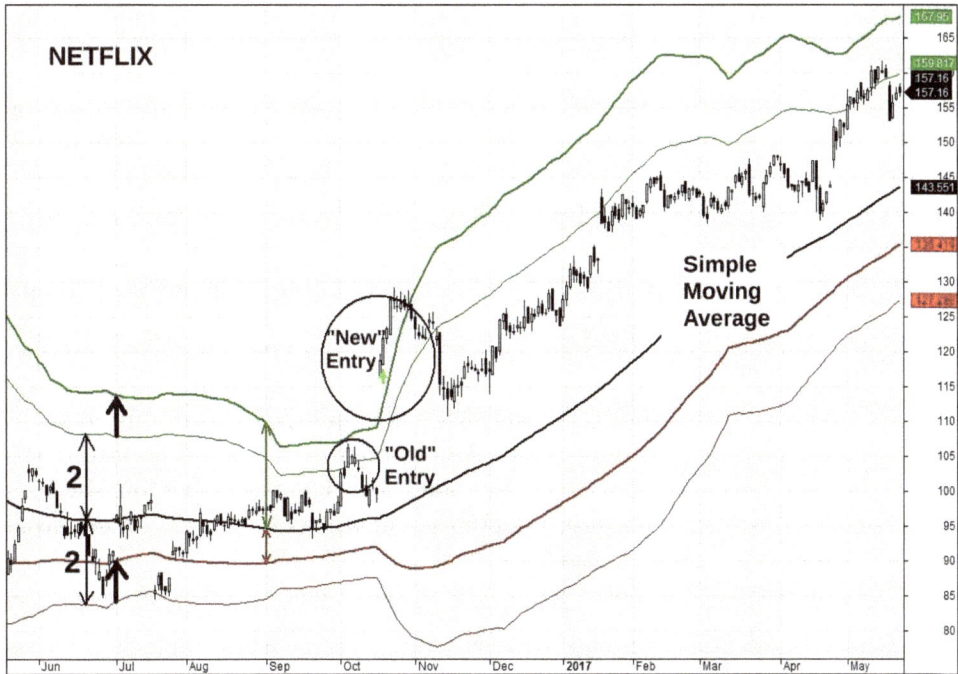

Remember the Bollinger Band system for FOREX has symmetrical entries and exits for long and short positions (compare with fig. 5.4A). This makes sense for currency markets because both trade directions, long and short, have in principle the same probability and the same features.

But now we are dealing with stock markets, which have a different behaviour. They are trending upwards about 70% of the time and in between they sometimes suffer huge declines – see for example the excellent book by Meb Faber [18]. There are different reasons for this. Companies produce returns year after year. They reinvest this money with stock buy-back programmes, pay dividends to their shareholders, etc. That's why in the long term, up until now, they have been the best asset class. Although this topic is beyond the scope of this book, it is reasonable to assume that stock markets are not symmetric like currency markets, but have an uptrending bias.

As a consequence of this upside bias of the stock markets, it could be a good idea to move both the Bollinger Bands, for entry and exit, to the upside. Like this you get a new entry point which is slightly higher than the old entry point for FOREX currencies was, where the upper band was closer to the simple moving average.

To start with, for stocks, we shift both bands one full standard deviation to the upside. This means that the upper band is now three standard deviations over the simple moving average (SMA) and the bottom band is one standard deviation below it.

After this shify, entries are now more difficult, they occur later at higher prices and the system has to wait for bigger breakouts. This should make false breakouts more unlikely since you are further away from the general stock market noise. Because the entry moves higher, it is logical to also move the exit higher, in order not to let the losing trades become too big.

Finally, we increase also the moving average length (from 60 for FOREX to 100 for stocks) to make the system more slow. Again, the idea for this measure is to avoid general stock market noise.

Certainly these will not be optimal parameters – they will just be our starting point, based on some plausible arguments. But before we start the optimisation of the SMA and all the other relevant parameters of the trading logic (entry, exit, position size, etc., see section 9.4) we want to explain the principle of the trading logic in more detail (fig. 9.2) – so that you get more familiar with it.

The better you know your system from the beginning, the more confidence you will have in it. This will be helpful in phases when you get some unavoidable drawdowns. You should trade with trading systems which you fully understand.

The Bollinger Band system – trading logic for stocks

Figure 9.2: Bollinger Band trading logic for stocks. Top band (green) for entry, bottom (red) for exit. The bands have different distances from the central line which represents a simple moving average (black). Entry: buy on the open of the day after the stock closed above the top Bollinger Band (green line). Here a long signal was triggered for Netflix on 19 October 2016. Exit: the bottom band (red line) acts as a trailing stop. Exit on the open of the day after the stock closed below this red line.

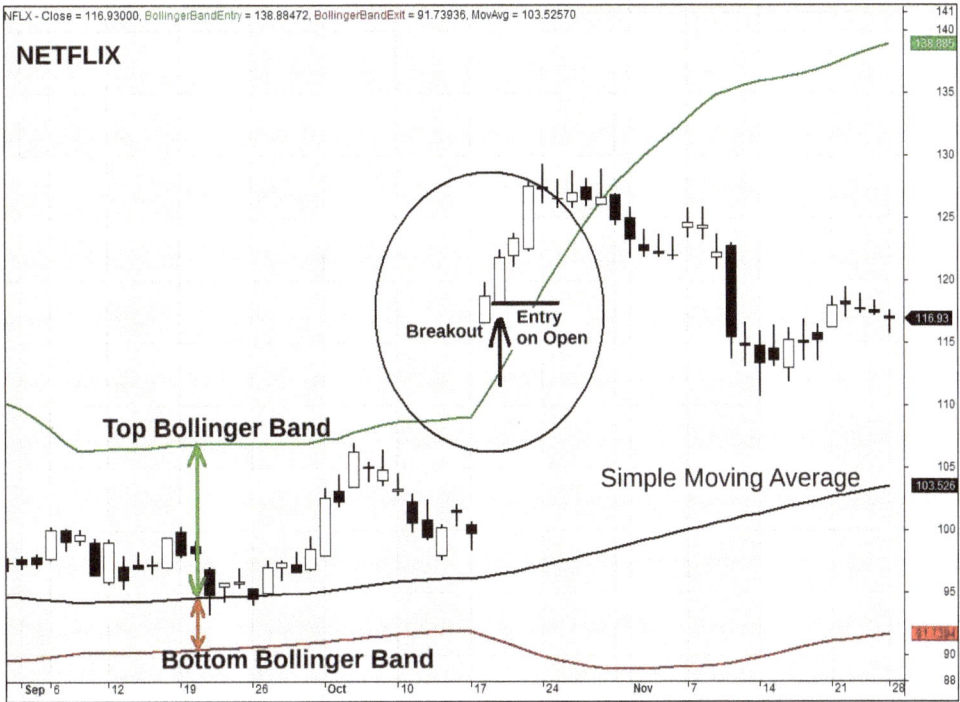

Because both Bollinger Bands have moved to the upside a bit, they have now different distances from the central simple moving average line (black).

You can see that the entry is triggered one day after the upper Bollinger Band was crossed. This gives you sufficient time to check your signals after the market close and place your orders for the next day. The same holds true for the exits.

The following figure (9.3) shows the same signal as the figure above on a longer time period. Like this you have an example of a full trade from entry until exit.

Figure 9.3: Bollinger system applied to the Netflix stock, same entry as fig. 9.2 on a longer time period. The entry takes place on October, 19th, 2016 after the top Bollinger Band has been crossed. Further long entry signals are triggered in July 2017 and January 2018. The exit takes place two years later, on October, 11th 2018. In the meantime the bottom Bollinger Band acts as a trailing stop and is not reached.

You can see that the Bollinger long breakout in October 2016 at a price of $118 was just the starting point of a long uptrend which followed in this volatile technology stock. A second and even a third long signal followed later in July 2017 and January 2018, while the exit was never reached but acted as a safety net to protect your profits. In late 2018 the trade was finally exited at around $325, when the stock tumbled sharply (remark, off topic: discretionary traders may notice the shoulder/head/shoulder formation confirming the necessary exit). So, all in all the stock has tripled from its entry until the exit.

Although such a high gain in one single trade is rather an exception, you will see in this chapter that the Bollinger strategy on stocks is worth taking a look at.

9.2 Examples: Results on single stocks

Before we apply the Bollinger strategy to complete portfolios of stocks, let's first check the strategy on some single stocks. Like this you get a better feeling about what happens when you use the system.

The following parameters are used for the shown tests in this chapter 9.2:

- Moving average length of Bollinger Bands: 100 days (SMA100)

- Entry point (top band): 3 standard deviations above SMA100

- Exit point (bottom band): 1 standard deviation below SMA100

- Money management: The equity curve is calculated by investing 5% of the equity into each position (this means $5,000 in the beginning and then equity value/20)

- Trading costs: 0.5% (0.25% at the entry and 0.25% at the exit)

So let's start to check some examples. Fig. 9.4 shows the equity curve of the trading logic systematically applied to Boeing over 70 years, from 1950–2018.

Figure 9.4: Equity curve of the Bollinger Band system applied to Boeing from 1950–2018. Result includes 0.5% trading costs.

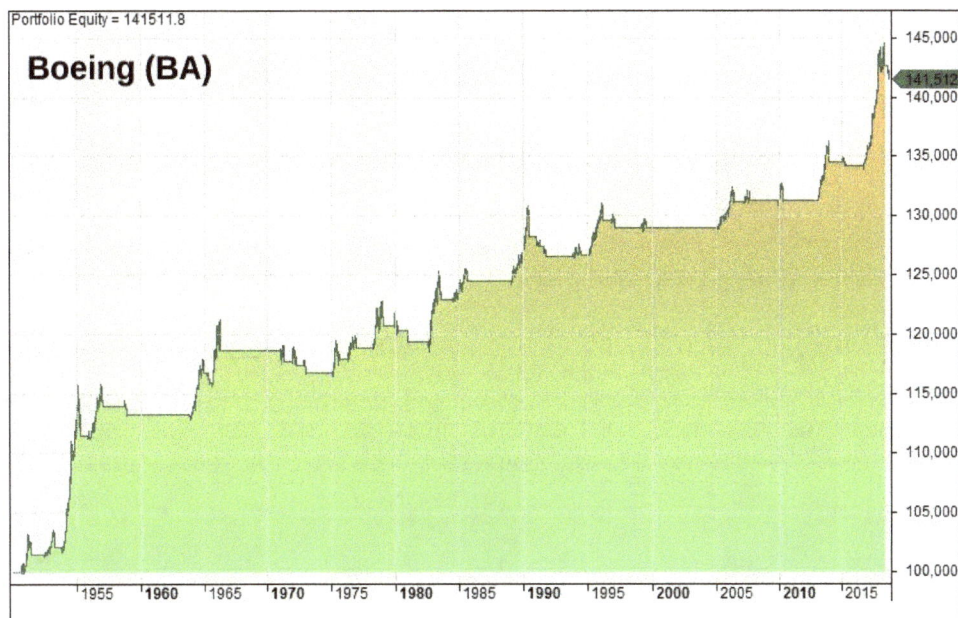

The system produced 32 signals in the 68 years of the test period (see table 9.1). On average a position was held for 173 days, which is more than half a year. Eighteen out of the 32 signals were winning trades and 14 were losing trades. As you can see, the equity curve is growing steadily, looking a bit like a stairway. This shows that signals appear rarely and in between you get long flat periods when nothing spectacular on the upside of this stock happens.

Thirty-two signals in 68 years means only one signal every two years. From these numbers it is clear that in real life nobody would like to trade this system with just one stock.

Let's see some further examples. The following pictures show six other stocks of the Dow Jones index with similar trade numbers in the same test period from 1950–2018 (Fig. 9.5 A–F).

Figure 9.5A–F: Equity curves of the Bollinger Band system applied to six Dow Jones stocks from 1950–2018. Result includes 0.5% trading costs.

Figure 9.5A: Caterpillar (CAT)

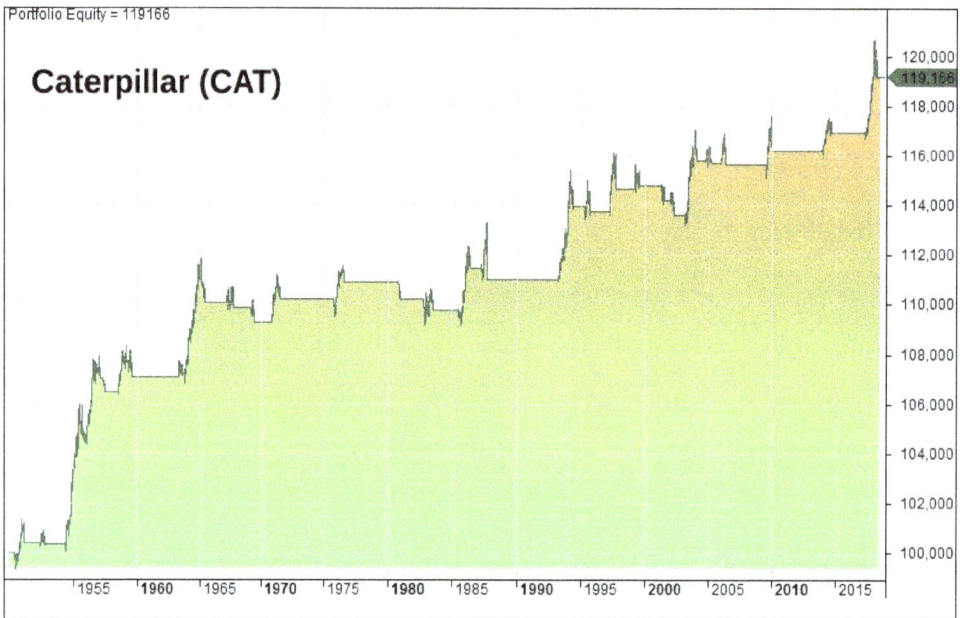

Figure 9.5B: IBM Corp. (IBM)

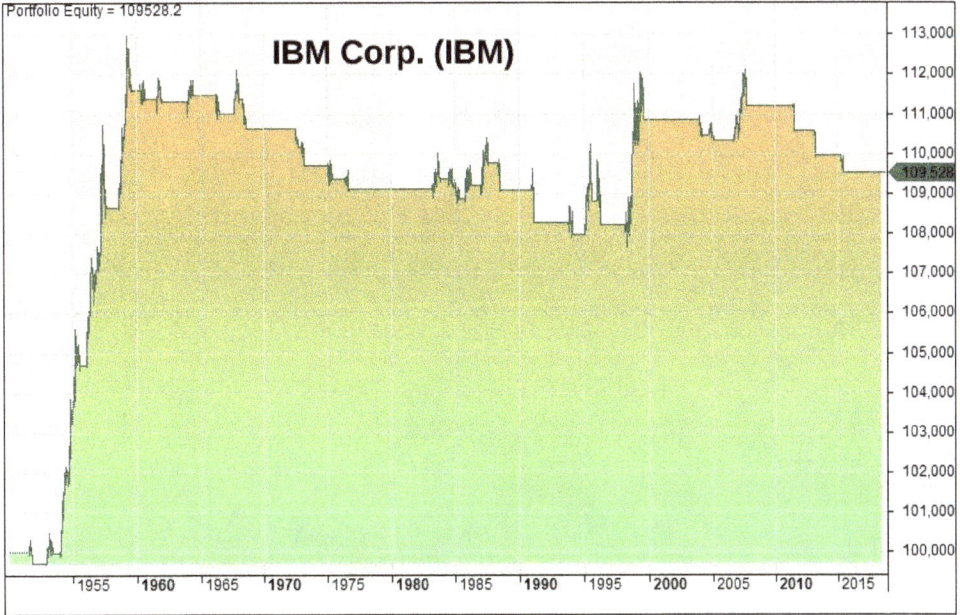

Figure 9.5C: Coca Cola (KO)

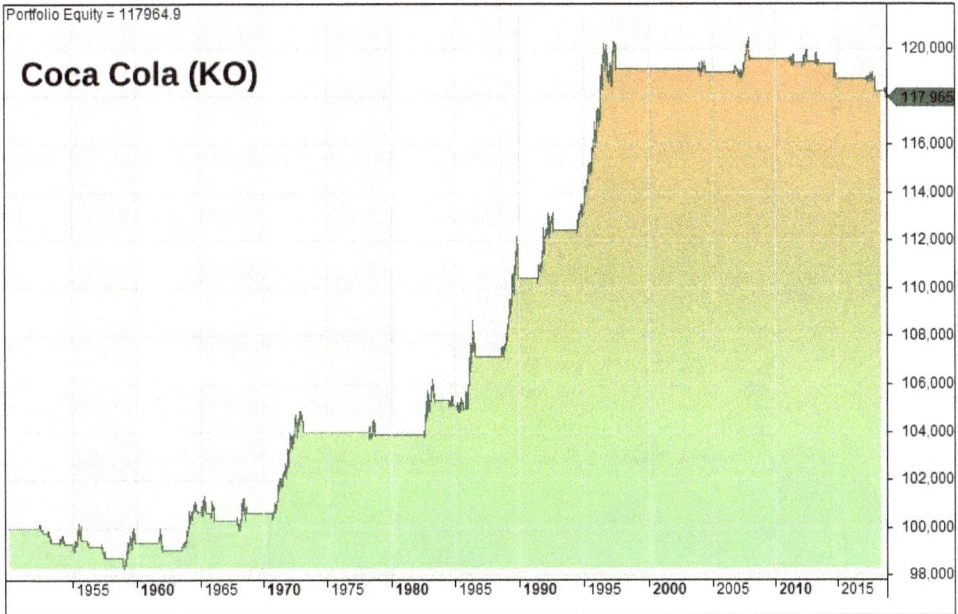

Figure 9.5D: Merck (MRK)

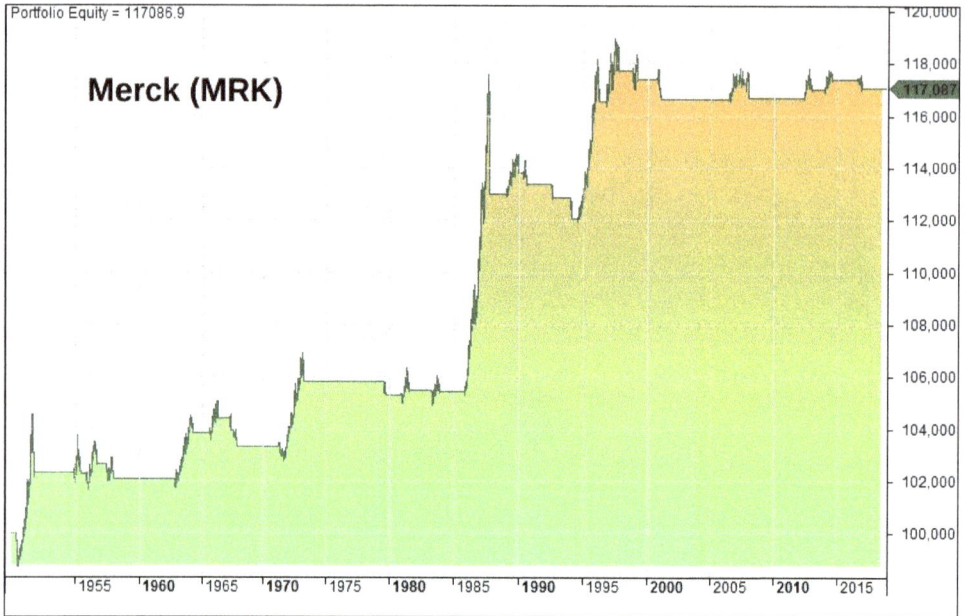

Figure 9.5D: Merck (MRK)

Figure 9.5E: Procter & Gamble (PG)

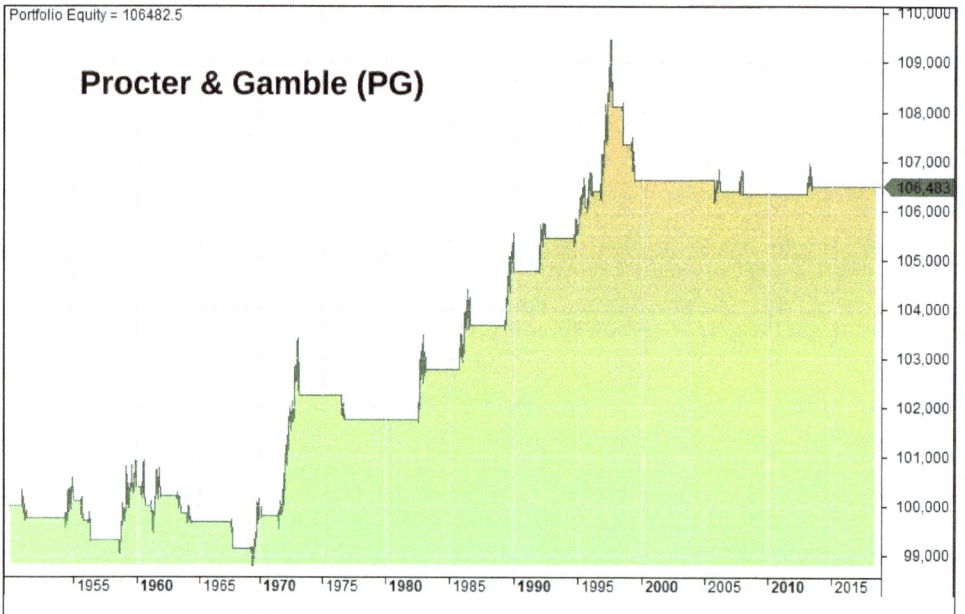

Figure 9.5E: Procter & Gamble (PG)

Figure 9.5F: Walgreens (WBA)

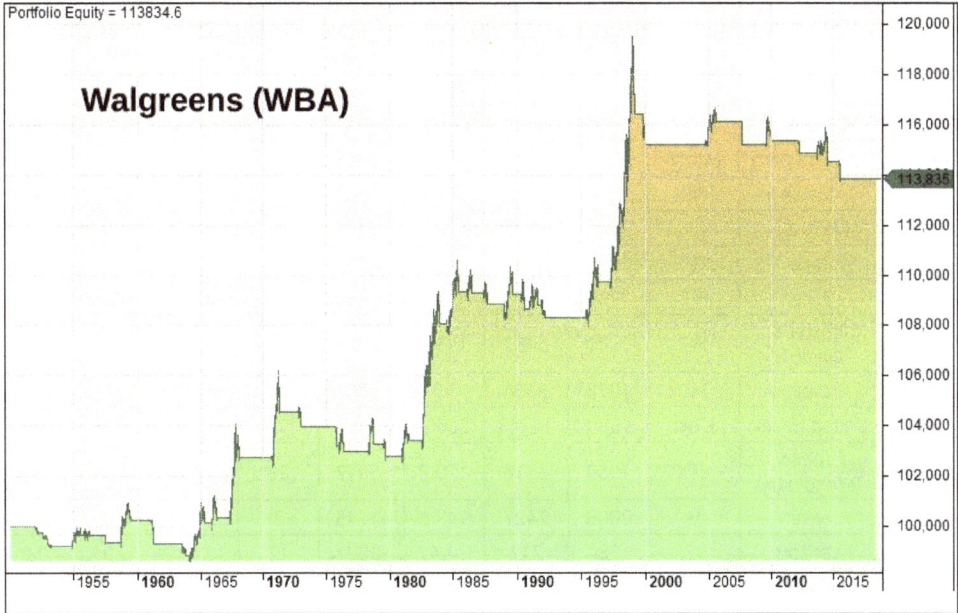

The following table shows how the system would have performed on all the 30 Dow Jones stocks of December 2018 (table 9.1).

Table 9.1: Statistics of the Bollinger Band system applied to the current 30 Dow Jones stocks from 1950–2018. Result includes 0.5% trading costs.

Number	Name	Symbol	DOW-Start	Net Profit	Net % Profit	Max. Sys DD	# Trades	Avg Profit/Loss	Avg Bars Held	% of Winners
1	Apple	AAPL	1981	25645	512.8	-10580	17	1509	171	65
2	American Express	AXP	1977	3229	64.6	-3884	21	154	135	48
3	Boeing	BA	1950	41512	830.2	-4807	32	1297	173	56
4	Caterpillar	CAT	1950	19166	383.4	-2898	30	639	156	53
5	Cisco Systems	CSCO	1990	19011	380.2	-6245	16	1188	151	50
6	Chevron	CVX	1950	4395	88	-2662	31	142	138	42
7	Walt Disney	DIS	1957	4180	83.6	-4429	28	149	116	43
8	Dow Dupont	DWDP	2017	x	x	x	x	x	x	x
9	Goldman Sachs	GS	1999	2457	49.2	-2855	5	491	159	100
10	Home Depot	HD	1981	16921	338.4	-7399	12	1410	157	58
11	IBM	IBM	1950	9528	190.6	-5357	33	289	122	39
12	Intel	INTC	1973	18780	375.6	-7415	22	854	143	50
13	Johnson & Johnson	JNJ	1950	3528	70.6	-3307	32	110	131	44

Number	Name	Symbol	DOW-Start	Net Profit	Net % Profit	Max. Sys DD	# Trades	Avg Profit/ Loss	Avg Bars Held	% of Winners
14	JPMorgan	JPM	1969	-1823	-36.4	-3708	17	-107	98	35
15	Coca Cola	KO	1950	17965	359.2	-2496	32	561	164	41
16	McDonald's	MCD	1966	4660	93.2	-3664	27	173	147	48
17	3M Company	MMM	1950	7522	150.4	-3741	35	215	131	49
18	Merck	MRK	1950	17087	341.8	-5701	28	610	167	46
19	Microsoft	MSFT	1986	21019	420.4	-7798	20	1051	159	55
20	Nike	NKE	1980	8537	170.8	-6603	19	449	150	37
21	Pfizer	PFE	1950	7448	149	-3159	27	276	129	52
22	Procter & Gamble	PG	1950	6483	129.6	-3287	25	259	143	52
23	Travelers	TRV	1975	2504	50	-2302	20	125	129	65
24	United Health	UNH	1984	14343	286.8	-2422	15	956	139	73
25	United Technologies	UTX	1950	8510	170.2	-5972	28	304	133	29
26	Visa	V	2008	7427	148.6	-1745	2	3714	463	100
27	Verizon	VZ	1984	217	4.4	-3097	12	18	129	50
28	Walgreens	WBA	1950	13835	276.6	-5798	37	374	129	43
29	Walmart	WMT	1972	6106	122.2	-8660	26	235	113	35
30	Exxon Mobil	XOM	1950	8927	178.6	-4102	31	288	158	42
	Average				220	-4693	23	611	153	52
	Total						680			

As you can see, other stocks behave in a similar way to the examples above concerning trade frequency (about one trade in two years) and time in the market (half a year in the market for each trade, represented in table 9.1 by 'avg. bars held': 153 days on average, with 252 days being one full year).

Further, this table shows that the Dow Jones index is not static. From time to time index constituents change their names in mergers and acquisitions, or they have to leave the index and are replaced by other stocks. Therefore, table 9.1 is quite heterogeneous. While some stocks are members of the Dow Jones since 1950, others just entered recently. It is clear that the younger members have less time to produce trading signals. One example is the DowDuPont stock (symbol DWDP, number 8 in table 9.1). It was formed after the merger of Dow Chemical and DuPont on 31 August 2017 and has not produced any Bollinger breakout since then.

The combined equity curve from these 30 stocks looks promising at the first glance (fig. 9.6).

Figure 9.6: Theoretical, combined equity curve if you had traded all the 30 Dow Jones stocks (universe of December 2018) with the Bollinger Band system.

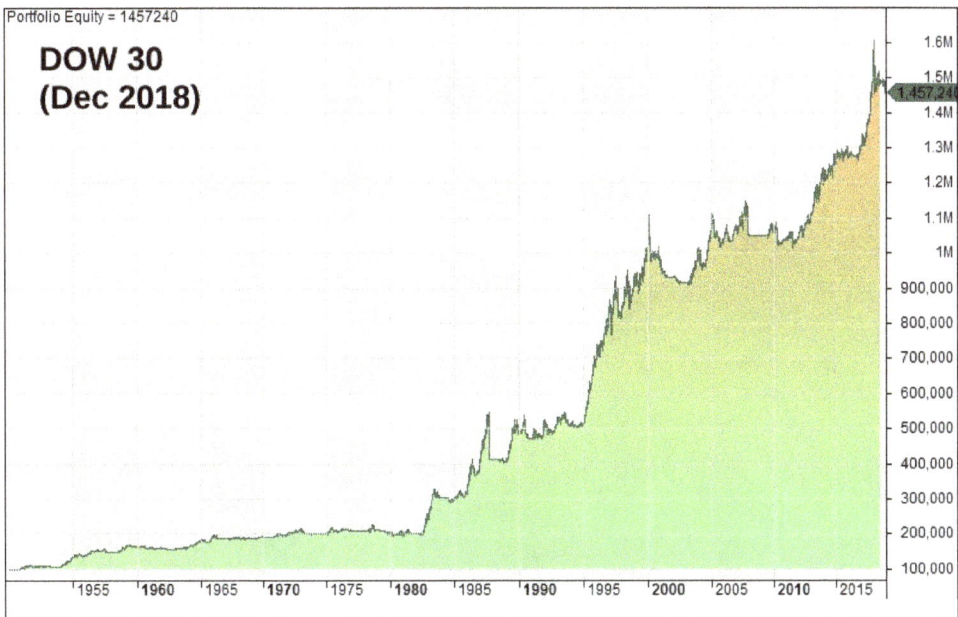

However, please don't look at this equity curve and think this result is achievable. At first, you have many stocks in recent times contributing to this equity line while you have fewer stocks earlier. But there is another, much more important point to consider: survivorship bias!

Since this topic is indispensable when developing trading systems on portfolios of stocks we'll discuss it in the next section before we can start with more serious portfolio back-tests.

9.3 Survivorship bias in portfolio back-tests

Why are your test results too good if you test on the current index constituents?

As you know, the main index of a country usually contains its biggest companies. And from time to time index constituents are replaced. Companies who lose market value are replaced by companies who gain.

Let's take for example the Nasdaq 100 stock index. At the end of 2018 the largest stocks therein were Amazon, Apple, Alphabet (=Google) and Facebook. If you had invested $10,000 into these four stocks 20 years ago, you would be multi-millionaire today. But the problem is that not all the current stocks have been in the Nasdaq Index all that time. Some did not exist and some have changed names in the meantime, etc. So you immediately see the problem of such simple considerations.

In the Nasdaq 100, since 1995 every year on average 16 of the 100 stocks have been replaced by new ones. This means that in the year 2018 less than 15 are left from the 100 stocks that were listed in the Nasdaq 100 index in 1995! (To find out more see [24].)

Let's have a look at two examples of how stocks perform inside versus outside the Nasdaq 100 index (fig. 9.7 A and B).

Figure 9.7: Two stocks and their performance in the Nasdaq 100. A: Dentsply Sirona (XRAX). B: Apollo Education Group (APOL).

Figure 9.7A: X-RAY time in ND 100 index

Dentsply Sirona Corp (XRAY) entered the Nasdaq 100 on 20 June 2016 (fig 9.7 A). The chart shows that the stock performed well before it entered the index (marked with point 1), but within the Nasdaq 100 index it performed quite poorly – so poorly that it was kicked out of the index again at the end of 2018 (marked with point 2).

The second example is the Apollo Education Group (symbol APOL, fig 9.7 B). The stock entered the Nasdaq 100 index in December 2001 after a phase of good performance. It continued to perform well for a certain time. But after some years of bad performance it was thrown out of the Nasdaq 100 in Dec 2012. Later on, in Feb 2017, the Apollo Education Group was completely delisted because of its acquisition by a consortium of investors. Therefore the data history ends here.

Figure 9.7B: APOL time in ND 100 index

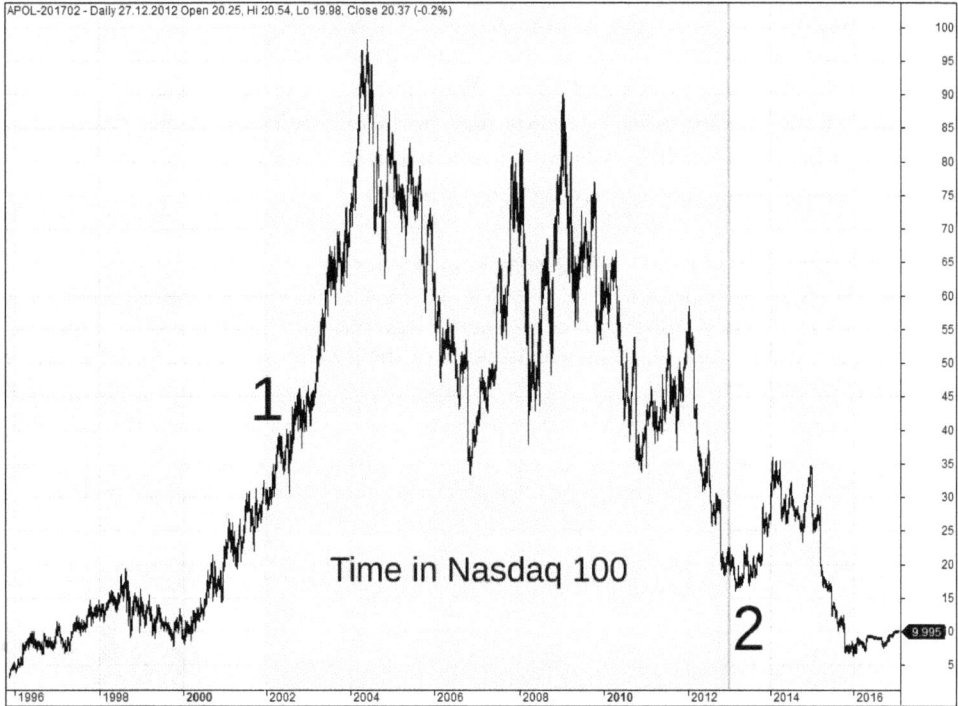

APOL-201702 - Daily 27.12.2012 Open 20.25, Hi 20.54, Lo 19.98, Close 20.37 (-0.2%)

If you test on the current Nasdaq 100 members only, you will not include stocks like these two above with their bad history in the index. But in a correctly performed back-test, you **must** include these stocks at each point of time when they were listed in the index.

This means that for the two above examples, XRAY must be included in your calculations from 20 June 2016 until the exact date end of 2018 when it left the Nasdaq 100 index, and APOL must be included from December 2001 until December 2012.

If you don't do this then your back-test will be far too optimistic – especially in long-only strategies, like the one which we investigate in this whole chapter 9.

The error which you get when you perform your back-test in this wrong way, on just the members which are there today in the index, is called *survivorship bias*.

Let's investigate how big this effect usually is.

Fig. 9.8 shows an example. This is the equity curve of a long-only Bollinger Band trading system which is applied to all the stocks of the Nasdaq 100 index. You get the better, upper equity curve with over 23% (!) annual return when you apply your trading system to the current Nasdaq 100 index constituents only. The lower but more realistic curve (with about 9% annual return) is what you get when your trading system is applied to the 100 stocks which really are in the Nasdaq index at the time when the buy signals occur – the *point-in-time index* constituents.

So in this example the error which you make when you test on the incomplete universe of stocks is more than half of your back-tested performance!

This error may vary from strategy to strategy, dependent on the entry, the number of positions, the holding periods and so on. But the effect is always there. As a rule of thumb, if you ever perform back-tests on just the current index members: you have to divide your back-test result by a factor of two or three – then you get a more realistic idea of how your system in real trading could perform.

Figure 9.8: A Bollinger Band system tested on the Nasdaq 100 stock universe. Fig. A (1995–2001) is a small section of fig. B (1995–2018). Too optimistic, upper curves: test on only current Nasdaq 100 index constituents leads to 23% annual return. Realistic, lower curves: test on point-in-time constituents of the Nasdaq 100. This leads to a more realistic result of 9%.

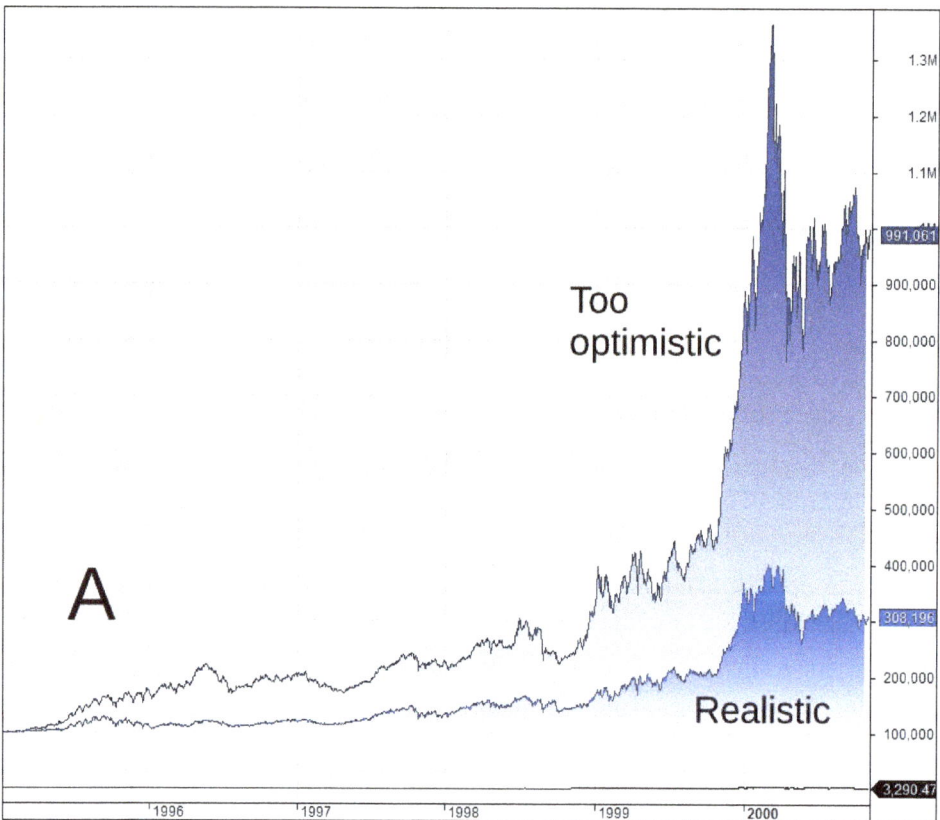

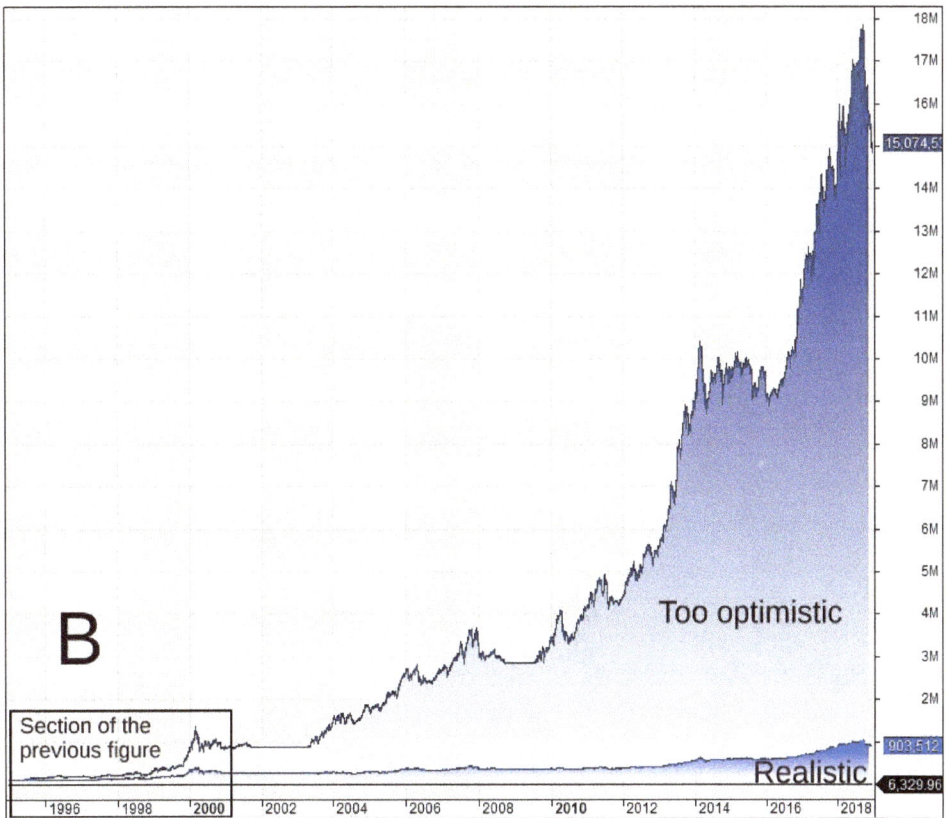

To be free from this survivorship bias, all our following tests on portfolios of stocks in this book are performed with the point-in-time index constituents on Norgate Data.

The Norgate database includes all stocks, the current index constituents and the ones that have been removed out of the index (fig. 9.9). As you can see, the correct universe consists of more delisted stocks than currently listed stocks.

At the time of writing (2019), Norgate is the only common data vendor which provides such professional data for a reasonable price to retail traders.

Figure 9.9: Screenshot of an AmiBroker workspace. Left side: index members of Nasdaq 100. Your database must keep besides the active symbols (green), also all dead or delisted symbols (red). From this database your trading system must select the point-in-time index constituents to generate realistic entry signals. Right side: Nasdaq 100 index around the year 2000.

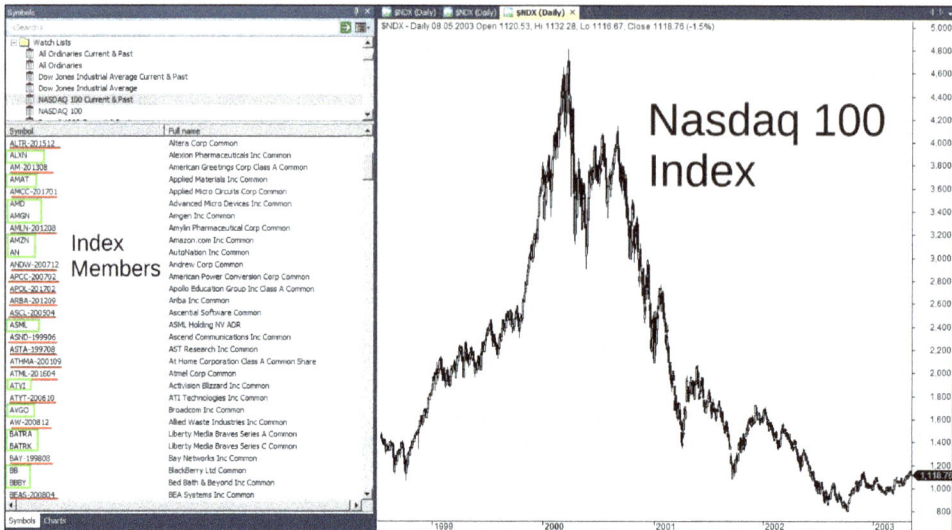

9.4 Application of the strategy to a portfolio of S&P 500 stocks

In this chapter we investigate our strategy on a portfolio of the stocks within the S&P 500 index. This index contains the top 500 US companies by market capitalisation.

Why do we now switch to the S&P 500 universe instead of the Dow Jones with which we started above (chapter 9.2)?

The answer is simple. Remember that each stock produced only about one Bollinger breakout signal every two years. Thus the 30 stocks of the DOW Jones index produce about 15 signals per year on average. With this few signals, you would not find any suitable settings in terms of risk and money management. If you take huge positions (e.g. 20% or 50% of your money) for each of the few signals then you increase drastically your risks.

For these reasons it is better to use bigger portfolios to trade, like the 500 stocks of the S&P 500, where you get more signals.

Before we start with the trading system development, we have a short look at the performance of the S&P 500 index itself, since this will be the benchmark to beat. (Compare with chapter 5.3 about market data bias.)

Please note: For simplification we don't include dividends into the calculations in this whole chapter. If you include them, the returns of the S&P 500 index and in all back-test results the annual performance increases on average about 1–1.5% per year. You can change this in the AmiBroker database settings as follows if you want: File -> Database settings-> configure -> Price and Volume Adjustment.

9.4.1 The S&P 500 index

Let's have a look at the performance of the S&P 500 index over the last 30 years (figs. 9.10 A and B).

Figure 9.10: Buy and hold result of the S&P 500 index. Daily data from 1/1/1989–31/12/2018. A: S&P 500 index; B: underwater equity curve.

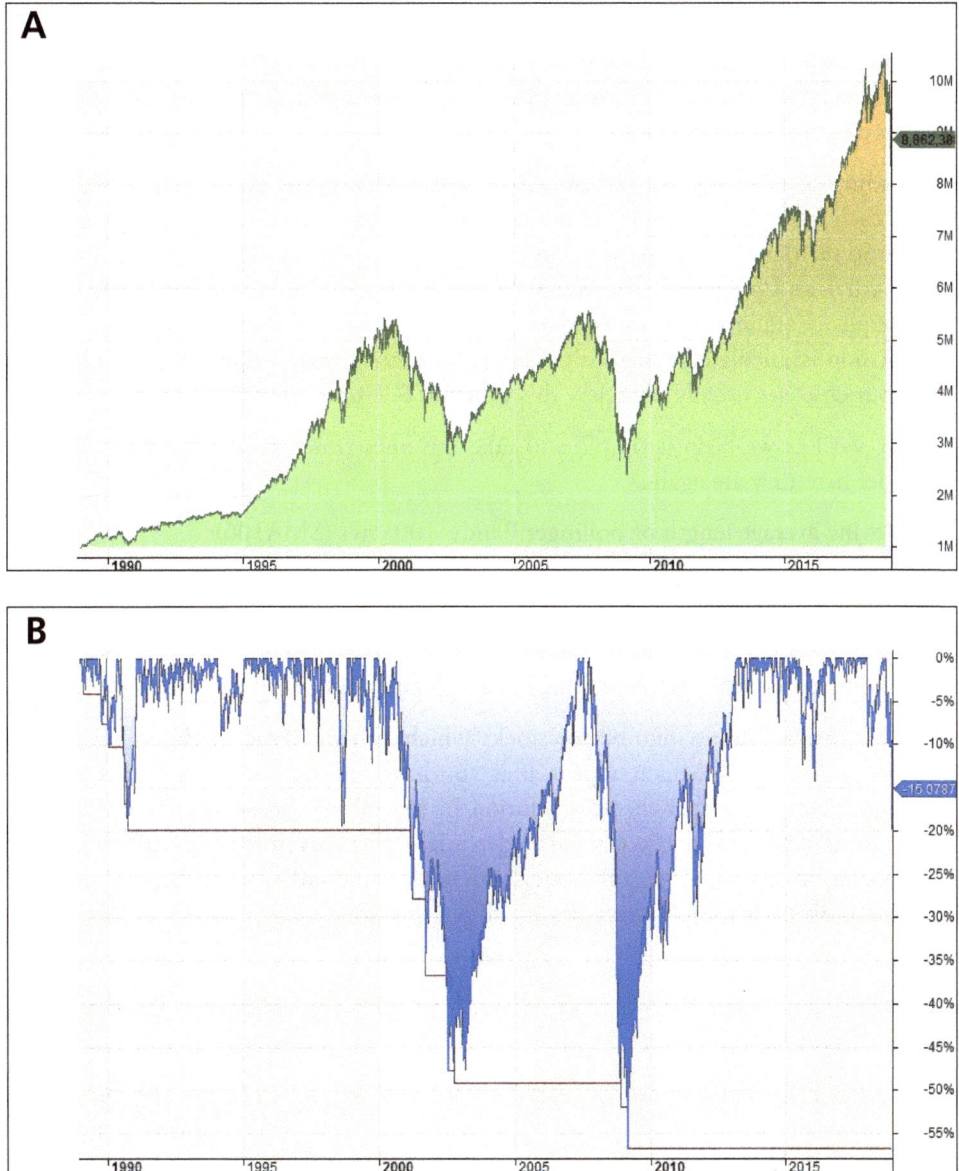

With a buy and hold strategy of the S&P 500, you get a compound annual return of 7.5%. Please note, however, that in between you suffer much pain. In the last 30 years you would have to withstand two big drawdowns. One of 48% capital loss between 2001 and 2003, and an even bigger loss of 56.7% in 2008.

9.4.2 Testing a portfolio of S&P 500 stocks

Now you have all the ingredients to start back-tests on portfolios of stocks. With the Bollinger Band you have a promising strategy, with Norgate you have a suitable data supplier and with AmiBroker a matching back-test software.

Instead of testing just one stock or a few, one after another – you can go now for hundreds and thousands different stocks at the same time. Day by day your system checks which stocks have such strong upside movements that the Bollinger Band system triggers a long signal for them.

For trading costs within our back-tests we take 0.25% at the entry and 0.25% at the exit of each trade. It is necessary to include trading costs in percentage terms (e.g. 0.5% per round turn) and not in fixed dollar amounts per trade (e.g. $10 per trade) since the equity curve and therefore the invested capital per trade (position size) is changing. As a consequence trading costs must adapt to these changes as well. Please note that 0.5% commission is calculated generously – with some stockbrokers like Interactive Brokers (IB) your costs are usually far below this value (at 0.2%) in the S&P 500.

As first settings we keep it simple and take the ones from above (chapter 9.2). As a reminder here they are again:

- Moving average length of Bollinger Bands: 100 days (SMA100)

- Entry point (top band): 3 standard deviations above SMA100

- Exit point (bottom band): 1 standard deviation below SMA100

- Trading costs: 0.5% per trade (0.25% at the entry and 0.25% at the exit)

We limit the maximum number of stocks which you can hold at the same time to 20. You ignore signals which appear after you have already got 20 positions in your portfolio. Please note that this is a solution in the middle between retail traders and institutional traders. Whereas a retail trader might prefer even fewer positions because it is easier to handle, professional money managers would rather prefer bigger portfolios in order to diversify more to have lower risk per position.

With the limitation of the maximum position number we must also decide now which stock to buy when the portfolio is nearly full and several entry signals from different stocks appear at the same time. We therefore include the following ranking method, which will be explained in detail and also optimised later (in chapter 9.4.7):

- Ranking: buy the stocks with the highest gain of the last 100 days when you get too many signals at the same time.

This is a common momentum approach which is well founded in existing literature (e.g., see [21]).

Finally, we remove the following four stocks out of the tested universe of initially 1,778 symbols because they are double: GOOG (Alphabet), FOX (Twenty-First Century Fox), DISCK (Discovery) and UA (Under Armour).

There are two ticker symbols each for these four stocks. For example, for Alphabet you got GOOGL (Alphabet A) and GOOG (Alphabet C). Since there's little price difference between the two, it does not make sense to keep them both. You don't want to enter a trade twice on the same day for the same stock.

Thus 1,774 stocks remain for testing. As you know from the last chapter, this is far more than 500 stocks since your database contains all the stocks expelled from the index as well.

Let's apply the Bollinger system with all these settings on the data, free of survivorship bias, for the S&P 500 stock universe of the last 30 years (fig. 9.11).

Figure 9.11: Bollinger Band system applied to a portfolio of the S&P 500 stocks. Point-in-time index constituents. Daily data from 1/1/1989–31/12/2018, including 0.5% commissions per position. A: equity curve of all trades; B: underwater equity curve.

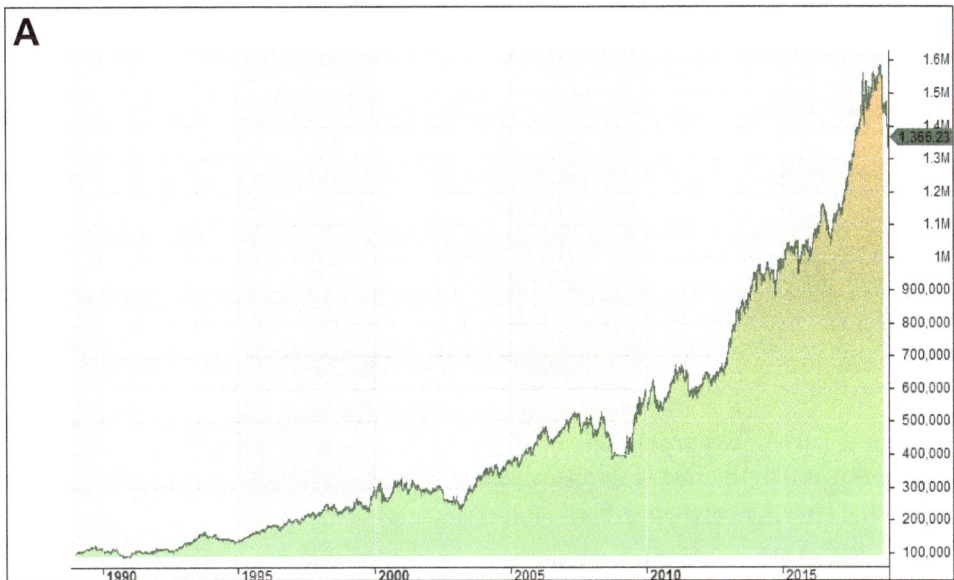

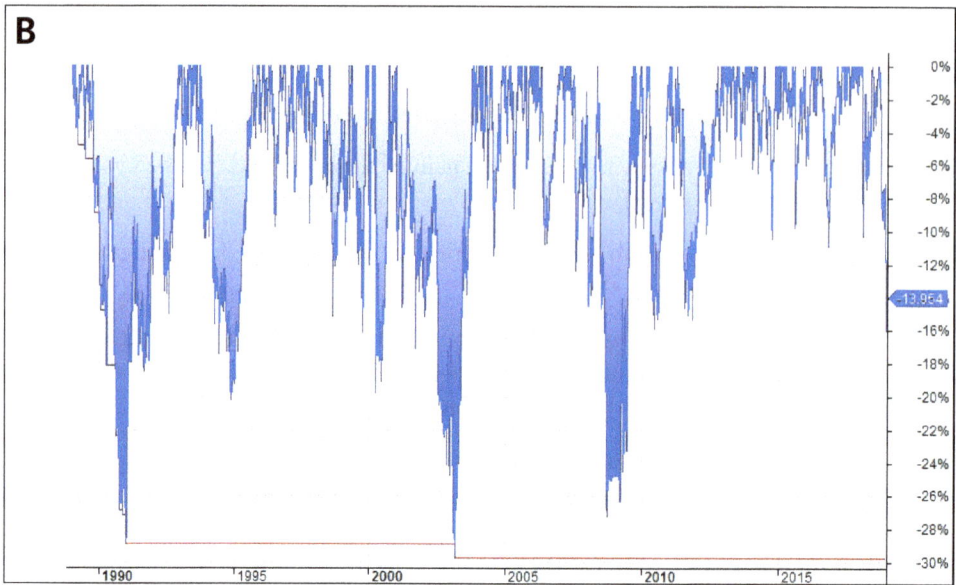

Figure 9.12 Logarithmic equity curve: Bollinger Band system applied to the S&P 500 stocks. Point-in-time index constituents. Daily data from 1/1/1989–31/12/2018.

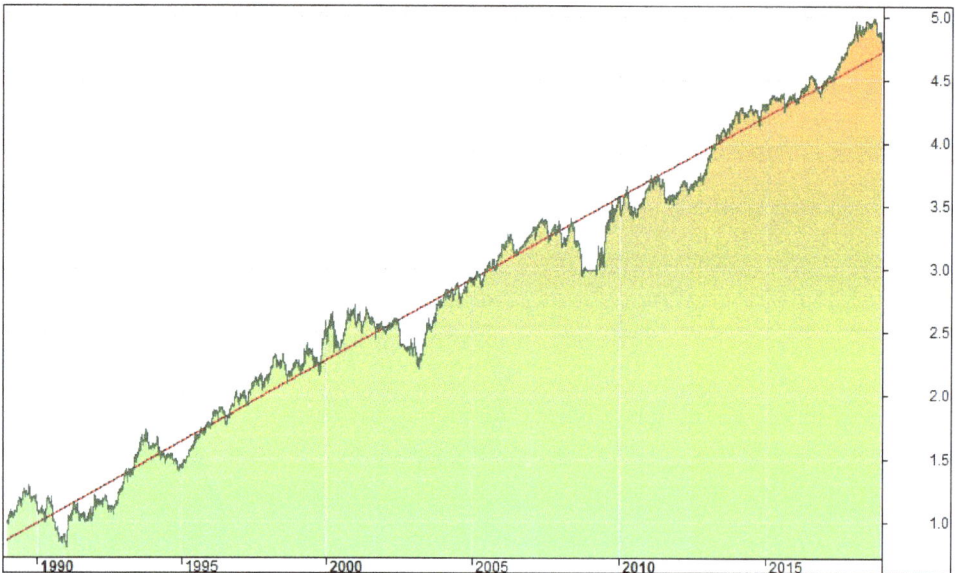

The equity curve looks promising. The system seems to confirm on this stock universe of the S&P 500 index, free of survivorship bias, our earlier simple indications which we got on the Dow Jones (chapter 9.2).

Keep in mind that with this back-test the gains from the trades are reinvested. As a consequence, the equity curve for profitable systems like the Bollinger grows exponentially.

Therefore, it is advantageous to look at the following logarithmic presentation of the equity curve as well (fig. 9.12).

This logarithmic presentation better shows the behaviour of the trading system, especially if you want to compare different years. You can see from it that the trading logic over the years more or less kept its behaviour, which is a good sign for its stability. The capital sometimes falls below and sometimes moves above the red line, which is a linear regression and shows the average growth of the capital within the test period.

Table 9.2: Returns per month and per year. Bollinger Band system applied to the S&P 500 stocks. Point-in-time index constituents. Daily data from 1/1/1989–31/12/2018.

Year	Jan	Feb	Mar	Apr	May	Jun	Jul	Aug	Sep	Oct	Nov	Dec	Yr%
1989	2.5%	1.0%	0.8%	1.7%	5.2%	-2.9%	8.1%	0.0%	-0.0%	-2.7%	0.0%	0.8%	14.8%
1990	-8.8%	0.7%	-0.4%	-2.8%	11.3%	-3.0%	-2.7%	-10.9%	-0.7%	-4.2%	0.4%	-0.5%	-20.9%
1991	5.1%	5.7%	3.8%	2.0%	3.4%	-8.7%	3.3%	-0.7%	-1.5%	3.8%	-4.2%	13.8%	27.0%
1992	-5.3%	3.4%	-1.9%	2.1%	1.1%	-6.0%	1.5%	-2.8%	5.5%	4.5%	1.5%	3.9%	7.0%
1993	6.8%	-1.5%	1.0%	-0.2%	7.1%	3.8%	2.6%	6.5%	-0.9%	3.5%	-7.9%	-0.2%	21.5%
1994	2.2%	-0.2%	-3.9%	-0.7%	-1.2%	-4.1%	4.1%	1.1%	-3.6%	0.7%	-5.2%	1.0%	-9.9%
1995	-0.2%	3.5%	1.8%	4.1%	2.8%	0.9%	3.5%	-0.1%	3.7%	-1.7%	4.7%	-0.1%	25.2%
1996	2.9%	3.0%	0.9%	3.7%	-1.4%	-0.3%	-7.4%	3.9%	6.1%	2.4%	5.9%	-5.5%	13.9%
1997	3.9%	-1.9%	-2.6%	2.8%	3.7%	1.9%	5.4%	-3.5%	3.6%	-5.3%	3.8%	3.9%	16.3%
1998	-1.5%	5.9%	5.8%	-2.2%	-2.3%	1.5%	-0.1%	-10.9%	4.7%	1.1%	3.2%	4.1%	8.3%
1999	0.1%	-5.3%	3.9%	5.4%	-0.0%	1.1%	-4.3%	-1.3%	-3.5%	5.4%	7.8%	14.3%	24.3%
2000	-8.4%	9.9%	-2.8%	-5.3%	-6.1%	-0.9%	3.8%	7.8%	10.2%	-0.4%	0.1%	2.2%	8.3%
2001	-7.2%	1.7%	-5.8%	4.5%	4.3%	-2.9%	-0.2%	-4.3%	-1.7%	-0.8%	2.8%	-1.9%	-11.7%
2002	-0.3%	-0.3%	3.1%	1.5%	1.5%	-3.3%	-10.2%	-0.9%	-1.6%	0.2%	4.3%	-7.9%	-13.9%
2003	1.3%	-4.6%	0.4%	8.2%	7.8%	2.1%	1.4%	3.6%	0.4%	9.5%	0.7%	1.4%	36.3%
2004	1.4%	1.6%	0.1%	-1.6%	2.4%	6.0%	-6.5%	-1.5%	4.3%	0.8%	5.0%	0.7%	13.0%
2005	-1.9%	2.3%	1.6%	-6.2%	4.3%	4.4%	3.1%	-0.1%	3.3%	-2.7%	3.5%	0.5%	12.2%
2006	6.8%	-0.8%	4.9%	-0.5%	-4.9%	-1.2%	-1.9%	3.0%	1.5%	1.9%	1.3%	2.0%	12.3%
2007	3.1%	-2.2%	2.8%	3.6%	0.8%	-2.0%	-4.2%	-2.8%	3.4%	3.8%	-2.8%	3.2%	6.5%
2008	-10.4%	1.9%	-0.6%	5.5%	4.3%	-1.6%	-7.7%	-2.0%	-7.9%	-4.0%	-0.7%	-0.5%	-22.4%
2009	0.0%	0.0%	-1.6%	10.7%	-2.2%	2.1%	13.8%	5.8%	4.5%	-4.8%	5.0%	7.1%	46.4%
2010	-7.0%	3.5%	5.9%	0.2%	-6.9%	-4.4%	3.4%	-2.1%	5.3%	2.3%	2.1%	4.7%	6.1%
2011	1.4%	3.6%	1.8%	1.8%	-1.7%	-3.3%	-3.5%	-4.4%	-2.1%	3.1%	1.3%	0.1%	-2.3%
2012	0.6%	4.5%	1.3%	-0.1%	-3.6%	2.5%	0.5%	0.4%	3.1%	-1.5%	3.3%	2.5%	14.1%
2013	6.2%	1.5%	7.5%	1.1%	2.8%	-0.5%	3.8%	-3.6%	4.4%	2.3%	3.5%	4.4%	38.5%
2014	-3.7%	5.5%	-0.9%	-2.3%	1.2%	2.8%	-3.4%	2.5%	-3.8%	1.4%	5.3%	-1.2%	2.7%
2015	-1.1%	5.3%	1.2%	-1.6%	0.6%	-1.2%	3.7%	-5.9%	1.7%	3.3%	0.6%	0.3%	6.5%
2016	-1.6%	0.4%	5.1%	-0.3%	0.5%	6.2%	1.0%	-4.5%	-1.2%	-3.1%	2.3%	2.2%	6.7%
2017	1.1%	1.9%	0.2%	1.7%	3.8%	0.7%	5.1%	1.3%	1.8%	4.2%	2.1%	0.5%	27.3%
2018	8.2%	-2.1%	-1.8%	-0.1%	2.7%	-0.0%	1.1%	2.9%	-0.7%	-7.4%	1.8%	-7.1%	-3.4%
Avg	-0.1%	1.6%	1.1%	1.2%	1.4%	-0.4%	0.6%	-0.8%	1.3%	0.5%	1.7%	1.6%	

When looking at the yearly returns (table 9.2), you can see that there are some years when the strategy has huge double-digit gains of 30% and more (e.g. 1991, 1995, 1999, 2009, 2013 and 2017). On the other side you also get some years when the strategy suffers drawdowns (1990, 1994, 2002 and 2008) – the biggest happens in the bear market 2001–2003 accounting for around 30% (figure 9.11B). In this bearish market phase, also the longest period of the system to recover to new equity highs took place (about three years).

Let's have a look into the system's statistics (table 9.3).

Table 9.3: Statistics of the Bollinger Band system applied to the S&P 500 stocks. Point-in-time index constituents. Daily data from 1/1/1989–31/12/2018.

	All trades	Long trades	Short trades
Initial capital	100000.00	100000.00	100000.00
Ending capital	1366237.00	1366237.00	100000.00
Net Profit	1266237.00	1266237.00	0.00
Net Profit %	1266.24%	1266.24%	å0.00%
Exposure %	92.75%	92.75%	0.00%
Net Risk Adjusted Return %	1365.16%	1365.16%	-nan(ind)%
Annual Return %	9.10%	9.10%	0.00%
Risk Adjusted Return %	9.81%	9.81%	-nan(ind)%
Transaction costs	114923.28	114923.28	0.00
All trades	1112	1112 (100.00 %)	0 (0.00 %)
Avg. Profit/Loss	1138.70	1138.70	-nan(ind)
Avg. Profit/Loss %	5.83%	5.83%	-nan(ind)%
Avg. Bars Held	126.62	126.62	-nan(ind)
Winners	511 (45.95 %)	511 (45.95 %)	0 (0.00 %)
Total Profit	2384329.41	2384329.41	0.00
Avg. Profit	4666.01	4666.01	-nan(ind)
Avg. Profit %	25.44%	25.44%	-nan(ind)%
Avg. Bars Held	190.36	190.36	-nan(ind)
Max. Consecutive	9	9	0
Largest win	92993.96	92993.96	0.00
# bars in largest win	499	499	0

Losers	601 (54.05 %)	601 (54.05 %)	0 (0.00 %)
Total Loss	-1118092.41	-1118092.41	0.00
Avg. Loss	-1860.39	-1860.39	-nan(ind)
Avg. Loss %	-10.84%	-10.84%	-nan(ind)%
Avg. Bars Held	72.43	72.43	-nan(ind)
Max. Consecutive	18	18	0
Largest loss	-13544.88	-13544.88	0.00
# bars in largest loss	17	17	0
Max. trade drawdown	-46109.55	-46109.55	0.00
Max. trade % drawdown	-54.26	-54.26	0.00
Max. system drawdown	-253309.78	-253309.78	0.00
Max. system % drawdown	-29.76%	-29.76%	0.00%

The average return per year is about 9%. Thus it beats the above shown buy and hold benchmark by about 1.5%. This does not look much, but keep in mind that also the drawdowns have become smaller: after 56.7% losses from buy and hold, you now got 30% with the base Bollinger logic.

In 30 years you get 1,112 trades, which means about 37 trades per year, or a bit less than one trade per week. The average holding period of all trades is 126 days – so about half a year. From the 1,115 trades, about 46% are profitable. This is a quite high number for a trend-following strategy, which often have less than 30% profitable trades.

The reason for this is that trend-following systems are mainly profitable because winners are much bigger than losers. With Bollinger this holds true: you get 25% average profit for all the winning trades versus a -11% loss with an average losing trade.

The profit per trade distribution also shows a typical profile of a trend-following system (fig. 9.13).

Figure 9.13: Profit distribution: Bollinger Band system applied to the S&P 500 stocks, point-in-time constituents. Daily data from 1/1/1989–31/12/2018.

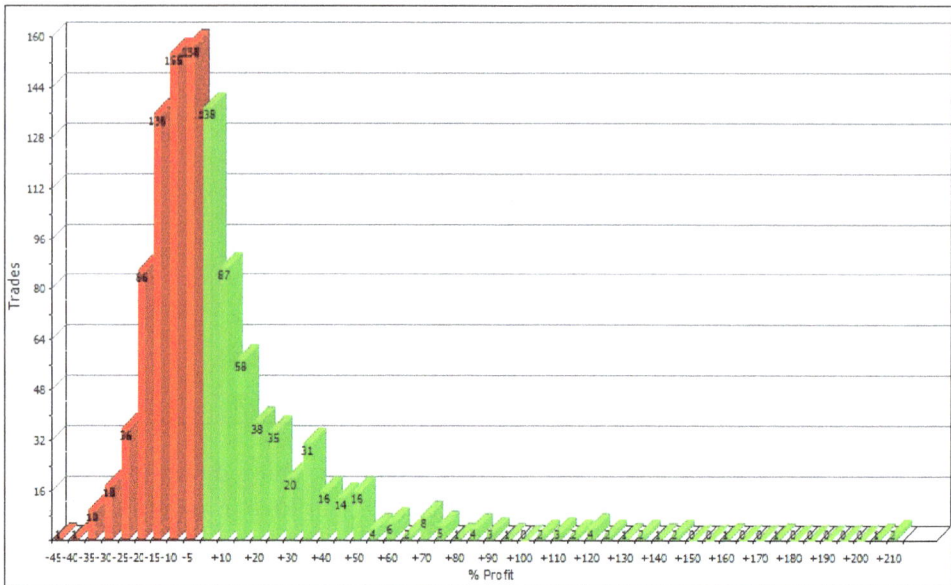

You get most of the losses between 0–30% per trade (red), compared to the wins which can go over 200% (green). Whereas losing trades are on average 72 bars long, you keep winning trades much longer, on average 190 days.

So the system does a good job in letting the profits run and cutting the losses short.

With these promising results as a starting point, we will now try to reduce the system's drawdowns.

9.4.3 Introducing a market filter

You can call it an index filter or a market filter. But how does it work?

As already mentioned, stock markets in the long term go up most of the time. But although the down times are much less, they often are destructive and painful. The experienced traders of you might remember the tech bubble crash in 2000–2003 and directly know what we mean. The ones who can't remember such a market phase where stock investors lost 50–80% within the short years of a bear market should just look at historical charts (e.g. the S&P 500, see chapter 9.4.1).

Many beginners often stop completely their activities on the stock markets after they have been hit by a mayor market decline. However, if you protect against it in advance, this is absolutely not necessary. Further investigations in the literature (e.g. [18]) show that in bear market phases nearly all stocks tend to go down at the same time. Such phases are therefore often called *irrational* since the market sometimes even seems to ignore the fundamentals behind the single stocks.

The purpose of an index filter is to stop your trading system early enough before it gets too big drawdowns when the ship begins to sink. This sinking can be measured in its simplest way by a moving average (fig. 9.14). There exist more sophisticated indicators for upcoming bear markets, like advance/decline lines and so forth, but in order to keep things simple we stay here with a simple moving average, as suggested by Richardson and Faber in their book [18]. When the market closes over its simple moving average (SMA), all is fine. Your trading system gets the green light to take any new long signal which appears. If the market slides below this SMA, however, you are not allowed to enter any new positions. In order to keep trading costs low, our trading system will not close all positions in such bearish market phases – it will instead just avoid any new position during those forbidden (red cross) times.

Figure 9.14: Introducing a market filter. S&P 500 index, with a simple moving average, in this case of 200 days (SMA200). When the market falls below the SMA200, you don't open any new positions (red crosses). You must only open new positions according to your trading logic when the market trades above the moving average SMA200 (green hooks).

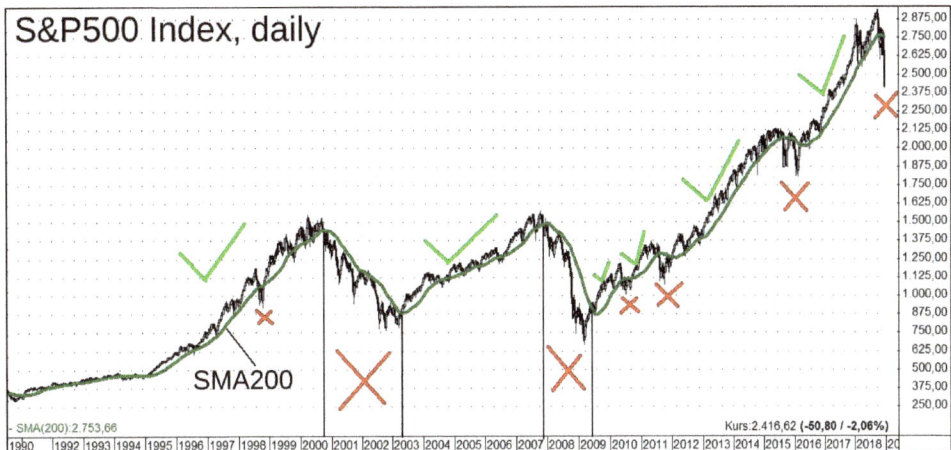

In the AmiBroker code for the entry you must add the following line to include a market filter like this:

```
Buy … AND NOT Ref(IndexDownTrend,-1); // Don't enter new positions in a
bear market
```

With the added index filter, let's perform an optimisation. Which filter lengths are appropriate in order to lower the drawdowns of more than 35% of the Bollinger system within the S&P 500 stock universe (fig. 9.15)?

At this point, the tremendous calculation speed of AmiBroker is worthy to mention. Such an optimisation of all 1,719 stock symbols (the point-in-time constituents S&P 500 stocks) over 30 years (which means about 7,500 data points per stock) with those 50 optimisation runs takes only a few minutes on a normal Intel Pentium PC!

Figure 9.15: Optimisation of index filter length (= SMA length). S&P 500 stock universe, daily data from 1/1/1989–31/12/2018. Point-in-time index constituents. A: Maximum Drawdown; B: Ratio of Annual Return/Max Drawdown (CAR/MDD).

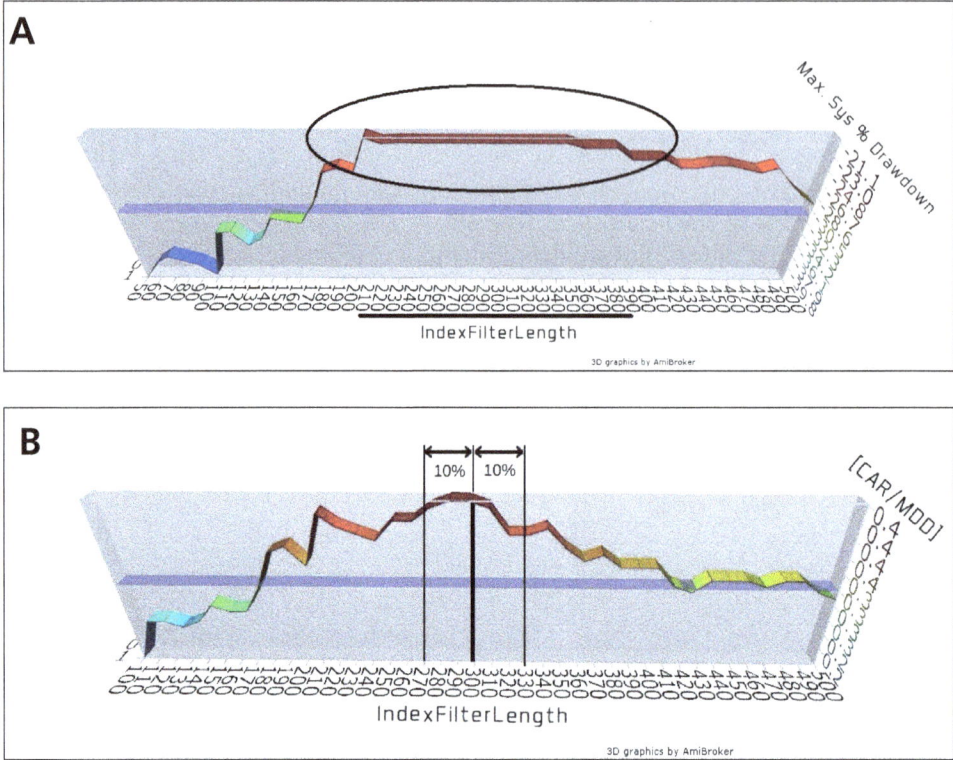

You can see from these two optimisation graphs that any index filter length between 200 and 400 days reduces the maximum drawdown (fig. 9.15A) from 30% down to about 20%. (Please note that AmiBroker plots such drawdown-optimisation graphs in a way that lowest drawdowns are at the highest peaks – this is the opposite to the underwater-equity curves used earlier in this book with the TradeStation examples.) The plot of the Ratio of Annual Return/Max Drawdown (CAR/MDD) shows that the optimal value is just in the middle of this drawdown plateau, at 300 days (fig. 9.15B).

For the robustness of the strategy it is however necessary not just to have a spike at the optimal value (here 300 days). It is important that if you go up and down from this optimum a bit – e.g., by 10% (here to 270 days and to 330 days) – your result does not change a lot. In this case this seems fine, since for 270 and 330 days index filter length all the main system figures (average return, drawdown, average trade net profit, etc.) are not much different from the optimal value at 300.

It may be irritating that the market filter will sometimes stop you for months and years from opening new positions. But your patience will be rewarded in the end because what you miss are usually not the big gains, but more often the big losses. This is according to the findings of one of the greatest speculators of all time, Jesse Livermore. He mentioned that "money is not made by trading, but by sitting." (See the highly recommended book about Livermore written by Richard Smitten: *Trade like Jesse Livermore* [19].)

Let's not indulge in nostalgia any further, but instead have a quick look at the equity curve and main system figures with the index filter of 300 days in place, while all other parameters stay the same as before (figs. 9.16 A, B).

Figure 9.16: The Bollinger system with applied index filter of 300 days (SMA300). S&P 500 stock universe, point-in-time index constituents, daily data from 1/1/1989–31/12/2018. A: equity curve; B: underwater equity curve.

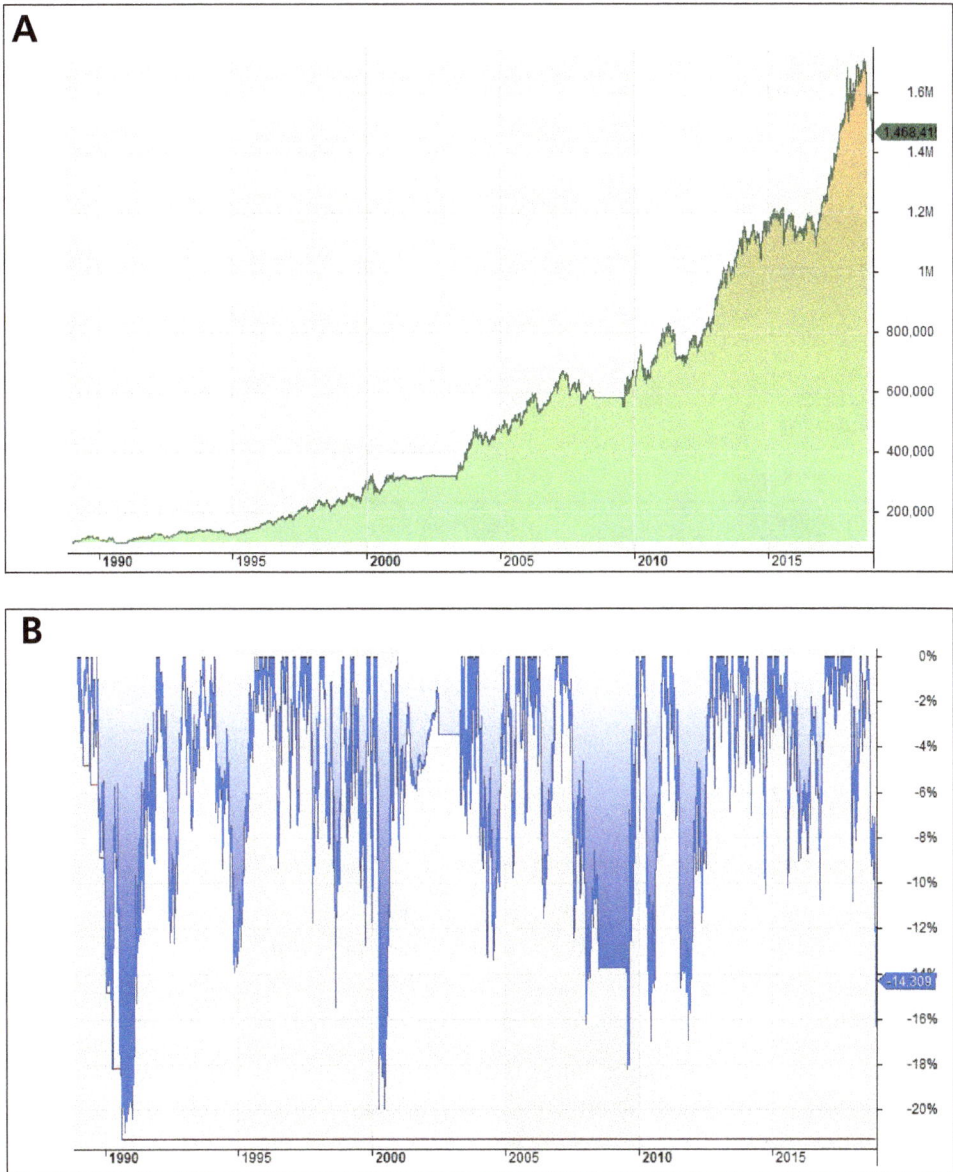

From the equity curve and test results you can see that following the Bollinger system with the index filter in place feels more comfortable (table 9.4).

Table 9.4. Statistics of the Bollinger system with applied index filter of 300 days (SMA300). S&P 500 stock universe, point-in-time index constituents, daily data from 1/1/1989–31/12/2018.

Initial capital	100000
Ending capital	1468415.02
Net Profit	1368415.02
Net Profit %	1368.42%
Exposure %	82.18%
Net Risk Adjusted Return %	1665.18%
Annual Return %	9.37%
Risk Adjusted Return %	11.40%
Transaction costs	118209.83
All trades	953
Avg. Profit/Loss	1435.9
Avg. Profit/Loss %	6.75%
Avg. Bars Held	130.25
Winners	458 (48.06 %)
Total Profit	2432895.25
Avg. Profit	5312
Avg. Profit %	24.75%
Avg. Bars Held	191.11
Max. Consecutive	9
Largest win	99186.4
# bars in largest win	499
Losers	495 (51.94 %)
Total Loss	−1064480.23
Avg. Loss	−2150.47
Avg. Loss %	−9.90%
Avg. Bars Held	73.95
Max. Consecutive	18
Largest loss	−16442.25
# bars in largest loss	67
Max. trade drawdown	−49179.97
Max. trade % drawdown	−50
Max. system drawdown	−279412.02
Max. system % drawdown	−21.30%

The strategy produces similar yearly returns to those without the index filter, above 9%. Also most other trading figures like average trade net profit, etc., have not changed much, although you get about 160 trades fewer because the market filter prohibits entries during bearish market phases (953 trades compared to 1,112 before).

The main benefit of the market filter is the reduction of your drawdowns to about 21%. Remember that this is about one-third of buy and hold, which had a nearly 60% maximum drawdown.

Please note at this point that there is no strategy whatsoever which can exist without any drawdown. From our experience every successful trader has to suffer losses in between profitable phases. The important point which distinguishes the professional from the beginner is the *amount* of these losses, e.g. 20% instead of 60%. In the first case you just take a break and afterwards you continue stronger. In the second case you may not be able to come back again.

At the end of this chapter, let us again have a look at our performed optimisation (fig. 9.15 A and B). You have stable values around 300 days index filter length. And the most important: if you vary this parameter to its up- and downside the outcome of your trading system stays similar. E.g., if you take 270 days for the index filter or 330 days, it does not change much the maximum drawdown or the annual return.

Can you now be sure of having found an optimal value for the index filter?

This will be discussed further in the next chapter about two-dimensional optimisation.

9.4.4 Optimising two parameters together: index filter and Bollinger Band length

Let's look at a graph which shows the general principle of the optimisation of two parameters at the same time (fig. 9.17).

Figure 9.17: Optimisation of two parameters at the same time. Sometimes your strategy has different local maxima, bigger and smaller mountains or plateaus.

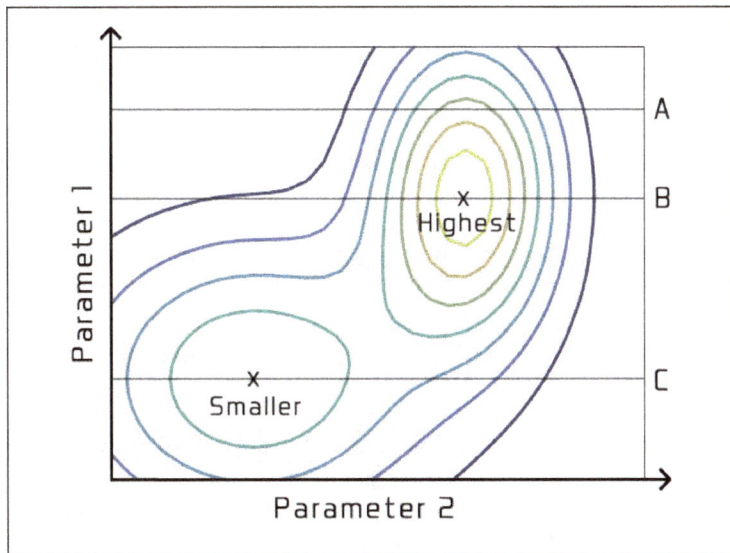

Figure created with MATLAB.

Let us assume that there are two different maxima. One absolute maximum ("Highest") and another smaller mountain.

If you optimise just Parameter 2 while holding Parameter 1 fixed at value A, B or C – you finally reach different plateaus. Only one optimisation (case B) would lead by accident to the highest mountain.

Therefore, in our case, the optimisation from the last chapter (fig. 9.15) does not guarantee that we found the highest value – it could well be a smaller plateau like C or even A.

From these findings it is clear that it is better to optimise more parameters of the system at the same time. How much you can do depends among other factors on the calculation performance of your PC and the software.

We know professionals who optimise five or six parameters at the same time! This may take months of computer calculation power and the interpretation of the results is not easy either. (And of course they have to avoid the over-optimisation trap – compare with chapter 5.4–5.6.) But like this, they can be more sure to find the highest mountains and plateaus. Once they have got a good parameter set they take it and apply it to out-of-sample data for verification (e.g. other stock universes like Nasdaq 100, Australian market, etc., or data from other years).

Of course, the more parameters you optimise, the longer your calculation will take. On a normal PC the one-dimensional optimisation on the S&P 500 stocks of the last 30 years takes a few minutes (e.g., fig. 9.15). Every added optimisation parameter multiplies the time by the factor of the tested different parameters. Therefore, the optimisation of two parameters like the figures 9.17 below takes about 30 minutes to one hour on a normal PC – whereas the optimisation of three parameters could take one full day, and four parameters could take some weeks.

The high calculation speed of AmiBroker is a main reason to use this professional platform if you plan such multiparameter optimisations.

In order to keep the optimisation process more transparent, we will not optimise more than two parameters at the same time in this book. Two parameters can be displayed in a three-dimensional chart. To display three parameters at the same time, you would need to create a fourth dimension. This is really hard to imagine, not to mention adding even more parameters.

Let's have a look at the results for the case where you optimise the following two parameters at the same time. We keep the index filter length in this optimisation because we want to look at this parameter in isolation, but we also want to look at it under the influence of another parameter (to check if we have a situation like in fig. 9.17). The Bollinger period seems to be the most appropriate since it, like the index filter, is also a time-dependent parameter.

Let's see some important trading figures as a function of these two parameters: index filter periods and Bollinger Band periods (figs. 9.18 A–D).

Figure 9.18 A-D: Optimising two parameters at the same time. Index filter length and Bollinger Band periods. Optimisation performed on S&P 500 stock universe, point-in-time index constituents, daily data from 1/1/1989–31/12/2018.

Figure 9.18A: Maximum System Drawdown

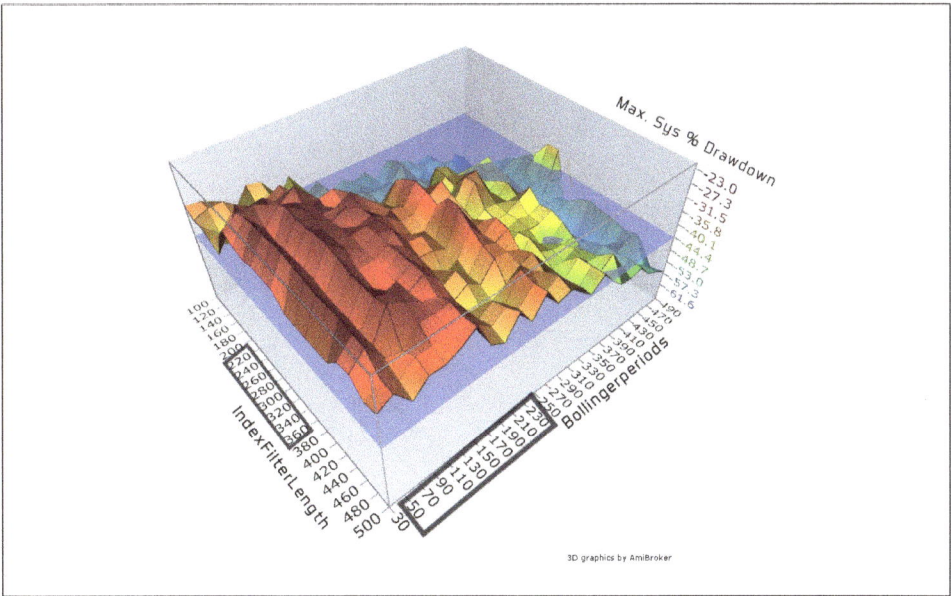

Figure 9.18B: CAR = Compounded Annual Return (=Average yearly net profit)

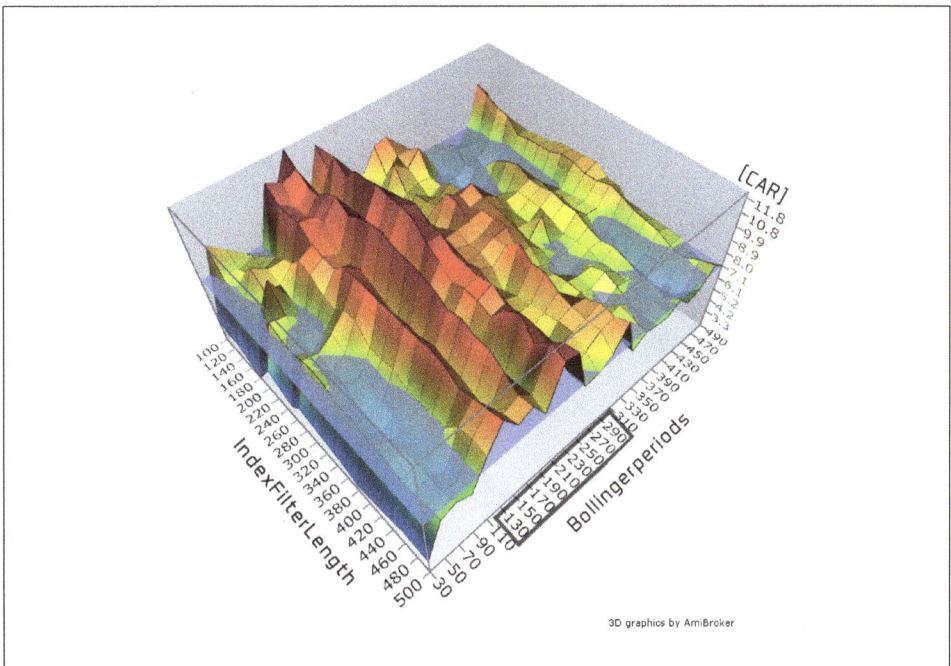

Figure 9.18C: Ratio Annual Return/Max Maximum System Drawdown (CAR/MDD)

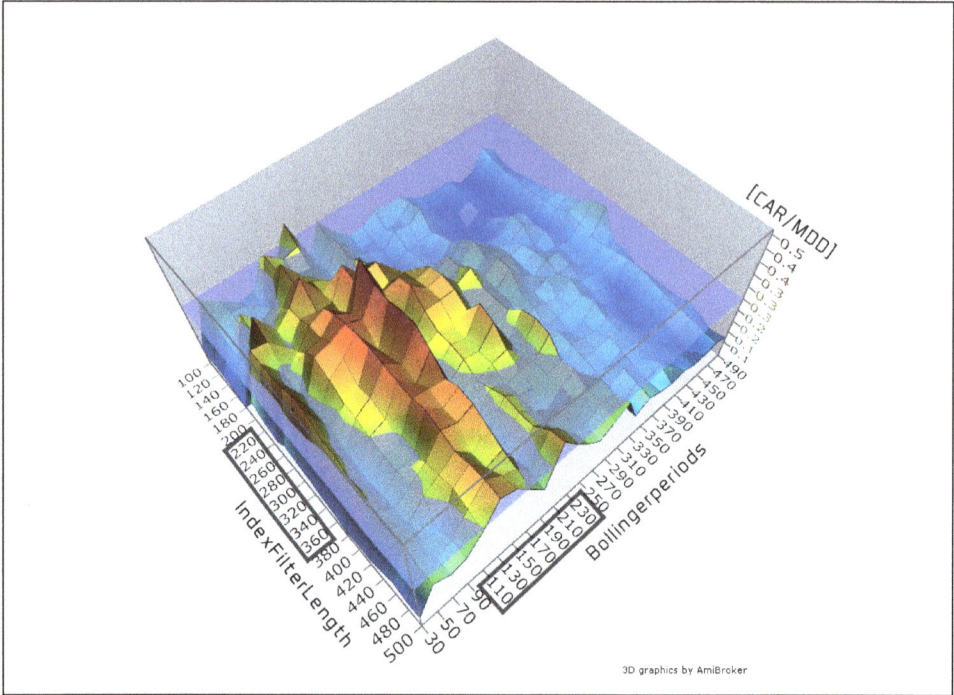

3D graphics by AmiBroker

Figure 9.18D: Number of total trades

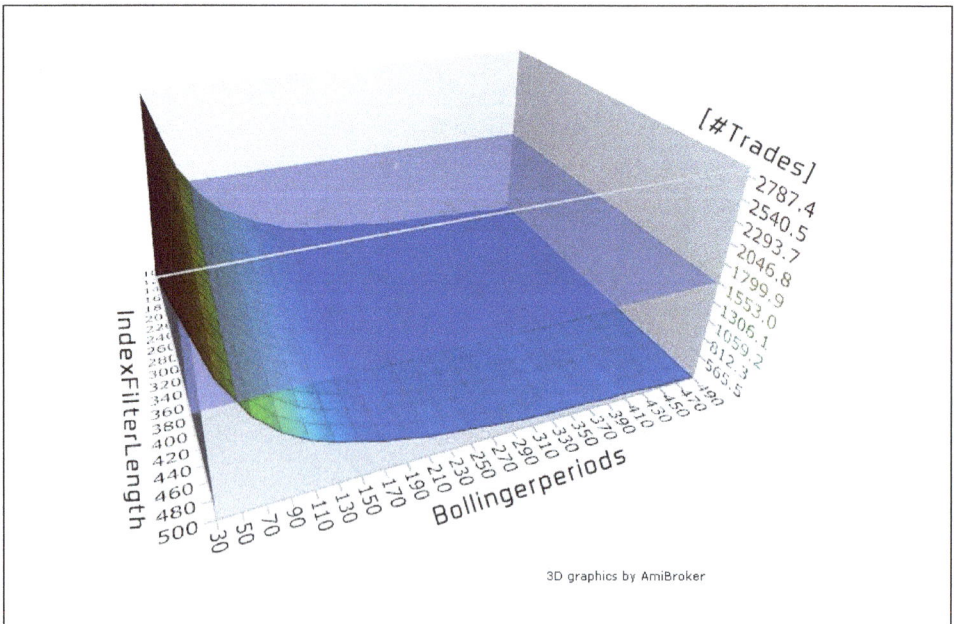

3D graphics by AmiBroker

The first good news here is that there seems to be only one higher mountain concerning maximum drawdown and concerning annual net profit (CAR). This makes the interpretation and selection of good parameters a bit easier. Furthermore, the two-dimensional optimisation confirms the results of the one-parameter optimisation of the index filter length from the last chapter (figs. 9.18 A and C).

But let us go through the four figures one after another.

The maximum drawdown (fig. 9.18A) confirms that the plateau is broad around 300 days of index filter length for different Bollinger Band periods. Further it shows that the lowest drawdowns you get are with shorter Bollinger periods between around 50 and 230 days.

The annual return (CAR, fig. 9.18B) reveals other points. First it confirms that there are many similar good parameters for variation of the index filter length. More importantly, it shows a maximum for the Bollinger periods between 130 and 270 days.

The Ratio Annual Return/Max Maximum System DrawDown (CAR/MDD, fig. 9.18C), confirms the best parameter areas for both inputs. Index filter length at around 300 and Bollinger Band periods of about 180 days.

Finally, you can see from the number of trades (fig. 9.18D) an obvious thing. The smaller the Bollinger period, the more trades you get. This is clear because the smaller this period, the closer the bands move to the current prices. On the other hand, the trade number seems to be nearly independent from the index filter length. This seems strange at first glance because the more often the S&P 500 trades under the index filter, the more often you can not trade. This reduces the number of signals. But: the market appears to be about the same number of days above or below its moving average, regardless of the length of this. And therefore its choice ultimately has no major impact. Only the fact, whether the filter is there or not, has of course decisive influence (see chapter 9.4.3).

From the performed optimisations we finally conclude the following:

1. We stay with the index filter length of 300 days.

2. We continue with 180 days for the length of the Bollinger Band periods from now on (instead of the 100 which we had before). Please note that this parameter does not seem as robust as the index filter length.

9.4.5 Variation of the entry and exit point = upper and lower band distance

Unfortunately most beginners only look at the entry point. As you already know if you have read this book from the beginning, this alone will not help you much without suitable exits (=risk management) and appropriate rules for your position sizes (=money management). Here, let us focus on the entry and exit points.

In the Bollinger Band strategy these are given with the upper and lower Bollinger Bands. As a short reminder, see the trading logic again (fig. 9.19).

Figure 9.19: System logic of the Bollinger Band strategy. The entry takes place after a breakout above the top Bollinger Band (next day). The trade is exited after the close is below the bottom Bollinger Band (again next day).

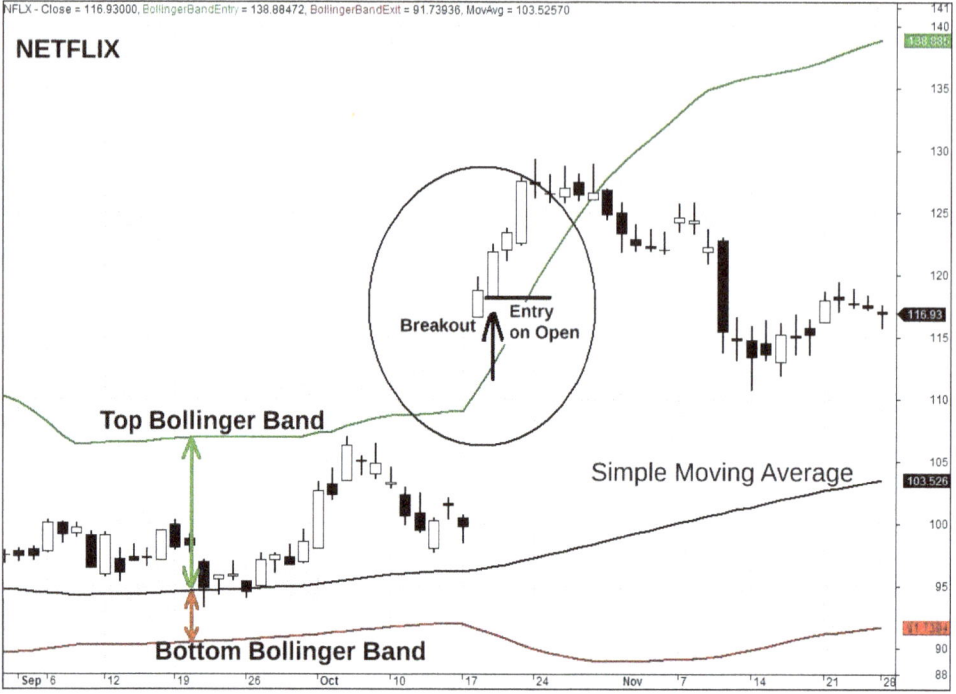

These two bands, which set the entry and exit points, are now simultaneously shifted up and down by different amounts. First, we concentrate on the entry point and on high returns. Therefore, we look how the compound annual return (CAR) depends on the Bollinger top width (fig. 9.19A).

Figure 9.19A: Annual Return (CAR) as a function of Bollinger top width and bottom width. S&P 500 stock universe, 1/1/1989–31/12/2018.

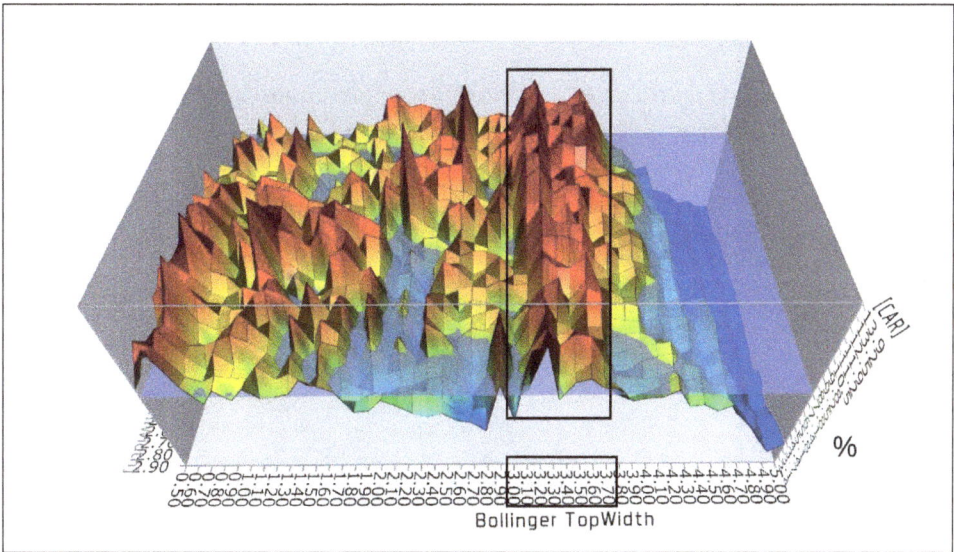

You find a small area between 3 and 3.7 Bollinger top periods for an optimal entry point. This area seems to be stable, regardless of what values we take for the exit (bottom Bollinger Band width).

Now let's look at it from a different side. We check how different exit distances (given by the bottom Bollinger Band width) change the maximum drawdown of the strategy (fig. 9.19B).

Figure 9.19B: Maximum system drawdown as a function of Bollinger top width and bottom width. S&P 500 stock universe, 1/1/1989–31/12/2018.

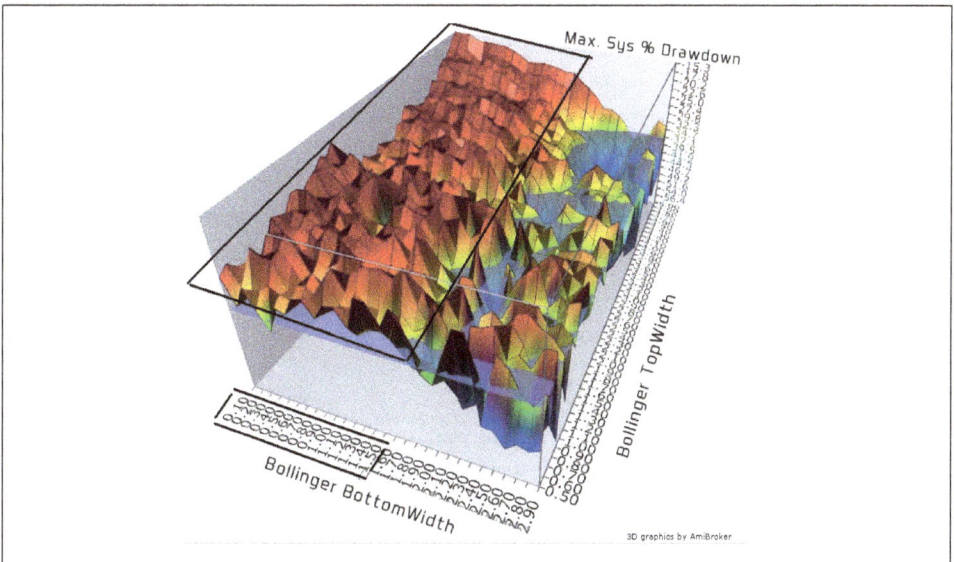

Lowest drawdowns are displayed with red mountains. The result is not surprising: closer stops, means smaller Bollinger bottom width lower the drawdowns. Independent from the Bollinger top width, the area between 0.1 and 1.5 (bottom width) seems to produce the lowest drawdowns.

Finally, let's combine return and risk into one single optimisation graph. You can display CAR/MDD (return divided by drawdown) as a function of our two optimised parameters, upper and lower Bollinger distances (fig. 9.19C).

Figure 9.19C: CAR/MDD as a function of Bollinger top width and bottom width. S&P 500 stock universe, 1/1/1989–31/12/2018.

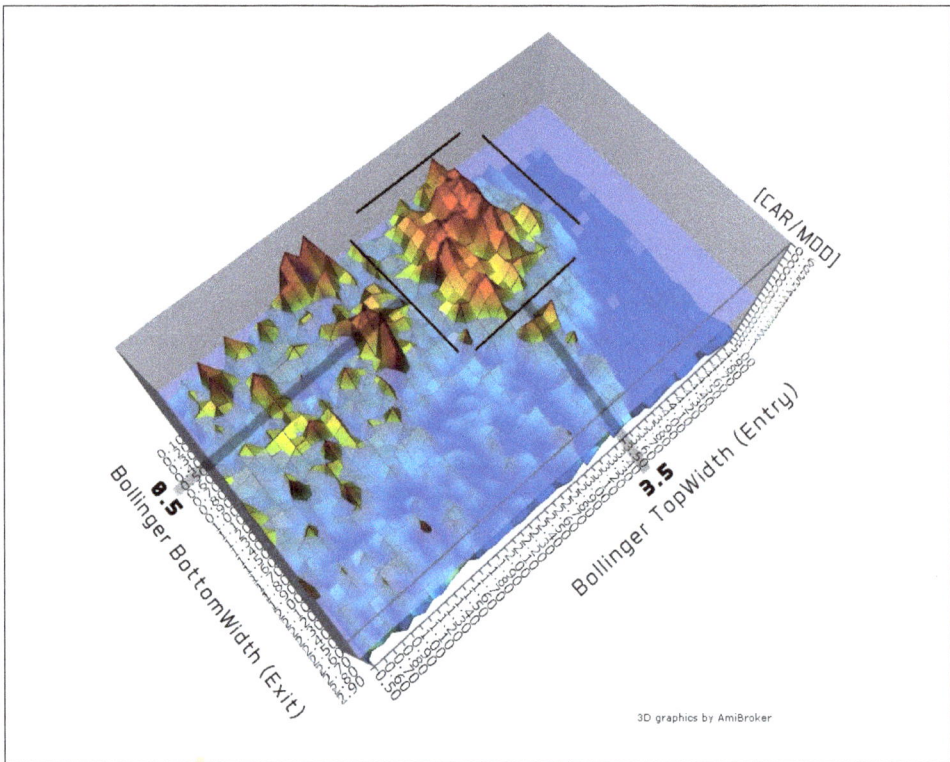

You see that to find a broad plateau of stable parameters is not so easy. You have different mountains and you may end up on the wrong one easily. From our findings in this chapter we select the following two parameters and continue our tests with them:

1. Bollinger Top Width (entry point) = 3.5

2. Bollinger Bottom Width (exit point) = 0.5

This is a small shift of both Bollinger Bands half a period to the upside, compared with our initially taken parameters in this chapter. We will keep these new parameters in the following.

9.4.6 Ranking methods in case multiple signals occur on the same day

In an ideal case a Bollinger buy signal for stock XY appears because this stock moves up on a special day when all other stocks don't. The reason could be an announcement of the management of company XY, insider trading, just fake news or whatever – in any case a stock moves up and therefore your breakout system chooses it to buy the next day.

Such isolated breakouts happen sometimes, but often stocks (or rather the buyers of these stocks) act like a flock of sheep which like to move together.

When dealing with portfolios of stocks like the S&P 500 you need to be aware of high correlations. In a bear market most stocks will go down and in a bull market most stocks will go up. And because of these existing correlations there will be some days when you get several buy signals for different stocks simultaneously.

Which stocks are you going to buy then?

You have different choices. One good idea would be to look at liquidity and spreads. In order to reduce your trading costs in such cases you could buy the stocks which have the smallest spreads. (This is not so important in the big indices like the S&P 500, but may play a role especially if you plan to trade smaller stocks.) You could instead look at the fundamentals, e.g. buy the stocks with the highest dividends, etc. Or you could prefer stocks which had the lowest volatility within the last years – to apply mean variance methods.

As you can see there are endless possibilities. Whatever you finally decide, it is advisable to be prepared in advance for this case. Additionally, for practical reasons: when back-testing you must tell the computer clearly how it should rank securities in case of multiple signals.

In this short section we only check two different ranking methods as common examples. In the first case you choose the stocks with the highest gains within the last X days, e.g. 100 days, which we have used so far in this chapter, indicated by the Rate of Change indicator (ROC). ROC simply checks the price difference between today's price and the price of 100 days before. The more the stock has moved upwards in the last 100 days, the higher is the value of the ROC.

The second method uses the same selection principle, but now instead of selecting the best performing stocks over the last X days, it selects the worst performing by preferring lowest ROC stocks.

There are also more sophisticated methods to rank this relative strength or momentum of stocks. Instead of the simple price change indicated by the ROC, you could use for example a linear regression line or whatever other indicator you like. But let's keep it simple at this point.

The following figures show the result of the two different selection methods (figs. 9.20A, B).

Figure 9.20: Compound annual return in percent (CAR) as a function of the score-length. S&P 500 stock universe, 1/1/1989–31/12/2018. A: buy the stocks first with highest returns the last X days; B: buy the stocks first with lowest returns the last X days.

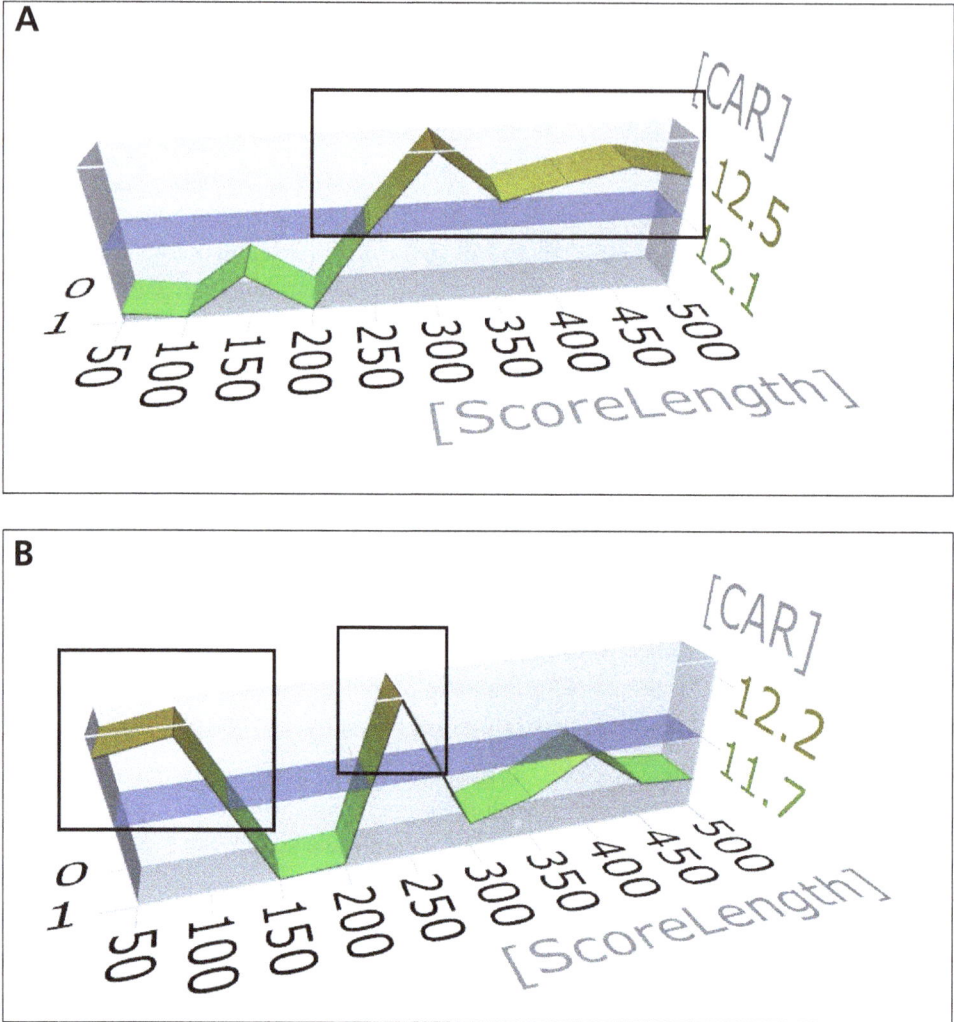

The first point to mention is that we are discussing here a minor effect. The days when multiple signals appear change your compound annual return only by about 1%. You see that the scales on the figures are all in the range from 11.5–12.5% compound profit per year (CAR).

If you look a bit deeper inside your tests then you see that in general the stocks with the highest momentum over the last X days (fig. 9.20A) are superior to the stocks with the lowest momentum (fig. 9.20B). They rather gain 12–12.5% instead of 11.5–12.2%. So, although the effect is small, it is there.

Within these strongest stocks the longer periods (250–500 days) are the better choice than our above suggested 100 days lookback period, in case you get several signals on the same day. These findings are also confirmed when you look at the return/risk ratios (figs. 9.21A, B)

Figure 9.21: Return/risk ratio (CAR/MDD) as a function of the score-length. S&P 500 stock universe, 1/1/1989–31/12/2018. A: buy the stocks first with highest returns the last X days; B: buy the stocks first with lowest returns the last X days.

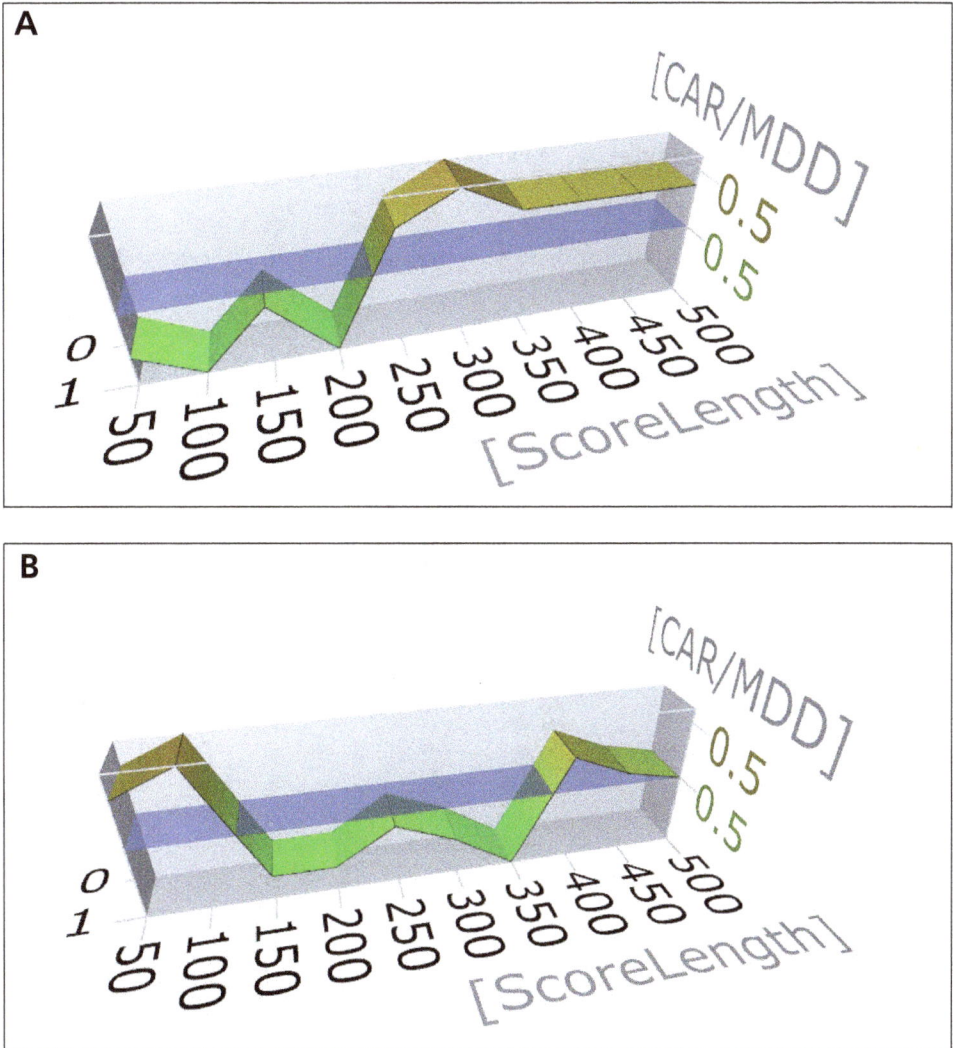

Conclusion

From these optimisation results we decide to stay from now on with 300 days for the ranking and with the method that takes the best performing stocks (highest price change within the last 300 days indicated by the ROC = Rate of Change).

Differences in stock selection between the two ranking methods

We close this chapter with a small example which compares the two presented ranking methods.

Let's have a look at a day when multiple signals occur. This does not happen that often, maybe once every two or three years. But it happens sometimes, like on 9 November 2016. On this day the overall S&P 500 is strongly bullish and the following seven stocks generate a Bollinger Band breakout signal for the next days:

GS, KEY, LNC, MTBV, PBCT, PRU and R (alphabetic row).

The following figure shows one of these seven stocks with its Bollinger breakout signal as an example (fig. 9.22).

Figure 9.22: Upper part: The PRU stock closes on 9.11.2016 at 93.51 above the top Bollinger Band (93.38). Therefore a Bollinger long breakout signal is generated. This stock is one out of seven which you can buy the next day. Lower part: The ROC(300) indicator decides in comparison with the other six stocks if you buy this stock the next day or not.

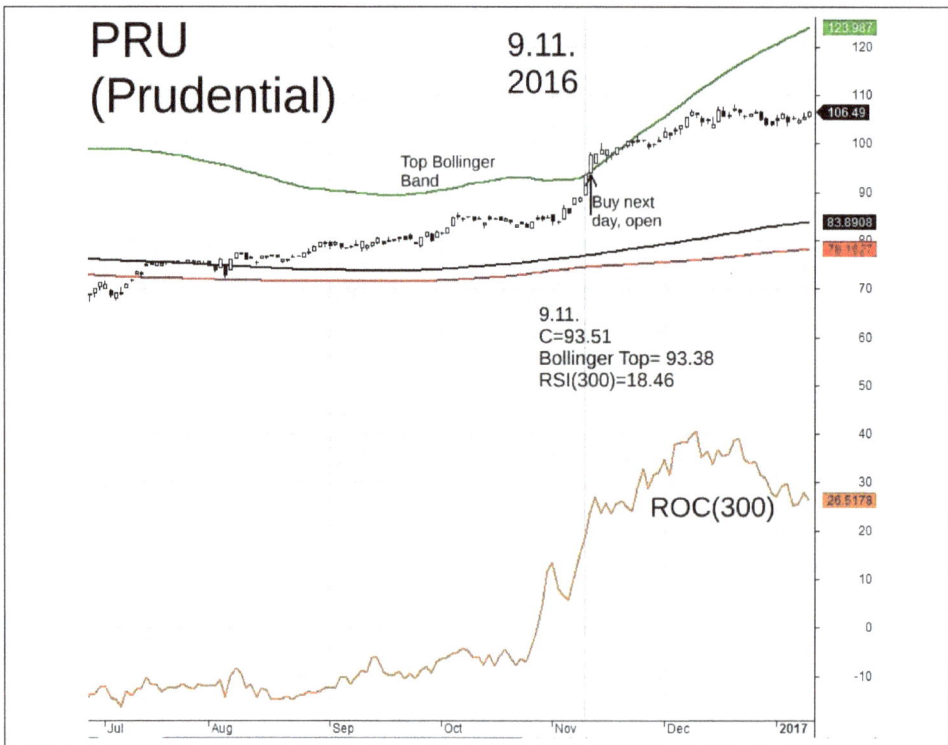

The figure shows that the PRU stock closes on 9/11/2016 at 93.51, only slightly above the top Bollinger Band which is at 93.38 that day (green line). (The small difference is not visible in this figure here, but we checked it.) Therefore you have a Bollinger long breakout signal. This stock is one out of seven which you can buy the next day on open.

Now on that day the portfolio already contains 16 stocks, which means that you can buy only four more stocks the next day according to your trading system (to have 20 in total). So which four stocks out of these seven do you choose?

To decide this, the system ranks according the Rate of Change of these stocks within the past 300 trading days (ROC300), on the day when the signal occurs (table 9.5.).

Table 9.5: ROC(300) of the seven stocks which show all simultaneously a Bollinger breakout signal on the same day (9 November 2016)

Symbol	ROC (300) on 9.11.2016
PRU	18.46
LNC	17.00
PBCT	15.87
KEY	14.33
MTBV	14.11
GS	4.40
R	−5.65

The trading system sorts these seven stocks from highest to lowest ROC(300). In case you have the method which chooses the stocks with the highest ROC(300) you must buy the next day the top four stocks: PRU, LNC, MTBV and KEY. In the other case of the method which chooses the lowest ROC(300), you buy the stocks from bottom of the table to the top: R, GS, MTBV and KEY. That's all.

So, you see from this example that on some days you will buy different stocks with different ranking methods. The two ranking approaches would only have one stock from seven in common: KEY (KeyCorp). The other three selected stocks are different.

The fewer positions you allow in your portfolio, the more often the ranking method will have to decide which stocks to buy and therefore the more important it will be.

9.4.7 Conclusion: Development of a trading system on the S&P 500 stocks

This chapter has shown on the case of the S&P 500 stock universe how you can develop a trading system step by step. As you have seen in the course of the optimisation process, this is not always a straightforward process.

Finally, we ended up with a set of parameters which seems stable enough to produce useful results. Let us repeat these main settings because they will be used as a basis for the following chapters of this book:

- Back-test software: AmiBroker

- Data supplier: Norgate

- Data universe: S&P 500 point-in-time constituents

- Back-test and optimisation period 1/1/1989–31/12/2018

- Commissions included: 0.5% per position

- Market filter in place: Moving average length of 300 days (do not open any new position if market is below 300 day SMA; but keep your existing positions until they are stopped out)

- Bollinger Band length: 180 days

- Top Bollinger Band distance = 3.5 standard deviations (entry point)

- Bottom Bollinger Band distance = 0.5 standard deviations below (exit point)

- Maximum number of positions in the portfolio = 20

- Ranking method in case you have multiple signals: highest momentum indicated with ROC (300)

- Trade execution: Next day on open if the day before you got the entry/exit signal at market close

You will also find these parameters inserted into the free AmiBroker code in Appendix 5.

Please note that our found parameters may not be the best in terms of return and risk. That is not our goal. Rather, we want to show how optimisation works in principle. We are sure that with a little patience you will find better parameters than those shown here.

Let's look again at the equity curves and statistics which you get with these optimised parameters (fig. 9.23 A–D, table 9.6 and 9.7).

Figure 9.23. Result of the Bollinger system, S&P 500 stock universe, point-in-time index constituents, daily data from 1/1/1989–31/12/2018. A: equity curve; B: underwater equity curve; C: logarithmic equity curve; D: profit distribution.

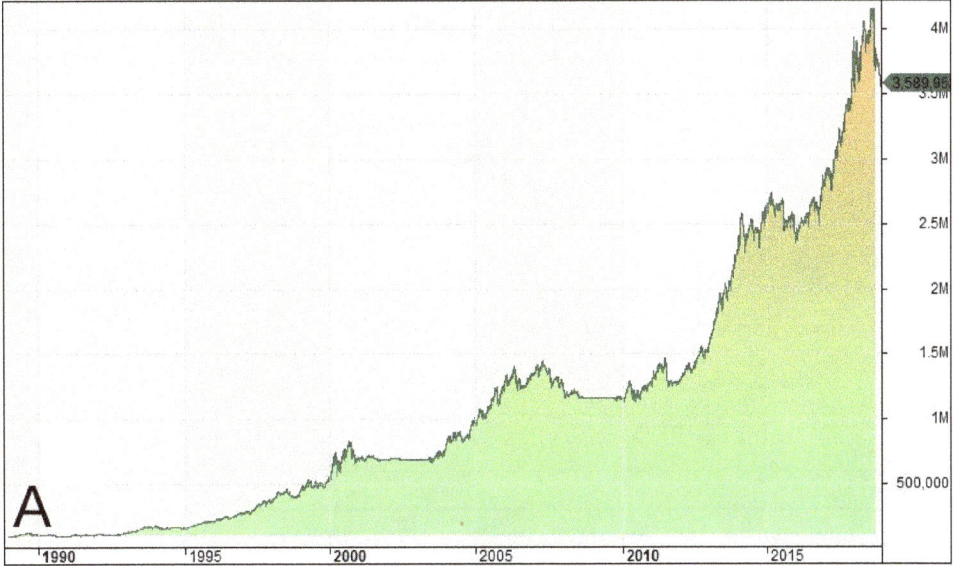

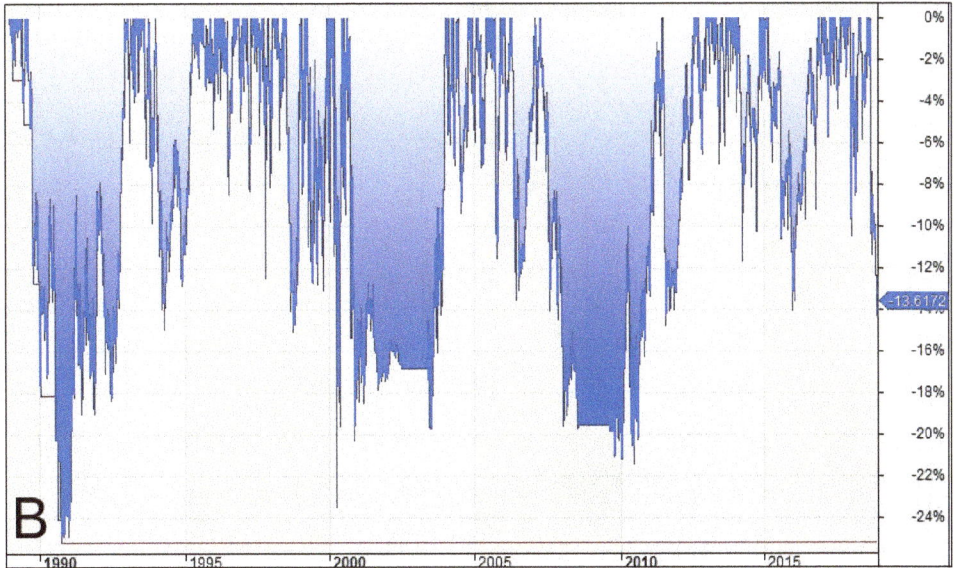

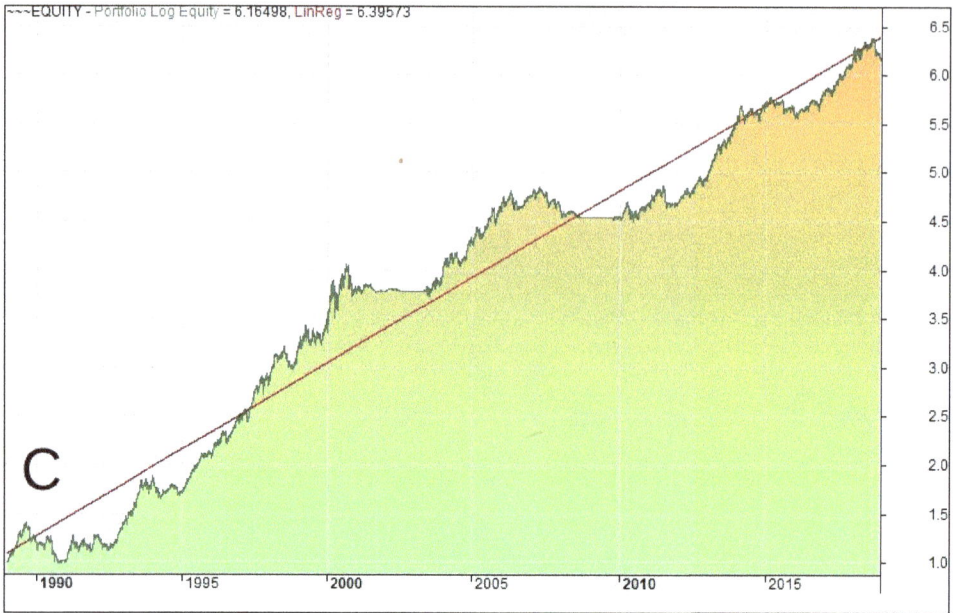

~~~EQUITY - Portfolio Log Equity = 6.16498, LinReg = 6.39573

C

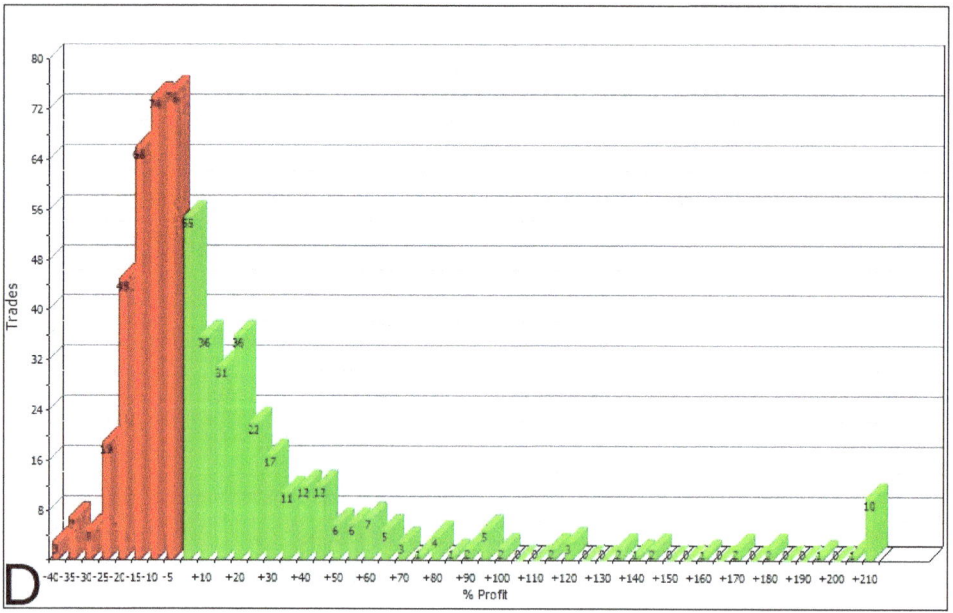

D

Table 9.6: Return per month and per year of the Bollinger system, S&P 500 stock universe, point-in-time index constituents, daily data from 1/1/1989–31/12/2018.

Year	Jan	Feb	Mar	Apr	May	Jun	Jul	Aug	Sep	Oct	Nov	Dec	Yr%
1989	2.6%	1.4%	3.8%	4.2%	7.5%	-2.0%	6.4%	3.8%	-3.4%	-7.2%	1.3%	0.7%	19.8%
1990	-8.3%	4.1%	-1.6%	-1.2%	7.5%	-2.5%	-1.9%	-9.5%	-1.9%	-1.8%	1.1%	0.4%	-15.7%
1991	1.3%	5.8%	7.4%	-2.3%	1.8%	-6.4%	7.4%	1.3%	-4.5%	0.0%	-3.8%	12.2%	20.2%
1992	-2.1%	1.1%	-4.6%	-1.3%	0.2%	-2.9%	3.6%	-2.1%	5.3%	3.2%	4.4%	3.9%	8.5%
1993	2.4%	0.8%	4.7%	-1.2%	7.3%	4.4%	6.3%	6.6%	-3.4%	2.6%	-8.0%	4.9%	29.7%
1994	2.3%	-4.8%	-3.4%	-1.0%	3.6%	-1.1%	2.5%	3.4%	-0.4%	-0.4%	-4.8%	1.1%	-3.6%
1995	0.0%	3.6%	4.1%	3.1%	5.0%	1.6%	3.1%	2.6%	3.6%	-0.8%	1.3%	1.2%	32.3%
1996	1.6%	2.1%	2.1%	3.5%	4.2%	0.9%	-5.5%	3.1%	4.1%	4.2%	6.0%	-2.2%	26.2%
1997	2.9%	1.5%	-4.3%	5.7%	4.6%	4.5%	10.2%	-4.0%	7.8%	-2.9%	4.4%	1.0%	34.9%
1998	-0.4%	8.9%	7.9%	-1.5%	-0.3%	2.3%	0.5%	-9.0%	0.1%	-0.3%	1.7%	9.7%	19.8%
1999	11.5%	-5.0%	5.3%	0.8%	-3.4%	4.7%	-2.2%	0.3%	-1.5%	-0.5%	3.4%	10.7%	25.0%
2000	1.0%	21.2%	1.7%	-1.9%	-6.3%	11.5%	1.4%	15.2%	-3.0%	-4.8%	-12.6%	5.6%	26.9%
2001	-1.1%	-0.7%	0.1%	3.0%	0.1%	0.0%	-1.7%	-1.3%	-1.3%	0.1%	0.7%	-0.2%	-2.3%
2002	0.3%	1.3%	-0.0%	-0.7%	0.1%	-0.2%	-0.6%	0.0%	0.0%	0.0%	0.0%	0.0%	0.2%
2003	0.0%	0.0%	0.0%	0.0%	0.6%	-3.9%	4.5%	3.0%	-2.9%	4.6%	2.0%	4.0%	12.0%
2004	9.2%	0.9%	2.0%	-1.1%	2.9%	3.0%	-6.1%	-0.9%	3.2%	2.3%	9.5%	3.6%	31.0%
2005	-3.3%	7.0%	0.6%	-4.1%	3.4%	2.4%	5.9%	5.8%	4.0%	-6.6%	3.8%	0.5%	20.0%
2006	10.2%	-4.4%	3.2%	2.7%	-3.6%	0.4%	-5.2%	0.6%	0.4%	4.3%	1.1%	1.4%	10.6%
2007	1.8%	-0.4%	0.8%	3.3%	-0.8%	-4.1%	-3.5%	-1.7%	2.1%	1.0%	-3.1%	-0.5%	-5.3%
2008	-6.8%	0.2%	-0.4%	1.0%	1.0%	-0.3%	-3.0%	0.2%	-0.7%	0.0%	0.0%	0.0%	-8.7%
2009	0.0%	0.0%	0.0%	0.0%	0.0%	0.0%	0.0%	0.2%	-0.2%	-1.9%	2.6%	-0.7%	0.0%
2010	-2.0%	3.6%	5.1%	1.2%	-5.3%	-4.2%	5.9%	-4.3%	6.7%	-0.1%	-0.3%	3.9%	9.7%
2011	-1.0%	5.9%	4.0%	2.8%	-0.4%	0.4%	-3.3%	-6.6%	-1.9%	1.4%	0.1%	0.2%	1.0%
2012	2.2%	2.7%	3.2%	2.4%	-3.7%	2.8%	1.9%	3.1%	3.0%	-2.7%	3.0%	0.2%	19.3%
2013	5.2%	4.2%	6.1%	2.7%	5.8%	-2.7%	5.9%	-3.7%	5.6%	4.4%	5.9%	2.0%	49.7%
2014	2.7%	8.4%	-4.2%	-1.9%	2.0%	1.7%	-2.6%	1.6%	-1.5%	1.7%	4.7%	-0.2%	12.5%
2015	-0.3%	4.9%	-1.5%	-4.1%	3.0%	-0.8%	2.9%	-6.4%	-0.7%	1.3%	1.1%	-1.1%	-2.2%
2016	-2.6%	-0.4%	3.0%	-1.4%	2.8%	0.5%	3.6%	0.2%	-0.1%	-3.4%	4.8%	3.1%	10.2%
2017	2.6%	0.6%	0.3%	-0.8%	4.6%	0.7%	6.2%	-0.7%	2.7%	4.2%	0.4%	0.1%	22.7%
2018	12.8%	-1.8%	-2.5%	0.7%	5.7%	-2.8%	1.9%	5.9%	-0.6%	-9.1%	0.3%	-4.0%	4.9%
Avg	1.5%	2.4%	1.4%	0.4%	1.7%	0.3%	1.5%	0.2%	0.7%	-0.2%	1.0%	2.1%	

Table 9.7: Main system figures of the Bollinger system. Green rectangle: The exposure indicates what percentage of the account is filled with shares on average. S&P 500 stock universe, point-in-time index constituents, daily data from 1/1/1989–31/12/2018.

Initial capital	100000
Ending capital	3589952.06
Net Profit	3489952.06
Net Profit %	3489.95%
Exposure %	77.71%
Net Risk Adjusted Return %	4490.87%
Annual Return %	12.67%
Risk Adjusted Return %	16.31%
Transaction costs	150338.68
All trades	595
Avg. Profit/Loss	5865.47
Avg. Profit/Loss %	15.47%
Avg. Bars Held	192.8
Winners	301 (50.59 %)
Total Profit	4914426.62
Avg. Profit	16327
Avg. Profit %	41.25%
Avg. Bars Held	271.16
Max. Consecutive	10
Largest win	872132.89
# bars in largest win	738
Losers	294 (49.41 %)
Total Loss	-1424474.55
Avg. Loss	-4845.15
Avg. Loss %	-10.93%
Avg. Bars Held	112.57
Max. Consecutive	16
Largest loss	-38498.54
# bars in largest loss	90
Max. trade drawdown	-220894.7
Max. trade % drawdown	-58.09
Max. system drawdown	-594086.65
Max. system % drawdown	-25.22%

With 12.67% annual return (including trading costs) and 25% maximum drawdown, the system outperforms the S&P 500 index which has an annual return of 7.5% and a maximum drawdown of 56.7%.

Please note you are not all the time fully invested. Your exposure (this means the percentage of money of your total portfolio which is invested in stocks) is only 77.7% (table 9.7 marked with the green rectangle). Thus, you have on average more than 20% of your money free to invest in other ways, e.g. in short-term US treasury bills, etc. Therefore your real return, the risk-adjusted return, will be even higher, here 16.31% (marked again with the green rectangle).

At the end of this chapter, we have a quick look at how the optimised Bollinger system would have performed on the S&P 500 stocks on a much longer time period.

We take the whole period for which Norgate provides point-in-time information for S&P 500 index membership, from 1/9/1962 until 31/12/2018.

Of course, this raises the question of whether it makes sense to test on such old data at all. Experience shows that some trading systems only work on data in which PCs were not active as a calculation aid in the markets. In 1980, for example, it would not have been possible to trade the market with a Bollinger system.

We perform our tests nevertheless, but remain with the knowledge that the test period from the sixties to the eighties should be taken less seriously (figs. 9.24A, B).

Figure 9.24: Result of the Bollinger system with all the same parameters as above on daily data from 1/9/1962–31/12/2018 (max 20 positions, Bollinger Band length = 180; top width = 3.5, bottom width = 0.5, index filter = 300 days; 0.5% commissions per position) S&P 500 stock universe, point-in-time index constituents. A: equity curve, logarithmic; B: underwater equity curve.

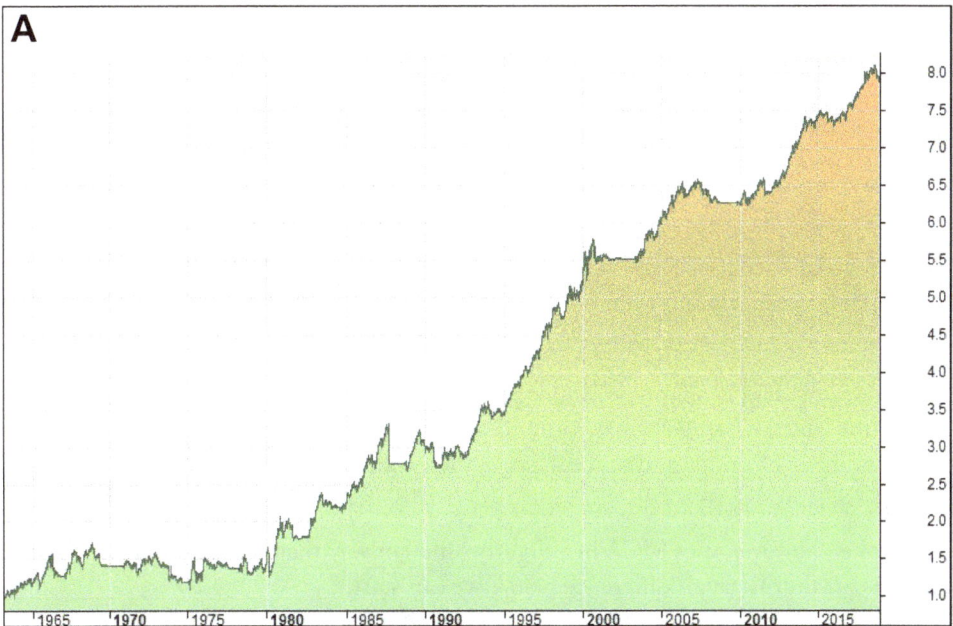

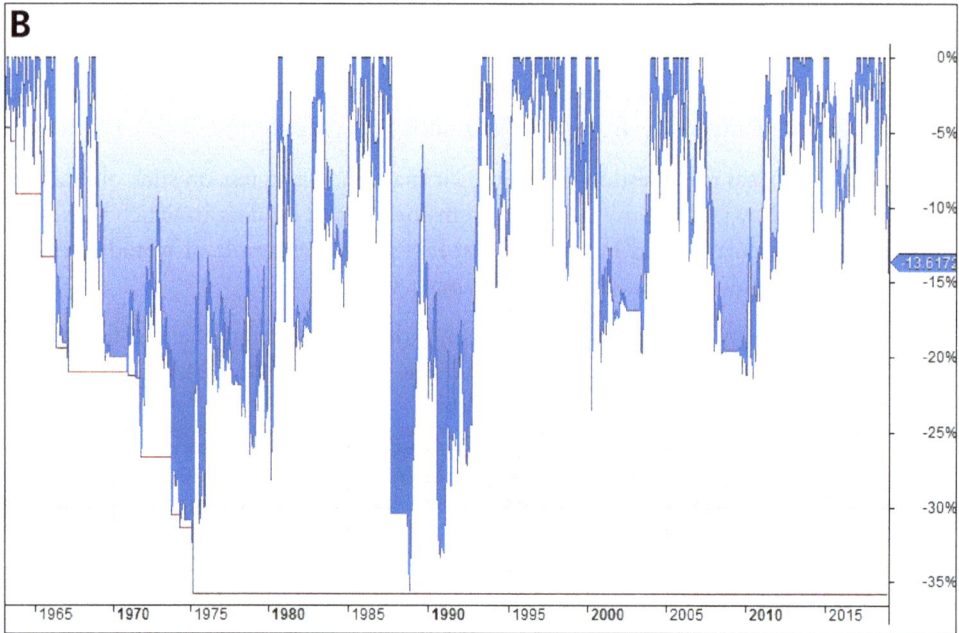

The graphs show that this system also works in the 30 years before our optimisation period. It seems to be stable over many decades, surviving several recessions with its biggest drawdown of around 35%.

9.5 Monte Carlo analysis of the Bollinger Band system

You know the principles of Monte Carlo analysis (MCA) already from chapter 4.2.

But whereas we had in chapter 4.2. an equity line of one market symbol, we now have an equity line which is based on many hundreds. The principle stays the same however. You have a number of trades and you exchange their different positions in many hundreds of different runs.

AmiBroker, however, uses MCA in a slightly different way than TradeStation. So we first have to explain this small difference before we can start.

*There are sampling schemes **without replacement**, which means no element can be selected more than once in the same sample – this is like shaking a ladder, see chapter 4.2 – or **with replacement**, which means an element may appear multiple times in the one sample. For example, if you catch fish, measure them, and immediately return them to the water before continuing with the sample, this is a with replacement design, because you might end up catching and measuring the same fish more than once. However, if you do not return the fish to the water, or tag and release each fish after catching it, this becomes a without replacement design [26].*

TradeStation MCA uses a sampling scheme without replacement, whereas AmiBroker uses by default a scheme with replacement.

Figure 9.25 shows the setup page for MCA in AmiBroker.

Figure 9.25: Monte Carlo analysis window in AmiBroker (version 6.28)

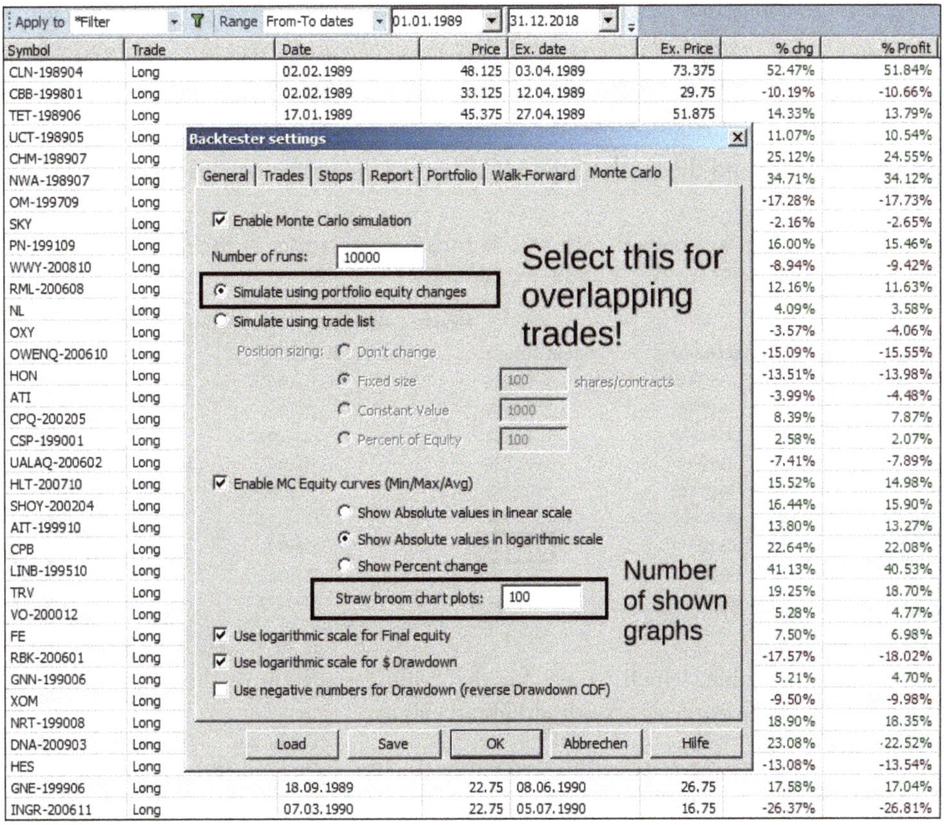

If you have activated this window, MCA happens when you press the **Back-test** button in the analysis window. AmiBroker's Monte Carlo simulator is so fast that it usually adds just a fraction of a second on top of normal back-test procedure.

It is easy and straightforward – but there are some minor details which you should take care with. The most important is that you select **Simulate using portfolio equity changes** in case you have overlapping trades, which we certainly have here with the Bollinger portfolio. This option makes sure that it takes the daily equity returns and randomizes that. So there is no randomizing of the single trades.

You can find more details on this topic in the AmiBroker help section, as follows:

Simulate using portfolio equity changes:

This option causes the MC simulation to use bar-by-bar portfolio equity percentage changes instead of individual trades. Those individual equity changes are randomly picked and permuted to create the simulation run. In this mode, bar-by-bar equity changes are computed as ratios (so a 10% increase is represented as 1.1), selected randomly and multiplied cumulatively. This setting allows the handling of situations when you have multiple overlapping trades in your system and do not require any special setting for position sizing.

After the test, you find the result of the MCA within the performance report (table 9.8).

Table 9.8: Monte Carlo analysis with 10,000 runs on the stocks of the S&P 500 with the Bollinger Band system from 1/1/1989–31/12/2018.

		Monte Carlo		
Percentile	Final Equity	Annual Return	Max. Drawdown $	Max. Drawdown %
1%	484415	5.40%	120960	20.54%
5%	897994	7.59%	207440	23.20%
10%	1191278	8.61%	274207	24.89%
25%	1999469	10.50%	428863	28.08%
50%	3588438	12.67%	725702	32.39%
75%	6327497	14.82%	1252522	37.55%
90%	10622374	16.82%	2084749	43.40%
95%	14268739	17.97%	2839412	47.26%
99%	24991658	20.20%	4790770	55.37%

Let's explain this table, which we get for the Bollinger system in the S&P 500 stock universe, with some examples. See highlighted values.

The annual return value at the 90th percentile (in this case 16.82%) means that 90% of all tests (which are 10,000 runs) had an annual profit less or equal than the shown 16.82%. So you can say that there is about a 10% chance that the strategy would make more than 16.8% per year. On the other hand, this means that there is also a chance of 10% that the system generates a maximum drawdown of 43.4%. But on the other hand, with 90% certainty, the drawdown will be lower than 43.4%.

In the same way, the MCA tells you that only with a chance of 1% the Bollinger strategy produces a maximum drawdown of over 50% (55.37%).

AmiBroker gives you more than just this useful table of worst-case scenarios and their probabilities. It also shows you typical equity curves of the performed Monte Carlo runs (fig. 9.26).

Figure 9.26: Monte Carlo analysis of the Bollinger Band system on the stocks of the S&P 500 from 1/1/1989–31/12/2018. Blue line: Average from all equity lines (all 10,000 runs). Green/Red lines: Min/max equity. Gray lines represent 100 individual test equities.

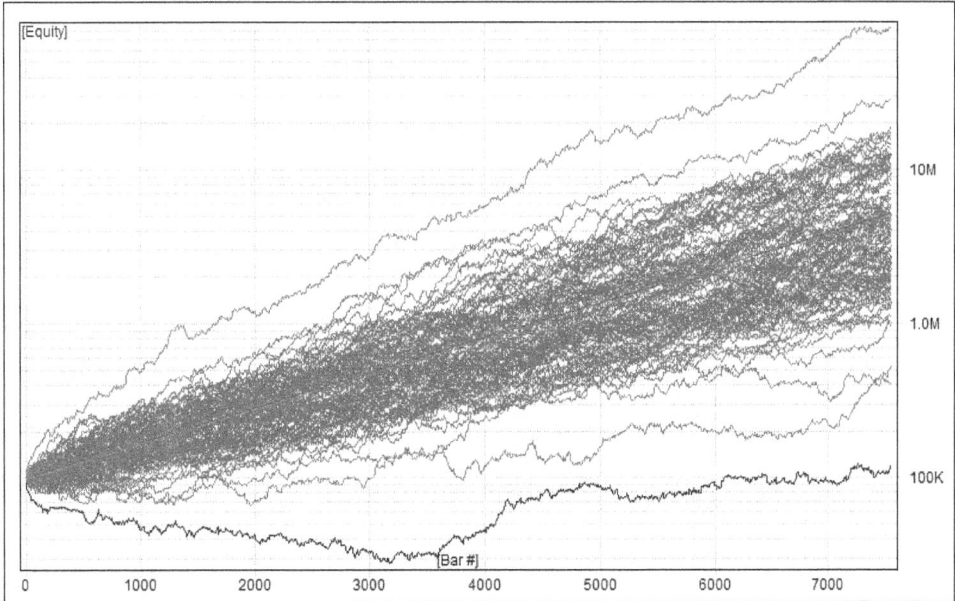

You see on the lower axis the number of tested bars. In this case we had 30 years of data in our back-test. One year has about 250 trading days (dependent on holidays, etc.). Most often 252 days are taken. So 30 × 250 days = 7500 days. This means a chart of the Bollinger Band system within the last 30 years contains 7,500 days (bars).

Note that green and red lines (min/max equity) are not really single best and worst equities. They are bar-by-bar highest (max) and lowest (min) points of **all** equities generated during MCA. So they are actually best points from all equities and worst points from all equities. And blue line (avg) is the average from all equity lines (all runs). The cloud of gray lines represents individual test equities.

All these lines could give you a better feeling of how your trading system could behave in reality when market conditions change. MCA attempts to simulate various outcomes and provide you with statistical information on how bad/good it may be.

As you can see, in the Bollinger Band system, even with the worst equity line of the MCA – which shows a drawdown of 55% in between – your trading account would survive. This is a good sign of stability. But remember that what happened to the LUXOR system in 2010 can and will (!) always happen to every trading system sooner or later.

Remark: When you compare this figure with fig. 4.9 of chapter 4.2 you notice that here the equity curves all end in different points whereas in fig. 4.9 they ended in the same point. This is because in fig. 4.9 you had a sampling without replacement and now you have a sampling with replacement – but everything else stays the same.

9.6 Periodic reoptimisation/walk-forward analysis (WFA)

Periodic reoptimisation/walk-forward analysis (WFA) is the same principle on portfolios of stocks as on single symbols. You can use the explanation in chapter 6 for the single symbol of GBPUSD (cable) and apply it now on portfolios of stocks instead.

Programmes like AmiBroker have nowadays become so fast that WFA, which was ten, 20 years ago only possible in the industry with huge PC centres, can today be performed by everyone on a home PC in minutes (fig. 9.27).

Figure 9.27: Principle of rolling WFA. IS = In Sample, is the optimisation period. OOS = Out Of Sample, means the test afterwards with the IS-parameters on unseen data.

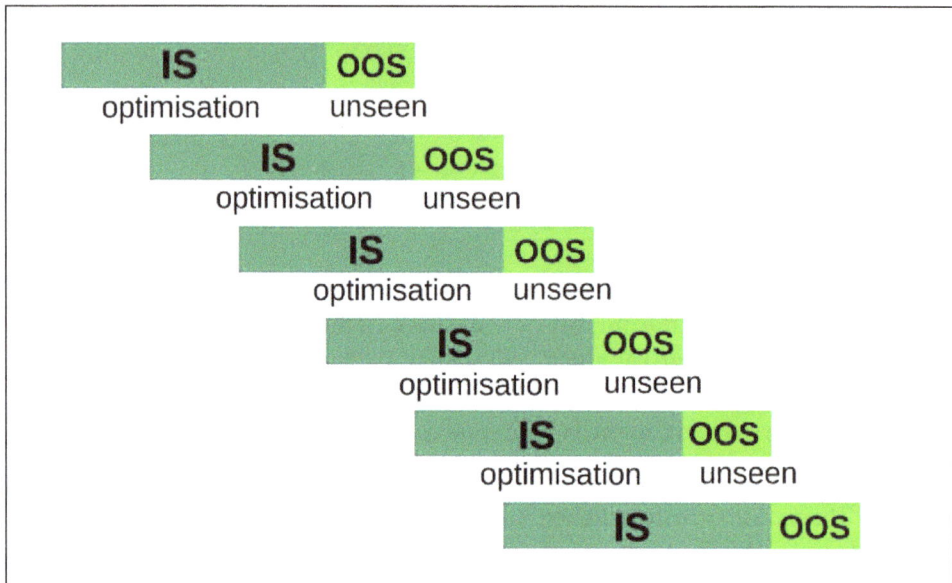

We do not want to go too deep into the details here. For transparency reasons, we prefer to stay in the whole chapter with normal optimisations. Here we would just like to give you one example of how it works so that you can then repeat and use it yourself later whenever you need it.

Interested readers can further study this fundamentally important topic. A brief introduction into walk-forward analysis with AmiBroker, especially for older AmiBroker versions, can be found in the book of Howard B. Bandy *Quantitative Trading Systems* [27]. The masterpiece about walk forward is certainly the classic book from Robert Pardo [4].

We will perform period reoptimisation on one of the main parameters of the trading system – the Bollinger Band top width. This parameter is the key for each new entry because it sets the distance of the observed breakout. Based on this distance the Bollinger strategy decides to enter a position or not (fig. 9.28).

Figure 9.28: Apple, daily, with Bollinger Bands. The level at which you set the entry (green line, 2, 4, 6 distances above the price) decides whether you buy a stock at a certain point or not.

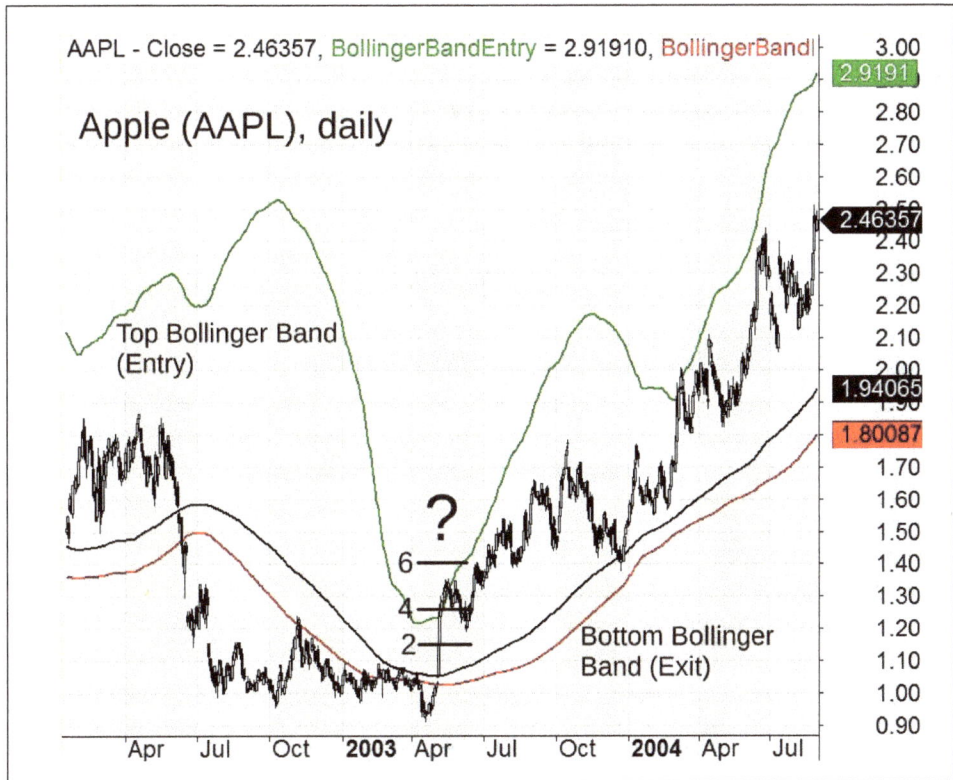

So the first thing you have to do is to change the AmiBroker code as following:

- NumberPositions = 20;

- BollingerTopPeriods = 180;

- BollingerTopWidth = Optimise ('BollingerTopWidth', 3.5, 0.5, 5, 0.1); // (default, min, max, step)

- BollingerBottomWidth = 0.5;

- IndexFilterLength = 300;

- ScoreLength = 300;

- CommissionAmount = 0.25;

All input variables must be fixed, except the one you want to optimise – in this case the 'BollingerTopWidth'.

Next you can define your settings in the AmiBroker back-tester window, see fig. 9.29.

Figure 9.29: Setting up for periodic reoptimisation (WFA) in the AmiBroker back-tester settings window. In this case you optimise the return/risk ratio (CAR/MDD). Our rolling optimisation window is three years and rolls every new year one year forward. Unseen, out-of-sample data, is always the subsequent year thereafter. Detailed explanation for AmiBroker version 6: 1: Choose back-tester settings. 2: Select Walk-Forward. 3: Select "Easy mode (end of day)" or "Advanced mode". 4: Set the optimisation period ("in sample" = IS-window). This will roll forward each year. 5. Leave the option 'Anchored' unchecked. 6. Define your step – here one year. 7: Here you see the first OOS-window, which means unseen data. 8: Set the parameter which you want to optimise, here CAR/MDD = ratio of annual return/maximum drawdown. 9: You see the first periods of IS and OOS periods, how the test will be performed.

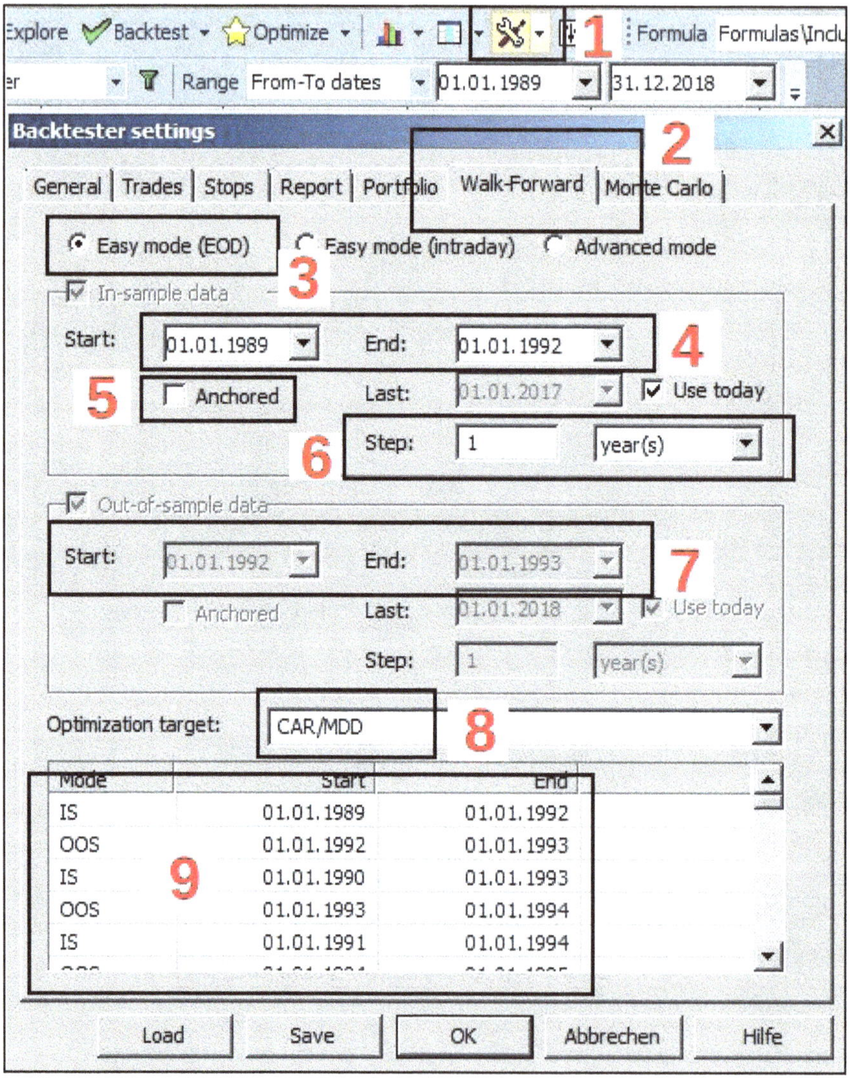

First you define the time ranges which you want to optimise (IS) and those which you want to test afterwards with these optimised settings (OOS). In our case the optimisation period is always three years, starting from 1/1/1989–1/1/1992. The out-of-sample test period is always the year thereafter.

We are looking for optimal values of CAR/MDD (compound annual return/maximum drawdown). So we are searching for optimal return/risk ratios. AmiBroker lets you optimise on net profit, maximum drawdown, average trade, or whatever you like.

Before you start the WFA, it is advisable to check if everything is set-up correctly. Therefore, first perform a normal back-test again – this takes ten seconds and is a useful confirmation to quickly re-check if you have the right code and settings (fig. 9.30).

Figure 9.30: Before you start with the periodic reoptimisation (WFA), just make a short back-test for reference purposes.

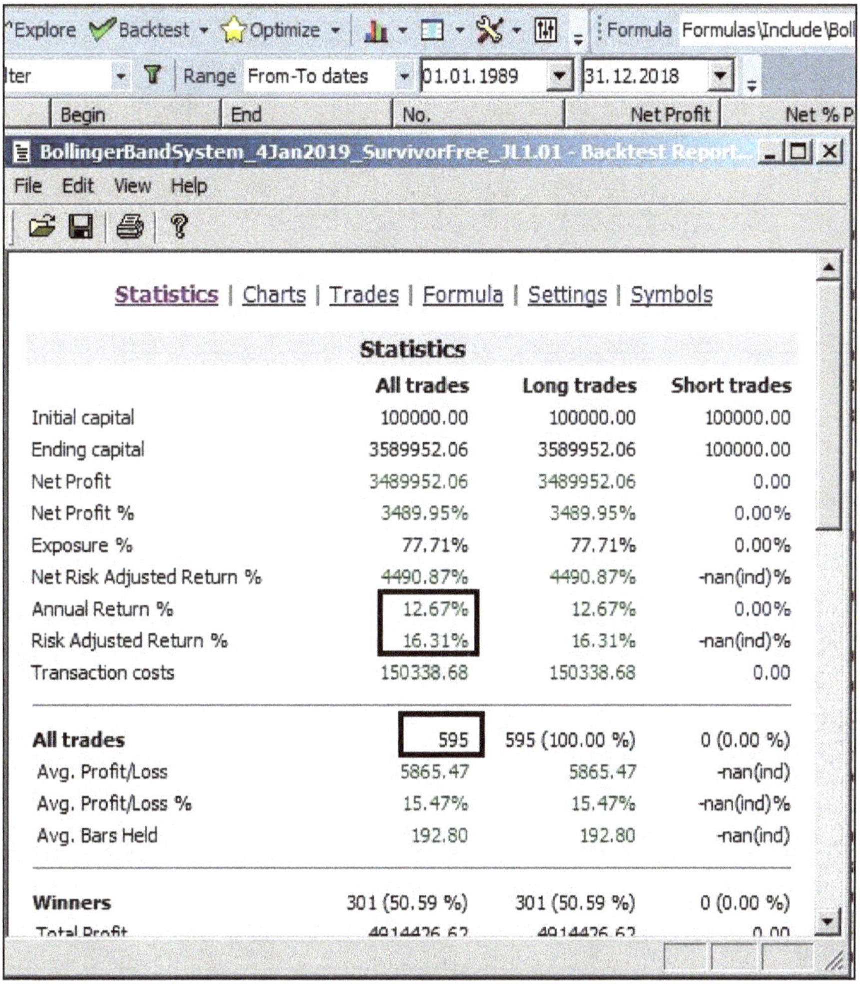

After this quick check, which you then have as a reference, it is time to press the button 'optimise' ---> 'walk forward' and start the periodic reoptimisation.

This can take much more time now, dependent on your optimisation settings – how many parameters you optimise at the same time and which step sizes you choose.

When you export the gained trades list to Excel and plot it there, you see a first result of the periodic reoptimisation: the optimal value for the Bollinger top width changes a lot from year to year (fig. 9.31).

Figure 9.31: Changing, optimised, result for Bollinger top width. In sample optimisation length for each point was three years.

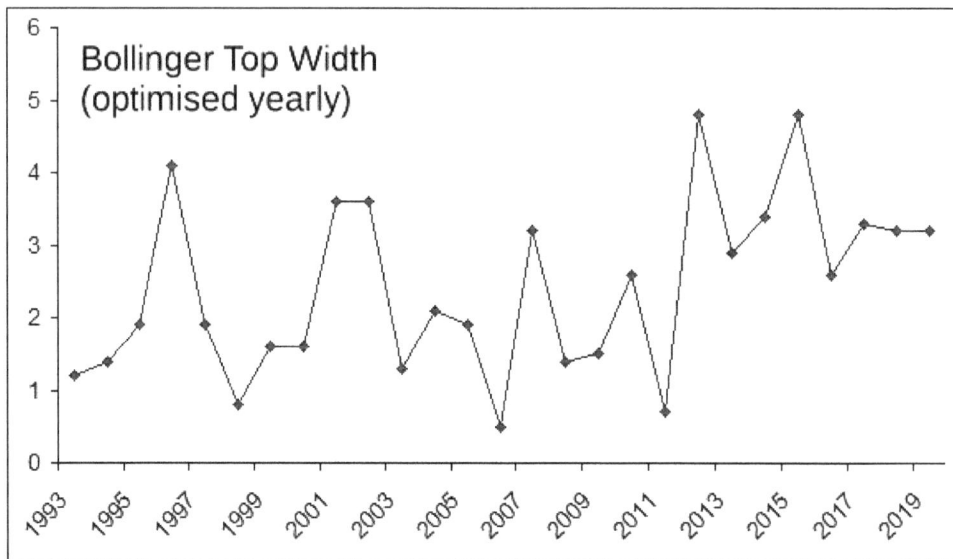

Chart created with Excel

Remember that the optimal value for the whole interval has been 3.5. And now we get variations from 0.5 up to 5. But this is not unusual, since in our reoptimisation we just *blindly* (or better, automatically) optimised, whereas in the analysis above we looked for peaks and valleys with experience (compare with fig. 9.19).

After these first thoughts, let's have a look at the most interesting question, for which a WFA is performed: how will the Bollinger Band system behave out of sample on before unseen data?

Let's look at the OOS results and compare them with the gained values from chapter 9.4, especially table 9.7.

The OOS test results are provided by AmiBroker like the normal back-tests, with all the same charts like normal equity curve, underwater equity curve and statistics (fig. 9.32 and table 9.9).

Figure 9.32: Rolling walk-forward result. Bollinger Band system on S&P 500 stocks out of sample (OOS), from 1/1/1992–31/12/2018. A: log equity curve; B: underwater equity curve.

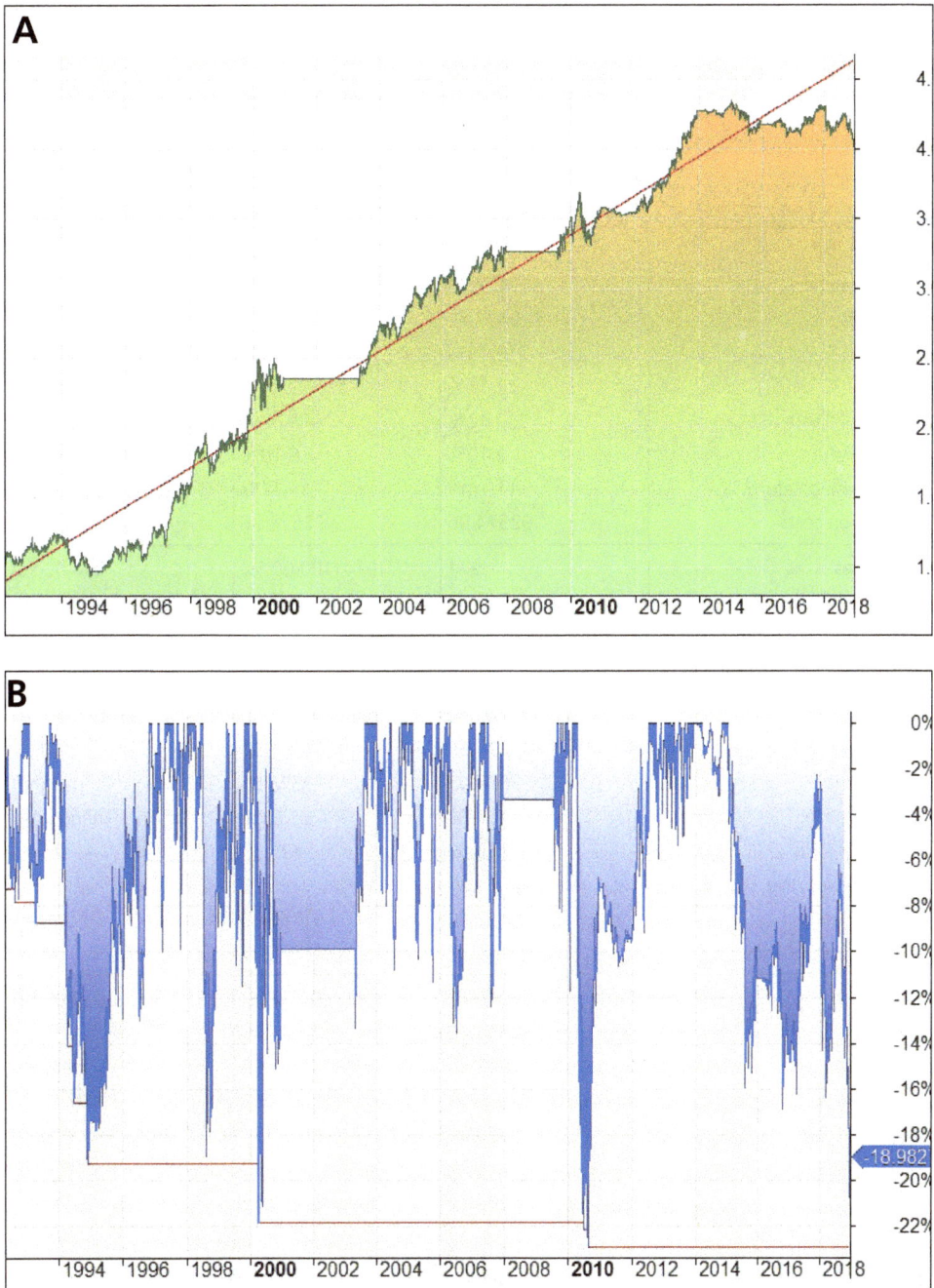

You see that the equity curve still looks steady and that the maximum drawdown stays in an acceptable range also. The results start to get a bit worse and the equity curve starts to go sideways towards the end. This seems a bit disappointing at a first glance, but keep in mind that 2018 was a difficult year in the stock markets and in this environment at least bigger draw-downs were avoided. Finally let's have a look at the system figures in this OOS test (table 9.9).

Table 9.9: System figures: Bollinger Band system on S&P 500 stocks out of sample (OOS), from 1/1/1992–31/12/2018.

	All trades	Long trades	Short trades
Initial capital	100000.00	100000.00	100000.00
Ending capital	819427.76	819427.76	100000.00
Net Profit	719427.76	719427.76	0.00
Net Profit %	719.43%	719.43%	0.00%
Exposure %	72.71%	72.71%	0.00%
Net Risk Adjusted Return %	989.42%	989.42%	-nan(ind)%
Annual Return %	**8.10%**	8.10%	0.00%
Risk Adjusted Return %	11.14%	11.14%	-nan(ind)%
Transaction costs	92574.96	92574.96	0.00
All trades	**974**	974 (100.00 %)	0 (0.00 %)
Avg. Profit/Loss	738.63	738.63	-nan(ind)
Avg. Profit/Loss %	5.15%	5.15%	-nan(ind)%
Avg. Bars Held	101.72	101.72	-nan(ind)
Winners	**461 (47.33 %)**	461 (47.33 %)	0 (0.00 %)
Total Profit	1649471.91	1649471.91	0.00
Avg. Profit	3578.03	3578.03	-nan(ind)
Avg. Profit %	21.87%	21.87%	-nan(ind)%
Avg. Bars Held	136.59	136.59	-nan(ind)
Max. Consecutive	21	21	0
Largest win	51752.56	51752.56	0.00
# bars in largest win	237	237	0
Losers	**513 (52.67 %)**	513 (52.67 %)	0 (0.00 %)
Total Loss	-930044.16	-930044.16	0.00
Avg. Loss	-1812.95	-1812.95	-nan(ind)
Avg. Loss %	-9.87%	-9.87%	-nan(ind)%
Avg. Bars Held	70.38	70.38	-nan(ind)
Max. Consecutive	27	27	0
Largest loss	-14464.16	-14464.16	0.00
# bars in largest loss	14	14	0
Max. trade drawdown	-18965.94	-18965.94	0.00
Max. trade % drawdown	-68.91	-68.91	0.00
Max. system drawdown	-209853.68	-209853.68	0.00
Max. system % drawdown	**-22.93%**		

The first point to look at is the annual return. It is no longer 12%, but 8% is not a bad result for an OOS test. Furthermore, the maximum drawdown with 22.93% is now better than it was before (25%).

You may notice that you now have many more trades – nearly 1,000 instead of 595 before. The reason for this is that when the Bollinger top width is smaller (e.g. 1 instead of 3.5), then you enter positions earlier. And this leads to a higher trade frequency because positions might be a bit worse, get stopped out, etc. As a consequence, the winning percentage goes down (from over 50% to 47%). So, the results seem to be logical and consistent.

Conclusion

A proper WFA is important to get more insight into your trading system. With AmiBroker it has become easily manageable, even for bigger portfolios.

When you perform many WFAs on different systems, you will notice that most mediocre trading systems will collapse completely in a WFA. Therefore a result like the one of the Bollinger system (for this one parameter of Bollinger top width only) is not the worst we have ever seen.

9.7 Results on other portfolios of stocks

We now take the optimised trading system from the S&P 500 and apply it to different other portfolios of stocks: the Nasdaq 100, S&P 1500, Russell 3000, Russell 2000 and the Australian stock market (All Ordinaries: 500 stocks).

In general, we will keep all the same parameters which we found in the S&P 500 and apply it unchanged to all other markets. Where there are deviations from this for specific reasons, we will point this out separately.

Of course, all tests are performed again on point-in-time index constituents with data free of survivorship bias from Norgate. (See [22] for their data catalogue.)

9.7.1 Nasdaq 100 – technology at work

Before we start to apply the Bollinger system logic on this market, let's first have a look at this impressive index itself (fig. 9.33).

Figure 9.33: The Nasdaq 100 index from 1/1/1995–31/12/2018. A: Buy and hold the Nasdaq 100: how $100.000 would increase its value to $1.5 Mio; B: the underwater equity curve shows that in the year 2002 you would lose 82.9% of your money.

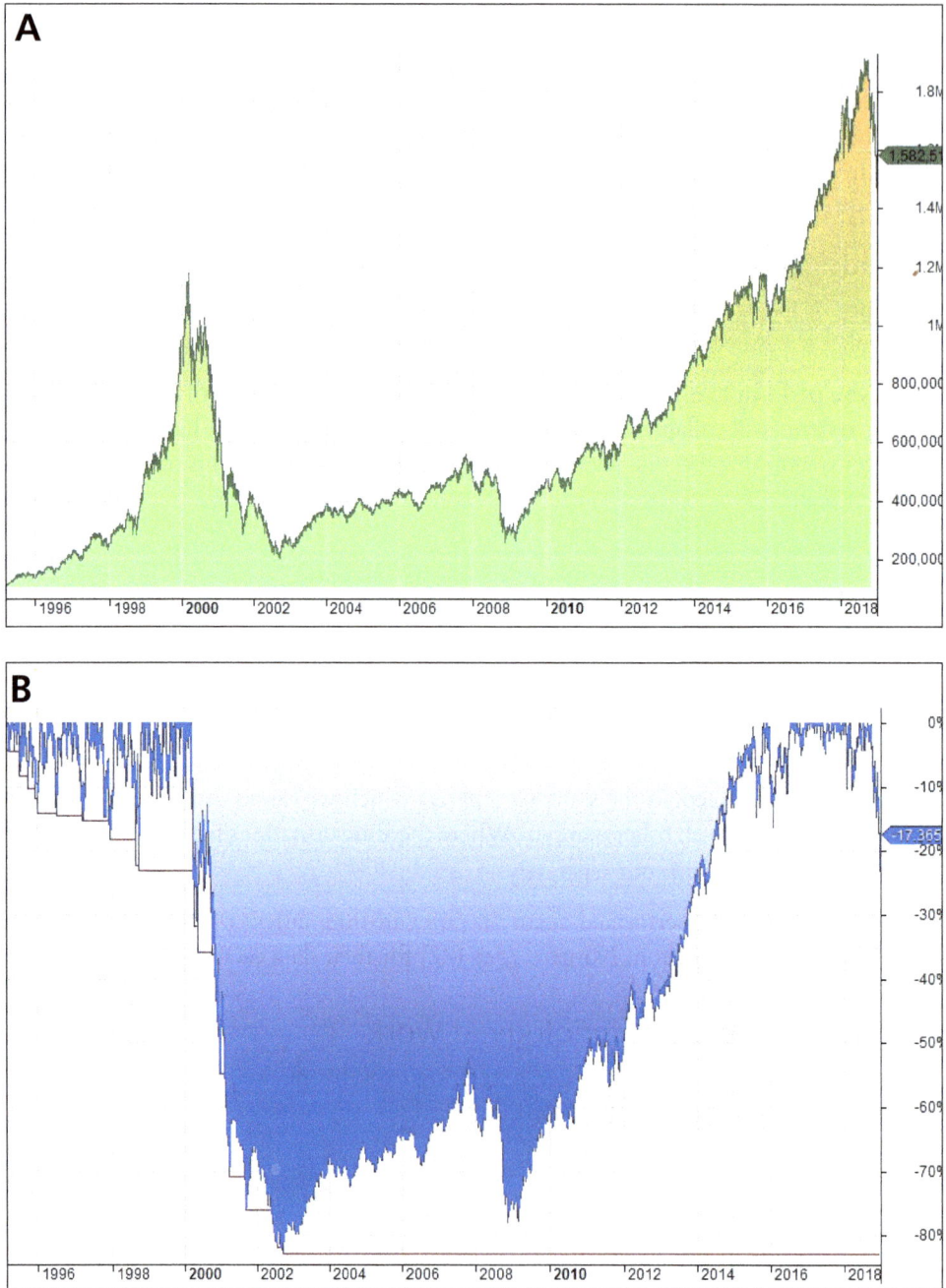

You have here an index with a massive growth rate of 12.2% annual return on the one side. But this comes with huge drawdowns on the other side. Especially the technology bubble around the year 2000 some will never forget. The maximum drawdown was 82.9% and it took about 15 years (!) to reach the 2000 peak again – and afterwards the market climbed further to new highs until the middle of 2018. As you can see the Nasdaq 100 is a roller coaster – a challenge for every trader.

This index consists of the top 100 NASDAQ companies by market cap. From our experience with the Bollinger system this number of stocks is the minimum to have in order to get enough trading signals. From all tested universes the Nasdaq 100 is the smallest. For the shown tests and optimisations, we use the longest available data history that is free of survivorship bias, which starts at 1/1/1995.

Like we did in the S&P 500 we remove all stocks which are double in the Nasdaq 100: These are GOOG, FOXA, DISCK, LBTYK, LMCK and LILAK.

First we check how the Bollinger system performs within the Nasdaq 100 stock universe with exactly the same parameters which we found in the S&P 500. With all these settings you get on the Nasdaq 100 a copound annual return (CAR) of 9.6% and a maximum system drawdown of –36.8% (see table 9.10, last line).

Please note that with the Bollinger system on average only half of your money is invested in the market, shown by the exposure of 54.3%. Therefore about half of the time you could invest the money in short-term treasury bills in the bond market and, by doing this, increase the annual return to 17.7% (RAR = risk-adjusted return). So you are much better than the benchmark buy and hold, even without further optimisation. You have a higher return and a far smaller drawdown.

The smaller size of the Nasdaq 100 and the higher volatility of its stocks suggest that there might be better settings for this index, not just the same as for the S&P 500. However, we don't want to add in this book now for every new index again the complete optimisation procedure as shown above for the S&P 500. First, it could be too boring for you and, second, the results would be optimal, but probably not robust.

But as an example, to give you an idea what is possible on this index with a breakout system like the Bollinger, we will just check other numbers of allowed positions and different entry points, which are defined by the top Bollinger Band width.

When you leave all parameters as above with the S&P 500 and vary these two parameters again you get the following result (table 9.10).

Table 9.10: Optimisation results on Nasdaq 100 stock universe, 1/1/1995–31/12/2018. Results of optimisation of Bollinger top width and number of position, sorted from highest return/risk ratio (CAR/MDD) to lowest. Bottom row: Results for above optimised S&P 500 parameters (marked green).

Para 1	Para 2								
Number of positions	Bollinger Top Width	Comp. Annual Return % (CAR)	Exposure %	RAR	Max. Sys % DrawDown	CAR/ MDD	No. of Trades	% of Winners	Winners Avg. Bars Held
5	1.5	19.5	81.7	23.9	-33.7	0.58	154	50.7	245.9
6	1.5	19.9	81.6	24.4	-35.8	0.56	185	51.9	242.8
7	1.5	19.4	81.8	23.7	-34.6	0.56	217	50.2	247.9
5	1.7	20.6	81.1	25.4	-38.9	0.53	154	50.0	247.8
7	2	18.6	80.5	23.2	-36.8	0.51	190	47.4	273.3
8	1.5	18.9	81.9	23.1	-36.8	0.51	245	50.6	245.2
9	2.9	18.9	78.2	24.2	-36.9	0.51	210	51.0	289.1
9	1.5	18.5	81.6	22.6	-36.7	0.5	279	50.9	239.8
6	1.7	19.4	81.3	23.8	-38.5	0.5	188	47.9	247.4
5	3.6	21.4	69.7	30.7	-42.8	0.5	104	55.8	265.6
12	2.8	19.6	77.5	25.3	-39.3	0.5	265	53.2	295.9
9	2.7	19.0	78.7	24.2	-38.7	0.49	221	50.2	282.8
5	2.2	19.4	80.7	24.0	-39.9	0.49	150	45.3	260.2
5	2.6	20.1	81.1	24.8	-41.1	0.49	136	43.4	295.6
8	1.7	19.0	81.9	23.2	-38.6	0.49	246	48.4	251.4
13	2.9	18.3	76.1	24.0	-37.3	0.49	290	52.4	285.4
11	2.8	19.6	78.1	25.1	-40.4	0.49	248	52.8	293.5
12	2.9	18.3	76.6	23.9	-37.7	0.49	271	51.3	290.8
8	2	18.3	80.3	22.8	-37.2	0.49	216	50.0	262.6
7	1.6	17.1	81.1	21.1	-34.7	0.49	217	51.2	239.7
10	1.5	17.9	81.6	21.9	-37.1	0.48	312	50.3	238.9
8	0.5	16.4	82.5	19.9	-34.3	0.48	340	37.9	240.8
9	0.5	15.8	82.5	19.1	-33.1	0.48	386	37.8	235.7
6	2.7	19.7	79.7	24.8	-40.8	0.48	160	50.0	271.2
12	2.7	18.2	77.5	23.5	-38.0	0.48	289	51.6	278.9
19	2.4	17.5	77.6	22.6	-36.8	0.48	456	54.0	264.4
7	2.6	17.6	80.3	21.9	-36.8	0.48	194	45.4	277.1
5	2.7	21.1	80.0	26.3	-43.5	0.48	130	51.5	277.6
...	...	...	...	...	...	...	...	...	...
...	...	...	...	...	...	...	...	...	...
Result with S&P 500 parameters from above									
20	3.5	9.6	54.3	17.7	-36.8	0.26	313	48.6	255.6

The table starts at the top with the highest CAR/MDD ratios and goes to the lower. Please note that there are in total 3,000 optimisation rows in this table, so you can only see a small part of it.

The result which we had before (green row) can be found somewhere in the middle of the table. So there are much better parameters for the Nasdaq 100 stocks than the previously obtained.

You can see from the following optimisation graphs where the best profit/risk parameters are located (fig. 9.34).

Figure 9.34: CAR/MDD as a function of position number and Bollinger top width. Nasdaq 100 stock universe, 1/1/1995–31/12/2018. A: side view. B: front view.

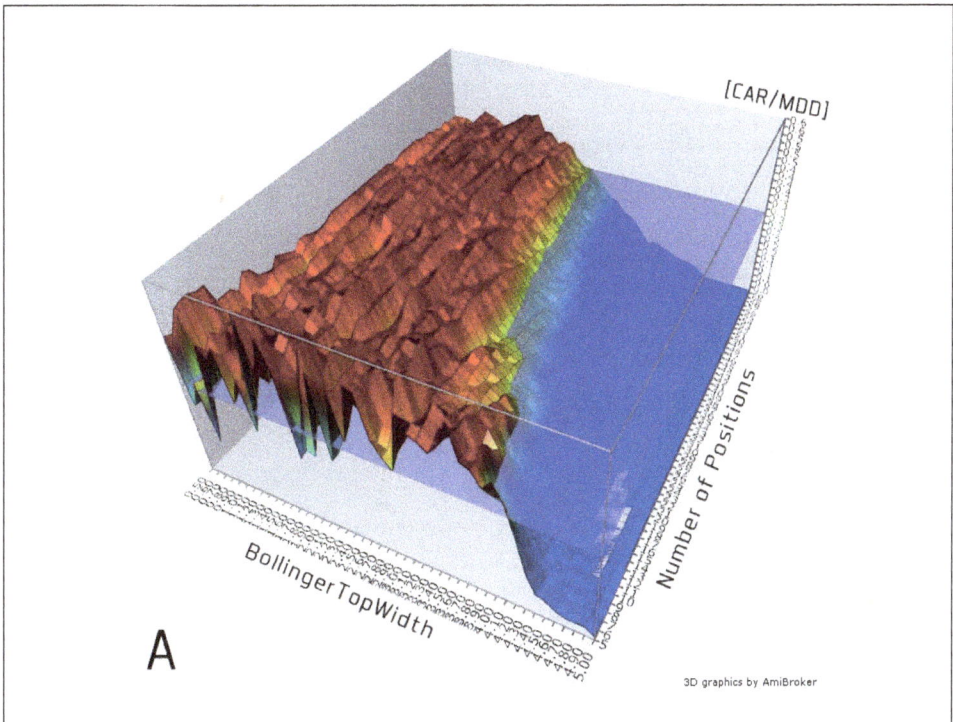

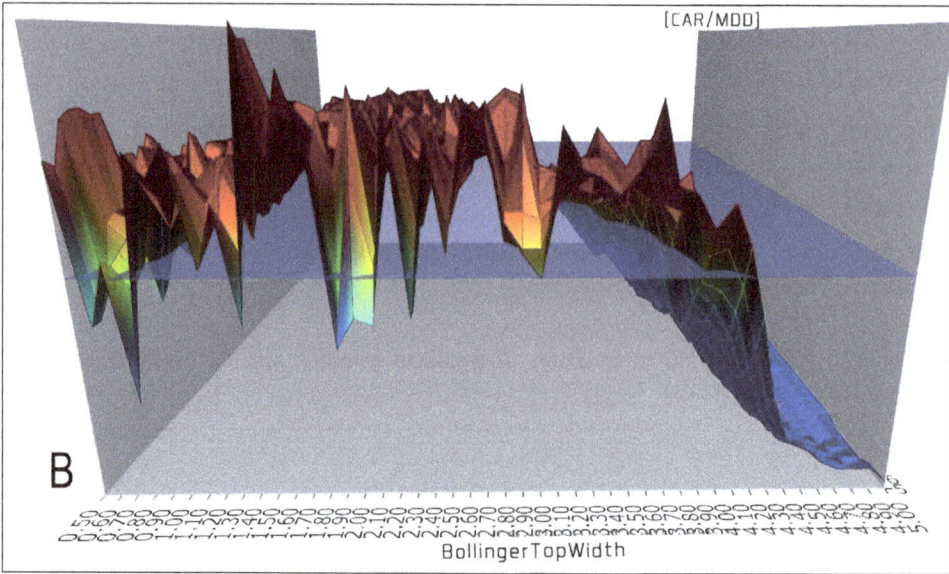

The figures show that you get the highest values in the front, left corner of the 3D graph. This means low numbers of positions around 5–10 and Bollinger top width between 1–3 are to be preferred.

But as you can see from fig. 9.34B, smaller position numbers come with a bigger uncertainty. These parameters are in general a bit better, but they are less stable.

The best values are around the following:

• CAR: around 20%

• RAR: around 25%

• Max System Drawdown: –35%

But instead of choosing these optimised values, let's stay more conservative. Therefore let's have a look at the equity curves with the original parameter set, taken over from the S&P 500 (fig. 9.35).

Figure 9.35: Bollinger Band system. Results on the Nasdaq 100 stock universe. Back-test period 1/1/1995–31/12/2018. All settings kept like test on S&P 500 (see chapter 9.4.7). Back-tests performed with AmiBroker and Norgate Data, on point-in-time index constituents. A: equity curve; B: underwater equity curve; C: logarithmic equity curve; D: profit distribution.

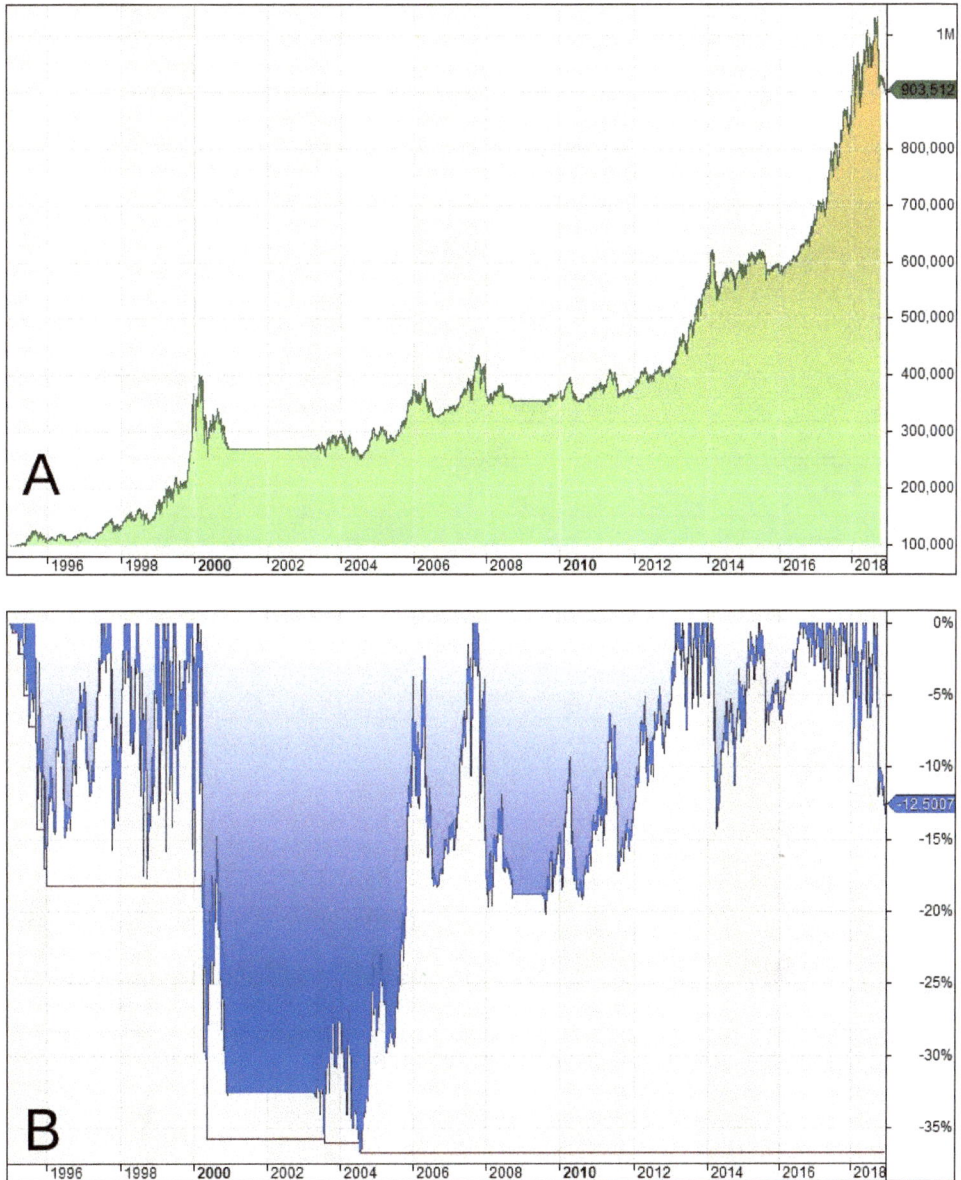

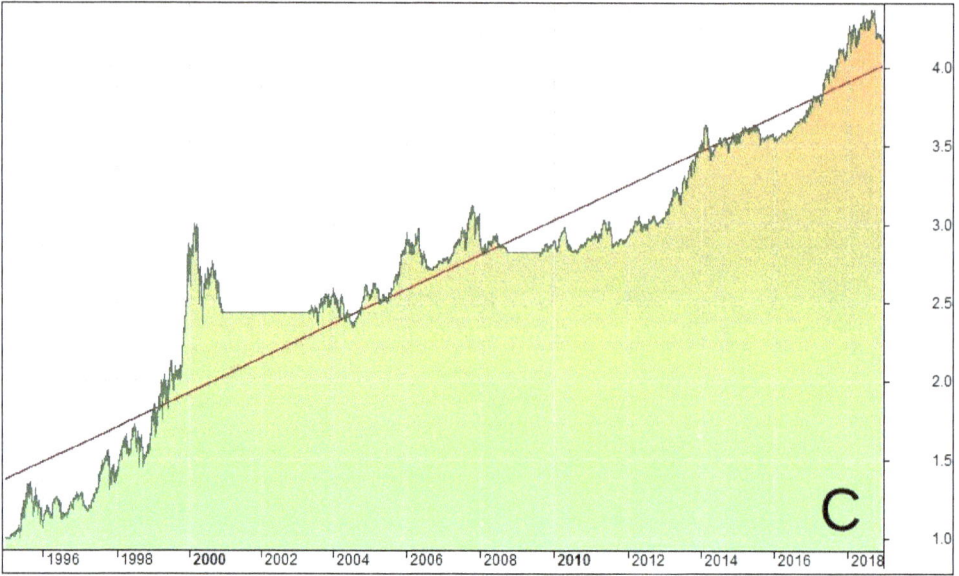

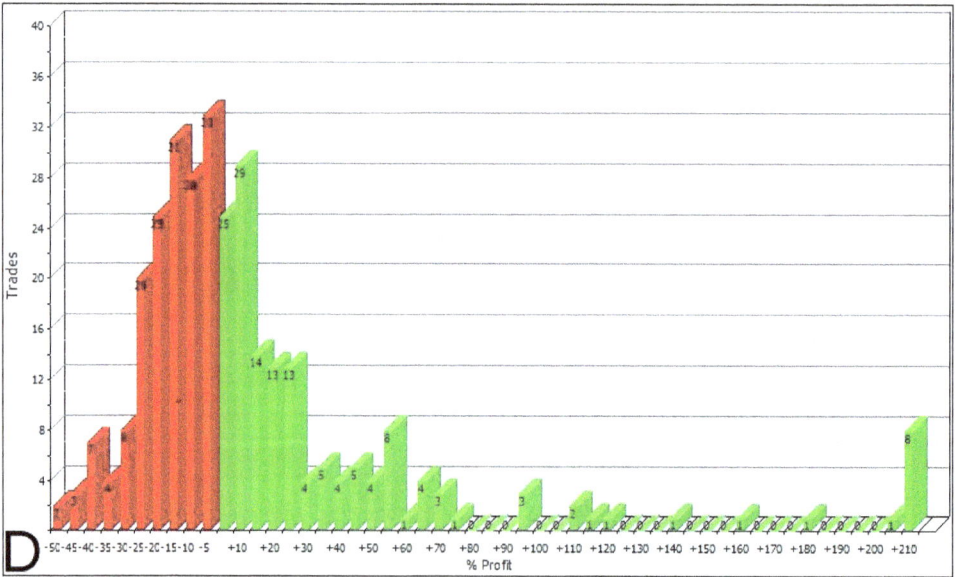

Table 9.11: Bollinger Band system. Results on the Nasdaq 100 stock universe. Back-test period 1/1/1995–31/12/2018. All settings kept like test on S&P 500 (see chapter 9.4.7). Back-tests performed with AmiBroker and Norgate Data, on point-in-time index constituents.

Table 9.11A: Results per month and year

Year	Jan	Feb	Mar	Apr	May	Jun	Jul	Aug	Sep	Oct	Nov	Dec	Yr%
1995	-0.4%	0.9%	0.3%	2.7%	-2.4%	8.9%	9.1%	0.4%	1.6%	-2.8%	-1.9%	-3.1%	13.1%
1996	-1.4%	2.3%	-2.8%	6.6%	0.9%	-2.7%	-4.3%	0.1%	3.0%	1.2%	3.1%	0.2%	5.7%
1997	2.0%	-5.9%	-1.8%	2.0%	5.4%	0.8%	9.5%	1.3%	4.5%	-8.3%	2.5%	0.2%	11.6%
1998	2.2%	6.6%	6.2%	-0.5%	-5.2%	9.1%	-1.8%	-12.2%	14.3%	-8.1%	1.2%	10.4%	20.6%
1999	12.5%	-7.4%	11.3%	1.8%	0.5%	9.5%	-3.6%	4.8%	-3.4%	4.7%	16.4%	42.9%	121.1%
2000	-8.8%	20.1%	-1.2%	-14.0%	-16.2%	11.4%	0.7%	10.0%	-7.4%	-3.4%	-11.5%	-0.0%	-24.0%
2001	0.0%	0.0%	0.0%	0.0%	0.0%	0.0%	0.0%	0.0%	0.0%	0.0%	0.0%	0.0%	0.0%
2002	0.0%	0.0%	0.0%	0.0%	0.0%	0.0%	0.0%	0.0%	0.0%	0.0%	0.0%	0.0%	0.0%
2003	0.0%	0.0%	0.0%	0.0%	2.1%	-2.8%	2.1%	1.6%	-2.9%	7.6%	-0.7%	0.6%	7.5%
2004	-2.2%	-1.3%	-0.2%	-5.1%	1.5%	-0.4%	-3.5%	0.7%	3.0%	4.7%	7.1%	-1.5%	2.2%
2005	-0.5%	4.1%	-3.3%	-4.7%	3.1%	-2.8%	3.6%	2.9%	5.3%	2.7%	6.3%	1.5%	18.8%
2006	5.6%	-2.3%	-0.2%	3.0%	-7.1%	1.4%	-5.8%	-1.1%	-0.0%	1.0%	2.1%	-0.5%	-4.5%
2007	1.9%	-0.6%	1.0%	4.4%	2.9%	1.0%	1.1%	4.2%	6.1%	3.3%	-6.1%	0.5%	21.0%
2008	-12.3%	0.8%	1.4%	0.0%	3.7%	-3.7%	-0.1%	-0.9%	-2.0%	0.0%	0.0%	0.0%	-13.2%
2009	0.0%	0.0%	0.0%	0.0%	0.0%	0.0%	-0.0%	-0.4%	1.9%	-0.9%	1.4%	2.0%	4.0%
2010	-2.1%	1.6%	5.2%	0.9%	-6.1%	-2.6%	0.4%	-0.6%	2.6%	0.9%	0.5%	1.5%	1.6%
2011	0.6%	1.4%	0.0%	3.7%	3.1%	-1.8%	-4.6%	-3.9%	-0.3%	2.3%	-0.3%	0.7%	0.4%
2012	2.0%	1.5%	3.6%	2.0%	-4.0%	0.8%	0.7%	0.8%	1.7%	-2.6%	1.6%	0.2%	8.4%
2013	2.9%	1.8%	4.8%	1.6%	1.3%	-2.0%	8.7%	-2.9%	8.6%	2.1%	3.5%	3.0%	38.2%
2014	1.1%	8.0%	-6.9%	-5.0%	3.2%	2.1%	-0.1%	2.2%	-1.5%	0.4%	4.0%	-2.5%	4.2%
2015	-1.8%	5.7%	0.1%	-2.0%	2.5%	-0.9%	1.0%	-4.7%	-0.6%	0.7%	1.1%	0.5%	1.2%
2016	-0.5%	-0.6%	1.8%	-0.8%	2.6%	-0.7%	2.1%	1.7%	1.8%	0.4%	2.5%	1.5%	12.5%
2017	3.4%	-0.2%	2.0%	0.5%	9.3%	-1.5%	5.7%	-0.0%	2.8%	5.0%	-2.3%	-0.6%	26.2%
2018	12.7%	-2.0%	-2.3%	-0.5%	7.4%	-1.8%	-0.6%	8.3%	-0.5%	-10.1%	0.2%	-2.0%	7.2%
Avg	0.7%	1.4%	0.8%	-0.1%	0.4%	0.9%	0.8%	0.5%	1.6%	0.0%	1.3%	2.3%	

Table 9.11B: Statistics

	All trades
Initial capital	100000
Ending capital	903511.86
Net Profit	803511.86
Net Profit %	803.51%
Exposure %	54.26%
Net Risk Adjusted Return %	1480.91%
Annual Return %	**9.60%**
Risk Adjusted Return %	**17.70%**
Transaction costs	28811.92
All trades	313
Avg. Profit/Loss	2567.13
Avg. Profit/Loss %	16.74%
Avg. Bars Held	178.74
Winners	152 (48.56 %)
Total Profit	1163548.24
Avg. Profit	7654.92
Avg. Profit %	50.04%
Avg. Bars Held	255.59
Max. Consecutive	8
Largest win	231635.17
# bars in largest win	755
Losers	161 (51.44 %)
Total Loss	-360036.39
Avg. Loss	-2236.25
Avg. Loss %	-14.71%
Avg. Bars Held	106.19
Max. Consecutive	8
Largest loss	-10300.21
# bars in largest loss	113
Max. trade drawdown	-77421.68
Max. trade % drawdown	-69.67
Max. system drawdown	-147297.98
Max. system % drawdown	**-36.77%**

At first glance, the total profit now remains behind the buy and hold strategy. But keep in mind that the equity curve shows just the money which you earn from the money which is invested in stocks. Since this is only about half, the other half you would invest otherwise, e.g., in bonds (or in other trading strategies, etc.). So finally you would end with a higher equity, even with the conservative parameter setup from the S&P 500. Because your risk-adjusted return with 17.7% is much higher than it was with buy and hold (12.2%).

Additionally, your drawdowns of 37%, which is much better than the incredible 82% of buy and hold, would be further reduced if you invest half of your money otherwise.

9.7.2 The S&P 1500 – a large index

Having tested only the best-known US indices so far, we would like to examine to what extent our strategy works with the same parameters on other stock universes. We start with the S&P 1500, which includes the 1,500 US companies with the largest market capitalisation. We take the maximum time period at which Norgate provides data free of survivorship bias – from 1/11/1994–31/12/2018 (fig. 9.36 A–D and table 9.12 A and B).

Figure 9.36: Results of the Bollinger Band system on the point-in-time index constituents of the S&P 1500 index. All settings as above (max 20 positions; Bollinger Band length = 180; top width = 3.5; bottom width = 0.5; index filter = 300 days; 0.5% commissions per position) daily data from 1/11/1994–31/12/2018. A: equity curve. B: underwater equity curve. C: logarithmic equity curve. D: profit distribution of all trades.

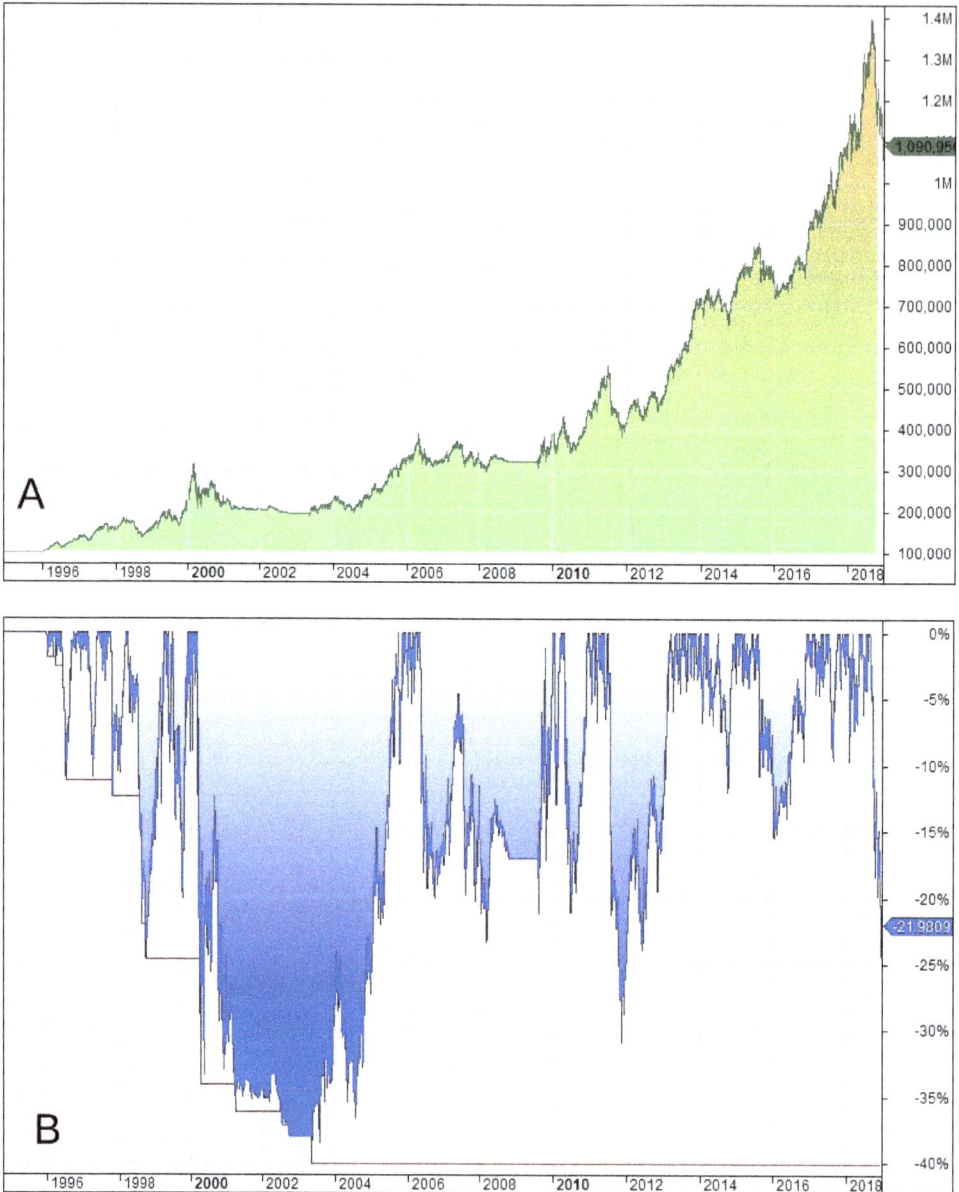

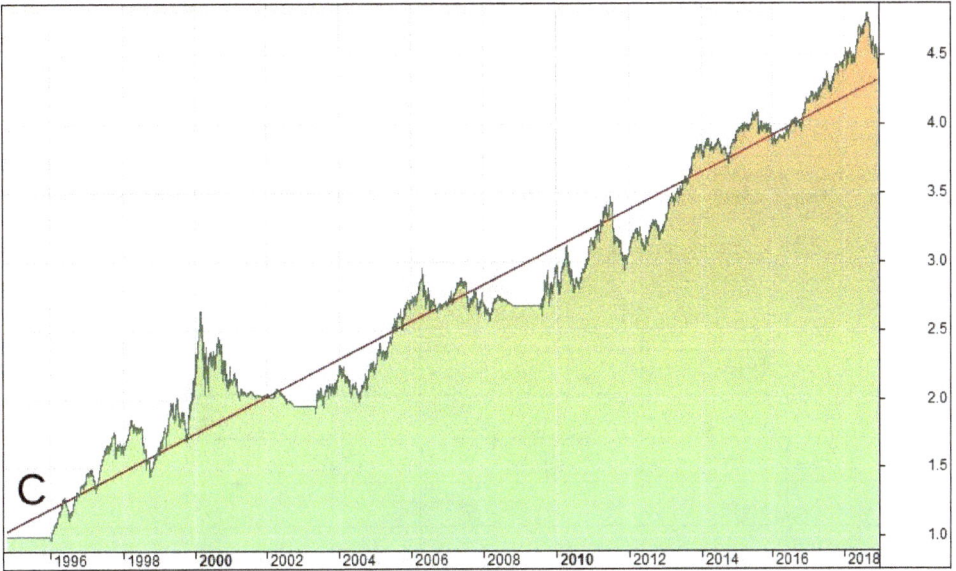

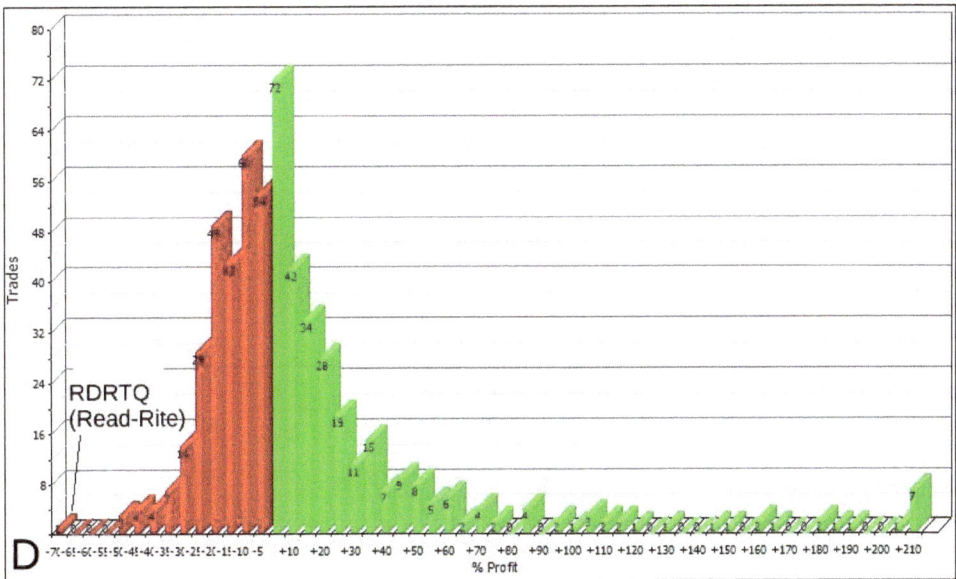

Table 9.12: Results of the Bollinger Band system on the point-in-time index constituents of the S&P 1500 index. All settings as above (max 20 positions; Bollinger Band length = 180; top width = 3.5; bottom width = 0.5; index filter = 300 days; 0.5% commissions per position) daily data from 1/11/1994–31/12/2018.

Figure 9.12A: Profits per month and year

Year	Jan	Feb	Mar	Apr	May	Jun	Jul	Aug	Sep	Oct	Nov	Dec	Yr%
1994	N/A	N/A	N/A	N/A	N/A	N/A	N/A	N/A	N/A	N/A	0.0%	0.0%	0.0%
1995	0.0%	0.0%	0.0%	0.0%	0.0%	0.0%	0.0%	0.0%	0.0%	0.0%	0.0%	0.0%	0.0%
1996	1.9%	3.3%	4.5%	5.2%	4.7%	-4.0%	-5.1%	6.1%	5.0%	1.5%	3.6%	2.7%	32.8%
1997	4.5%	-1.5%	-6.0%	1.7%	8.5%	6.4%	4.2%	-0.5%	6.3%	-7.2%	1.1%	1.1%	18.7%
1998	-0.5%	4.4%	7.3%	0.2%	-4.2%	1.1%	-7.7%	-10.7%	4.1%	-4.0%	5.3%	5.7%	-0.7%
1999	4.0%	1.4%	0.6%	12.7%	5.4%	-1.0%	-9.0%	0.8%	-1.2%	-2.1%	9.2%	17.7%	42.3%
2000	2.9%	27.8%	-10.8%	-1.9%	-13.2%	10.8%	-4.5%	13.9%	-4.5%	-6.2%	-12.9%	10.6%	3.9%
2001	-3.3%	-4.0%	-4.6%	2.3%	-2.5%	1.0%	0.5%	-1.4%	0.0%	-0.4%	-0.5%	0.7%	-11.7%
2002	-0.9%	0.0%	0.3%	3.0%	-1.3%	-1.2%	-2.9%	-0.7%	-0.5%	-1.2%	0.0%	0.0%	-5.3%
2003	0.0%	0.0%	0.0%	0.0%	1.5%	2.5%	1.4%	2.5%	-3.0%	4.7%	0.9%	2.4%	13.3%
2004	3.6%	0.0%	-1.9%	-5.6%	1.3%	2.2%	-5.9%	1.4%	4.9%	0.5%	9.2%	-0.2%	8.9%
2005	3.1%	4.1%	-1.9%	-1.9%	5.7%	3.0%	7.8%	4.1%	3.7%	-3.7%	6.2%	-2.3%	30.9%
2006	7.4%	-2.3%	7.6%	3.3%	-5.1%	0.1%	-4.7%	-1.8%	-3.9%	2.4%	0.1%	1.4%	3.5%
2007	1.6%	0.9%	2.3%	3.8%	3.9%	-3.4%	-5.4%	-1.1%	-0.6%	4.3%	-7.5%	3.9%	1.7%
2008	-5.5%	-1.3%	0.1%	6.5%	3.0%	-2.2%	0.3%	-0.7%	-0.9%	-1.4%	0.0%	0.0%	-2.7%
2009	0.0%	0.0%	0.0%	0.0%	0.0%	0.0%	0.0%	2.4%	8.4%	-10.1%	6.0%	10.1%	16.6%
2010	-5.4%	-0.5%	10.9%	6.8%	-8.5%	-8.5%	3.2%	-2.3%	8.3%	2.7%	5.0%	6.9%	17.6%
2011	-1.4%	6.4%	5.1%	4.8%	4.8%	0.1%	-1.9%	-13.8%	-3.3%	-6.4%	1.3%	-0.4%	-6.4%
2012	6.5%	3.8%	3.4%	-0.0%	-6.8%	0.9%	2.8%	5.3%	1.4%	-1.3%	-1.6%	0.1%	14.7%
2013	5.5%	7.1%	5.4%	-2.0%	2.8%	0.4%	5.4%	-1.8%	8.0%	7.5%	5.6%	-0.7%	51.6%
2014	-3.6%	5.7%	1.2%	-3.3%	0.1%	3.3%	-6.5%	2.3%	-3.5%	4.6%	3.7%	2.3%	5.6%
2015	1.3%	3.6%	-0.4%	-1.4%	1.7%	3.9%	2.3%	-6.4%	-1.0%	0.1%	1.4%	-2.4%	2.3%
2016	-2.1%	-3.0%	2.8%	-1.2%	2.7%	1.8%	4.7%	0.3%	-0.9%	-3.2%	7.8%	5.2%	15.3%
2017	0.7%	2.1%	2.0%	1.1%	-0.0%	3.6%	1.1%	-2.6%	5.4%	5.5%	1.4%	-2.3%	19.1%
2018	6.3%	-1.2%	-0.2%	-1.1%	9.0%	3.2%	3.0%	9.9%	-4.8%	-9.8%	-1.9%	-7.4%	3.0%
Avg	1.1%	2.4%	1.2%	1.4%	0.6%	1.0%	-0.7%	0.2%	1.1%	-1.0%	1.7%	2.2%	

Figure 9.12B: System statistics

Initial capital	100000
Ending capital	1090955.95
Net Profit	**990955.95**
Net Profit %	**990.96%**
Exposure %	78.27%
Net Risk Adjusted Return %	**1266.07%**
Annual Return %	10.39%
Risk Adjusted Return %	13.27%
Transaction costs	53378.29
All trades	565
Avg. Profit/Loss	**1753.9**
Avg. Profit/Loss %	**10.99%**
Avg. Bars Held	**168.09**
Winners	297 (52.57 %)
Total Profit	1628572.04
Avg. Profit	5483.41
Avg. Profit %	33.63%
Avg. Bars Held	226.47
Max. Consecutive	**10**
Largest win	75092.82
# bars in largest win	438
Losers	268 (47.43 %)
Total Loss	−637616.09
Avg. Loss	−2379.16
Avg. Loss %	−14.09%
Avg. Bars Held	103.4
Max. Consecutive	12
Largest loss	−26227.03
# bars in largest loss	34
Max. trade drawdown	−61513.01
Max. trade % drawdown	−74.61
Max. system drawdown	−339782.41
Max. system % drawdown	−40.11%

The Bollinger Band system produces a compound annual return (CAR) of 10.39% and a risk-adjusted return of 13.27%. Remember, the risk-adjusted return is higher than the CAR when your system is less than 100% in the market, shown by its exposure. The money which is not used in the stock market can be invested on the bond market. The system produces 565 trades of which over 50% are profitable. Its biggest drawdown is 40.1%.

Again, also in this bigger market with 1,500 stocks, the Bollinger strategy beats buy and hold which would produce 7.4% annual return with a far higher maximum drawdown of −56.77%.

Like with the S&P 500 and the Nasdaq stocks, the main profits from the system again are produced by the big winners, whereas losing trades are cut at typically around 30%–40% at the latest (see profit distribution, fig. 9.36D).

However, in this bigger universe which also contains some smaller stocks, drawdowns of single trades tend to be bigger than in the two earlier tested indexes. As an example we show here the largest loss event, which occurred in the RDRTQ stock. This stock was taken out of the S&P 1500 index in 2005, but previously in the year 2000 produced a loss signal of nearly 70% (fig. 9.37)!

Figure 9.37: RDRTQ (Read-Rite Corp) with a Bollinger Band entry and exit. This was the biggest loss signal of the strategy within the S&P 1500 universe.

This happens seldom, but it can happen in the worst case.

Not least because of such trades, it is important to better trade smaller position sizes and take a bigger number of positions into your portfolio. (With 20 positions this trade would be a loss of -3.5% in your portfolio, whereas with only five positions it would mean 14%, etc.)

9.7.3 Overview: Bollinger Band System vs. buy and hold

Besides the above shown universes of the S&P 500, the Nasdaq 100 and the S&P 1500 we also applied the strategy to further indices: the Russell 1000, 2000, 3000 and to the biggest 500 companies of the Australian stock market.

The following table gives a brief summary of all these test results, keeping the same parameter settings for all tested stock universes (table 9.13).

Table 9.13: Bollinger Band system: return and maximum drawdown on all tested markets vs. buy and hold. Settings: Bollinger-periods = 180; BollingerTopWidth = 3.5; BollingerBottomWidth = 0.5; IndexFilterLength = 300; ScoreLength = 300; CommissionAmount = 0.5% (per position). Tested on point-in-time constituents with AmiBroker.

Stock Universe	Test period	Number of positions	Bollinger Breakout System (%)			Buy and Hold (%)	
			Comp. Annual Return (CAR)	Risk Adj. Return (RAR)	Max Sys. Drawdown	Comp. Annual Return (CAR) = RAR	Max Sys. Drawdown
S&P 500	1/1/1989–31/12/2018	20	12.67	16.31	-25.22	7.50	-56.70
Nasdaq 100	1/1/1995–31/12/2018	20	9.60	17.70	-36.80	12.20	-82.90
S&P 1500	1/11/1994–31/12/2018	20	10.39	13.27	-40.11	7.40	-56.77
Russell 1000	1/7/1990–31/12/2018	20	9.55	11.75	-32.88	7.25	-56.88
Russell 1000	1/7/1990–31/12/2018	50	9.20	12.14	-35.16	7.25	-56.88
Russell 2000	1/7/1990–31/12/2018	20	15.36	17.82	-51.90	7.54	-59.89
Russell 2000	1/7/1990–31/12/2018	100	11.66	14.21	-40.74	7.54	-59.89
Russell 3000	1/7/1990–31/12/2018	20	10.85	12.78	-40.74	7.25	-57.07
Russell 3000	1/7/1990–31/12/2018	100	11.56	14.02	-39.08	7.25	-57.07
All Ordinaries 500 (AUS)	1/6/1992–31/12/2018	20	19.44	24.39	-33.64	4.50	-63.80

As you can see, the Bollinger system beats all buy and hold strategies (with the same parameters) concerning annual return and maximum drawdown. This is an indication of the good robustness of the strategy.

Especially as a beginner it might be a good idea to trade stocks of the S&P 500 and the Nasdaq 100. These two worldwide known indices are already a good selection of the best performing stocks.

First of all, these universes historically have had the best performances for good reasons. Second these markets have a better liquidity – trading costs and bid/ask spreads will be lower and it is easier for you to find a suitable broker who offers them to trade. Third, these US indices contain companies from many different industry sectors, thus you are highly diversified, and the chances are good that the Bollinger system picks the strength of each sector whenever it appears.

Although the smaller stocks in the huge indices like the S&P 1500, Russell 2000 or 3000 sometimes might have a better performance, this comes often at the cost of higher risks.

If you like to diversify your trading portfolio further, the Australian stock market is a good universe to add. The Bollinger strategy shows a huge outperformance on this index which has an emphasis on the banking sector, but also contains a bunch of commodity-related stocks from a different region outside the US.

Of course, you can and should test this strategy (and your own modifications and new ideas!) on other stock universes as well: European stocks, Asian stocks, emerging market stocks, etc. When you do so, always be aware of the data quality/survivorship bias.

9.8 Position management with five stocks on the Nasdaq 100 – practical example

In this section we want to show you daily position management with a practical example. For reasons of clarity and better visualisation, we limit ourselves to a small portfolio, which consists of a maximum of five different positions each. All other system parameters we keep from the initial optimisation on the S&P 500 above (compare with chapter 9.4). See here again:

- Number of positions = 5;

- Bollinger-Periods = 180;

- BollingerTopWidth = 3.5;

- BollingerBottomWidth = 0.5;

- IndexFilterLength = 300;

- ScoreLength = 300;

- CommissionAmount = 0.5% (per position)

Please note that only five positions means higher risks. If you are focused on profits, trading just two or three positions would be even better. Fund managers, however, typically work with at least 20 positions to control better their risks and drawdowns (see, for example, [21]).

Once you have set your position number to five, which equals 20% of invested capital per new position, you must determine the starting capital. For demonstration purposes let's take a small amount of only $5,000 here, so you can imagine better how the money could change over time.

Before we continue, we want to answer a question in advance, which often arises in such portfolios. What happens after you start with your account and in the very beginning a losing position has to be sold and replaced with a new one? For the new position, first of all, there is not the same amount of money as was available for the first positions (because a position is usually closed by a stop loss and therefore you have lost money).

The answer is: You have to keep a small amount of money besides the $5,000 – otherwise your new positions will be too small. This is one difference between back-testing and real trading or investment. In back-test mode, the software just always takes the same position sizes and lets them grow – money to invest is always there. In reality you must always have the money available on your account when your next buy signal appears.

Having clarified the position sizes and account size, let us have a look at the daily procedure of following a system like Bollinger. Before you start, be aware that this system needs discipline to trade, like every successful trading strategy.

Each evening you have to check if there are new Bollinger signals and place your orders for the next morning. Never forget to do this, because it is one of the worst things which can happen to systematic traders.

Imagine you missed an entry signal and you see how this position is already in profit. Will you now still go in or not? Psychologically this is a much more difficult situation than at the moment the signals appear. Therefore we recommend that you have a daily notifier which reminds you – e.g. an app on your mobile phone like ToDoReminder or whatever – to avoid such uncomfortable situations.

To keep a better overview about what happens in your $5,000 account we look at two recent ten-year periods in the Nasdaq 100. We start with 1/1/1999–1/1/2009, in which the Nasdaq 100 first collapsed around the year 2000 and afterwards slowly recovered (fig. 9.38). You have a difficult market phase here for every long-only stock trading strategy.

Figure 9.38: Nasdaq 100 index 1999–2009 with simple moving average of 300 days (SMA300, green line). New positions are not allowed when the market trades below the SMA300 (red crosses).

269

Let us see how your $5,000 would have developed in that period (fig. 9.39).

Figure 9.39: Equity of $5,000 when trading the Bollinger Band system on the Nasdaq 100, allowing five stocks at the same time. Ten-year period from 1/1/1999–31/12/2008. Back-test including 0.5% slippage and commissions per position. Red crosses: When the Nasdaq 100 index trades below the 300-day moving average, new positions are prohibited.

As you can see from the equity line, the $5,000 would grow to finally $34,140 (see also table 9.14).

Table 9.14: System figures: trading the Bollinger Band system on the Nasdaq 100, allowing five stocks at the same time. Ten-year period from 1/1/1999–31/12/2008. Back-test including 0.5% slippage and commissions per position.

	All trades
Initial capital	5000
Ending capital	34140.1
Net Profit	29140.1
Net Profit %	582.80%
Exposure %	55.72%
Net Risk Adjusted Return %	1045.89%
Annual Return %	21.19%
Risk Adjusted Return %	38.02%
Transaction costs	546.73

	All trades
All trades	35
Avg. Profit/Loss	832.57
Avg. Profit/Loss %	39.01%
Avg. Bars Held	174.86
Winners	**19 (54.29 %)**
Total Profit	34984.4
Avg. Profit	1841.28
Avg. Profit %	85.22%
Avg. Bars Held	221.79
Max. Consecutive	6
Largest win	13373.24
# bars in largest win	773
Losers	16 (45.71 %)
Total Loss	-5844.3
Avg. Loss	-365.27
Avg. Loss %	-15.85%
Avg. Bars Held	119.13
Max. Consecutive	5
Largest loss	-1313.51
# bars in largest loss	88
Max. trade drawdown	-8962.46
Max. trade % drawdown	-57.44
Max. system drawdown	-12153.41
Max. system % drawdown	**-51.36%**

This gain includes $546 trading costs. This result is a good additional income in a market which moved sideways – just compare the starting point (1999) with the end point (2009) of the Nasdaq and the huge drawdown of 80% there in 2002. You would have 35 trades only in the ten years and you suffer five consecutive losses at one point. Your maximum drawdown is $8,962.

Please especially note the importance of the market filter (red crosses). When the Nasdaq 100 index trades below the 300-day moving average, new positions are prohibited – there are such periods in 2000, 2004, 2005, 2006 and 2008. In these phases you keep your existing positions until they fall individually below their bottom Bollinger Band. This happens quite quickly in the years 2000 and 2008 so you had long flat periods in your account in which you were prohibited to open new positions. During the minor declines of 2004, 2005 and 2006 the market recovered early enough, so you could stay in your positions.

Keep in mind that this market filter, although it may seem frustrating to wait for two years for the next action, saved your money. It finally was the main reason for your success because it prevented your losses from getting too big. Never forget: all you can control in a trade is the amount which you are willing to lose!

As a comparison to the first market phase, let's have a look at the last ten years, the period from 1/1/2009–31/12/2018 (fig. 9.40).

This market phase seems easier to trade since the Nasdaq 100 index was bullish nearly all the time. The uptrend started after the financial crisis of 2008 and lasted until the middle of 2018. This means that most of the time your Bollinger system was free to take new stock positions. Only in the beginning of 2009 and end of 2018 the market traded below its 300-day moving average and therefore new positions are prevented by the market filter.

To make the position management a bit more transparent we insert all the traded stock symbols into the Nasdaq 100 during the whole year 2018 chart (fig. 9.41).

Figure 9.41: Nasdaq 100 index in 2018 with maximum five stock positions simultaneously traded. Coloured symbols and lines represent the held positions. As usual, new trades can only be taken when the index is above its SMA300 (green line).

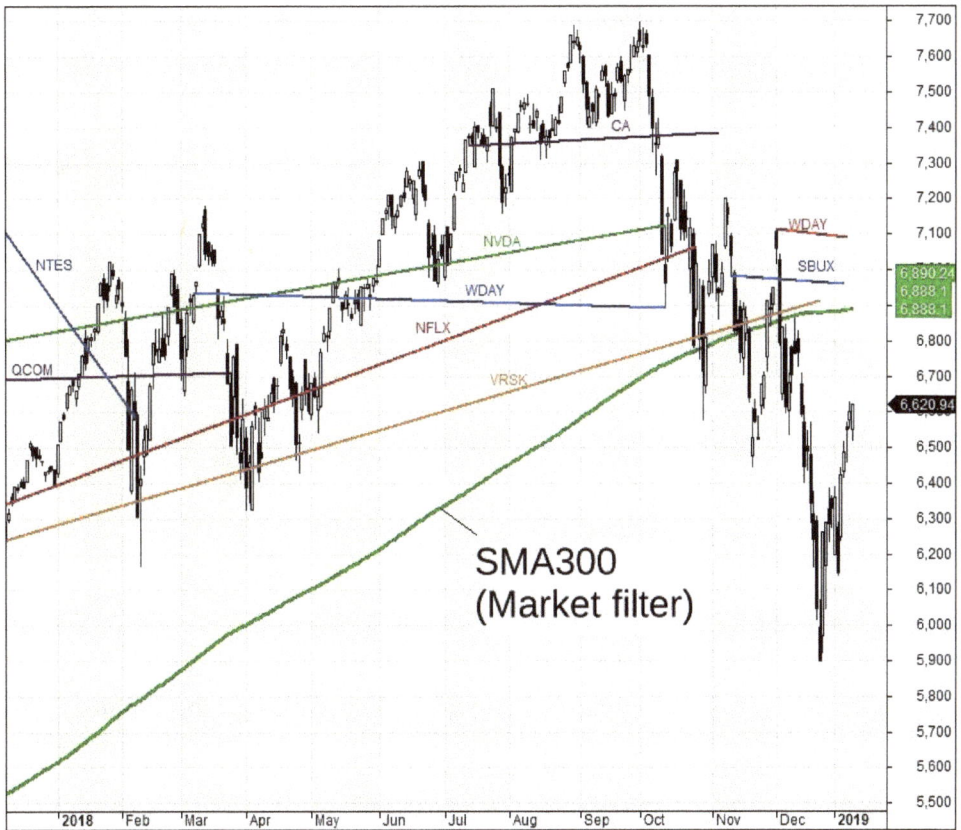

You can see that your trading logic makes sure that you never have more than five positions in the portfolio at the same time. Often you have less, since positions fall out and your strategy waits until a new Bollinger breakout signal occurs. At the beginning of 2019 you have just two stocks left in your portfolio, SBUX (Starbucks) and WDAY (Workday), because the Nasdaq 100 index trades below its 300 day simple moving average (SMA300).

The following figure shows the gained equity curve in this last ten-year period between 1/1/2009 and 31/12/2018 (fig. 9.42).

Figure 9.42: Equity of $5,000 when trading the Bollinger Band system on the Nasdaq 100, allowing five stocks at the same time. Ten-year period from 1/1/2009–31/12/2018. Back-test including 0.5% slippage and commissions per position. Red cross: When the Nasdaq 100 index trades below the 300-day moving average in the first half of 2009, new positions are prohibited. Therefore the equity line stays flat for a while.

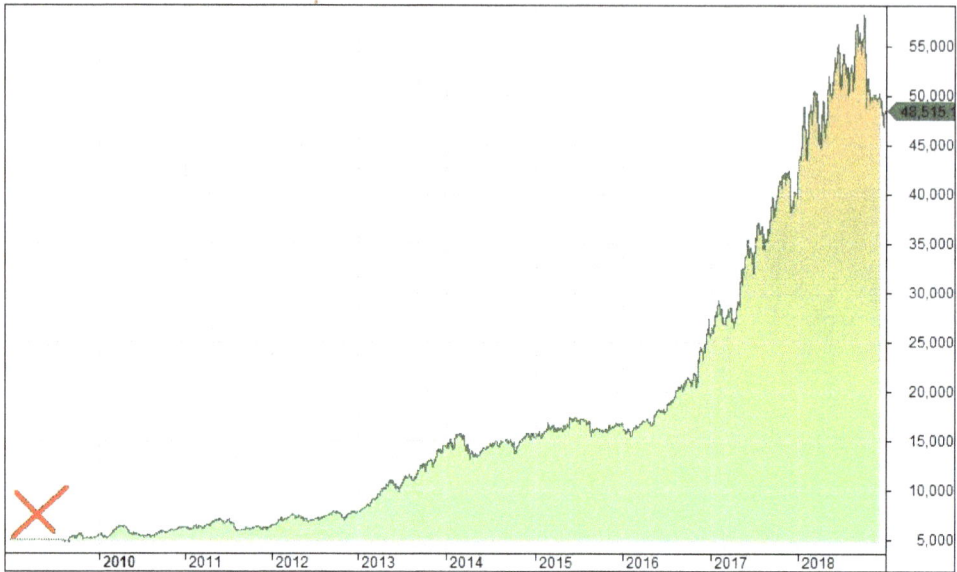

Table 9.15: Statistics of trading the Bollinger system with maximum five positions with $5,000, 1/1/2009–31/12/2018, including 0.5% slippage and commissions per position.

	All trades
Initial capital	5000
Ending capital	48515.11
Net Profit	43515.11
Net Profit %	870.30%
Exposure %	81.59%
Net Risk Adjusted Return %	1066.72%
Annual Return %	25.51%
Risk Adjusted Return %	31.27%
Transaction costs	640.22
All trades	43
Avg. Profit/Loss	1011.98
Avg. Profit/Loss %	40.40%
Avg. Bars Held	233.95

	All trades
Winners	25 (58.14 %)
Total Profit	47634.53
Avg. Profit	1905.38
Avg. Profit %	76.37%
Avg. Bars Held	322.24
Max. Consecutive	8
Largest win	25373.23
# bars in largest win	755
Losers	18 (41.86 %)
Total Loss	-4119.42
Avg. Loss	-228.86
Avg. Loss %	-9.55%
Avg. Bars Held	111.33
Max. Consecutive	3
Largest loss	-958.35
# bars in largest loss	56
Max. trade drawdown	-6313.06
Max. trade % drawdown	-32.79
Max. system drawdown	**-11406.94**
Max. system % drawdown	**-19.56%**

The portfolio equity ends at $48,415 so your overall gain is $43,415. From the 43 trades, more than half are profitable (25 trades). The biggest drawdown takes place in the sharp stock market correction at the end of 2018. At the worst point you lose $11,406 from your equity high (around $57,000), which is about 20% of your money.

You can see in the profit distribution of the single trades that your biggest losing trades are around 25% per position (fig. 9.43 and table 9.16).

Figure 9.43: Profit distribution of your trades. Red: Losing trades between -5% and -25%. Green: Winning trades between 5% and 800%. Biggest winners are AABA (95%), NFLX (159%), GILD (177%), BIIB (209%) and NVDA (795%).

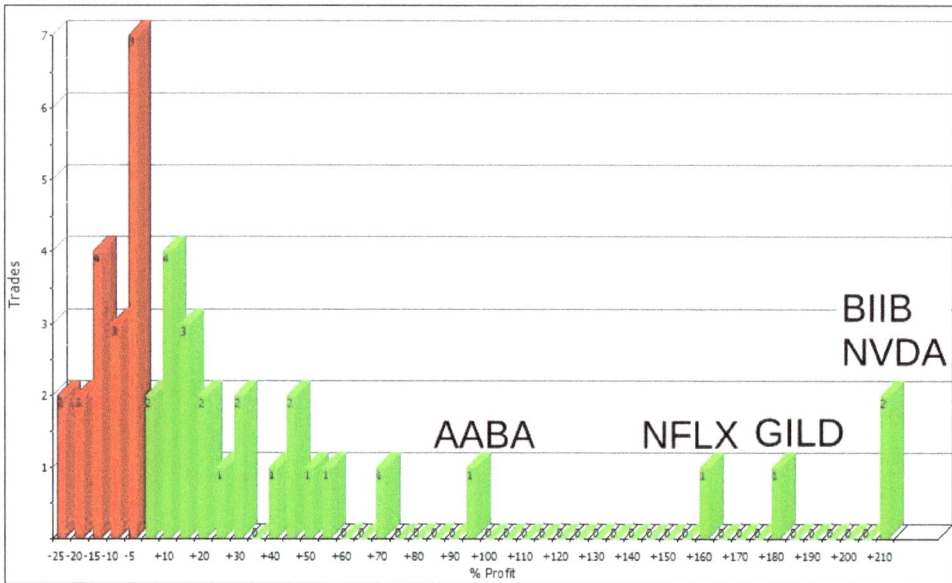

Table 9.16: Statistics of performed trades. Biggest winners are marked bold. The trades are sorted by the exit days (when profits and losses are realised).

Symbol	Entry Date	Entry Price	Exit Date	Exit Price	% Profit	$ Profit	Bars Hold	Cum. Profit
CA-201811	27/07/09	20.57	05/05/10	22.17	7.78%	72.59	196	72.59
GRMN	06/08/09	32.89913	27/05/10	32.49	-1.24%	-17.48	204	55.11
TEVA	30/07/09	54.69	02/06/10	53.9	-1.44%	-19.52	212	35.6
QRTEA	13/08/09	7.662766	29/06/10	8.428291	9.99%	92.95	221	128.54
URBN	10/08/09	27.71	15/07/10	33.27	20.06%	194.35	235	322.89
GENZ-201104	26/07/10	65.51	04/04/11	76.21	16.33%	168.12	176	491.01
VMED-201306	30/07/10	20.61	19/07/11	26.79	29.99%	316.59	245	807.6
CHRW	05/08/10	67.1	28/07/11	73.61	9.70%	100.53	248	908.14
BMC-201309	18/10/10	44.47	29/07/11	44.27	-0.45%	-9.47	198	898.67
CTXS	30/07/10	43.40572	03/08/11	55.23061	27.24%	286.85	256	1185.52
ATVI	24/10/11	13.5	02/03/12	11.68	-13.48%	-174.91	90	1010.61
FAST	04/11/11	19.67416	06/06/12	19.37771	-1.51%	-25.35	147	985.26
WCRX-201309	01/05/12	16.32728	18/09/12	12.85	-21.30%	-234.74	98	750.52
AAPL	26/07/11	57.1428	05/11/12	83.35992	45.88%	597.87	323	1348.39
GILD	**18/01/12**	**23.16**	**11/04/14**	**64.19**	**177.16%**	**1933.83**	**562**	**3282.22**
AABA	**06/11/12**	**17.44**	**12/05/14**	**33.99**	**94.90%**	**1365.16**	**380**	**4647.38**
VIAB	20/09/12	53.31	01/08/14	82.81	55.34%	863.85	468	5511.24

Symbol	Entry Date	Entry Price	Exit Date	Exit Price	% Profit	$ Profit	Bars Hold	Cum. Profit
ADBE	17/12/12	37.07	13/10/14	63.01	69.98%	674.79	459	6186.03
BIIB	25/04/11	91.84296	14/10/14	284.0306	209.26%	2566.03	875	8752.05
INTC	16/06/14	29.72	09/03/15	33.2	11.71%	315.77	184	9067.82
PAYX	28/10/14	46	30/06/15	47.1	2.39%	54.88	169	9122.7
ADP	03/11/14	81.5	30/06/15	81.39	-0.13%	-16.04	165	9106.66
CELG	17/07/15	134.41	25/08/15	118.64	-11.73%	-422.86	28	8683.8
ILMN	20/07/15	240.84	25/08/15	196.13	-18.56%	-382.71	27	8301.09
ALTR-201512	30/03/15	43.82	07/10/15	50.12	14.38%	434.52	134	8735.61
MNST	18/08/14	30.6633	15/10/15	43.07329	40.47%	1059.73	294	9795.33
BRCM-201601	04/06/14	35.74	11/11/15	51.84	45.05%	1242.73	365	11038.06
MSFT	27/10/15	53.99	14/06/16	49.9	-7.58%	-258.5	159	10779.56
LLTC-201703	27/07/16	60.5	19/10/16	58.83	-2.76%	-124.83	60	10654.73
NTAP	19/08/16	33.57	19/12/16	36.46	8.61%	326.44	85	10981.17
AKAM	27/10/16	68.09	04/05/17	53.13	-21.97%	-140.56	130	10840.61
SYMC	24/06/16	20.41	03/11/17	29.01	42.14%	1493.94	345	12334.55
QRTEA	10/05/17	23.94	08/11/17	20.93	-12.57%	-63.49	128	12271.06
CSX	20/01/17	44.5	14/11/17	49.46	11.15%	463.17	208	12734.24
NTES	20/11/17	362	09/02/18	291.72	-19.41%	-958.35	56	11775.89
QCOM	08/11/17	64.21	23/03/18	55.63	-13.36%	-58.57	93	11717.32
WDAY	07/03/18	134.67	11/10/18	124.05	-7.89%	-323.62	153	11393.71
NVDA	15/10/15	27.41	12/10/18	245.5066	795.68%	25373.23	755	36766.93
NFLX	19/10/16	118.25	25/10/18	307.12	159.72%	6600.86	509	43367.8
CA-201811	13/07/18	44.11	02/11/18	44.44	0.75%	0.9	80	43368.7
VRSK	03/11/17	91.08	20/12/18	110.11	20.89%	1034.85	284	44403.55
SBUX	08/11/18	67.775	31/12/18	64.4	-4.98%	-341.96	36	43857.07
WDAY	03/12/18	164.49	31/12/18	159.68	-2.92%	-546.48	20	43515.11

This means at the beginning of your journey when your position size is $1,000 you could lose about $250 per position and later when your position size is over $10,000 you could lose about $2,500 (because the equity is more than $50,000 and you trade 20% per every new position).

Keep in mind, however, that you let your positions grow. You don't sell your gains. In the extreme case where you have such a big winning trade like NVDA (Nvdia), you must not touch it. It grows and grows and grows – and finally collapses. And this collapse of your biggest position means that you give back $6,313 of your profit with it (see table 9.15 maximum trade drawdown).

But we recommend that you don't sell such positions of momentum stocks which bring you large gains; not even part of the position. This is because your overall gains mainly result from these big winners. The Nvdia trade alone makes $25,373 profit! But also the other three big winners are not bad: NFLX (Netflix) brings $6,600, BIIB (Biogen) $2,566 and GILD (Gilead Sciences) another $1,933. Please notice that with Netflix you earn far more than with Biogen or Gilead, because you have a much larger position size near the end of the ten-year period than at its beginning or in the middle. So although the percentage gain is less with Netflix than Biogen, your profit is bigger because of the bigger position size.

At the end of this chapter let's look at the biggest win which was captured by the Bollinger system in the Nasdaq 100 on NVDA (Nvidia) (fig. 9.44).

Figure 9.44: NVDA (Nvidia) stock 2013–2019 with Bollinger Bands and two entry and exit signals. Note the scale on the right side: this is a logarithmic chart.

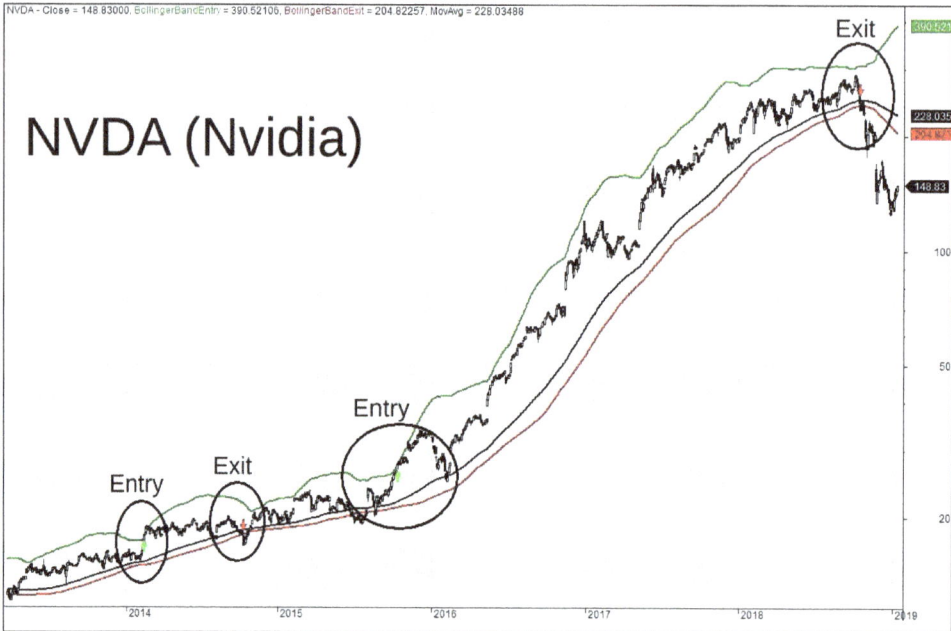

Chart created with AmiBroker.

After a minor trade which ends in a small loss (left side) the Bollinger system finally captures a big trend (entry at 15/10/2015) and gains 795% with one trade. This trade lasts about three years (755 trading days). Please also note the good exit on 12/10/2018. Without it you would give back about half of the profits in just six weeks! (Note that this is a logarithmic chart.)

Be aware that these huge profits and especially the Nvidia trade also show the danger when you just allow five positions for the system: if you miss some of these big winning trades, because your portfolio is already full when a signal like the Nvidia breakout occurs, then your trading account may stay mediocre!

But to capture these huge profits is psychologically not as easy as it looks. This will be the topic of the next section.

9.9 The psychological phenomenon of loss aversion

With the Bollinger Band breakout system, your overall profit usually is the result of a few winning trades, as outlined with the examples in the last chapters. This is common for most other trend-following and momentum-based strategies as well.

Usually in such systems, only about 30% – and sometimes even fewer – of the trades are winners. But these winners are, on average, bigger by a huge factor than the losses. These winners allow your account to grow.

So when you trade trend-following strategies, you have to do the following:

Let the profits run and cut your losses short.

Why is it difficult to follow this simple rule, which you hear from nearly every successful trader?

The reason is the psychological phenomenon of *loss aversion*, which was first discovered by the Israeli-American psychologists Daniel Kahneman and Amos Tversky, and described in their *Prospect Theory* [23]. They have found that losses hurt us more than gains make us happy.

For most, the discomfort that comes from losing $100 is greater than the happiness that comes from winning $100. It is thought that the pain of losing is psychologically about twice as powerful as the pleasure of gaining!

Before Kahnemann found that phenomenon, it had been common sense to believe that man was a rational decision-maker who always chooses the option with the highest expected utility, like a so called *homo economicus*. But simple examples show that this is absolutely not true. We are not always rational, logical and economical – especially not in situations when we could loose or gain a lot of money!

Psychologist Colin Camerer investigated in the 1990s the behaviour of New York taxi drivers. He found that they set themselves a daily specific sales target. When the sum was reached, the drivers turned off their taxis and went home. On good days they finished their job earlier, while on bad days they drove through the streets of New York for a long time. The other way around would be more rational: to drive longer with a lot of customers on busy days, and to end earlier on bad days. The drivers did not act rationally, however. They were afraid of days when they would not earn any money and they failed to make the most of the days when they could make bigger profits, which could easily have saved them a lot of time and work overall.

How loss aversion affects your trading can be shown with a diagram on which one axis shows the amount of gains and losses of a trade, and the other axis shows your feelings of joy and pain at the same time (fig. 9.45).

Figure 9.45: How traders feel losses and gains. The bottom red square shows how you feel with a loss of $500. The top green square shows how you feel with a profitable trade of $500. Important: The diagram is not symmetric because of loss aversion.

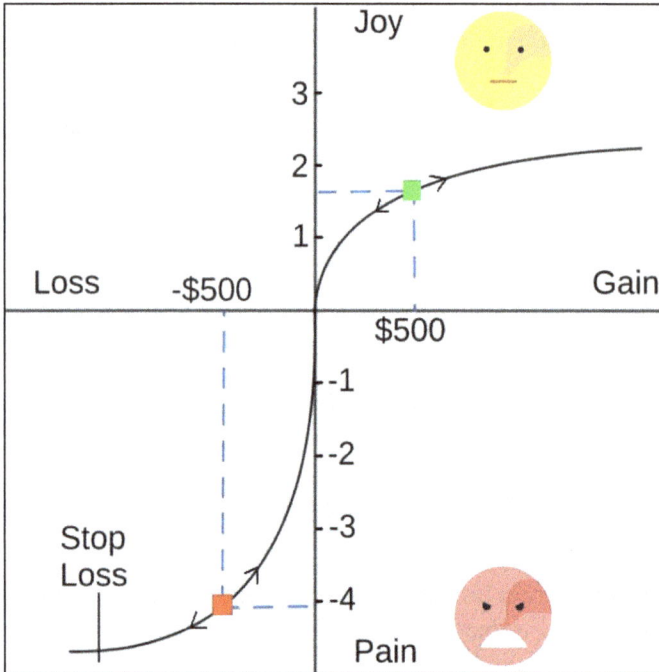

Picture created with prezi.com.

Let's first see what happens when you are in a losing position (red square). In the beginning you feel pain. And this pain is bigger if you lose $500 than the joy you feel if you win the same amount because of the asymmetry of the diagram, caused by *loss aversion*. Your bad feelings are not damaging at this point, however. You know as a trader that (small) losses will always happen.

Let us have a look at how you feel when this position goes ahead. If the trade comes back a little bit and leads you away from the losses, your pain gets less quickly. This is again just fine. The problem starts if this losing position moves further against you. Now that your pain is already so big, it does not increase further linearly. Therefore when you reach the Stop Loss point, you nearly become ignorant at this position, since the pain does not increase any more.

This is dangerous because the position needs action – otherwise a position of a normal loss could escalate to a huge loss.

Let's look at the gains, in the case where your trade is in profit with $500 (green square). You are happy because you've just made a profit. So far everything is fine. Your problem is that this trade is not finished yet. Again, there are two possibilities at this point. The profit could further increase, or you could lose the money which you've just earned.

As you can see from the diagram, when you gain further, the joy does not increase with the same speed according to your profits, because the curve is not linear! The bigger the profits become, the less your joy will grow. On the other hand, if you go left from the green point: when you give profits back your joy quickly diminishes and the pain starts to grow quickly.

This shows how difficult it is to stay in your winning positions!

You feel more pain when you give a profit back than you feel the reward when it increases. As a consequence, as a non-systematic trader you'd tend to take profits in such situations too early.

Therefore, it is advantageous to have a clear strategy which tells you exactly when to stop your trades and when to let them run to produce more money.

You do not want to end up like the taxi driver?!

9.10 Different ways of daily execution

There are different possibilities for you to put portfolio trading systems into practice. What possibility you choose depends first of all on your programming skills and the level on which you want to back-test. Some of you maybe just want to execute strategies without back-testing them by yourself.

Whatever level you plan to use, the daily implementation of systems like Bollinger at first requires you to define the universe of stocks which you want to trade. This seems simple, but it is an important point. If your universe is too small, you don't get enough signals. If it is bigger, you might have too many stocks which don't have enough liquidity or poor spreads, and therefore produce higher costs. It is advantegous if your data supplier provides predifined index universes like the Nasdaq 100, S&P 500, Nifty 50, Shanghai Composite, Nikkei 225, etc. If your data supplier or your backtest software don't supply such predifined universes, the work to build useful universes by yourself can become a time-consuming job.

So take care which stock universes you want to trade and which data supplier you choose for back-testing and for daily signal generation with the chosen universes. The following are some general thoughts from our experience. Your possibilities will increase and change quickly within the following years.

a) Professional back-testing and daily implementation, all in one

Use a professional platform like AmiBroker which allows portfolio back-testing. Then look for an adequate data supplier. Especially if you want to focus on the US markets and the Australian markets, Norgate Data is the first choice. It includes survivorship free, high-quality market data.

For other worldwide regions like Europe and Asia, survivorship free data is mainly available for institutional traders. As a retail trader this is a difficult task. Starting points to find adequate data are the forums of AmiBroker, etc.

b) Professional back-testing and daily implementation, separated

You could do your back-tests with AmiBroker on professional data like Norgate. But daily execution you perform with AmiBroker on stock portfolios which you have not back-tested. AmiBroker allows you to get data from several datafeeds without any problems. So you could get your data from the internet for free, or from your local data supplier at a lower price. You build your portfolio in AmiBroker, check for new signals every day and afterwards execute your trades. Some software suppliers will even allow you to do this automatically. Of course, if you plan to implement this, be sure that you 100% understand what your software does.

c) Daily implementation without back-testing

You can again use AmiBroker and data which stream in automatically every day to scan for your daily signals without performing any back-tests.

But if you don't want to back-test, you could also use cheaper software solutions. If you are a programmer, you could implement eveything in Excel lists or in any other programming language.

If you don't want to do this work, there are also simple solutions by different software and data suppliers. One of them you see as an example in the following screenshot (fig. 9.46).

Figure 9.46: Example of a software scan for Bollinger signals. Left side: you check in a list of stocks on which Bollinger signals appear (green: all stocks which are currently above the upper Bollinger Band); Right side: chart display of a stock from that list with two Bollinger signals (green).

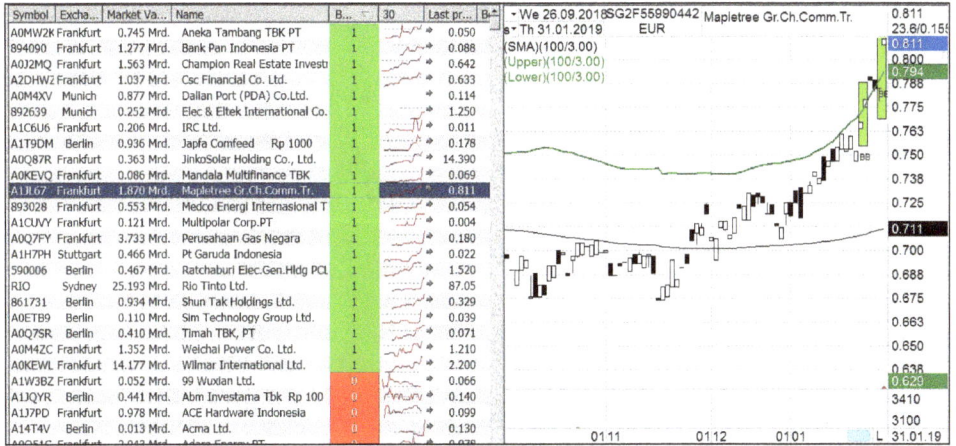

Charts created with software TAI-PAN (tai-pan.lp-software.de/stocks).

Within your predefined stock universe the software scans for Bollinger signals. They are displayed in a list – if you like in real-time. The figure shows a stock universe example which includes different stocks from Asia – Hong Kong, China, Taiwan, Japan, India, Singapore, etc. We believe that this is the region in the world which will become one of the most interesting the next few decades.

Of course, you can exchange markets and possible symbols as you like and scan any markets you want in Europe, USA, Brazil, or wherever. You can then have a deeper look into the chart of each symbol and decide if you want to trade a special signal or not.

Such software packages are often a cheaper and easier solution if you do not need to back-test. Prices start at about $50 per month and include most worldwide stock symbols with just a 15-minute delay from real time.

Conclusion

The trading system's code: is this the pivotal issue in quantitative trading? We believe that programming is just one of the many factors involved in trading systems development. The proof of this statement comes from experience in the field: in 25 years we have seen many successful systematic traders, but in only a few instances were they professional programmers.

So where was the edge?

We believe the edge was in understanding how and when to apply a system and understanding when to stop it. No system is forever. Markets change, traders change, systems change. Nothing is everlasting. Success is easy to reach with a code and a limited period, but really rare over five or ten years. So if you think that systematic trading is a job for life please do not overrate the importance of programming skill.

Let's make a comparison with a lawyer: is the knowledge of law important for a lawyer? Of course it is. But also social relations, character and the family background are equally important. If you are a lawyer and you know the law perfectly, but you run your business in a little town, you will seldom become involved with a nationwide criminal case that will project you into the stratosphere. If your social environment is comprised of little shopkeepers and retired persons, you will care about minor civil suits. If you play golf in New York with famous bankers and financial directors, it is likely that you will care more about high-profile cases.

The same applies with trading system development: it is important to have some basic programming capability, but if you want to be successful, a lot of other skills are required, such as networking with other systematic traders, following publications and seminars on the topic, purchasing and trying new software, and attending scientific meetings and the conferences of professional organisations, like those of IFTA (International Federation of Technical Analysis).

But most importantly: the internet has dramatically changed the world of trading within the last decade. It allows you easily to join live webinars of traders and system developers worldwide, to watch their YouTube videos and to network with other traders via social media.

Now we know what you think: if your ideas are disclosed to a programmer then he will make money with them. But there are many points against this idea. The first is that if your programmer makes money with your ideas, this will not prevent you from making money with them all the same. We have already discussed that you can publish your system in the *Wall Street Journal* (or on YouTube) and people will not trade it. So do not be scared about giving away some secrets, provided these are really such as you presume they are.

Second, it is rare that a programmer will have the time, the feeling or the capability to understand if a code is really important. Programming and testing are two different jobs. It often happens that testing is not done in a systematic way. All traders believe they have a feeling with some particular markets and timeframes and there are few traders that test a system over 70 markets and ten timeframes. So even if the programmer has the intention to steal something, it may be that he will not grasp what he is really stealing. To test a system over many markets and timeframes, to understand if something is missing, how to cure its shortcomings and how to improve its efficiency, is something that is a big job on its own, far away from the programming skill. The best systems we developed were fixed by professional programmers that we are sure did not understand what they were programming. Then, a last consideration: if you come up with two ideas per day and your programmer puts them into a code at the end of the year, there will be so many ideas and codes that he will be bored and never check anything more from you.

Testing and fine-tuning a code is a really time-consuming job, and expensive also, because you need to have many data sources and many data providers in order to easily cover all the markets and all the timeframes. A good systematic trader does not have a single code, but dozens of viable trading system codes that he selects and applies according to the current market conditions. So a really good systematic trader will never refuse to exchange codes with you. If you have 40 systems and you exchange some systems (it is better not to exchange the best performing systems on sensible time frames, e.g. 1–3 minutes), with some other systems, you will end up with more systems and no harm to your systems farm. A mediocre systematic trader has just one or two systems and he thinks that their codes will bring him success, so he keeps them in a safe and he would prefer to die rather than give them away.

The more complex the system, the more easily it will be over-optimised with too many variables or inputs. If you are not a sophisticated programmer this could be good luck because you will never run the risk of writing codes that are too lengthy.

Another point comes to mind when you are considering our professional activity in the last 25 years from a historical point of view: codes and ideas are almost the same, there is nothing really conceptually new in trading systems. You have tons of opening range breakout codes, pivot points, channel breakouts, etc. The same stories are oft-repeated but still work intermittently in today's markets. You can find thousands of these formulas for free on the internet with little effort. You can even know that Jim Simons, the best quant trader around, who made a huge personal fortune with his Magellan Fund, is trading mostly with Markov chains and on an intraday basis.

Would this be enough for you to emulate his success? No, it can help you in going in a precise direction, but it will never allow you to have any practical tips on the feeling, the approach and the theory that lies in his trading systems. So the key point is not the code, the key point is how to adapt existing codes to the current market conditions, how to build a portfolio, and how to know when the moment comes to stop a system and start another one.

But let's add another point which is more human than strictly technical. Like in many other human endeavours, persistence and determination are those qualities that sooner or later lead to success. The programming capability, the mathematical background, the creativity are all factors that surely help in algorithmic trading, but the most important thing will be the feeling you have with the markets, the trades and the systems. And this feeling is the relentless result of persistence and determination. To gauge systems, to develop systems, to evaluate quantitative trades, it takes years. It could not be possible in any other way: success is always difficult to reach and for a systematic trader success is money.

The thread that occurred to us during this book is clear: do not think that a powerful trading platform can transform you into a successful trader, do not think that one piece of code instead of another will bring you to success. It will take a lot of hard work and a little bit of chance. This is why we did not merely write down our recipe for success, we did not fill the book with codes, and we did not use complex concepts to explain the simple steps for successful systematic trading.

We recommend that you are always in control of what you do: do not listen to the sirens that pretend you will make money with their complicated software, their academic seminars and their 1,000-page books. Be flexible, cynical and scared: a systematic trader is always sitting on the bomb that will sooner or later explode and kill him. As Thomas Stridsman put it, probabilities are that we all will go bust sooner or later. If you start from this point, chances are that you will survive a long time.

*   *   *

Each methodology we highlighted in this book alone will not be the ultimate key for a profitable systematic trading, but all put together they will paint a clearer picture in which you can move comfortably just owning a simple trading system's code.

Let's review all the methodologies and try to summarise the pros and cons of each of them.

Rule complexity

It is better to trade with a system with few inputs, few variables and an equity line that is not historically exhilarating, instead of 100 inputs or variables and a super equity line.

Testing

Do not put your focus on a bunch of markets and forget the other ones. Nobody could tell you that a system does not perform on a market but could be the winning tool for trading the remaining 50 markets. Subscribe to a data vendor such as Norgate (norgatedata.com), CSI data (www.csidata.com) or TAI-PAN data (tai-pan.lp-software.

de/stocks) and then apply your systems on at least 70 different futures daily price series, or some hundred stocks, before arriving at the conclusion that the code does not work.

Optimisation

Optimisation is good if it is performed in a savvy way. You should re-optimise regularly, after a fixed time period, in order to keep the system in synchronisation with the market.

Monte Carlo analysis

This is a good process in order to check the stability of the system in a probabilistic way, but its importance should not be over-stressed. If the system is over-optimised the Monte Carlo analysis will be perfect, but this does not mean anything.

Portfolio building

In this book we have shown two different ways to approach this task: One with the combination of different trading systems for single markets; and one with the application of one trading system (Bollinger) to huge portfolios of stocks. Both approaches could be successful if applied in the correct way.

Whichever way you choose, the final solution will depend more on your experience as a trader than on the precise rules.

Dynamic risk management

Do not rely on a fixed rule in order to activate or stop a system from trading. You need to run a farm of a dozen trading systems and then activate those that are fit for the current trading environment. The moving average equity line crossover is this kind of tool, which can transform a mediocre system into a powerful trading machine.

Money management

This is one of the most important factors in trading – always keep your risk exposure less than 1% from the entry point per every trade, better to be 0.5% if you are able to afford such a low risk level.

As you can see from the above mentioned points, the systematic trader has at his disposal a long list of tools that can overcome the would-be higher efficacy of the programming complexity without hurting the profit attractiveness of a trading system. And we stress that you should pay heed to this list in order to improve results.

Appendices

Systems and Ideas

In these appendices we have included three trading systems based on TradeStation and two systems based on AmiBroker. Concerning the systems for TradeStation, these were left in the original state as they were written in our first edition around the year 2008. We explained the first two of these systems in articles in *Traders* magazine and the third one was extensively treated within this book. These three systems can be used as a starting point to build portfolios with trading systems, mainly on the futures and FOREX markets.

Concerning the two AmiBroker systems which came new into the updated book edition in 2019: both are discussed extensively within this book (see chapter 5.6. 'Beginning of Month system' for the main stock indices and chapter 9 'Bollinger Band system').

This last one, the Bollinger Band system, could be a starting point if you want to develop trading strategies which work on portfolios of stocks.

Appendix 1. Bollinger Band System

1.1 Idea

In this book we have explained a Bollinger Band system extensively. First, on a small example we showed with it the effect of out-of-sample deterioration (chapter 5.2).

Later on we took this Bollinger system and changed it in some parts in order to trade it on portfolios of stocks (chapter 9).

The Bollinger Band which we use now to build a simple but robust portfolio was first presented in detail in an earlier article in *Traders* magazine [14]. Its trading logic is explained again with fig. A1.1.

The first third of the graph (August to October 2004) shows a phase of lower market activity. The volatility drops and the Bollinger Bands become narrower. During this period of lower volatility the market often tends sideways without any direction. Many market participants are unsure about the further development and stay on the sidelines.

Such phases of decreasing interest of market participants form the basis of succeeding movements. The longer the indecisive phase, the stronger the subsequent breakout (see fig. A1.1, mid-October until December 2004). After the breakout the Bollinger Bands widen and follow the trending price very quickly. From fig. A1.1 you can calculate the profit of the trade which uses this impulsive long breakout. It brings 6 cents (=7,500 US dollars in the euro future) although some of the gains have been given away. Shortly after the long exit a short signal was triggered (February 2005) which turned out to be a false breakout and was soon exited by the moving average stop.

1.2 Entry logic and EasyLanguage code

```
Long entry:

If the price crosses above the higher Bollinger Band. Enter the
market intraday with a buy stop:

Enter long: next bar at HigherBand stop;


Short entry:

The short entry is symmetrical to the long entry, enter intraday
if the price crosses below the lower Bollinger Band.

Enter short: next bar at LowerBand stop;


Exit:

Exit if the price crosses the moving average between the
Bollinger Bands:

Exit: next bar at Average(Close,60) stop;
```

The exact position of the higher and the lower Bollinger Band is determined by taking the simple moving average and adding (higher band) or subtracting (lower band) the following, volatility dependent amount: Distance * Standard deviation. The volatility dependent component is located within the standard deviation, whereas the distance is a fixed parameter which can be varied.

The EasyLanguage Code is just some lines:

```
Inputs: Length(60), Distance(2);

Vars: HigherBand(0),LowerBand(0);


HigherBand = Average(Close, Length) + Distance * StdDev(Close,
Length);

LowerBand = Average(Close, Length) - Distance * StdDev(Close,
Length);


Buy next bar at HigherBand stop;

Sell next bar at LowerBand stop;


ExitLong next bar at Average(Close, Length) stop;

ExitShort next bar at Average(Close, Length) stop;
```

The system has two input parameters, which are bold typed. One represents the length of the moving average, the other determines the distance (or width) of how far away from this moving average the Bollinger Bands are placed. Their default values are set to a length of 60 and distance of 2. By changing these parameters you can adjust the trade frequency. The smaller you set the length for the moving average, and the smaller you choose the distance of the Bollinger Bands, the faster the system will react to market changes and the more signals you will get. As well as this possibility to adjust the system code to your personal needs Bollinger Bands have further advantages for building mechanical trading systems. Due to their volatility-based component they can easily adapt to different market conditions. Additionally they provide a natural exit point by using the moving average between the Bollinger Bands.

1.3 Application of the strategy to seven markets with same parameters

The strategy is now applied to daily data of seven markets from three different market groups:

- Three stock index futures: Nasdaq-MINI, EURO STOXX 50 and Swiss Market Index

- Two bond index futures: Bund, US-T-Note (10year)

- Two currency futures: Euro and Swiss Franc

Daily data was taken from mid-1994 until mid-2005. Data source for the end-of-day data was CSI Unfair Advantage (csidata.com).

For all the performed tests exactly the same parameters (default: length=60, distance=2) were taken in order to minimise the effect of curve fitting. All results are based on a one contract per market basis and are presented without subtraction of slippage and commissions.

1.4 Results and conclusions

The combined equity line of the seven markets looks like a good starting point for a viable trading system (fig. A1.2). For more detailed information have a look at the system figures (table A1.1). You can take this system and combine it with other uncorrelated systems/markets within a bigger portfolio.

As mentioned, the system was not optimised concerning the input parameters for the entries. More important to note, however, is that we have not inserted and optimised any special exits into the system. If you do this in the way it was shown in chapter 3.5 of this book, results can be improved, especially concerning risks and drawdowns.

Figure A1.1: Euro in US dollar, daily, with Bollinger Bands and 60-day moving average of closing prices. The entry and exit points are marked with circles. The crossing of the price and the Bollinger Bands generate the long and short entries. The crossing of the price and the moving average triggers the exits. Chart created with TradeStation 2000i.

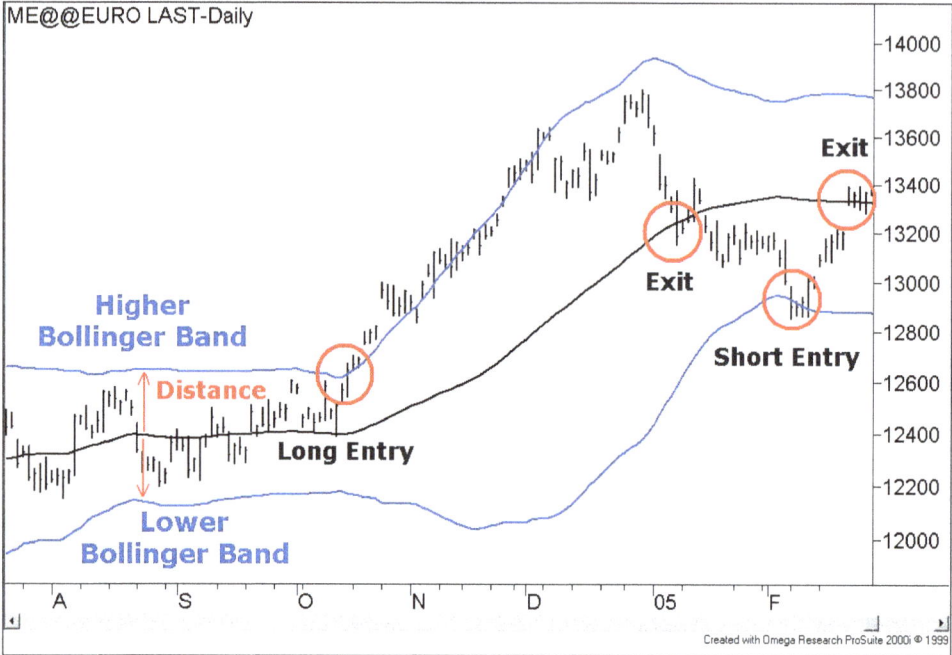

Figure A1.2: Combined equity line of the Bollinger Band system for the portfolio of seven markets, 08/1994–09/2005, for daily data. The figure shows the added net profit on a bar-by-bar basis of all trades on these markets without slippage and commissions. Chart created with RINA Systems.

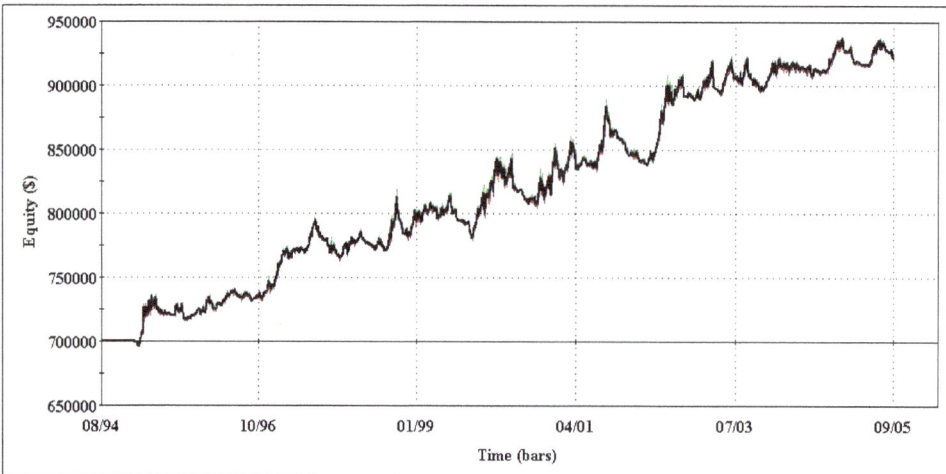

Table A1.1: Key figures of the system tests based on end-of-day data. The second table below shows the main figures of the Bollinger Band system for the portfolio of seven markets, 08/1994–09/2005, applied to daily data. The table shows the added results of all trades on these markets without slippage and commissions.

Bollinger Band System	
Seven market portfolio	
System Analysis	
Net profit	$220,943.00
Gross profit	$451,455.50
Gross loss	($230,512.50)
percent profitable trades	42.15%
Avg. Win/ avg loss.	2.69
profit factor	1.96
maximum drawdown	($8,120.00)
average drawdown	($1,424.51)
number of trades	261
average trade	$846.52

Time Analysis (Days)	
percent in the market	82.28%
longest period out (days)	77.00
Average time in market	59.53
average time between trades	2.14
average time in winning trades	103.71
average time in losing trades	27.34
average time to reach new high	120.10

Appendix 2. The Triangle System

'The symmetric triangle is one of the most profitable patterns for short-term trading.' [15]

2.1 Idea

Fig. A2.1 shows a chart of the continuous, back-adjusted euro/dollar future contract (Globex) at the end of January 2007. You see that within three days a nice, symmetrical triangle developed. The triangle pattern is a very strong, profitable pattern since the logic behind it is sound.

It uses a similar idea to the Bollinger system presented in Appendix A1. The triangle system is more exact in its entry however. Again, as with the Bollinger system, a phase of uncertainty leads at first to a compression in the market. The volatility decreases while the triangle pattern gets narrower. And again like in the Bollinger system, this phase of decreasing interest of the market participants is the reason for the succeeding movement. The longer the indecisive phase lasts, the stronger the subsequent breakout is. At a certain point, when the consolidation has continued for a longer time while many market participants are unsure about the further development, any distortion, e.g., a news event, can create a strong breakout. Many traders who had been standing on the sidelines before are now in a hurry to jump onto the driving train, and like this they amplify the emerging trend. This is underlined by the increasing volume when the breakout happens.

2.2 Programming and coding

Please note that we do not disclose this code but just describe its logic.

But, as you might have recognised, before that final breakout occurred smaller movements out of the boundaries of the triangular figure took place. While a good discretionary trader might ignore the false breakouts, such spikes are difficult to program on a computer. First of all it is difficult to identify such a triangular pattern. Then if your algorithm has found it, to draw the legs of the triangle you must tell the PC where the triangle starts and which points define the legs. Will you ignore the spikes in your calculations or will you include them? This will be different for each situation. Furthermore when will the triangle end and how will you calculate the profit target from the triangular shape? For the discretionary trader these points are easy to see, but on a PC it is a long list of programming tasks.

To overcome these issues we took a different, more abstract approach. We add a simple moving average of the last 200 closing prices and a volatility indicator of the last 300 bars to the same euro, 5-minute chart (fig. A2.2). On this example you see how the symmetrical triangle can be programmed. The figure shows that shortly before the breakout occurred, at the position of the black vertical line (called set-up point), two conditions were true at the same time:

1. The volatility indicator of the last 300 bars has dropped to its lowest point.

2. The moving average of the last 200 closing prices is moving nearly horizontal.

With these two clear simple conditions we can program the set-up of the triangle pattern, or better call it the low volatility/flat moving average pattern. Because like this we do not program a pattern recognition logic which is identifying symmetrical triangles. Instead we are only looking for low volatility phases and for phases in which the market tends sideways at the same time, described by the horizontal movement of the moving average. This is a much weaker condition than the exact pattern recognition but helps us to simplify our programmed trading system logic to put it into reality. Our two set-up conditions could well occur in other patterns, e.g. if the market consolidates within a rectangular small trading range.

Now the entry logic can be completed as follows. If our set-up with the two conditions is true we place a long entry stop order a fixed amount above the current market price and symmetrically a short entry stop order the same amount below the current market price. The long and short entry levels act as a natural stop loss and reversal point of our initiated positions. So if we have entered the market long and the market shortly after proves us wrong and changes to the down side, we exit our long position and enter the market in the opposite direction short. Thus our logic lets the market decide about its breakout direction and just follows it. We exit the position at a profit target which we determine from the difference of the high and the low within the last 300 bars (see yellow vertical lines in fig. A2.2). If the profit target is not reached shortly after the breakout we exit the position with a trailing stop instead.

2.3 Application to different liquid futures markets with same parameters

We apply our gained system code to 5-minute data of four different markets from different liquid futures markets groups: the euro/dollar future as a currency market, the S&P 400 MidCap future as a stock index, the US-T-Bond-Future as a bond market and Light Crude Oil as a liquid commodity future. As data supplier we took the intraday data feed of TradeStation 8. We tested our system within the period of the last five years on back-adjusted futures data from January 2002–January 2007 on all four markets with same system parameters. Our computer simulation is calculated with $30 slippage and commissions per round turn ($30 S&C per RT).

The equity curves all grow steadily with only minor drawdowns (figs. A2.3a–d). The best equity line seems to be Light Crude Oil. Also very steady over the tested five years were S&P 400 MidCap and US T-Bond Future. On the other side the euro future had a sideway phase for the last two years with its biggest drawdown happening just recently, in January 2007 (-$4,575). Overall the equity line, which you get by adding all trades, is however still clearly positive. If you watch the equity curves of the single markets more closely you see that they look a bit like stairs. The reasons for this behaviour are long lasting, flat periods between the signals. The system is only about 1–2% of the total time in the market, the rest of the time it is flat.

It is an important characteristic of our system that signals occur rarely, but when trades are taken they tend to result in big profits.

2.4 Advantages in building a portfolio

A positive side effect of the system's low market exposure is a low correlation of the system's results when applied to the four different markets simultaneously (table A2.1). You can see that the correlations of all four systems' results are nearly 0, they vary between a very small negative correlation of –0.002 and a small positive coefficient of 0.024. This practically uncorrelated behaviour of the four markets helps to build a high return/ low risk portfolio when combining them. You can also see that while the maximum equity drawdowns of the four single markets vary between –$2,440 (S&P 400 MidCap) and –$4,590 (US Treasury Bond Future) the maximum equity drawdown of the four-market portfolio is in the same area with –$3,275. So while the profit of the portfolio grows in a linear way with the added markets to over $58,000, the maximum drawdown is kept in the area of one single market. This results in a very steady portfolio equity curve (fig. A2.4). It is worth mentioning that even within the four-market portfolio the system is only in the market for 10% of the time. So the market exposure is very low, which would allow you to add further systems or markets to the portfolio.

The trade statistics reveal that the gains of the system don't come from a high winning percentage (53%), but from the fact that the average winning trade is a huge amount bigger (factor 1.4) than the average losing trade. Furthermore, the average time in trades is short, at 0.3 days. This shows that the system captures mainly dynamic breakouts which happen quickly and only last for a short time.

The system figures reveal a further quality of the triangle system: the equal weight of long and short trades. From the total 625 trades long and shorts nearly have the same number (322 vs. 303) and the profits are nearly divided equally between the long and short side. This applies for the single markets and as well for the combined portfolio. This feature is the result of the construction of the trading logic, which lets the market itself decide in which direction it goes and just follows it, with the same probability in the long and in the short direction.

2.5 Conclusion

The example of the triangular pattern clearly shows the different tasks of discretionary and systematic traders. While discretionary traders can rely on their experiences and their ability to estimate the market correctly, systematic traders need to act in a different way. As many patterns which are easily visible with the human eye cannot be programmed directly, we took a different approach and simulated the pattern with common indicators: a moving average, the volatility and the price itself. With this approach we could not exactly simulate the triangular pattern but we created a trading system which comes close to the conditions which are true within such a triangle pattern: decreasing volatility and sideways market direction. Like this our trading logic was gained by pure market observation and not by optimisation or curve fitting. We are rewarded with a very robust system which stays profitable over different markets with the same input parameters. At the first glance it seems to be a disadvantage that signals occur very rarely and that the time in the market is very low, but it is this fact which makes different markets completely uncorrelated for our trading logic and allows us to build a profitable low risk portfolio.

Figure A2.1: Principle of the symmetrical triangle pattern, discretionary view. Euro, Globex, 5 minute, 21–24 January 2007. A natural profit target can be derived from the width of the triangle. False breakouts usually occur which make triangles difficult to program for systematic trading. The final breakout takes place with volume increase and leads the price into the target region.

Figure A2.2: Principle of programmed triangle system. At the point before the breakout occurs (set-up point) the volatility is extremely low and the moving average tends sideways. If these two conditions are true, a long stop and a short stop entry order is placed. These entry levels also work as natural initial stop and reverse points. A profit target is derived from recent highs and lows (yellow lines).

Figures A2.3a-d: Result of triangle system on four different markets: 6/2/2002–6/2/2007, $30 S&C per RT, on a day-to-day basis.

A2.3a: Euro/dollar Future (TradeStation symbol @EC)

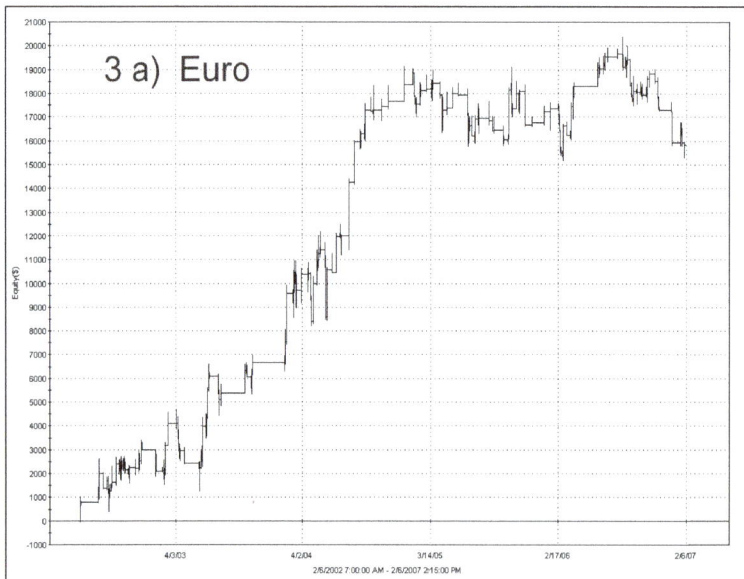

A2.3b: S&P 400 MidCap Future (TradeStation symbol @EMD.D)

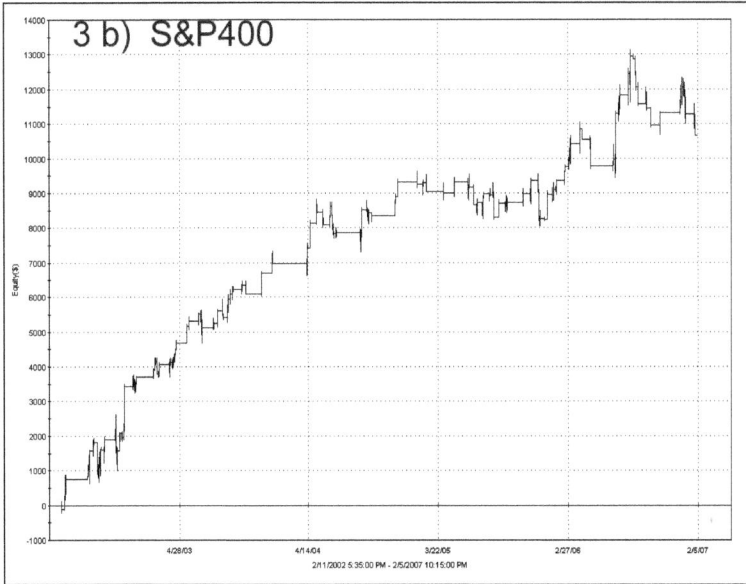

A2.3c: US T-Bond Future (TradeStation symbol @US.P)

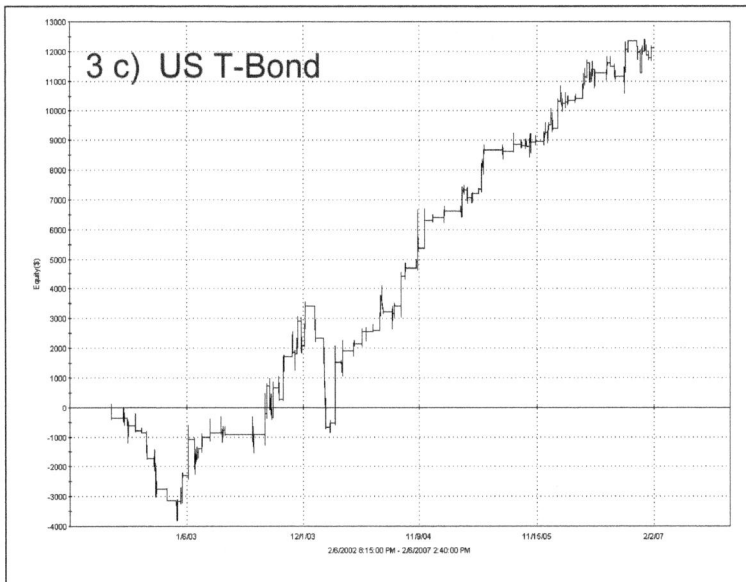

A2.3d: Light Crude Oil Future (TradeStation symbol @CL.C)

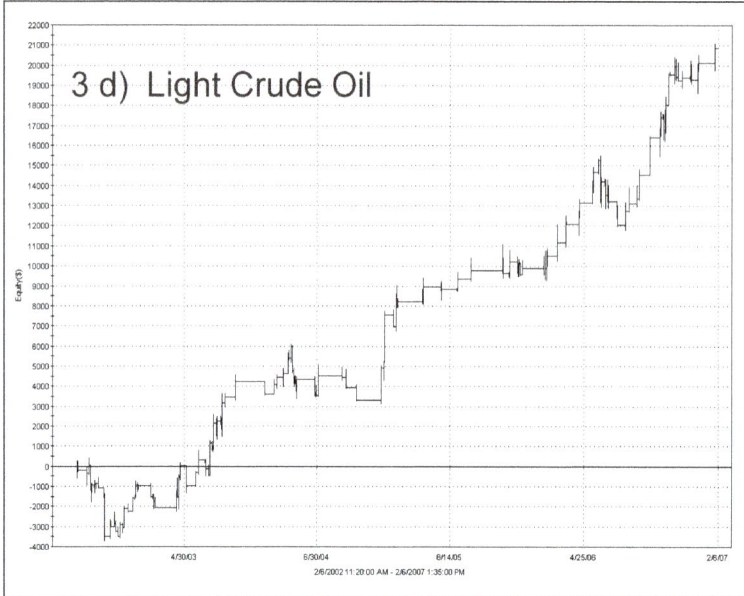

Figure A2.4: Equity curve of four-market portfolio. Triangle system applied with same system parameters to the following markets: euro/dollar Future, S&P 400 MidCap Future, US T-Bond Future and Light Crude Oil Future. Equally weighted on a one-contract basis, including $30 S&C per RT, Jan 2002–Jan 2007, calculated on a day-to-day basis. Chart created with RINA Systems.

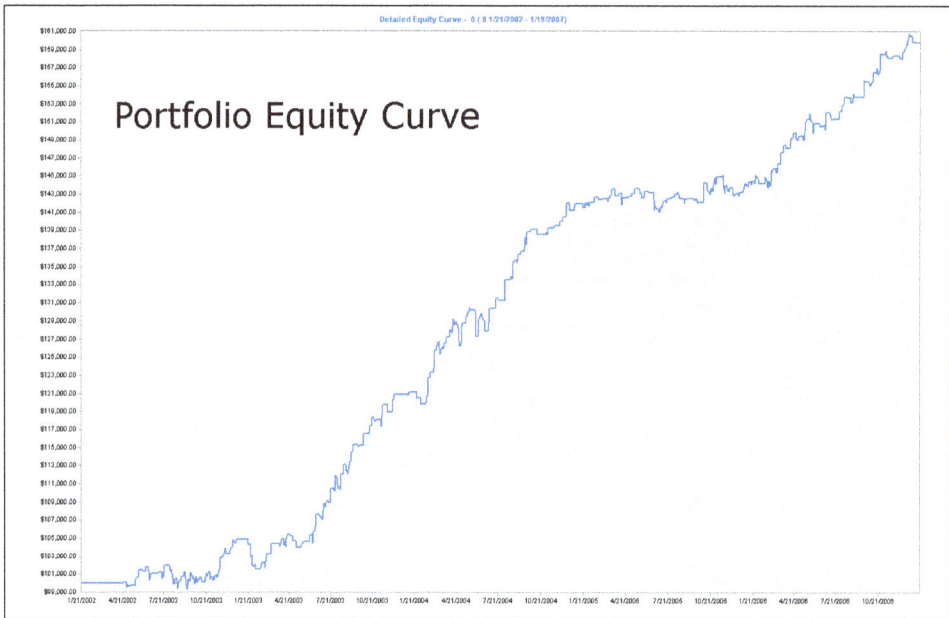

Table A2.1: Portfolio figures, Jan 2002–Jan 2007. Portfolio figures of Triangle system applied to the following markets: Euro/dollar Future, S&P 400 MidCap future, US T-Bond-Future and Light Crude Oil Future. Same system parameters for all markets, $30 S&C per RT, calculated on a day-to-day basis.

Market	Net Profit	Max. Drawdown	Net Profit Long	Net Profit Short	Number of Trades	Average Trade	Percent Profitable
1. Euro	$15,915	-$4,575	$8,693	$7,222	197	$81	49%
2. S&P 400	$11,280	-$2,440	$6,810	$4,470	149	$76	54%
3. US-T-Bond	$12,019	-$4,590	$9,556	$2,463	140	$86	57%
4. Light Crude Oil	$19,040	-$3,050	$9,570	$9,470	139	$137	53%
Portfolio	$58,254	-$3,275	$34,629	$23,625	625	$93	53%

Correlations	S&P 400	Euro	Light Crude Oil	US-T-Bond
S&P 400		0.019	0.020	-0.002
Euro	0.019		-0.002	0.024
Light Crude Oil	0.020	-0.002		0.006
US-T-Bond	-0.002	0.024	0.006	

Appendix 3. Portfolios with the LUXOR Trading System

In chapter 3 we presented the trend-following system called LUXOR and tested it extensively on the British pound/US dollar pair.

Now we are going to check this trading logic on other markets. We will outline how this strategy works on various bond markets and how to use it to construct robust portfolios.[5]

3.1 Idea

Before trying to code an idea with the purpose of building a systematic trading methodology it is important to understand the inner nature of the different markets you are going to trade. The market most appreciated by traders is the equity indexes universe. Stocks, that are the components of the equity indexes, move more following psychology than real events. Just think how an event could impact a stock: it is always an indirect influence, very seldom a direct one. Oil prices are going up? An oil stock can benefit from this situation but it will benefit more or less depending on its corporate efficiency, from the relative competitive position in the industry, from the intelligence of its management, and so on. Surely it will benefit but how much it will benefit is always a matter of discussion. But if we are talking about oil, the true commodity, the real black gold, this is another story.

Commodity prices are influenced by real demand and real offer. Psychology is still important but not dominant. If China is growing 10% per year in the following ten years, the demand of all kinds of commodities will perhaps double or triple, nobody knows for sure. This is a direct effect: Chinese importers are bidding for oil on the international cash markets and prices are going up. Nothing is more easy to understand. This is why psychology will be more important on stocks than on commodities.

But there will be another aspect to consider also. If we are talking about indirect effects, it means that there will be few events that everybody will agree will modify the picture of the equity indexes. On the equity indexes everything is smoothed by discussion, interpretation, indirect effects, and so on. When, on the contrary, news directly affects demands and offers, and the news is dramatic, there is no room for discussion and interpretation. Prices jump or they crash. *Tertium non datur.* So you will have limit up

---

[5] More information about this topic can be found in [16].

and limit down days, you will have huge price swings in one direction or another. But in this black and white world, in between psychology and real demand and offer, you have a third environment: bonds.

Monetary policy has a steady nature, no climax, no sudden changes. Economic swings are slow and seldom do they surprise markets. In a period of economic recession interest rates will go down for months after months, in a period of economic expansion interest rates will go up smoothly. Take for example the 17 interest rate increases in the US: at a certain point the market discounted them and it was obvious that they would then have to go up once again. A misunderstanding could only really have occurred if you were at the very beginning of the 17 interest rate increases or at the end of them. Please note, though, that we are talking about two situations out of 17.

In a more serious way we can say that elements of a macroeconomic series are quite auto-correlated, so that if they start rising they will go on for a while, if they will go down they will go continue down for a while. Monetary policy is not a kind of situation where one day you have an increase of 2% and tomorrow a decrease of 3% and then tomorrow again an increase of 1% and so on. This is why prices in bonds tend to follow the same direction without much noise and this is why moving averages on bonds are a good predictive tool, because they are simply able to catch this smoothing behaviour of prices. You should have no fear in trading bonds with moving averages. From all our performed quantitative tests and experience we can conclude: they work!

3.2 The trading logic

You can find all the details on the logic of the LUXOR system in chapter 3 of this book, so we won't discuss it further here, but will focus on the results of the strategy.

Please note that we do not apply any additional exits to the strategy at this point. Trades are only exited when the price crosses the slower moving average of the entry logic (in case of long positions). The system is built symmetrically concerning long and short trades.

Of course you can and should add exits which meet your personal needs to the strategy. You will find the appropriate methods on how to adjust them in chapter 3.5 of this book.

3.3 Results in the bond markets

Let's see how the LUXOR system works on the major bond markets. We want to check if bond markets really fit well with trend-following systems as we expected from our fundamental argumentation above.

All the following tests are based on a one-contract basis and are performed with the following input parameters of the system (fast moving average length=7, slow moving average length=26). No adaptation of the parameters to the different markets was performed in order to keep the results comparable and to avoid the effect of curve fitting.

The strategy is applied to the daily data which was provided by CSI Unfair Advantage (csidata.com). The futures data was point-based back-adjusted to get rid of artificial gaps between different contract months. All results in the figures and tables are based on a one contract per market basis.

If you apply the LUXOR system to the bond markets, you see that in all of them you get more or less steady equity curves (fig. A3.1). Some work better, like the US T-Bond, the US T-Note (10-year) and the German Bund, and some look a little bit worse, like the not so well known Australian 10-year Treasury Bond or the Korean 3-year Government Bond. But with all of them you get positive results.

In order to add the results of all tested bond markets to a combined portfolio, you have different possibilities. You could first convert the point values and currency of each market and build a portfolio in US dollars. For this you must convert the Korean bond, Japanese bond etc., by using the dollar conversion rates $/won, $/yen etc., and then add all equity-lines. To simplify these calculations we used another method here. We tested all the single bond markets in points. We made a simplification to add these point equity curves of all 12 markets to get a portfolio. This is not 100% mathematically correct but the result comes very close to what it would be if you were to use the exact currency conversion rates (for example 1 point in the Bund future is 1,000 euro, 1 point in the US T-Bond and US T-Note is $1,000 and so on).

The equity line becomes very nice and steady, you only get minor drawdowns (fig. A3.2). The most significant one happened in 1994 during the bond market crash, when all markets turned their trend from upside to downside more or less at the same time. But on the combined, long-term equity line it looks more like a small accident than a big issue.

If you have the capability you could trade this portfolio in the three different time zones with all included markets. There is, however, one reason why we won't advise you to do this, even if the equity line looks good enough: correlation! All the bond markets are so highly correlated that the possibility exists that the system might crash for all the markets at the same time, as happened partially in the year 1994 – just imagine if you were long in all 12 bond-markets and then they all go down at the same time. The high correlation increases the risk of your bond portfolio drastically.

In order to build a high return/low risk portfolio, the concept should be as follows: take a mixture of different systems and apply them to different markets in different timeframes. For example you could choose some liquid markets from the bond group and apply a medium-term trend-following system, like the one described here. Then you would add, for example, swing-trading systems for the currencies and day-trading systems for the

Mini S&P and so on. Various possibilities exist which you must fit to your personality and your trading style. The whole topic is too big to treat it seriously here.

3.4 Diversification with other market groups

Here, to stay with our trend-following logic and to get a better feeling for it, we build a small portfolio of different market groups.

We use two bond markets, the German Bund and the US T-Note (10 year) but add other markets from different market groups: the euro/dollar as a currency, the Mini S&P as a stock index plus Gold and Light Crude oil as famous commodities. So we have a portfolio in which the successful bond markets still build the core but which is diversified with less correlated markets. It is important to mention here that the Mini S&P produces a negative equity line, the Gold goes just sideways and the euro/dollar weakened in the last three years as well (the equity lines are not shown here).

Even with these markets included the overall portfolio shows a steady upward equity line, since the two bond markets and the crude oil kept the portfolio running well. The equity line does not look as steady as for the complete bond portfolio, but that's what we expected.

The idea here is to have a portfolio of less correlated markets in which there are always one or two that have big gains that compensate the losses of other markets.

Let's have a look at the portfolio's main figures (table A3.1). The system figures which we get are typical for a trend-following system. Only 37% of all the 3168 performed have been profitable. The overall big gains of the system result from the high ratio of average win/average losing trade which is nearly 2.5. A very important fact to mention is the following: the system's gains resulted from the 63 positive outlier trades. These outliers produced more profit ($606.487) than the final total net profit ($526.259)! This means that the extreme big winning trades made the profit of the system. This underlines again how important it is in trend-following systems to let the profits run. If you missed the positive outliers you would have no gain at all. The annoying point for you as a trader is, however, that such big gains occur very seldom, but when they do occur, you must catch them.

An interesting fact of the system is also that the average time in winning trades is more than four times longer than the average time which the system stays in losing trades (25 days versus 6 days). This shows again how the trend-following logic cuts the losses short and lets the profits run.

3.5 Conclusion

With the examples presented above we wanted to show you how important it is for successful trading to select the right systems for the right markets. With the bonds we have identified a group which could have been exploited perfectly with trend-following methods lasting recent decades. From the fundamental point of view the chances are good that they will continue to behave like this. We are aware that a trend-following system is not suited for every trader. It's annoying to have only a small amount of profitable trades and to wait most of the time until the big moves take place but trend-following strategies work too well in bond markets to not use them. They are a key part in the most successful existing hedge funds. In our opinion they should be at least one component of your trading systems if you want to be successful in the long run.

Figure A3.1: Equity Lines of 12 major bond markets, in points. Conversion from point values to base currency: German Bund: 1 point = 1,000 euro; US T-Bond, US T-Note (10 year) and US T-Note (5 year): 1 point = $1,000; US T-Note (2 year): 1 point = $2,000; Eurodollar (3 month) 1 point = $2,500; Long Gilts: 1 point = £1,000; Canadian Government Bond (10 year): 1 point = C$1,000; Canadian Bankers Acceptance (3 month): 1 point = C$2,500; Japanese Government Bond (10 year): 1 point = 10,000 yen; Australian Bond (10 year): 1 point = AU$1,000; Korean Government Bond (3 year): 1 point = 1m. Korean won. End of test period in all markets: April 2006. Charts created with TradeStation 2000i.

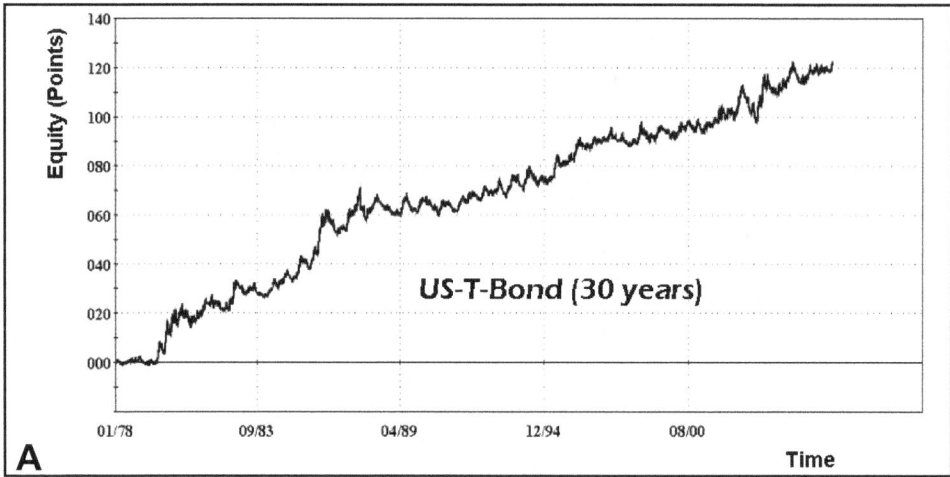

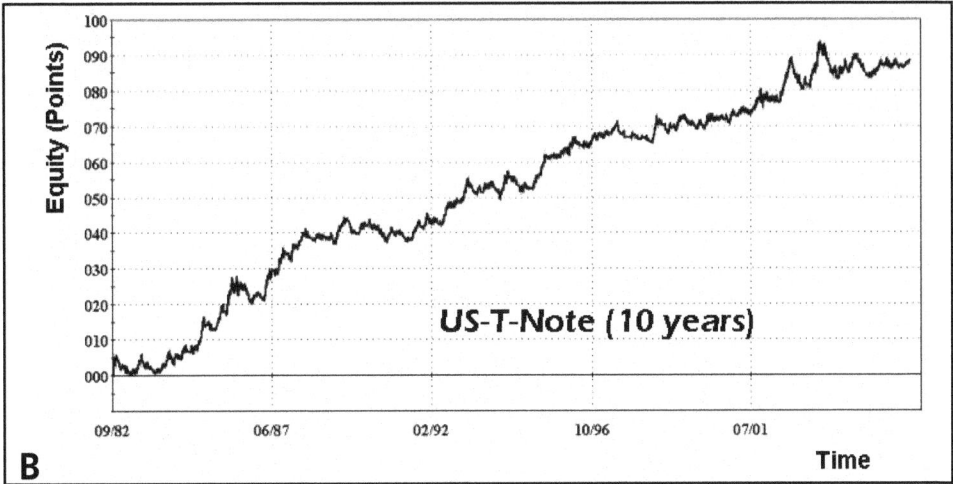

B

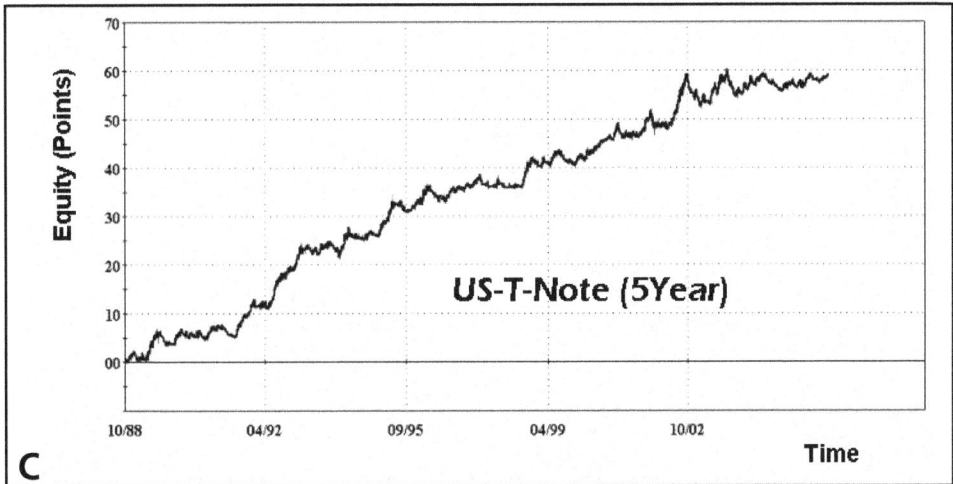

C

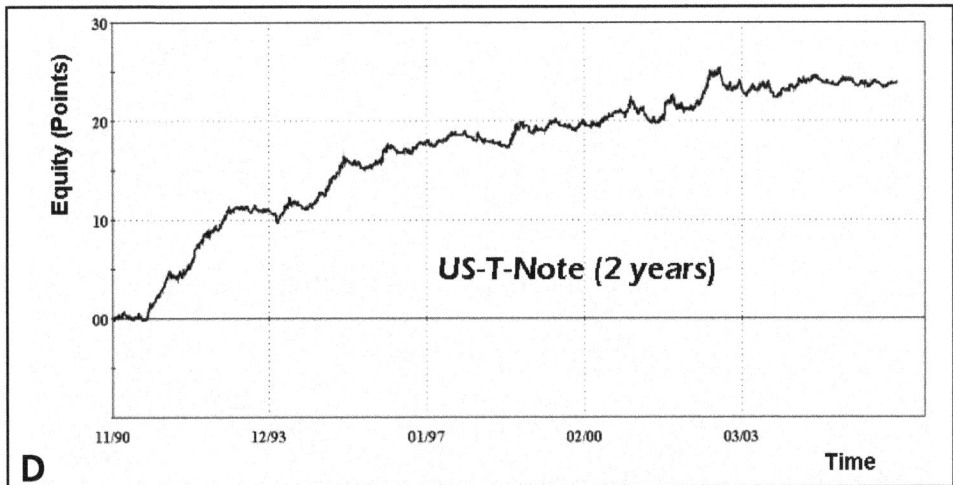

D

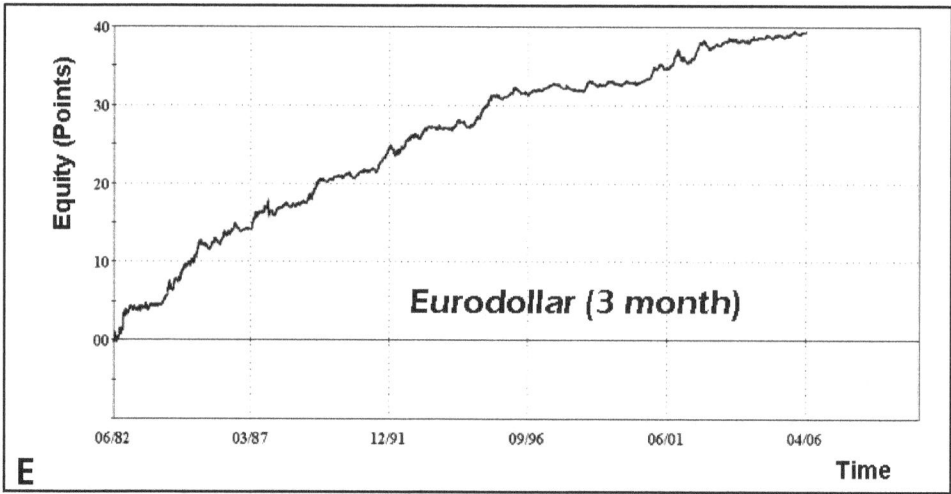

E

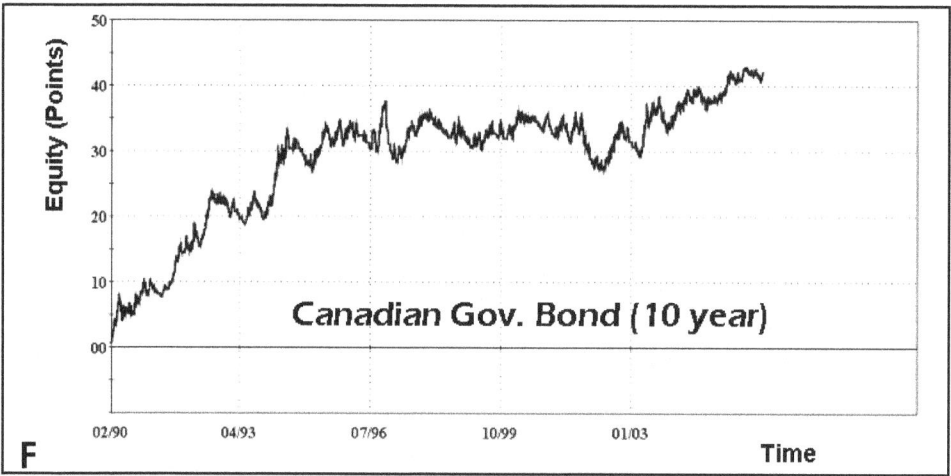

F

G

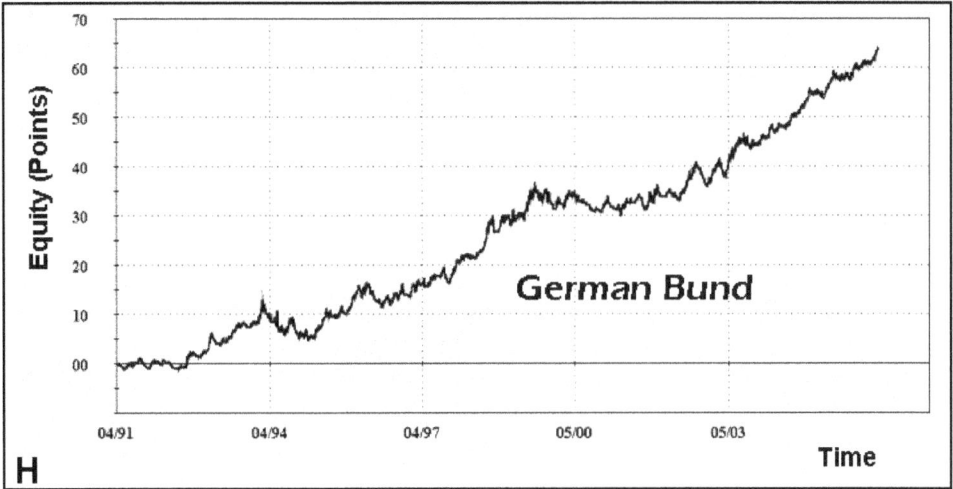

German Bund

H

Long Gilts (8.75 years)

I

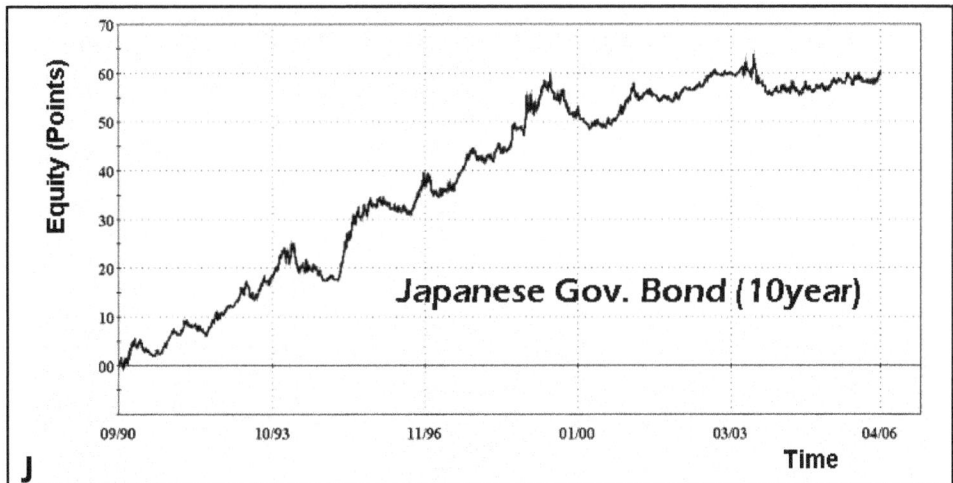

Japanese Gov. Bond (10year)

J

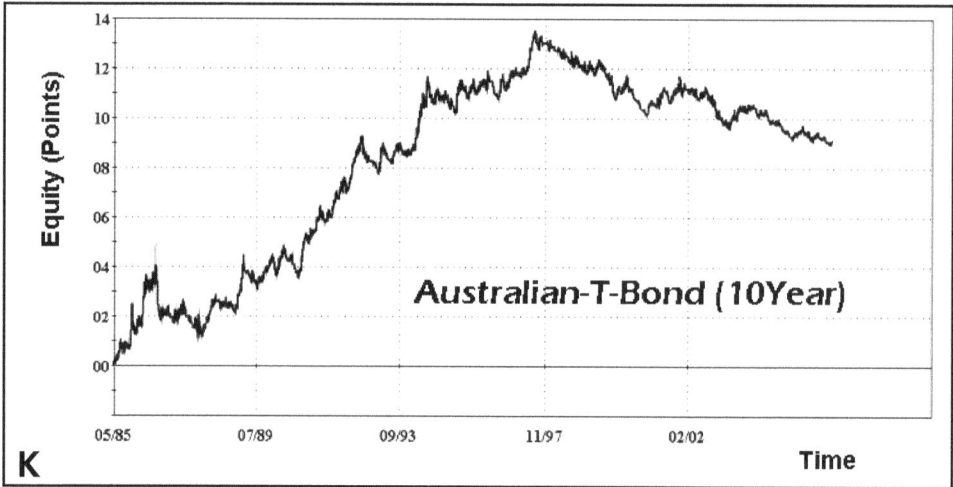

K

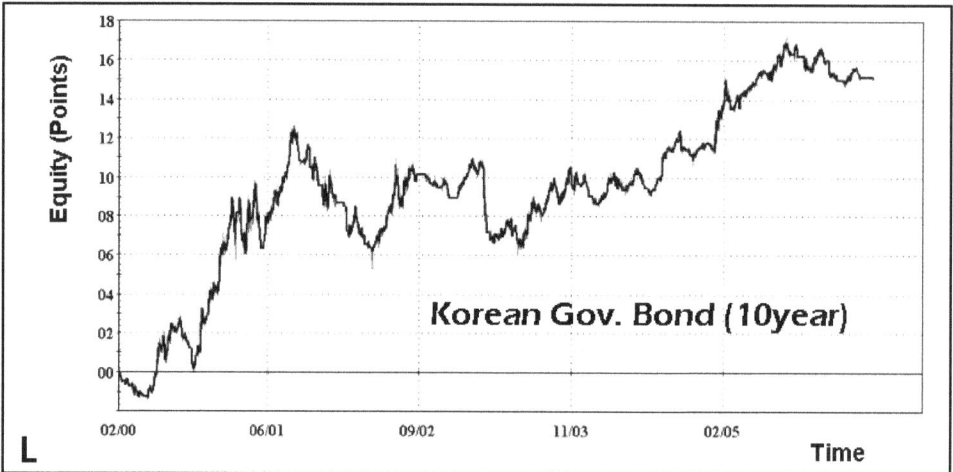

L

Figure A3.2: Portfolio of 12 combined bond-markets. The system equities in points of the following markets were summarised: German Bund, Long Gilt, US T-Bond (30 year, electronic), US T-Note (10 year, electronic), US-T-Note (5 year, electronic), US-T-Note (2 year, electronic), Eurodollar (3 month, electronic), Canadian Government Bond (10 year), Canadian Bankers Acceptance (3 month), Australian 10-year Bond, Japanese Government Bond (10 year), Korean Government Bond (3 year). August 1977–April 2006. Chart created with RINA Systems.

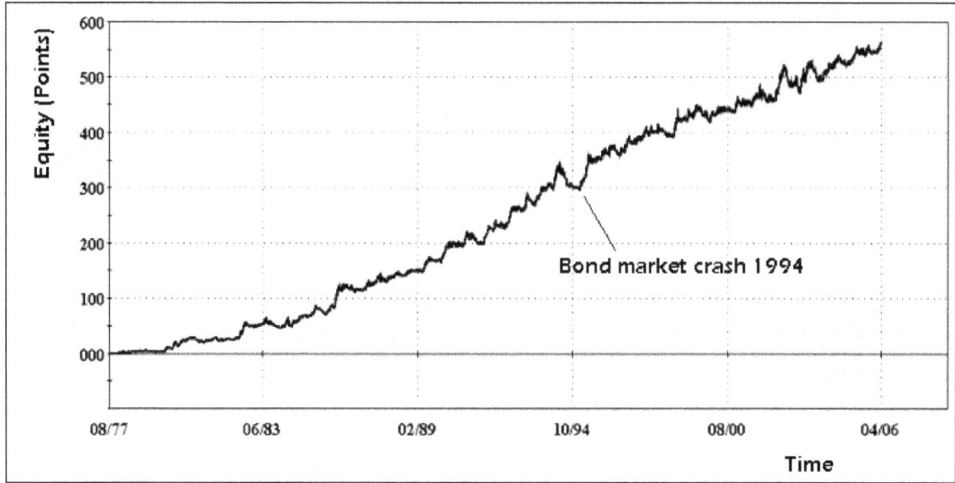

Figure A3.3: Portfolio of 2 bond markets and 4 markets of different groups: German Bund, US T-Note (10 year), Mini S&P, Gold, Light Crude Oil, euro/dollar. $30 slippage and commissions per trade subtracted. May 1972–April 2006. Chart created with RINA Systems.

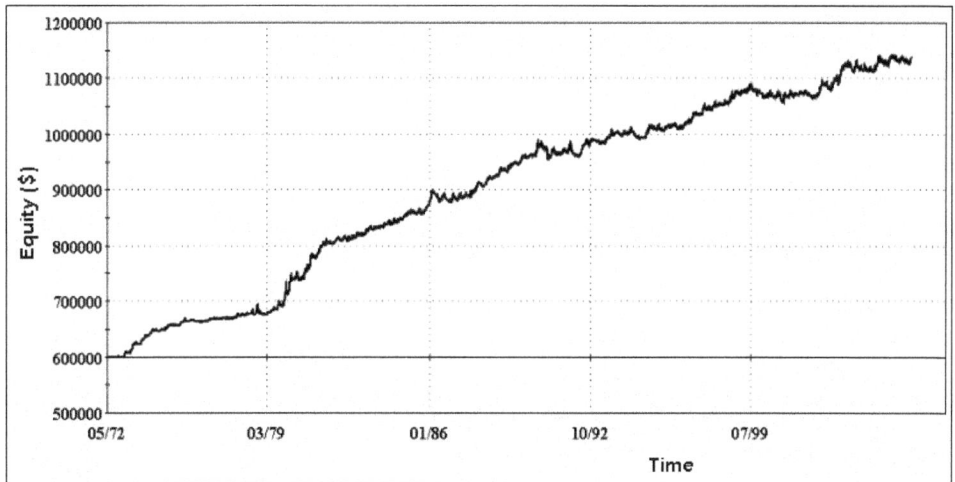

Table A3.1: System figures for the six-market portfolio consisting of German Bund, US T-Note (10 year), Mini S&P, Gold, Light Crude Oil, euro/dollar. May 1972–April 2006. All numbers are calculated with $30 slippage and commissions per trade.

System Analysis			
Net Profit	$526,259.20		
Gross Profit	$1,620,546.45		
Gross Loss	($1,094,287.25)	Total Slippage & Commission	$95,040.00

Percent profitable	37.59%	Profit factor	1.48
Ratio avg. win/avg. loss	2.46		

Annual Rate of Return	1.90%	Sharpe Ratio	0.92
Return on Initial Capital	87.71%		
Return on Max. Drawdown	1337.42%		

Total Trade Analysis	
Number of total trades	3,168
Average trade	$166.12

Outlier Trades	Total Trades	Profit/Loss
Positive outliers	63	$606,487.35
Negative outliers	4	($24,871.00)
Total outliers	67	$581,616.35

Time Analysis	
Percent in the market	86.51%
Longest flat period	24

Avg. time in trades	12.95
Avg. time between trades	0.48

Avg. time in winning trades	24.92
Avg. time between winning trades	2.27

Avg. time in losing trades	5.74
Avg. time between losing trades	2.67

Equity Curve Analysis	
Avg. time between peaks (days)	73.32
Maximum Equity Drawdown (daily)	($39,348.75)
Date of Maximum Drawdown	13/12/2000

Appendix 4. EasyLanguage Code Section

Here you find the free EasyLanguage codes for TradeStation, MultiCharts, etc., of the systems which we described and used in this book as examples. You can find the codes in electronic form to copy/paste on the website www.urban-stocks.com.

- LUXOR (see chapter 3.1)

- Beginning of Month (chapter 5.6)

- Bollinger Band System (chapter 9)

4.1 Beginning of Month (chapter 5.6)

```
[LegacyColorValue = true];

{ FOR EDUCATIONAL USE ONLY

Coded by Urban Jaekle, 20 Feb 2018

// wwww.urban-stocks.com

This system is called "time" because time (!) is the only important
parameter for it

Some facts about the system:

Only end-of-day data is needed to trade the system

It produces long entries for any stock index future, e.g. S&P 500, Nasdaq,
Russel 2000, EuroStoxx, DAX, Nikkei, HangSeng, KOSPI, SMI etc.

All trades are exited after a hold period of 4 days or if being stopped
out by the initial stop

// Idea: Buy a stock index on each last day of the month on close, if it
trades above the 40

// day moving average. Hold it for 4 days.

// Exit on the fourth trading day on close or when the market closes below
the 40 day moving

// average}

{####### Let's start with the inputs for the initial stop #######}

Inputs: MovAvgPeriods(40);

Variables: BullishPoint(0);
```

```
BullishPoint= Average( Close, MovAvgPeriods );

{###### The entry is only allowed at the last trading day of the month##}

If C > BullishPoint AND

((DayOfMonth(Date)=29 AND DayOfWeek(Date)=5) OR

(DayOfMonth(Date)=30 AND

(Month(Date)=4 OR Month(Date)=6 OR Month(Date)=9 OR Month(Date)=11))

OR

DayOfMonth(Date)=31 OR

(DayOfMonth(Date)=28 AND Month(Date)=2) OR

(DayOfMonth(Date)=28 AND (Month(Date)=4 OR Month(Date)=6 OR
Month(Date)=9 OR Month(Date)=11) AND DayOfWeek(Date)=5)

OR (DayOfMonth(Date)=30 AND DayOfWeek(Date)=5)

OR (DayOfMonth(Date)=29 AND Month(Date)=2)

OR (DayOfMonth(Date)=27 AND Month(Date)=2 AND DayOfWeek(Date)=5)

OR (DayOfMonth(Date)=26 AND Month(Date)=2 AND DayOfWeek(Date)=5))

then Buy("BuyDay") this bar on close;

{#### And finally the exit:

If the market closes below the 40day average: exit next bar on close

After 4 days if not being stopped out before#######}

If C<BullishPoint then Sell("MovAvgExit") this bar on close;

If BarsSinceEntry=4 then Sell("4days") this bar on close;
```

4.2 Bollinger Band System (chapter 9)

```
{*********************************************************************

Description: Bollinger Band System

Coded by Urban Jaekle, 20 Dec 2018 // wwww.urban-stocks.com

FOR EDUCATIONAL USE ONLY

*********************************************************************}

[LegacyColorValue = true];

Inputs#####################}

Inputs: BarsBlw(2), Length( 180 ),NumDevsUp( 3 ) ,       NumDevsDn( 1 );

{Define Bollinger Bands ###############################}

variables: UpperBand( 0 ), LowerBand( 0 ) ;

UpperBand = BollingerBand( C, Length, NumDevsUp ) ;
```

```
LowerBand = BollingerBand( C, Length, NumDevsDn ) ;
{###############buy ###################################}
If CountIF(Close < UpperBand, BarsBlw) = BarsBlw Then
    Buy ("BB") Next Bar at UpperBand Stop;
if CurrentBar > 1 and C crosses under LowerBand then
{ CB > 1 check used to avoid spurious cross confirmation at CB = 1 }
    sell ( "BBandexit" ) next bar at LowerBand stop ;
```

Appendix 5: AmiBroker Code Section

Here you find the free AmiBroker codes for the two systems which we described and used in this book as examples. You can also find these codes in electronic form to copy & paste on the website, www.urban-stocks.com:

- Beginning of Month (chapter 5.6)
- Bollinger Band System (chapter 9)

5.1 Beginning of Month

```
/*

Beginning of Month Trading System
FOR EDUCATIONAL USE ONLY


Coded for AmiBroker by Urban Jaekle, 9 Sept 2018
wwww.urban-stocks.com


Idea: Buy a stock index on each last day of the month on close, if it
trades above the 40 day moving average. Hold it for 4 days.
Exit on the fourth trading day on close or when the market closes
below the 40 day moving // average Apply to daily data,
stock indices like S&P500, DAX, Nifty50, World ex US, REIT etc.


##########     general settings     ################
number of positions, initial equity, commission amount etc.


*/


NumberPositions = 1;
SetOption("MaxOpenPositions", NumberPositions);
```

```
PositionSize = -100 / NumberPositions;


InitialEquity = 100000;
CompoundedProfits = 1; /*1 = yes, 0 = no  */
CommissionAmount = 20; /* means 40$ per round turn */


SetOption( "InitialEquity", InitialEquity );


SetOption( "CommissionMode", 2 ); /*  1 = percent, 2 = fixed */
SetOption( "CommissionAmount", CommissionAmount );



/*   define the last trading day opf the month for the entry   */


isLastOfMonth = TimeframeExpand(1, inMonthly, expandPoint);


/* for exit and entry filter: optimization of mov. average length */


MAExit = optimize( "MAExit", 40, 10,300, 10 );


IndexFilterLength = MAExit;
IndexUPTrend = C > MA(C,IndexFilterLength);


PositionScore = 100 + Ref(ROC(C, 252),-1);
/* Add this line for selecting the strongest
Index within an index portfolio */



Buy= isLastOfMonth AND IndexUPTrend;


Sell = Cross( MA( Close,MAExit ), Close) ;



BuyPrice=SellPrice=Close;
```

```
Short=Cover=0;


/* Exit Trade after X Bars; default = 4 days */


/*NumBarExit = optimize( "NumBarExit", 4, 1, 20, 1 );
   if you want to optimize */


NumBarExit = 4;
ApplyStop( stopTypeNBar, stopModeBars, NumBarExit );


/*    For visualization */


Plot(C,"Close", colorBlack, styleCandle);
Plot(MA( Close,MAExit ),"MA Exit", colorBlue, styleThick);
```

5.2 Bollinger Band System (chapter 9)

```
/* Bollinger Band Trading System

 FOR EDUCATIONAL USE ONLY


 Coded for AmiBroker by Urban Jaekle, 20 Nov 2018
 wwww.urban-stocks.com


 The system buys on the OPEN of today if yesterday's close was above
 the Bollinger Band Top


 Apply to daily data, e.g. all stocks incl. delisted of the S&P500,
 Nasdaq100, Russell2000 etc.


 For optimisation:
 variable = optimize( "Description", default, min, max, step );
 see also this: https://norgatedata.com/AmiBroker-usage.php */




 /*include all Norgate functions for survivorship free backtests */
```

```
#include_once "Formulas\Norgate Data\Norgate Data Functions.afl";


/* General settings */


index           = "$SPX";   /* choose index which you test;
don't forget this to set also in backtester settings "pad and align"!
e.g. Norgate symbols $SPX=S&P500, $SP1500=S&P1500,
 $NDX=Nadaq100, $DJI=DowJones 30, $RUT=Russell 2000,
 $RUA= Russell 3000, $XAO.au = Sidney All Ordinaries 500
more see https://norgatedata.com/data-content-tables.php; */


/* Strategy parameters */


NumberPositions      = 20;
/* Number of positions which you can hold at the same time*/
BollTopPrds          = 180;
/*compare with Appendix 1. Futures: default = 60 */
BollingerTopWidth    = 3.5;
/* For entry, compare with Appendix 1. Futures: default = 2 */
BollBottWdth         = 0.5;
/*For exit, compare with Appendix 1. Futures: default = 2 (for shorts) */
IndexFilterLength    = 300;   /*set Filter Length*/
ScoreLength          = 300;   /*Score length */



BollBottPrds    = BollTopPrds;


SetOption("MaxOpenPositions", NumberPositions);
SetPositionSize(100 / NumberPositions, spsPercentOfEquity);


InitialEquity = 100000;
CommissionAmount = 0.25;
/*this means 0.25% at entry AND 0.25% at exit of a position */


SetOption( "InitialEquity", InitialEquity );
```

```
SetOption( "CommissionMode", 1 ); /*1 = percent, 2 = fixed */

SetOption( "CommissionAmount", CommissionAmount );

RoundLotSize = 0;

/* 0: fractional number of shares are allowed */



/* Preparation for Entry and Exit */

indexFilter     = NorgateIndexConstituentTimeSeries(index);

upperBand = BBandTop(C, BollTopPrds, BollingerTopWidth);



LongEntry = C >upperBand     /* Price is above the upper Bollinger band */

AND Ref(C<upperBand, -1)

/* Price the day before is below the upper Bollinger band */

AND indexFilter;

/* make sure you have the correct stock universe */

LongExit = C < BBandBot(C, BollBottPrds, BollBottWdth);

/* price is below the bottom Bollinger band */



/* Market index filter. Allow positions only when index is in uptrend,

defined by a simple moving average of 300 days*/



SetForeign(index);

/*Norgate $SPX, $SP1500, $NDX, $DJI, $RUT=Russell 2000,

$RUA= Russell 3000, Sidney All Ordinaries

(Australian stock market)     $XAO.au

see here https://norgatedata.com/data-content-tables.php;

                                 */

IndexDownTrend = C < MA(C,IndexFilterLength);

/*IndexDownTrend = LinRegSlope(C, IndexFilterLength) ;

//   another possible option to define trend */

RestorePriceArrays();



/* In the case you get many different signals, buy the
```

stocks with the highest momentum over the last 300 days first*/

```
Rank = 100 + Ref(ROC(C, ScoreLength),-1);
PositionScore = Rank;
```

/* The entry and exit trigger */

```
Buy =      Ref(LongEntry,-1)
```
/* Price is today above the Bollinger band */
```
AND !Ref(IndexDownTrend,-1);
```
/* Index Filter: Don't enter new positions in a bear market */

```
Sell =      Ref(LongExit,-1)
OR DateTime()==GetFnData("DelistingDate")
```
 /* sell if stock is de-listed */
```
OR !indexFilter ;
```
/* sell if stock has to leave the index   */

```
BuyPrice=SellPrice=Open;      /* Buy and Sell on the next days open;
```

Close instead of open could improve performance */
```
Short = Cover = 0;
```

/* for visualisation */

```
/* Plot(C,"Close", colorBlack, styleCandle);
Plot(BBandTop(C, BollTopPrds, BollingerTopWidth),
"BollEntry", colorGreen, styleThick);
Plot(BBandBot(C, BollBottPrds, BollBottWdth),"BollExit"
, colorRed, styleThick);
Plot(ma(CLOSE, BollTopPrds),"MovAvg", colorBlack, styleThick); */
```

Bibliography

[1]   Stridsman, Thomas, *Trading Systems That Work* (McGraw-Hill Professional, 2000).

[2]   Aronson, David, *Evidence-Based Technical Analysis* (Wiley, 2006).

[3]   You, Dr. Alex, http://elsmar.com/pdf_files/Degrees_of_Freedom.pdf

[4]   Pardo, Robert, *Design, Testing and Optimization of Trading Systems* (Wiley, 1992).

[5]   Jaekle & Tomasini, 'Channel Breakout – Part 4: Light Crude Oil', *Traders* (2008), www.urban-stocks.com.

[6]   Stridsman, Thomas, *Trading Systems and Money Management* (Wiley, 2003).

[7]   Collins, Art, *Market Beaters* (Traders Press, 2004).

[8]   Jaekle & Tomasini, 'The importance of time for short-term trading', *Traders* (November 2006), www.urban-stocks.com.

[9]   Sweeney, John, *Maximum Adverse Excursion: Analyzing Price Fluctuations for Trading Management* (Wiley, 1997).

[10]   Farrell, Christopher, 'Monte Carlo models simulate all kinds of scenarios', *Business Week* (2001).

[11]   Williams, Larry, *The Definitive Guide to Futures Trading, Volume II* (Brown Co, 1990).

[12]   Vince, Ralph, *Portfolio Management Formulas: Mathematical Trading Methods for the Futures, Options and Stock Markets* (Wiley, 1990).

[13]   Jones, Ryan, *The Trading Game: Playing by the Numbers to Make Millions* (Wiley, 1999).

[14]   Jaekle & Tomasini, 'Bollinger Band System', *Traders* (2006), www.urban-stocks.com.

[15]   Jaekle & Tomasini, 'The Triangle System', *Traders* (2007), www.urban-stocks.com.

[16]   Jaekle & Tomasini, 'Trend following in the bond markets, Part 1 and 2', *Traders* (2006), www.urban-stocks.com.

[17]   www.bollingerbands.com

[18]   Faber, Mebane T. and Richardson, Eric W., *The Ivy Portfolio: How to Invest Like the Top Endowments and Avoid Bear Markets* (Wiley, 2011).

[19]   Smitten, Richard, *Trade like Jesse Livermore* (Wiley, 2004).

[20]   'Momentum crashes', *Journal of Financial Economics* Volume 122, Issue 2, November 2016, Pages 221–247 Kent Daniel, Tobias J. Moskowitz, doi.org/10.1016/j.jfineco.2015.12.002

[21]   Clenow, Andreas, *Stocks on the Move: Beating the Market with Hedge Fund Momentum Strategies* (CreateSpace Independent Publishing Platform, 2015).

[22]   norgatedata.com/data-content-tables.php

[23]   'Prospect Theory: An Analysis of Decision under Risk', Daniel Kahneman and Amos Tversky. Source: *Econometrica*, Vol. 47, No. 2 (Mar., 1979), pp. 263–291 Published by: The Econometric Society; stable URL: www.jstor.org/stable/1914185

[24]   e.g. see here: www.nasdaq.com or: en.wikipedia.org/wiki/NASDAQ-100

[25]   Kaepel, Jay, *Seasonal Stock Market Trends* (Wiley Trading, 2009).

[26]   'An Introduction to the Bootstrap', Efron, B.;Tibshirani, R. (1993). Boca Raton, FL: Chapman & Hall/CRC.ISBN 0-412-04231-2.softwareArchived 2012-07-12 at Archive.today

[27]   Bandy, Howard B., *Quantitative Trading Systems: Practical Methods for Design, Testing, and Validation* (Blue Owl Press, 2011).

Index

www.ingramcontent.com/pod-product-compliance
Lightning Source LLC
Chambersburg PA
CBHW081048220326
41598CB00038B/7025